Immigration Law for Paralegals

THIRD EDITION

by MARIA ISABEL CASABLANCA, ESQ.
GLORIA ROA BODIN, ESQ.

CAROLINA ACADEMIC PRESS
Durham, North Carolina

Library of Congress Cataloging-in-Publication Data

Casablanca, Maria Isabel.
  Immigration law for paralegals / by Maria Isabel Casablanca and Gloria Roa Bodin. -- 3rd ed.
      p. cm.
  Includes bibliographical references.
  ISBN 978-1-59460-817-9 (alk. paper)
  1. Emigration and immigration law--United States. 2. Legal assistants--United States. I. Bodin, Gloria Roa.
II. Title.

  KF4819.85.C375 2010
  342.7308'2--dc22   2010012354

Carolina Academic Press
700 Kent St.
Durham, NC 27701
Telephone (919) 489-7486
Fax (919) 493-5668
www.cap-press.com

Printed in the United States of America

This book is dedicated to my mother, Berta Muller de Casablanca,
who always wanted me to be a writer, and to the memory of my father,
Carlos Roberto Casablanca, who taught me to respect and be generous with those less fortunate.
This book is also dedicated to my siblings, Marta Casablanca and Jose Casablanca,
whose faith in me has never wavered, and to my son Mauricio Lopez-Aldazabal, my inspiration.

Maria I. Casablanca, Esq.

This book is dedicated to my father, Clement Roa,
and mother, Josefina Roa Morales, who as immigrants
nurtured my ambition to achieve the American Dream.
I am grateful to my husband, Eric A. Bodin,
for his love, support and encouragement.

Gloria Roa Bodin, Esq.

Contents

AUTHORS' ACKNOWLEDGMENTS   xi

INTRODUCTION   1

CHAPTER 1   Meeting with the Client   3

    I.   Interview Techniques   3

    II. Interviewing Tips   3

    III. Procedure for Opening a File   4

    IV. Procedure for the Tickler System   4

    Appendix   5

CHAPTER 2   Visitors for Business (B-1 Visa) and Pleasure (B-2 Visa)   19

    I.   Introduction   19

    II. General Requirements   19

        A. List of Permissible Activities for B-1 Visa — Visitors for Business   19

        B. List of Permissible Activities for B-2 Visa — Visitors for Pleasure   20

        C. The Visa Waiver Program (VWP)   20

    III. Conditions of Admission   21

        A. Consular Process for B-1/B-2 Visas   21

        B. Extensions for B-1/B-2 Visas   21

        Appendix   21

CHAPTER 3   Temporary Visas for Working   31

    I.   Introduction   31

    II. The H Visa — Temporary Worker   31

        A. The H-1B Visa — Specialty Occupation — Professional Visa and Fashion Models   31

        B. The H-2A Visa — Agricultural Worker   32

        C. The H-2B Visa — Unskilled Foreign Worker   32

        D. The H-3 Visa — Trainee   33

        E. The TN Status   34

    III. The E Visa   35

        A. The E-1 Visa — Treaty Trader   36

        B. The E-2 Visa — Investor   36

        C. The E-3 Visa — Specialty Occupation — Australian Aliens   37

IV. The L Visa   37

    A. The L-1A Visa — Intracompany Transferee   38

    B. The L-1B Visa — Specialized Knowledge Employee   39

    Appendix   40

CHAPTER 4   TEMPORARY VISAS FOR STUDYING   79

I.   Introduction   79

II.   The F-1 Visa   79

III. The J Visa   80

IV.   The M Visa   81

    Appendix   82

**CHAPTER 5   TEMPORARY VISAS FOR PARTICULAR OCCUPATIONS —
O, P, Q AND R VISAS   91**

I.   Introduction   91

II.   The O Visas — Extraordinary Ability Artists/Entertainers, Business People,
Scientists, Educators and Athletes   91

    A. The O-1 Visa — Science, Education, Business and Athletics   91

    B. Artists   91

    C. Star in Motion Pictures and Television   91

    D. The O-2 Visa — Support Staff of Artists and Athletes   92

    E. Peer Group Consultation   93

    F. Self-Employment   93

III. The P Visas   93

    A. The P-1 Visa — Athletes, Athletic Teams and Entertainment Groups 93

    B. The P-2 Visa — Artists and Entertainer Reciprocal Exchange   93

    C. The P-3 Visa — Artists and Entertainers Integral to Performance 94

    D. Peer Group Consultation   95

IV.   The Q-1 Visa   95

V.   The R-1 Visa   96

    Appendix   97

CHAPTER 6   Temporary and Permanent Visas for Victims — T and U Visas   121

I.   Introduction   121

II.   T Visa   121

    A. Nonimmigrant Visa   121

    B. Immigrant Visa   122

III. U Visa   122

    A. Non-Immigrant Visa   123

    B. Immigrant Visa   123

    Appendix   124

CHAPTER 7   **Family-Based Residency and Visas**   **189**

   I.   Introduction   189

   II. The Quota System for Residency   189

   III. Categories of Family Based Residency   189

      A. Immediate Relative — Spouse, Children and Parents of U.S. Citizens   189

      B. First Preference — Unmarried Sons and Daughters of U.S. Citizens   190

      C. Second Preference — Family of Lawful Permanent Residents — F-2A and F-2B   190

      D. Third Preference — Married Sons and Daughters of U.S. Citizens   190

      E. Fourth Preference — Brothers and Sisters of U.S. Citizens   190

   IV. Processing Residency   190

      A. The Petition Process   190

      B. Adjustment of Status   191

      C. Consular Processing   192

      D. Preparing Forms I-864 and I-864(a) — Affidavit of Support   192

   V. Conditional Residence   193

   VI. The K-1 Visa   193

      A. Evidence Required   193

      B. Application for Residency   194

   VII. The K-3 Visa   194

      A. Evidence Required   194

      B. Application for Residency   194

   VIII. The V Visa   194

      A. Evidence Required   195

      B. Application for Residency   195

      Appendix   195

CHAPTER 8   **EMPLOYMENT-BASED AND INVESTOR IMMIGRANT PREFERENCES**   **221**

   I.   Introduction   221

   II. First Preference — EB-1 — Priority Workers   221

      A. Extraordinary Ability in the Sciences, Arts, Education, Business or Athletics   221

      B. Outstanding Professors and Researchers   222

      C. International Executives and Managers   222

   III. Second Preference — EB-2 — Professionals with Advanced Degrees or Exceptional Ability   223

   IV. Third Preference — EB-3 — Labor Certification — PERM-Skilled Workers, Professionals and Other Workers; Schedule A; Visa Retrogression   224

      A. Labor Certification — PERM-Skilled Workers, Professionals and Other Workers   224

      B. Schedule A   229

      C. Visa Retrogression   229

   V. Evidence Required for Categories EB-1, -2 and -3   230

VI. Fourth Preference — Special Immigrants — Religious Worker   231

VII. Fifth Preference — EB-5 — Investors   232

    A. Employment Creation Visa   232

    B. Summary of Statutory Requirements   232

    C. Regional Centers   233

    D. Documents Required   233

    Appendix   233

CHAPTER 9   CLAIMING ASYLUM OR PROTECTION IN THE UNITED STATES   251

I.   Legal Standard for Asylum/Refugee Protection   251

    A. International Definition of Refugee   251

    B. Definition of Persecution   251

    C. Well-Founded Fear Test   251

II. Other Relief   252

    A. Withholding Standard   252

    B. Convention against Torture (CAT)   252

    C. Bars to Eligibility for Asylum   253

    D. Bar for Failure to File within One Year of Entry   253

III. Procedure for Filing Asylum Application   254

    "Affirmative" Asylum Application Filed with USCIS   254

    "Defensive" Asylum Process   254

IV. Required Documents   255

V.   Filing Documents with Government Agencies   255

VI. Status of Family Members, Adjustment of Status, Work Authorization and Travel Permit   256

    A. Derivative Status   256

    B. Aged Out or Reaching 21 Years of Age after Filing Application   257

    C. Obtaining Work Authorization   257

    D. Permission to Travel   257

    E. Unlawful Presence   257

    F. Adjustment of Status to Permanent Residency   258

    Appendix   258

CHAPTER 10   SEEKING RELIEF BEFORE THE COURTS (IJ, BIA AND FEDERAL COURTS)   277

I.   Introduction   277

II. The Immigration Court   277

    A. The Charging Document   277

    B. Master Calendar   277

    C. Individual Hearing   278

III. The Board of Immigration Appeals   278

IV. Federal Court Relief   278

    A. Writ of Mandamus   278

                    B. Writ of Habeas Corpus   278

                    C. Petition for Certiorari   279

                    Appendix   279

CHAPTER 11   CITIZENSHIP IN THE UNITED STATES   301

            I.   Introduction   301

                    A. Statutory Requirements   301

                    B. Bars to Naturalization   301

                    C. Exemptions to English or Government and History Requirement   302

                    D. Filing for Naturalization   302

                    Appendix   303

**CHAPTER 12   REPRESENTATION BEFORE DEPARTMENT OF HOMELAND
                SECURITY AGENCIES   315**

            I.   Introduction   315

            II.   USCIS   315

                    A. Requests for Evidence   315

                    B. Motions to Reopen   316

                    C. Motions to Reconsider   316

                    D. H1B and L1A Audits   316

            III. Appeals before the Administrative Appeals Office (AAO)   316

                    Appeals   317

            IV.   Customs and Border Protection (CBP)   317

            V.   Immigration and Customs Enforcement (ICE)   317

                    A. Enforcement Removal Operations (ERO)   317

                    B. Homeland Security Investigations   318

                    Appendix   319

GLOSSARY AND ACRONYMS   345

KEYWORDS   351

Authors' Acknowledgments

This book would not have been possible without the assistance of certain exemplary individuals. We would like to thank Walter Infante, Cyril Filipinas, Marilyn Dalocanog, Miles Strebeck, Melinda Hapca, Ana Aleman, Alex Rangel, Patricia Gonzalez, and Christina Carr for their top-notch technical processing.

Special thanks go to Bob Conrow, Beth Hall, Keith Potter, and the staff at Carolina Academic Press for their outstanding support and assistance.

Introduction

This book is designed with both the classroom setting and the paralegal practicing immigration in mind. When paralegals are provided with the skills necessary to manage cases, attorneys are able to increase productivity and enhance the quality of representation.

Throughout this book, step-by-step instructions guide the paralegal through each major visa category, including sample forms and correspondence.

Immigration Law for Paralegals includes:

1. Interviewing techniques and caseload management
2. Temporary visas for investing, studying or employment
3. Family-based residency
4. Employment-based permanent residency
5. Political asylum
6. Citizenship
7. Appeal process
8. T and U visas for victims
9. Representation before DHS agencies

Now more than ever, the practitioners and their legal staff must be current regarding legal standards and procedures. Government officials such as senators, congressmen and even the President of the United States are constantly making proposals and/or introducing bills relating to immigration issues. The creation of the Department of Homeland Security (DHS) in response to the terrorist attacks of September 11, 2001, represented the single largest reorganization within the federal government in 69 years. The now-defunct Immigration and Naturalization Service (INS) has been divided into three departments under the DHS: U.S. Citizenship and Immigration Service (USCIS); Immigration and Custom Enforcement (ICE); and Customs and Border Protection (CBP).

One caveat: This book should be utilized by the paralegal while working under the supervision of an attorney. A paralegal who offers his/her services and who is not working under an attorney's guidance is engaged in the unlicensed practice of law and may be subject to sanctions and criminal penalties.

Maria I. Casablanca, Esq.
Gloria Roa Bodin, Esq.

CHAPTER 1

Meeting with the Client

I. Interview Techniques

The client's initial call to the office generates the beginning of the interview process. The receptionist, paralegal or person in charge of fielding calls should identify the area of immigration law involved. This is important because in many offices the cases are assigned to the paralegal according to the type of case.

Once the appointment is made, a notation regarding the type of case should be placed next to the caller's name in the appointment book or computerized case management system (e.g., if it is a labor certification, write "L.C." next to the name). This will ensure that the paralegal who handles labor certifications will be prepared to assist the attorney during the interview.

The client should be told to bring his/her passport, Form I-94 and copies of any documents pertaining to the immigration matter to the initial interview. Also, the cost of the initial consultation fee should be discussed at the time the appointment is made. If the firm takes credit cards, the caller should be informed.

At the appointment, the client should be greeted in a friendly and respectful manner and made to feel comfortable. S/he should be asked to fill out a Client Interview/Intake Sheet.

Initially, the interview should be conducted by the attorney in private, as all conversations are confidential. The attorney should quickly run through the interview/intake sheet to determine what issues are involved. This is to avoid having the attorney use his/her time on a case involving a simple form.

For example, if a client needs an extension of a tourist visa, the attorney's time will be limited to a short review of the documents and the client's intentions to determine if s/he qualifies. Thereafter, the matter can be turned over to the paralegal. In any event, at the close of the discussion, fees and costs should be quoted. When the client decides to hire the law firm, the contract for services (Retainer Agreement) should be executed.

II. Interviewing Tips

The following information should be noted in the interview/intake sheet. The first documents to be reviewed should be the passport and departure record (Form I-94), if available. It is important to determine whether the client was admitted by an immigration officer at the port of entry or entered illegally without being inspected (i.e., EWI: Entry Without Inspection). The passport and Form I-94, if any, will reflect the client's current status as well as any visas, entries and departures. If the entry is just for 90 days under the Visa Waiver Program (VWP), no change of status or extension(s) is permitted.

An expired Form I-94 triggers issues such as unlawful presence and bar to adjustment under most circumstances. If the client's status has expired, any period of unauthorized presence violates the "3/10 Rule." Under this rule, a person who is unlawfully present in the United States for a period of more than 180 consecutive days after his/her authorized stay, but less than one year, who voluntarily leaves the United States, may be barred from re-entering for three years from the date of the person's departure or removal. A person who has been unlawfully present in the United States for one year or more may be barred for 10 years from the date of the person's departure or removal from the United States.

After the questions regarding entry and status are completed, the client should be asked about his/her major concerns. The client should be guided through the problems or issues by asking relevant questions.

A talkative person will, by nature, want to disclose his/her whole life story. The attorney or paralegal must maintain control of the interview by narrowing the issues (e.g., ascertain the most recent date of entry). This is an important question that may not be easily answered if the client did not bring his/her passport or Form I-94. It is one of the best methods of determining the alien's status.

The attorney, as well as the paralegal, should review the interview/intake sheet to determine whether the client has ever committed a crime. Minor infractions such as driving under the influence, shoplifting or domestic aggravated battery may have negative immigration consequences. As mentioned, unlawful presence is important in determining whether there are any bars.

In assisting the attorney, no legal advice should be given by the paralegal until instructed by the attorney. If the client does not initially retain the firm, the interview/intake sheet should be filed in a file box marked "Interviews." Once the client returns for a second interview or to start the case, the interview/intake sheet should be pulled from this box and reviewed to help the interviewer recall what transpired at the initial interview and what fees were quoted. A copy of the signed retainer and a receipt for any monies received should be given to the client.

III. Procedure for Opening a File

In the New Case Management Form, a sequential file number should be assigned and the color coded file should be opened. The interview/intake sheet should be the first document placed in the file, on the right-hand side of the folder, together with a photocopy of the client's passport, Form I-94 and any other relevant documents. On the left-hand side of the folder, attach any documents filed with a government agency, including certified mail, return receipt requested or courier receipts and copies of the filing fee checks. The employee in charge of assigning the file should fill out an assignment sheet and assign the case to an attorney and/or paralegal and the matter should be entered into a follow-up (tickler) system.

IV. Procedure for the Tickler System

All deadlines, USCIS interview and Executive Office for Immigration Review (EOIR) hearings, Form I-94 expiration dates and any other appointments or requests for information should be recorded in the tickler system.

The following is an example of the tickler system for a USCIS Request for Additional Evidence (RFE):

1. The RFE will indicate the date the additional evidence was requested by USCIS.

2. The deadline to submit the requested information to USCIS.

3. The amount of time given to respond must be calculated from the stated date on the RFE letter.

RFE Stamp:

Received — RFE/Other

Due Date: _____

Follow-up Date: _____

Assigned To: _____

4. The following is the description of the stamp:

    a. The Due Date is the date the response to the RFE must reach USCIS.

    b. The Follow-up Date is the date that the attorney follows up with the paralegal to determine whether the response to the RFE has been prepared and whether new follow-up should be assigned.

5. Once the document has tickler stamp affixed to the back of the RFE cover letter, the following information must be placed on the Case Management RFE Due List:

    a. Type of case and name of client;

    b. Due date of the RFE; and

    c. The initials of the person who will be preparing and submitting the response to the RFE.

This tickler system can be used to monitor other deadlines. There are sophisticated computerized case management systems for volume immigration practice.

Appendix

1. Case Codes
2. Sample Visa and Form I-94
3. Form I-797 C (Approval-Attorney Copy)
4. Form I-797 A (Approval-Client Copy)
5. Form I-797 (Receipt)
6. Client Interview/Intake Sheet
7. Retainer Agreement
8. Sample Sequential Receipt
9. New Case Management Form
10. Color-Coded File

Case Codes

TYPE OF CASE	CODE
B-1	B
B-2	B
E-1	E
E-2	E
F-1	F
H-1 to H-3	H
I	I
J-1	J
K-1 to K-3	K
L-1 to L-2	L
M	M
O-1 to O-3	O
P	P
Q	Q
R	R
V	V
Relative Petition	RP
Labor Certification	LC
Political Asylum	PA
Citizenship	C

Sample Visa

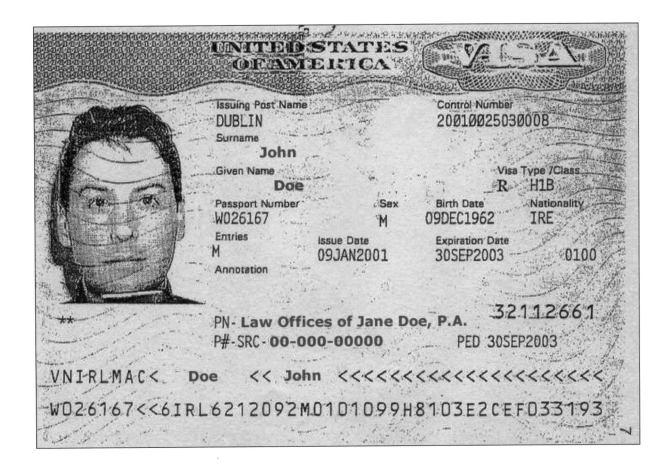

Form I-94

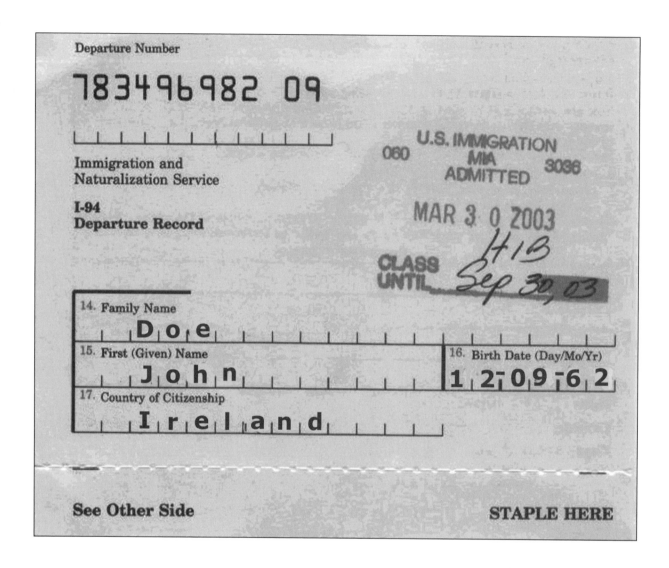

Form I-797 C (Approval-Attorney Copy)

U.S. Department of Justice
Immigration and Naturalization Service

Notice of Action

THE UNITED STATES OF AMERICA

RECEIPT NUMBER		CASE TYPE I129
SRC-00-000-00000		PETITION FOR A NONIMMIGRANT WORKER

RECEIPT DATE	PRIORITY DATE	PETITIONER
August 23, 2002		Law Offices of Jane Doe, P.A.

NOTICE DATE	PAGE	BENEFICIARY A-000-000-00
October 29, 2002	1 of 1	John Doe

Jane Doe, Esq.
Law Offices of Jane Doe, P.A.
123 Arch Avenue
Coral Gables, FL 33145

Notice Type: Approval Notice
Class: H3
Valid from 08/25/2002 **to** 08/24/2003

Courtesy Copy: Original sent to: **Law Offices of Jane Doe, P.A.**

This courtesy notice is to advise you of action taken on this case. The official notice has been mailed to the attorney or representative indicated above. Any relevant documentation included in the notice was also mailed as part of the official notice.

The above petition and extension of stay have been approved. The status of the named foreign worker(s) in this classification is valid as indicated above. The foreign worker(s) can work for the petitioner, but only as detailed in the petition and for the period authorized. Any change in employment requires a new petition. Since this employment authorization stems from the filing of this petition, separate employment authorization documentation is not required. Please contact the IRS with any questions about tax withholding.

The petitioner should keep the upper portion of this notice. The lower portion should be given to the worker. He or she should keep the right part with his or her Form I-94, *Arrival-Departure Record*. This should be turned in with the I-94 when departing the U.S. The left part is for his or her records. A person granted an extension of stay who leaves the U.S. must normally obtain a new visa before returning. The left part can be used in applying for the new visa. If a visa is not required, he or she should present it, along with any other required documentation, when applying for reentry in this new classification at a port of entry or pre-flight inspection station. The petitioner may also file Form I-824, *Application for Action on an Approved Application or Petition*, with this office to request that we notify a consulate, port of entry, or pre-flight inspection office of this approval.

This courtesy copy may not be used in lieu of official notification to demonstrate the filing or processing action taken on this case.

THIS FORM IS NOT A VISA NOR MAY IT BE USED IN PLACE OF A VISA.

Please see the additional information on the back. You will be notified separately about any other cases you filed.
IMMIGRATION & NATURALIZATION SERVICE
TEXAS SERVICE CENTER
P O BOX 851488 - DEPT A
MESQUITE TX 75185-1488
Customer Service Telephone: (214) 381-1423

Form I-797C (Rev. 09/07/93) N

Form I-797 A (Approval-Client Copy)

U.S. Department of Justice
Immigration and Naturalization Service

Notice of Action

THE UNITED STATES OF AMERICA

RECEIPT NUMBER	CASE TYPE I129
SRC -00-000-00000	PETITION FOR A NONIMMIGRANT WORKER

RECEIPT DATE	PRIORITY DATE	PETITIONER
October 2, 2003		LAW OFFICES OF Jane Doe, P.A.

NOTICE DATE	PAGE	BENEFICIARY A-000-000-00
March 26, 2004	1 of 1	John Doe

Jane Doe, Esq.
Law Offices of Jane Doe, P.A.
123 Arch Avenue
Coral Gables, FL 33145

Notice Type: Approval Notice
Class: H1B1
Valid from 10/01/2003 to 10/01/2006

The above petition and extension of stay have been approved. The status of the named foreign worker(s) in this classification is valid as indicated above. The foreign worker(s) can work for the petitioner, but only as detailed in the petition and for the period authorized. Any change in employment requires a new petition. Since this employment authorization stems from the filing of this petition, separate employment authorization documentation is not required. Please contact the IRS with any questions about tax withholding.

The petitioner should keep the upper portion of this notice. The lower portion should be given to the worker. He or she should keep the right part with his or her Form I-94, *Arrival-Departure Record*. This should be turned in with the I-94 when departing the U.S. The left part is for his or her records. A person granted an extension of stay who leaves the U.S. must normally obtain a new visa before returning. The left part can be used in applying for the new visa. If a visa is not required, he or she should present it, along with any other required documentation, when applying for reentry in this new classification at a port of entry or pre-flight inspection station. The petitioner may also file Form I-824, *Application for Action on an Approved Application or Petition*, with this office to request that we notify a consulate, port of entry, or pre-flight inspection office of this approval.

THIS FORM IS NOT A VISA NOR MAY IT BE USED IN PLACE OF A VISA.

Please see the additional information on the back. You will be notified separately about any other cases you filed.
IMMIGRATION & NATURALIZATION SERVICE
TEXAS SERVICE CENTER
P/O BOX 851488 - DEPT A
MESQUITE TX 75185-1488
Customer Service Telephone: (800) 375-5283

Form I797A (Rev. 09/07/93)N

PLEASE TEAR OFF FORM I-94 PRINTED BELOW, AND STAPLE TO ORIGINAL I-94 IF AVAILABLE

Detach This Half for Personal Records

Receipt # SRC--00-000-00000
I-94# 783496982 09
NAME   John Doe
CLASS H1B1

VALID FROM 10/01/2003 UNTIL 10/01/2006

PETITIONER:

Jane Doe, Esq.
Law Offices of Jane Doe, P.A.
123 Arch Avenue
Coral Gables, FL 33145

783496982 09

Receipt Number SRC -00-000-00000
Immigration and
Naturalization Service
I-94
Departure Record   Petitioner: LAW OFFICES O

14. Family Name Doe	
15. First (Given) Name John	16. Date of Birth 12/09/1962
17. Country of Citizenship IRELAND	

Form I 797A (Rev. 09/07/93)N

Form I-797 (Receipt)

Department of Homeland Security
U.S. Citizenship and Immigration Services

I-797, Notice of Action

THE UNITED STATES OF AMERICA

| RECEIPT NUMBER | | CASE TYPE I765 |
| SRC-00-000-00000 | | APPLICATION FOR EMPLOYMENT AUTHORIZATION |

| RECEIPT DATE | PRIORITY DATE | APPLICANT A 00 000 000 |
| May 3, 2004 | | **John Doe** |

| NOTICE DATE | PAGE |
| July 6, 2004 | 1 of 1 |

Jane Doe, Esq.
Law Offices of Jane Doe, P.A.
123 Arch Avenue
Coral Gables, FL 33145

Notice Type: Approval Notice
Class: C09
Valid from 06/29/2004 to 06/29/2005
Representative's Copy

Your application for employment authorization has been approved. The Form I-688B, Employment Authorization Document, was sent under separate cover to the beneficiary.

This card authorizes your employment in the United States. Show this card to your employer to verify authorization to work during the dates on the card.

If any information on the card is incorrect, please write the office listed below. Include your Employment Authorization Document, I-688B, a photocopy of this notice, and evidence to support the necessary corrections.

THIS FORM IS NOT A VISA OR EVIDENCE OF EMPLOYMENT AUTHORIZATION, NOR MAY IT BE USED IN PLACE OF A VISA OR FORM I-688B.

Please see the additional information on the back. You will be notified separately about any other cases you filed.
IMMIGRATION & NATURALIZATION SERVICE
TEXAS SERVICE CENTER
P O BOX 851488 - DEPT A
MESQUITE TX 75185-1488
Customer Service Telephone: (800) 375-5283

Form I-797 (Rev. 11/28/03) N

The following interview/intake sheet will assist the paralegal and attorney in interviewing a new client. The questions in this interview/intake form are presented in a logical order and are intended to serve as a guide. The interviewer may, of course, paraphrase the questions and present them in his/her own style. The interview sheet must be given to the receptionist at the end of the day to be filed alphabetically. When the client decides to retain the firm, this interview/intake sheet is reviewed to recall the type of immigration case, fee and pertinent notes taken by the attorney.

Client Interview/Intake Sheet

Consultation Fee: $75.00–$150.00 Consulta: $75.00–$150.00

If you do not wish to pay for the consultation, please advise prior to the interview.

Si usted no desea pagar por la consulta, por favor avise antes de la entrevista.

Date: _____   Referred by: _____

Name: _____
       Last   First   Middle

Address: _____ Zip: _____

Phone: _____   Fax: _____   E-mail: _____

Interviewed By: _____

Country of Birth: _____

Date Last Entered U.S. _____   Form I-94 Expiration Date: _____

Visa Expiration Date: _____   Current Type of Visa: _____   _____
                                                                 B-1   B-2

                                         _____ _____ _____ _____ _____
                                          F-1   H-1   L-1   E-1/2   Other

Ask client this general question:

Do you want to become a legal permanent resident in the United States?   _____   _____
                                                                            Yes   No

If the client wants to become a permanent resident, analyze whether s/he is eligible for any of the categories listed below. Usually, if there are other issues such as deportation or overstay the client will divulge it.

1. **Relative Petition:**
   Are you married or related to a U.S. citizen or permanent resident?

2. **Labor Certification:**
   Do you qualify for labor certification based on a special skill or profession?

3. **Intracompany Transferee**
   Are you employed by a company abroad that is transferring you in the capacity of executive, manager or specialized knowledge to a U.S. branch office, or do the owners of the foreign company wish to open a branch office in the United States?

4. **Treaty Trader (E-1) and Treaty Investor (E-2)**
   Are you importing or exporting substantial goods or investing more than $150,000.00? Only certain countries are eligible; consult list of treaty countries.

5. Professional

Are you a person holding a university degree or the equivalent years of professional or managerial experience? Three years of progressive managerial experience is equivalent to one year of university studies (e.g., 12 years of progressive managerial experience is required to complete a bachelor's degree).

6. Entrepreneur-Investor

Are you able to invest $1,000.00 or $500,000.00 in a targeted high unemployment area?

7. Religious Worker

Are you minister or religious worker?

8. Suspension of Deportation/Cancellation of Removal

Have you resided in the United States for at least seven or ten years and/or have U.S. citizen or permanent resident relatives?

9. Political Asylum

Analyze country conditions. Are you escaping persecution on account of membership in one of five enumerated groups: race, religion, nationality, membership in a particular social group, or political opinion?

10. Other _____

If the client desires to be a permanent resident, s/he must fall into one or more of the above categories. These categories are composed of almost all of the important sections of the law that concern the interviewer. Check the appropriate category and proceed to explain to the client the office procedure and method of handling the case.

Notes:

_____

_____

_____

_____

_____

_____

_____

_____

_____

_____

_____

_____

_____

_____

Potential Problems

The questions below all refer to the grounds of inadmissibility, which could bar a person from immigrating.

1. Have you ever been arrested or convicted of a crime?

2. Have you ever been deported, excluded, or removed?

3. Have you ever been accused of visa fraud or misrepresentation?

4. Have you ever falsely claimed to be a U.S. citizen?

5. Have you ever lived in the U.S. without being admitted (e.g., entered without an immigration officer issuing a Form I-94 at the border)?

6. Have you ever stayed longer than permitted on a nonimmigrant visa or stayed after violating the terms of a nonimmigrant visa; if so, how, when, and for how long?

7. Have you ever violated any immigration laws?

8. Have you ever used a false social security number or other false legal document?

9. Other _____

A nonimmigrant visa (NIV) is temporary; an immigrant visa (IV) is permanent. The permanent residency visa, Form I-551, is some times called a "Green Card," even though it is no longer green, but beige. Legal permanent residents are allowed to remain indefinitely in the United States, as long as they do not violate the terms of their residency (e.g., committing certain crimes or staying outside the United States too long). A legal permanent resident may apply to become a United States citizen after a specific amount of time. The process for legal permanent residency may take many years. While the goal of most immigrants is to obtain permanent residency, many times the individual must have a temporary visa in order to remain legally in the United States while s/he waits for his/her residency.

The following is a list of temporary visas:

B-1:	Tourist for business
B-2:	Tourist for pleasure
E-1:	Treaty trader
E-2:	Treaty investor
F-1:	Student
H-1:	Professional or person of distinguished ability; Registered Nurse, special occupation
H-2:	Unskilled temporary worker
H-3:	Trainee
I:	Media journalist
J:	Exchange visitor
K:	Fiancé(e); relative of U.S. citizen with approved I-130
L-1:	Multinational executive or manager of a foreign corporation
M:	Student vocational
O:	Alien of extraordinary ability in science, arts, education, business, or athletics; extraordinary achievements in the motion picture or television field
P:	Athlete, artist, or entertainer in a group
Q:	Exchange of cultural component
R:	Minister or religious worker
TN:	North American Free Trade Agreement (NAFTA) Professionals from Canada and Mexico based on trade agreements

Retainer Agreement

Name: _____ Date: _____
           Last   First   Middle

Address: _____

Telephone: _____ Fax: _____ E-mail: _____

I hereby retain the Law Firm of _____as immigration attorney to represent me for professional services to be rendered with respect to the United States immigration and visa procedures.

Type of case: _____We will provide our legal services in connection with this matter for a fee of $_____, plus costs.

In setting this fee, please consider the amount of time we will devote to your matter and the experience and expertise in the field of Immigration and Nationality Law.

$ _____ Initial payment

$ _____ Balance to be paid in equal monthly installments of $ _____ commencing on the 1st day of each and every month until balance has been paid in full. A 5% penalty will be assessed on payments received after the 15th day of the month.

$ _____ Balance to be paid within seven days after notification of receipt of approval

- One half of the balance is due upon approval of the labor certification.

- Payments are absolutely not refundable upon a file being assigned to the attorney for its processing.

I agree to pay the usual immigration filing fees, photocopy fees, translation fees, credential evaluation fee, courier or expedited mail charges (e.g., UPS, Federal Express), costs of advertisement(s) and/or any other disbursement in connection with the case such as long distance calls, which I agree may be charged to my U.S. home telephone number: _____.

Should the U.S. Citizenship and Immigration Services or any other government agency request further evidence, I will be billed at the rate of $ _____ per hour.

For any permission to travel, personal appearance or extraordinary services not contemplated at the time of the engagement, I agree that I will be billed at the rate of $ _____ per hour, plus expenses, in excess of initial fees.

In the event that there is a remaining balance at the completion of the case, I agree to pay the balance owed.

I agree that the U.S. Department of Labor and/or the Department of Homeland Security or any other relevant federal agency will rely on the truthfulness of any statement made by me, and I hereby affirm that all statements made by me are true and correct. Furthermore, any marriage entered into for the convenience of a Green Card and not for love and affection will fail the bona fide marriage test for permanent residency and I understand this constitutes fraud.

I have fully read this Retainer Agreement and accept the terms set forth in its entirety.

Date:_____ Signature: _____

Filing Fees:

USCIS   _____

Credential Evaluation   _____

Translations   _____

Miscellaneous   _____

Sample Sequential Receipt

Law Offices of Jane Doe, P.A.
123 Arch Avenue
Coral Gables, FL 33145

CUSTOMER'S ORDER NO.	PHONE		DATE	
NAME				
ADDRESS				

CASH	C.O.D.	CHARGE	ON ACCT.	MDSE. RET'D	PAID OUT	

QTY.	DESCRIPTION	PRICE	AMOUNT
		TAX	
SOLD BY	RECEIVED BY	TOTAL	

19993

All claims and returned goods
MUST be accompanied by this bill.

Thank You!

PRODUCT 2530   B

New Case Management Log

File No	Date	I-130/485	Labor Cert.	I-140	NIV/Misc.

Color-Coded File

Relative Petition	Red folder
Temporary Visas	
B-1/B-2 Extensions	Red folder
F-1/M	Green folder
H-1/H-2/H-3, E-1/2	Yellow folder
L-1A/B, TN	Light blue folder (cardboard)/accordion file
O/P/Q/R	Light blue folder (cardboard)/accordion file
Labor Certifications	Brown folder
Adjustment of Status	Red folder
Miscellaneous	Manila folder
Appeal	Blue folder

CHAPTER 2

Visitors for Business (B-1 Visa) and Pleasure (B-2 Visa)

I. Introduction

Individuals entering the United States as visitors for business (B-1) or pleasure (B-2) enter with a temporary nonimmigrant visa. The Visa Waiver Program (VWP) is another visitor classification. The VWP allows nationals from certain participating countries to enter the United States without applying for a B-2 visa at the consulate. This program automatically grants entry at the border or port of entry for 90 days. INA § 101(a)(15)(B), 8.U.S.C. § 1101(a)(15)(B), 8 C.F.R. § 214.2(b) 9 FAM § 41.31

The application for a B-1 and/or B-2 visa is filed with the consulate or embassy in the home country or current place of residence abroad. The process involves an interview with the consular officer who analyzes the application and interviews the individual. If the officer suspects preconceived intent such as intent to work or marry rather than visit, the application will be denied.

Once the consular officer is satisfied with applicant's true intent, a visa scanned stamp will be affixed to the passport, stating, among other things, the issuance date and expiration date. Some visas are granted for as little as 30 days and others for up to 10 years.

II. General Requirements

A. List of Permissible Activities for B-1 Visa— Visitors for Business

1. Commercial transactions that do not involve gainful U.S. employment (e.g., taking orders for foreign goods);

2. Contract negotiation;

3. Installation, service or repair of commercial/industrial equipment purchased from outside the United States and/or training of U.S. workers to perform such services (**Note:** Typically, a contract of sale requires the seller to provide such services, and the B-1 visitor must have the specialized knowledge essential to the contract's performance.);

4. Consultation with business associates;

5. Litigation;

6. Participation in scientific, educational, professional or business conventions, conferences or seminars;

7. Professional entertainers involved in cultural events paid for and sponsored by a sending country that will involve public appearance before a non-paying audience;

8. Investors seeking investments that may eventually qualify them for immigrant or E-2 nonimmigrant status;

9. Independent research or professional artistic activity;

10. Foreign airline employees who meet E Visa criteria, but are not nationals of a treaty country or of the airline's country of nationality;

11. Construction and set-up support by foreign employer in connection with exhibits at international fairs and exhibitions;

12. Certain religious and charitable activities (e.g., missionaries and recognized international volunteer efforts);

13. Certain athletes who are professional but intend to receive no salary;

14. Individuals or members of a foreign-based team in an internationally recognized sporting activity;

15. Amateur individuals or members of a foreign-based team who seek to try out with U.S. teams and who will pay only their incidental expenses; and

16. Servants of foreign employer temporarily in the United States.

B. List of Permissible Activities for B-2 Visa— Visitors for Pleasure

1. Usual tourist activities (e.g., visit tourist attractions, friends and/or relatives);

2. Medical treatment;

3. Participation in a conference, convention of social or fraternal organizations;

4. Short course of study incidental to tourist or social activities; and

5. Amateur entertainers or athletes who will compete or perform in a not-for-profit context without payment except for expenses.

C. The Visa Waiver Program (VWP)

Under the VWP for tourists and business visitors, nationals from the following countries can visit the United States for 90 days:

Andorra	Lithuania
Austria	Luxembourg
Australia	Malta
Belgium	Monaco
Brunei	The Netherlands
Czech Republic	New Zealand
Denmark	Norway
Estonia	Portugal
Finland	San Marino
France	Singapore
Germany	Slovakia
Hungary	Slovenia
Iceland	South Korea
Ireland	Spain
Italy	Sweden
Japan	Switzerland
Liechtenstein	United Kingdom

(**Note:** No change of status or extension may be obtained under this classification. Application for lawful permanent residency under adjustment of status is permitted under certain circumstances.)

III. Conditions of Admission

The arrival/departure document, Form I-94, is issued at the port of entry. The card is white for the B-1/B-2 visitor and green for the 90-day VWP visa. At the port of entry, the Form I-94 is completed to request permission for admission to the United States. The B-2 is initially granted for six months and can be extended for up to one year. The B-1 is granted for the time needed to complete business activities and may be extended for up to one year.

An individual's failure to maintain status or overstaying for the allotted time may trigger consequences under the Illegal Immigration Reform and Immigration Responsibility Act (IIRAIRA 1996). Under this law, nonimmigrant temporary visitors unlawfully present in the United States fall under the "3/10 Rule" as mentioned in Chapter 1.

If the alien is refused entry at the border or port of entry because of fraud, criminal activity, false documents, violation of prior authorized stay or pre-conceived intent, s/he will be removed immediately and held to be inadmissible to the United States.

A. Consular Process for B-1/B-2 Visas

Aliens seeking to enter the United States as visitors must make an application at the U.S. consulate, Nonimmigrant Visa (NIV) Section, in the country of residence and provide the following:

1. Forms Required:

   The Nonimmigrant Visa Application, DS-156 (DS-157 Supplement for male applicants ages 16–45);

2. Documents Required:

   a. Passport valid at least six months beyond intended stay(s) in the United States;

   b. One recent passport photo;

   c. Proof of ties to home country (e.g., savings account, employment, tax returns and/or real estate owned);

   d. (i) If visit is for business, a letter from the employer outlining temporary nature of business trip,

      (ii) If visit is for pleasure, a letter of invitation from friend or relative in the United States and notarized affidavit of support, together with a U.S. tax return;

   e. Copy of round trip airline ticket; and

   f. Proof of family relationship (e.g., marriage certificate and birth certificate(s)).

B. Extensions for B-1/B-2 Visas

Extensions of stays are obtained by filing the Application to Extend Status/Change Nonimmigrant Status (Form I-539) together with required filing fee and any supporting documents, with the USCIS Service Center having jurisdiction over the place of residence or employment (B-1) in the United States.

Appendix

1. Form DS-156 and 157
2. Form I-539
3. Form G-28

Form DS-156

U.S. Department of State
NONIMMIGRANT VISA APPLICATION

Approved OMB 1405-0018
Expires 09/30/2007
Estimated Burden 1 hour
See Page 2

PLEASE TYPE OR PRINT YOUR ANSWERS IN THE SPACE PROVIDED BELOW EACH ITEM

1. Passport Number
543789

2. Place of Issuance:
City: London
Country: United Kingdom
State/Province:

DO NOT WRITE IN THIS SPACE
B-1/B-2 MAX   B-1 MAX   B-2 MAX
Other _____ MAX
Visa Classification
Mult or _____
Number of Applications
Months _____
Validity
Issued/Refused
On _____ By _____
Under SEC.   214(b)   221(g)
Other _____ INA
Reviewed By _____

3. Issuing Country
United Kingdom

4. Issuance Date *(dd-mmm-yyyy)*
11-Oct-2008

5. Expiration Date *(dd-mmm-yyyy)*
10-Oct-2012

6. Surnames *(As in Passport)*
Smith

7. First and Middle Names *(As in Passport)*
John

8. Other Surnames Used *(Maiden, Religious, Professional, Aliases)*
None

9. Other First and Middle Names Used
None

10. Date of Birth *(dd-mmm-yyyy)*
20-May-1986

11. Place of Birth:
City: London
Country: United Kingdom
State/Province:

12. Nationality
English

13. Sex
☑ Male
☐ Female

14. National Identification Number *(If applicable)*

15. Home Address *(Include apartment number, street, city, state or province, postal zone and country)*
56 Mainstream Drive Apt. 25
London United Kingdom

16. Home Telephone Number
+44 08705 301530

Business Phone Number

Mobile/Cell Number

Fax Number

Business Fax Number

Pager Number

17. Marital Status
☐ Married ☑ Single (Never Married)
☐ Widowed ☐ Divorced ☐ Separated

18. Spouse's Full Name *(Even if divorced or separated. Include maiden name.)*

19. Spouse's DOB *(dd-mmm-yyyy)*

20. Name and Address of Present Employer or School
Name:
Address:

21. Present Occupation *(If retired, write "retired". If student, write "student".)*

22. When Do You Intend To Arrive In The U.S.? *(Provide specific date if known)*

23. E-Mail Address

24. At What Address Will You Stay in The U.S.?
222 SW 27 Drive
Weston Florida 33484

BARCODE

25. Name and Telephone Numbers of Person in U.S. Who You Will Be Staying With or Visiting for Tourism or Business
Name:
Home Phone:
Business Phone:
Cell Phone:

DO NOT WRITE IN THIS SPACE

26. How Long Do You Intend To Stay in The U.S.?
4 Months

27. What is The Purpose of Your Trip?
Visitor / Tourist

50 mm x 50 mm

PHOTO

staple or glue photo here

28. Who Will Pay For Your Trip?
Applicant

29. Have You Ever Been in The U.S.? ☐ Yes ☑ No
WHEN? _____
FOR HOW LONG? _____

Form DS-156

30. Have You Ever Been Issued a U.S. Visa? ☐ Yes ☑ No WHEN? _____ WHERE? _____ WHAT TYPE OF VISA? _____	31. Have You Ever Been Refused a U.S. Visa? ☐ Yes ☑ No WHEN? _____ WHERE? _____ WHAT TYPE OF VISA? _____
32. Do You Intend To Work in The U.S.? ☐ Yes ☑ No *(If YES, give the name and complete address of U.S. employer.)*	33. Do You Intend To Study in The U.S.? ☐ Yes ☑ No *(If YES, give the name and complete address of the school.)*

34. Names and Relationships of Persons Traveling With You

None

35. Has Your U.S. Visa Ever Been Cancelled or Revoked? ☐ Yes ☑ No	36. Has Anyone Ever Filed an Immigrant Visa Petition on Your Behalf? ☐ Yes ☑ No If Yes, Who?

37. Are Any of The Following Persons in The U.S., or Do They Have U.S. Legal Permanent Residence or U.S. Citizenship?
   Mark YES or NO and indicate that person's status in the U.S. (i.e., U.S. legal permanent resident, U.S. citizen, visiting, studying, working, etc.).

☐ YES ☑ NO Husband/Wife _____	☐ YES ☑ NO Fiance/Fiancee _____	☐ YES ☑ NO
☐ YES ☑ NO Father/Mother _____	☐ YES ☑ NO Son/Daughter _____	Brother/Sister _____

38. IMPORTANT: ALL APPLICANTS MUST READ AND CHECK THE APPROPRIATE BOX FOR EACH ITEM.
 A visa may not be issued to persons who are within specific categories defined by law as inadmissible to the United States (except when a waiver is obtained in advance). Is any of the following applicable to you?

- Have you ever been arrested or convicted for any offense or crime, even though subject of a pardon, amnesty or other similar legal action? Have you ever unlawfully distributed or sold a controlled substance (drug), or been a prostitute or procurer for prostitutes? ☐ YES ☑ NO

- Have you ever been refused admission to the U.S., or been the subject of a deportation hearing, or sought to obtain or assist others to obtain a visa, entry into the U.S., or any other U.S. immigration benefit by fraud or willful misrepresentation or other unlawful means? Have you attended a U.S. public elementary school on student (F) status or a public secondary school after November 30, 1996 without reimbursing the school? ☐ YES ☑ NO

- Do you seek to enter the United States to engage in export control violations, subversive or terrorist activities, or any other unlawful purpose? Are you a member or representative of a terrorist organization as currently designated by the U.S. Secretary of State? Have you ever participated in persecutions directed by the Nazi government of Germany; or have you ever participated in genocide? ☐ YES ☑ NO

- Have you ever violated the terms of a U.S. visa, or been unlawfully present in, or deported from, the United States? ☐ YES ☑ NO

- Have you ever withheld custody of a U.S. citizen child outside the United States from a person granted legal custody by a U.S. court, voted in the United States in violation of any law or regulation, or renounced U.S. citizenship for the purpose of avoiding taxation? ☐ YES ☑ NO

- Have you ever been afflicted with a communicable disease of public health significance or a dangerous physical or mental disorder, or ever been a drug abuser or addict? ☐ YES ☑ NO

While a YES answer does not automatically signify ineligibility for a visa, if you answered YES you may be required to personally appear before a consular officer.

39. Was this Application Prepared by Another Person on Your Behalf? (If answer is YES, then have that person complete item 40.)	☑ Yes ☐ No

40. Application Prepared By:

NAME: Blank Attorney, P.A. _____   Relationship to Applicant: Attorney _____

ADDRESS: 444 Brickell Ave Suite 1020 Miami FL 33131 _____

Signature of Person Preparing Form: _____   DATE *(dd-mmm-yyyy)* _____

41. I certify that I have read and understood all the questions set forth in this application and the answers I have furnished on this form are true and correct to the best of my knowledge and belief. I understand that any false or misleading statement may result in the permanent refusal of a visa or denial of entry into the United States. I understand that possession of a visa does not automatically entitle the bearer to enter the United States of America upon arrival at a port of entry if he or she is found inadmissible.

APPLICANT'S SIGNATURE _____   DATE *(dd-mmm-yyyy)* _____

Privacy Act and Paperwork Reduction Act Statements

Form DS-157

U.S. Department of State
SUPPLEMENTAL NONIMMIGRANT VISA APPLICATION

Approved OMB 1405-0134
Expires 11/30/2011
Estimated Burden 1 Hour*

PLEASE TYPE OR PRINT YOUR ANSWERS IN THE SPACE PROVIDED BELOW EACH ITEM
PLEASE ATTACH AN ADDITIONAL SHEET IF YOU NEED MORE SPACE TO CONTINUE YOUR ANSWERS

1. Last Name(s) (List all Spellings)	2. First Name(s) (List all Spellings)	3. Full Name (In Native Alphabet)
Smith	John	None

4. Clan or Tribe Name (If Applicable)

5. Spouse's Full Name (If Married)

6. Father's Full Name
Smith, Eric

7. Mother's Full Name
Di, Elena

8. Full Name and Address of Contact Person or Organization in the United States (Include Telephone Number)

Elena Di
222 S.W. 27 Drive, Weston, FL 33484 USA   Phone - (954)777-8855

9. List All Countries You have Entered in the Last Ten Years (Give the Year of Each Visit)	10. List All Countries That Have Ever Issued You a Passport	11. Have you ever lost a passport or had one stolen?
None	United Kingdom	☐ Yes ☒ No

12. Not Including Current Employer, List Your Last Two Employers

Name	Address	Telephone Number	Job Title	Supervisor's Name	Dates of Employment (mm-dd-yyyy) or "Present" From	To

13. List all Professional, Social and Charitable Organizations to Which You Belong (Belonged) or Contribute (Contributed) or with Which You Work (Have Worked).
None

14. Do you have any specialized skills or training, including firearms, explosives, nuclear, biological, or chemical experience?
☐ Yes ☒ No   If YES, please explain

15. Have you ever performed military service?   ☐ Yes ☒ No If yes, complete below.

Name of Country	Branch of Service	Rank/Position	Military Specialty	Dates of Service (mm-dd-yyyy) or "Present" From	To

16. Have you ever been in an armed conflict, either as a participant or victim?   ☐ Yes ☒ No   If YES, please explain.

17. List all educational institutions you attend or have attended. Include vocational institutions but not elementary schools.

Name of Institution	Address/Telephone Number	Course of Study	Dates of Attendance (mm-dd-yyyy) or "Present" From	To
University of London	London, United Kingdom	Business Administration	01-01-2008	Present

18. Have you made specific travel arrangements?   ☐ Yes ☒ No   If YES, please provide a complete itinerary for your travel, including arrival/departure dates, flight information, specific location you will visit, and a point of contact at each location.

DS-157
01-2009

Form I-539

OMB No. 1615-0003; Expires 02/29/12

Department of Homeland Security
U.S. Citizenship and Immigration Services

I-539, Application to Extend/
Change Nonimmigrant Status

START HERE - Please type or print in black ink | For USCIS Use Only

Part 1. Information About You

Family Name	Given Name	Middle Name
DOE	John	

Address -
In care of - Blank Attorney, P.A.

Street Number and Name	222 S.W. 27th Drive	Apt. Number

City	State	Zip Code	Daytime Phone Number
Weston	Florida	33484	(954) 777-8855

Country of Birth	Country of Citizenship
United Kingdom	United Kingdom

Date of Birth (mm/dd/yyyy) 05/20/1986	U. S. Social Security # (if any) None	A-Number (if any) None

Date of Last Arrival Into the U.S. 07/20/2009	I-94 Number 123456789 00

Current Nonimmigrant Status B2	Expires on (mm/dd/yyyy) 01/19/2010

For USCIS Use Only

Returned	Receipt
Date	
Resubmitted	
Date	
Reloc Sent	
Date	
Reloc Rec'd	
Date	

Part 2. Application Type (See instructions for fee)

1. I am applying for: (Check one)
 a. ☒ An extension of stay in my current status.
 b. ☐ A change of status. The new status I am requesting is: _____
 c. ☐ Reinstatement to student status.

2. Number of people included in this application: (Check one)
 a. ☒ I am the only applicant.
 b. ☐ Members of my family are filing this application with me. The total number of people (including me) in the application is: _____
 (Complete the supplement for each co-applicant.)

☐ Applicant Interviewed on _____ Date

Part 3. Processing Information

1. I/We request that my/our current or requested status be extended until (mm/dd/yyyy): 07/18/2010

2. Is this application based on an extension or change of status already granted to your spouse, child, or parent?
 ☒ No ☐ Yes. USCIS Receipt # _____

3. Is this application based on a separate petition or application to give your spouse, child, or parent an extension or change of status? ☒ No ☐ Yes, filed with this I-539.

 ☐ Yes, filed previously and pending with USCIS. Receipt #: _____

4. If you answered "Yes" to Question 3, give the name of the petitioner or applicant:

 N/A

 If the petition or application is pending with USCIS, also give the following data:

Office filed at N/A	Filed on (mm/dd/yyyy)

☐ Extension Granted to (Date): _____

Change of Status/Extension Granted
New Class: From (Date): _____
_____ To (Date): _____

If Denied:
☐ Still within period of stay
☐ S/D to: _____
☐ Place under docket control

Remarks:

Action Block

Part 4. Additional Information

1. For applicant #1, provide passport information: | Valid to: (mm/dd/yyyy)
 Country of Issuance: United Kingdom | 10/10/2012

2. Foreign Address: Street Number and Name | Apt. Number
 56 Mainstream Drive | 25

City or Town	State or Province
London	

Country	Zip/Postal Code
United Kingdom	E15 6PP

To Be Completed by
Attorney or Representative, if any

☐ Fill in box if G-28 is attached to represent the applicant.

ATTY State License #

Form I-539 (Rev. 06/12/09)Y

Form I-539

3. **Answer the following questions. If you answer "Yes" to any question, describe the circumstances in detail and explain on a separate sheet of paper.**

		Yes	No
a.	Are you, or any other person included on the application, an applicant for an immigrant visa?	☐	☒
b.	Has an immigrant petition ever been filed for you or for any other person included in this application?	☐	☒
c.	Has Form I-485, Application to Register Permanent Residence or Adjust Status, ever been filed by you or by any other person included in this application?	☐	☒
d. 1.	Have you, or any other person included in this application, ever been arrested or convicted of any criminal offense since last entering the United States?	☐	☒

d. 2. Have you EVER ordered, incited, called for, commited, assisted, helped with, or otherwise participated in any of the following:

    (a) Acts involving torture or genocide?

    (b) Killing any person?

    (c) Intentionally and severely injuring any person?

    (d) Engaging in any kind of sexual contact or relations with any person who was being forced or threatened?

    (e) Limiting or denying any person's ability to exercise religious beliefs?   ☐   ☒

d. 3. Have you EVER:

    (a) Served in, been a member of, assisted in, or participated in any military unit, paramilitary unit, police unit, self-defense unit, vigilante unit, rebel group, guerrilla group, militia, or insurgent organization?

    (b) Served in any prison, jail, prison camp, detention facility, labor camp, or any other situation that involved detaining persons?   ☐   ☒

d. 4. Have you EVER been a member of, assisted in, or participated in any group, unit, or organization of any kind in which you or other persons used any type of weapon against any person or threatened to do so?   ☐   ☒

d. 5. Have you EVER assisted or participated in selling or providing weapons to any person who to your knowledge used them against another person, or in transporting weapons to any person who to your knowledge used them against another person?   ☐   ☒

d. 6. Have you EVER received any type of military, paramilitary, or weapons training?   ☐   ☒

e.	Have you, or any other person included in this application, done anything that violated the terms of the nonimmigrant status you now hold?	☐	☒
f.	Are you, or any other person included in this application, now in removal proceedings?	☐	☒
g.	Have you, or any other person included in this application, been employed in the United States since last admitted or granted an extension or change of status?	☐	☒

1. If you answered "Yes" to Question 3f, give the following information concerning the removal proceedings on the attached page entitled "**Part 4. Additional information. Page for answers to 3f and 3g.**" Include the name of the person in removal proceedings and information on jurisdiction, date proceedings began, and status of proceedings.

2. If you answered "No" to Question 3g, fully describe how you are supporting yourself on the attached page entitled "**Part 4. Additional information. Page for answers to 3f and 3g.**" Include the source, amount, and basis for any income.

3. If you answered "Yes" to Question 3g, fully describe the employment on the attached page entitled "**Part 4. Additional information. Page for answers to 3f and 3g.**" Include the name of the person employed, name and address of the employer, weekly income, and whether the employment was specifically authorized by USCIS.

Form I-539

		Yes	No
h.	Are you currently or have you ever been a J-1 exchange visitor or a J-2 dependent of a J-1 exchange visitor?	☐	☒

If "Yes," you must provide the dates you maintained status as a J-1 exchange visitor or J-2 dependent. Willful failure to disclose this information (or other relevant information) can result in your application being denied. Also, provide proof of your J-1 or J-2 status, such as a copy of Form DS-2019, Certificate of Eligibility for Exchange Visitor Status, or a copy of your passport that includes the J visa stamp.

Part 5. Applicant's Statement and Signature (*Read the information on penalties in the instructions before completing this section. You must file this application while in the United States.*)

Applicant's Statement (Check One):

☒ I can read and understand English, and have read and understand each and every question and instruction on this form, as well as my answer to each question.

☐ Each and every question and instruction on this form, as well as my answer to each question, has been read to me by the person named below in _____, a language in which I am fluent. I understand each and every question and instruction on this form, as well as my answer to each question.

Applicant's Signature

I certify, under penalty of perjury under the laws of the United States of America, that this application and the evidence submitted with it is all true and correct. I authorize the release of any information from my records that U.S. Citizenship and Immigration Services needs to determine eligibility for the benefit I am seeking.

Signature	Print your Name	Date
	John Doe	
Daytime Telephone Number (954) 777-8855	E-Mail Address	

NOTE: *If you do not completely fill out this form or fail to submit required documents listed in the instructions, you may not be found eligible for the requested benefit and this application may be denied.*

Part 6. Interpreter's Statement

Language used: _____

I certify that I am fluent in English and the above-mentioned language. I further certify that I have read each and every question and instruction on this form, as well as the answer to each question, to this applicant in the above-mentioned language, and the applicant has understood each and every instruction and question on the form, as well as the answer to each question.

Signature	Print Your Name	Date
Firm Name (if applicable)	Daytime Telephone Number (*Area Code and Number*)	
Address	Fax Number (*Area Code and Number*)	E-Mail Address

Form I-539

Part 7. Signature of Person Preparing Form, if Other Than Above (Sign Below)

Signature	Print Your Name	Date

Firm Name (if applicable)	Blank Attorney, P.A,	Daytime Telephone Number *(Area Code and Number)* (954) 777-8855	
Address	222 S.W. 27th Drive Weston, FL 33751	Fax Number *(Area Code and Number)* (954) 777-8855	E-Mail Address attorney@attorney.com

I declare that I prepared this application at the request of the above person and it is based on all information of which I have knowledge.

Part 4. (Continued) Additional Information. (Page 2 for answers to 3f and 3g.)

If you answered "Yes" to Question 3f in Part 4 on Page 3 of this form, give the following information concerning the removal proceedings. Include the name of the person in removal proceedings and information on jurisdiction, date proceedings began, and status of proceedings.

```
N/A
```

If you answered "No" to Question 3g in Part 4 on Page 3 of this form, fully describe how you are supporting yourself. Include the source, amount and basis for any income.

```
Applicant will be supporting himself with personal funds and funds from family members. An
additional six months are being requested so applicant can continue sightseeing and visit family
members. Once stay has expired, applicant will be departing the United States by air. See copy of
return ticket attached.
```

If you answered "Yes" to Question 3g in Part 4 on Page 3 of this form, fully describe the employment. Include the name of the person employed, name and address of the employer, weekly income, and whether the employment was specifically authorized by USCIS.

```
N/A
```

Form I-539

Supplement -1
Attach to Form I-539 when more than one person is included in the petition or application.
(List each person separately. Do not include the person named in Form I-539.)

Family Name	Given Name	Middle Name	Date of Birth (mm/dd/yyyy)
Country of Birth	Country of Citizenship	U.S. Social Security # (if any)	A-Number (if any)

Date of Arrival (mm/dd/yyyy)	I-94 Number
Current Nonimmigrant Status:	Expires on (mm/dd/yyyy)
Country Where Passport Issued	Expiration Date (mm/dd/yyyy)

Family Name	Given Name	Middle Name	Date of Birth (mm/dd/yyyy)
Country of Birth	Country of Citizenship	U.S. Social Security # (if any)	A-Number (if any)

Date of Arrival (mm/dd/yyyy)	I-94 Number
Current Nonimmigrant Status:	Expires on (mm/dd/yyyy)
Country Where Passport Issued	Expiration Date (mm/dd/yyyy)

Family Name	Given Name	Middle Name	Date of Birth (mm/dd/yyyy)
Country of Birth	Country of Citizenship	U.S. Social Security # (if any)	A-Number (if any)

Date of Arrival (mm/dd/yyyy)	I-94 Number
Current Nonimmigrant Status:	Expires on (mm/dd/yyyy)
Country Where Passport Issued	Expiration Date (mm/dd/yyyy)

Family Name	Given Name	Middle Name	Date of Birth (mm/dd/yyyy)
Country of Birth	Country of Citizenship	U.S. Social Security # (if any)	A-Number (if any)

Date of Arrival (mm/dd/yyyy)	I-94 Number
Current Nonimmigrant Status:	Expires on (mm/dd/yyyy)
Country Where Passport Issued	Expiration Date (mm/dd/yyyy)

Family Name	Given Name	Middle Name	Date of Birth (mm/dd/yyyy)
Country of Birth	Country of Citizenship	U.S. Social Security # (if any)	A-Number (if any)

Date of Arrival (mm/dd/yyyy)	I-94 Number
Current Nonimmigrant Status:	Expires on (mm/dd/yyyy)
Country Where Passport Issued	Expiration Date (mm/dd/yyyy)

If you need additional space, attach a separate sheet of paper.
Place your name, A-Number, if any, date of birth, form number, and application date at the top of the sheet of paper.

Form G-28

OMB No. 1615-0105; Expires 04/30/2012

**G-28, Notice of Entry of Appearance
as Attorney or Accredited Representative**

Department of Homeland Security

Part 1. Notice of Appearance as Attorney or Accredited Representative

A. This appearance is in regard to immigration matters before:

[x] USCIS - List the form number(s): I-539   [ ] CBP - List the specific matter in which appearance is entered:

[ ] ICE - List the specific matter in which appearance is entered: _____

B. I hereby enter my appearance as attorney or accredited representative at the request of:

List Petitioner, Applicant, or Respondent. **NOTE:** Provide the mailing address of Petitioner, Applicant, or Respondent being represented, and **not** the address of the attorney or accredited representative, except when filed under VAWA.

Principal Petitioner, Applicant, or Respondent			A Number or Receipt Number, if any	
Name: Last	First	Middle		[ ] Petitioner
DOE	John		None	[x] Applicant
				[ ] Respondent

Address: Street Number and Street Name   Apt. No.   City   State   Zip Code

Applicant's Address

Pursuant to the Privacy Act of 1974 and DHS policy, I hereby consent to the disclosure to the named Attorney or Accredited Representative of any record pertaining to me that appears in any system of records of USCIS, USCBP, or USICE.

Signature of Petitioner, Applicant, or Respondent   **Date**
                                                                          11/08/2009

Part 2. Information about Attorney or Accredited Representative *(Check applicable items(s) below)*

A. [x]   I am an attorney and a member in good standing of the bar of the highest court(s) of the following State(s), possession(s), territory(ies), commonwealth(s), or the District of Columbia: State of _____   Supreme Court

   I am not [x] or [ ] **am subject to any order of any court or administrative agency disbarring, suspending, enjoining, restraining, or otherwise restricting me in the practice of law (If you are subject to any order(s), explain fully on reverse side).**

B. [ ]   I am an accredited representative of the following qualified non-profit religious, charitable, social service, or similar organization established in the United States, so recognized by the Department of Justice, Board of Immigration Appeals pursuant to 8 CFR 1292.2. Provide name of organization and expiration date of accreditation:

C. [ ]   I am associated with _____ .

   The attorney or accredited representative of record previously filed Form G-28 in this case, and my appearance as an attorney or accredited representative is at his or her request *(If you check this item, also complete item A or B above in **Part 2**, whichever is appropriate).*

Part 3. Name and Signature of Attorney or Accredited Representative

I have read and understand the regulations and conditions contained in 8 CFR 103.2 and 292 governing appearances and representation before the Department of Homeland Security. I declare under penalty of perjury under the laws of the United States that the information I have provided on this form is true and correct.

Name of Attorney or Accredited Representative	Attorney Bar Number(s), if any
Attorney or Accredited Representative's Name	
Signature of Attorney or Accredited Representative	Date 11/08/2009

Complete Address of Attorney or Organization of Accredited Representative (Street Number and Street Name, Suite No., City, State, Zip Code)

Attorney or Accredited Representative's Address

Phone Number *(Include area code)*	Fax Number, if any *(Include area code)*	E-Mail Address, if any
(305) 442-1322	(305) 444-7578	Valid E-mail Address

Form G-28 (Rev. 04/22/09)N

CHAPTER 3

Temporary Visas for Working

I. Introduction

Individuals may obtain a temporary visa to work in the United States. The U.S. government and practitioners refer to these types of visas as work visas. The prospective employee who is seeking the visa to work is the beneficiary. The prospective employer is the petitioner. The most utilized visas for working in the United States are the H visa, L visa, E visa and J visa. It is important to note that individuals are only allowed to work for the company or organization that files the petition. The petitioning company or organization may be a newly established company or organization or one that has been operating for a long time. The type of business to which the organization dedicates itself is not limited as long as the position being offered to the worker is related to the business of the company.

II. The H Visa—Temporary Worker

There are several types of H visas for temporary workers. Each type of visa allows the individual to perform a specific job. The H1-B is for professionals who are coming to work in a specialty occupation; the H1-C is for nurses who will work in particular positions; the H2-A is for agricultural workers; the H2-B is for non-agricultural workers; and the H-3 is for trainees (the H-4 is the accompanying visa granted to the spouses and children under 21 years old). INA § 101(a)(15)(H)(i)(b), 8 U.S.C. § 1101(a)(15)(H)(i)(b); 8 C.F.R. § 214.2(h)(1).

A. The H-1B Visa—Specialty Occupation—Professional Visa and Fashion Models

The H1-B visa is the most utilized H visa in the practice. This visa allows individuals who are offered a position with a U.S. employer to work for that employer as long as the position is in their field. It is important to note that while the position must be one that usually requires the attainment of at least a bachelor's degree, the worker does not necessarily have to have the degree. The worker may qualify based on years of employment experience that are determined to be the equivalent to a bachelor's degree. INA § 101(a)(15)(H)(i)(b), 8 C.F.R. § 214.2(h)(1).

The H1-B is initially valid for three years. The individual is in status as long as s/he remains employed with the same employer in the same professional occupation and as long as the underlying business on which the visa is based remains a viable entity. The maximum number of years an individual may remain with the H1-B status is six years. If a labor certification has been pending for more than 365 days, the petitioner can request further extensions (please refer to Chapter 7 for employment-based adjustments). If a Labor Certification has been approved and an I-140 has been approved as well, the petitioner can request extensions in three-year increments.

1. Forms Required:

   The Labor Condition Attestation, Form ETA 9035, must be electronically filed with DOL. The Petition for Non-Immigrant Worker, Form I-129, H Classification Supplement, H1B

Data Collection and Filling Fee Exception Supplement, G-28, certified Form ETA 9035 received from the DOL and Forms I-539 with G-28 (for the spouse and accompanying children) must be submitted to the USCIS Service Center.

2. Documents Required:

   a. Labor Condition Application (LCA), Form ETA 9035;

   b. University or post-graduate degree and/or certificates of applicant's education;

   c. Résumé;

   d. Letter of experience from previous employers;

   e. Passport;

   f. Form I-94; and

   g. Credential Evaluation if the degree is a foreign degree.

Congress has established an annual fiscal year limitation of 65,000 on the number of available H1-B visas, commonly referred to as the "H1-B cap." Under the terms of the legislation implementing the United States-Chile Free Trade Agreement and the United States-Singapore Free Trade Agreement, 6,800 of the 65,000 available H1-B visas are annually set aside for the Chile/Singapore H1-B program.

As directed by the H1-B Visa Reform Act of 2004, the first 20,000 H1-B petitions filed on behalf of aliens holding U.S.-earned master's or higher degrees will be exempt from any fiscal year cap on available H1-B visas. USCIS also notes that petitions for new H1-B employment are exempt from the annual cap if the aliens will be employed at institutions of higher education or related or affiliated not-for-profit entities, or not-for-profit research organizations or governmental research organizations. Thus, petitions for these exempt H1-B categories may be filed at any time during the fiscal year.

B. The H-2A Visa—Agricultural Worker

This type of visa allows agricultural workers to work in the United States in temporary or seasonal agricultural positions. An employer may file one application for multiple aliens. An H-2A petition may be filed by either the employer listed on the certification, the employer's agent or the association of the U.S. agricultural producer names as a joint employer on the certification. The petition may be extended for the validity of the labor certification or for a period of up to one year. The alien's total period of stay under this status may not exceed three years (an exception for the Virgin Islands exists that the total period of stay may not exceed 45 days.) INA § 101(a)(15)(H)(ii)(a); 8 USC § 1101(a)(H)(ii)(a); 8 C.F.R. § 214.2(h)(2).

1. Forms Required:

   Form ETA 9142 including Appendix A1 and A2 must be electronically filed with DOL. The Forms I-129, H Classification Supplement, G-28 and certified Form 9142 from the DOL and Forms I-539 with G-28 (for the spouse and accompanying children) must be submitted to the USCIS Service Center.

2. Documents Required:

   a. Passport; and

   b. Form I-94 (if in the United States).

C. The H-2B Visa—Unskilled Foreign Worker

This visa allows an individual to work in the United States for a temporary period to fill an offered non agricultural position that does not require any specific studies or experience. The employment must be on a one-time need based upon low U.S. worker availability, seasonal, peak load or intermittent needs. The petition may be extended for the validity of the labor certification or for a period of up to one year. The alien's total period of stay under this status may not exceed three years (an exception for the Virgin Islands exists that the total period of stay may not exceed 45 days.) An H-2B worker who has reached the three year maximum period of stay must wait outside the U. S. for three months before seeking extension, change of status, or admission under H or L status. INA § 101(a)(15)(H)(ii)(b); 8 USC § 1101 (a)(15)(H)(ii)(b); 8 C. F. R. § 214.2(h)(2)(iv).

Initially the DOL must certify the position. This is done by filing the ETA Form 9142 and Appendix B-1. The employer must request and obtain a prevailing wage determination (Form ETA 9141) that is valid either on the date recruitment begins or the filing date of the ETA Form 9142. No wage determination permits an employer to pay a wage lower than the highest wage required by any applicable Federal, State, or local wage law. Upon receipt of the certification, the employer must file the certified ETA Form 9142 received from Department of Labor, Form I-129, Supplement H and appropriate documentation to the USCIS Service Center (see www.uscis.gov for more information)

Employers receiving certification must retain records and documents supporting the ETA Form 9142. Retention period of documents is 3 years from date of certification.

There is a 66,000 annual limit or cap on new H-2B visas.

33,000 visas for new workers are reserved for employers whose seasonal needs start in the first half of the government fiscal year (October through March) and 33,000 are reserved for employers whose needs start in the second half of the fiscal year (April through September).

1. Forms Required:

   Forms ETA Form 9142 and ETA Form 9142, Appendix A.2 and the recruitment report must be filed with the Chicago National Processing Center, U.S. Department of Labor, Employment and Training Administration, Chicago National Processing Center, 844 N. Rush Street, 12th Floor, Chicago, IL 60611. However, before filing check for changes of filing address at *www.foreignlaborcert.doleta.gov*. Forms I-129, Supplement H, G-28 and certified Form ETA 9142 received from the DOL and Forms I-539 with G-28 (for the spouse and accompanying children) must be submitted to the USCIS Service Center.

2. Documents Required:

   a. Passport; and

   b. Form I-94 (if in the United States).

D. The H-3 Visa—Trainee

This visa allows individuals to come to the United States temporarily to receive instruction and training from a company or organization in the United States. The training must be necessary in order for them to use their skills abroad. The type of training they will be performing in the United States must not be available in their own country. This visa is valid for the period of the training program, but may not exceed two years. INA § 101(a)(15)(H)(iii); 8 USC § 1101(a)(15)(H)(iii); 8 C.F.R. § 214(h)(ii)(E).

The petitioner must demonstrate that:

- The proposed training is not available in the beneficiary's own country;
- The beneficiary will not be placed in a position that is in the normal operation of the business and in which citizens and resident workers are regularly employed;
- The beneficiary will not engage in productive employment unless such employment is incidental and necessary to the training; and
- The training will benefit the beneficiary in pursuing a career outside the United States.

   In addition, each petition must include a statement which:

- Describes the type of training and supervision to be given and the structure of the training program;
- Sets forth the proportion of time that will be devoted to productive employment;
- Shows the numbers of hours that will be spent, respectively, in classroom instruction and in on-the-job training;

- Describes the career abroad for which the training will be prepare the alien;
- Indicates the reasons why such training cannot be obtained in the alien's country and why it is necessary for him/her to be trained in the United States; and
- Indicates the source of any remuneration received by the trainee and any benefit that will accrue to the petitioner for providing the training.

A training program may not be approved which:

- Deals in generalities with no fixed schedule, objectives or means of evaluation;
- Is incompatible with the nature of the petitioner's business or enterprise;
- Is on behalf of a beneficiary who already possesses substantial training and expertise in the proposed field of training;
- Is in a field in which it is unlikely that the knowledge or skill will be used outside the United States;
- Will result in productive employment beyond that which is incidental and necessary to the training;
- Is designed to recruit and train aliens for the ultimate staffing of domestic operations in the United States;
- Does not establish that the petitioner has the physical plant and sufficiently trained manpower to provide the training specified; or
- Is designed to extend the total allowable period of training previously authorized a nonimmigrant student.

1. Forms Required:

   Petition for Non-Immigrant Worker, Form I-129, H Classification Supplement, G-28, and Forms I-539 with G-28 (for the spouse and accompanying children) must be submitted to the USCIS Service Center.

2. Documents Required:

   a. Training manual;

   b. Credentials of H-3 trainer;

   c. Color photographs of training facilities;

   d. Company literature;

   e. Necessity letter from employer;

   f. Proof of relationship with H-3 beneficiary (e.g., birth certificate or marriage certificate);

   g. Copy of all passport pages, of principal and its dependent members; and

   h. Form I-94.

E. The TN Status

TN status allows certain qualifying Canadian and Mexican citizens to temporarily work for an employer in the United States under the North American Free Trade Agreement (NAFTA). Employment must be temporary and the alien must demonstrate s/he has no intention to permanently reside in the United States. INA § 214(e); 8 C.F.R. § 214.6.

The position must be listed on a list of approvable occupations. A Canadian or Mexican citizen who has reached the maximum stay for H or L status may change to TN status as long as the intent to remain in the United States is temporary.

1. Forms Required:

   Non-Immigrant Visa Application Form (Mexicans only)

2. Documents Required:

   a. Proof of Canadian or Mexican citizenship;

b. Statement explaining position similar to H1-B1 petition statement;

c. University or post-graduate degree and license, if required;

d. Résumé;

e. Passport;

f. Current passport or if Canadian can provide birth certificate in lieu of passport; and

g. Credential evaluation if a foreign degree, except for degrees from Canada, Mexico or the United States.

The procedures for obtaining an initial TN visa for Mexican citizens are now very similar to obtaining a TN for a Canadian national; Mexican aliens must still apply for a nonimmigrant visa to request admission into the United States.

If spouse and/or children (unmarried children under 21 years of age) are accompanying or joining the TN professional, each will need proof of citizenship. Applicants must demonstrate a bona fide spousal or parent-child relationship to the principal TN visa holders. Dependents do not have to be Mexican citizens; they are considered a Trade Dependent (TD) and are not authorized to work (study is permitted).

The fees for dependents are paid by the TN professional. Dependents have to present copies of the TN's entry documents, Form I-94, proof of citizenship and evidence of a legal relationship (e.g., marriage certificate or long form birth certificate), which entitles them to be properly classified as TDs of a TN professional.

Please, check the American Embassy website for Mexico to determine processing time for the different consulates in Mexico.

III. The E Visa

A mandatory prerequisite to an E visa is a treaty between the United States for trade or commerce. Only citizens or nationals of certain countries are eligible for this type of visa. The list of countries varies depending on whether the visa will be for an E-1 visa or an E-2 visa. The E-1 visa is for an individual who is doing substantial trade with the United States. The E-2 visa is for an investor who is directing an investment. The E-2 visa is also the accompanying visa that is granted to the worker's spouses and children under 21 years old. Both types of E visas are issued for one year when the business enterprise is less than one year old. The visas will be extended indefinitely for five-year increments after the initial issuance. INA § 101(a)(15)(E); 8 C.F.R. § 214.2(e).

Treaty countries are as follows:

E-1
Australia, Austria, Belgium, Bosnia-Herzegovina, Brunei, Canada, China (Taiwan), Colombia, Costa Rica, Croatia, Denmark, Estonia, Ethiopia, Finland, France (includes Martinique, Guadalupe, French Guiana and Reunion), Germany, Greece, Honduras, Iran, Ireland, Israel, Italy, Japan, Jordan, Korea (South), Latvia, Liberia, Luxembourg, Macedonia, Mexico, Netherlands (includes Aruba and Netherlands Antilles), Norway, Oman, Pakistan, Paraguay, Philippines, Poland, Slovenia, Spain, Suriname, Sweden, Switzerland, Thailand, Togo, Turkey, United Kingdom and Yugoslavia.

E-2
Albania, Armenia, Australia, Austria, Azerbaijan, Bahrain, Bangladesh, Belgium, Bolivia, Bosnia-Herzegovina, Bulgaria, Cameroon, Canada, China (Taiwan), Colombia, Congo (Brazzaville), Congo (Kinshasa), Costa Rica, Croatia, Czech Republic, Ecuador, Egypt, Estonia, Ethiopia, Finland, France, Georgia, Germany, Grenada, Honduras, Iran, Ireland, Italy, Jamaica, Japan, Jordan, Kazakhstan, Korea (South), Kyrgyzstan, Latvia, Liberia, Lithuania, Luxembourg, Macedonia, Mexico, Moldova, Mongolia, Morocco, Netherlands, Norway, Oman, Pakistan, Panama, Paraguay, Philippines, Poland, Romania, Senegal, Slovak Republic, Slovenia, Spain, Sri Lanka, Suriname, Sweden, Switzerland, Thailand, Togo, Trinidad and Tobago, Tunisia, Turkey, Ukraine, United Kingdom and Yugoslavia.

A. The E-1 Visa—Treaty Trader

This visa is for individuals who have a company or business with which the volume of trade between the United States is 50 percent or more in purchases and sales. INA § 101(a)(15)(E)(i); 8 C.F.R. § 214.2(e)(1).

1. Forms Required:

   The Forms I-129, Supplement E, and G-28 with Forms I-539 and G-28 (for the spouse and accompanying children) must be submitted to the USCIS Service Center. For consular processing, submit OF-156E (treaty questionnaire).

2. Documents Required:

   a. Previous educational degrees and certificates;

   b. Résumé and/or experience letters reflecting experience as a director or executive of a foreign company;

   c. Invoices and receipts to show extent of trade with the United States;

   d. Business plan to show the future extent of trade with the United States;

   e. Passport; and

   f. Form I-94.

B. The E-2 Visa—Investor

This type of visa is issued to individuals who invest in the United States. The investment should be in a functioning business. It is not available for solely investing in real estate because investment in real estate does not generally require that a person operate the business. It is recommended that if there is a business operating outside the United States, the foreign company should continue operating in order for the individual to later immigrate to the United States under a multinational executive visa (EB-1), employment-based residence, which will be explained in another chapter. INA § 101(a)(15)(E)(ii); 8 C.F.R. § 214.2(e)(2).

1. Forms Required:

   The Forms I-129, Supplement E and G-28 with Forms I-539 and G-28 (for the spouse and accompanying children) must be submitted to the USCIS Service Center. For consular processing, submit DS-156E (treaty questionnaire).

2. Documents Required:

   a. Previous educational degrees and certificates;

   b. Proof of investment or income from sources other than the U. S. investment;

   c. Résumé and/or experience letters reflecting the ability of the individual to direct the enterprise;

   d. Documents of the U.S. company:

      1. Occupational License/permits to operate the U.S. company;

      2. Lease/deed for premises of U.S. company;

      3. Employer's wage and tax report and quarterly income reports;

      4. IRS Form SS-4 Application for Federal Employer Identification Number, which may be obtained from the Internal Revenue Service at *www.irs.gov*;

      5. Stock certificate and/or evidence of exact ownership of the U.S. and foreign companies;

      6. Bank letter (evidence showing authorization and/or transfer of funds to the United States);

      7. Articles of Incorporation and State Charter Number;

      8. Financial Statement;

9. Contracts, sale and purchase receipts, budget projections;

10. Business plan;

11. Photographs of the business premises; and

12. Brochures, advertisements.

e. Passport of the applicant valid for at least one year. Each member of the family needs a passport;

f. Visa application;

g. Two recent photographs of the applicant;

h. Wire transfers from the foreign country; and

i. Form I-94.

C. The E-3 Visa — Specialty Occupation — Australian Aliens

This type of visa is new and was created pursuant to the Australian Free Trade Agreement. The final rule was published in September 2005. The E-3 classification applies to nationals of Australia who are coming to the United States solely to perform services in a specialty occupation. The E-3 classification also applies to the principal beneficiary's spouses and children.

Generally, a specialty occupation is one that cannot be performed without a bachelor's degree or higher (or its equivalent) in a specific field of study or a narrow range of fields of study. The requirements for E-3s with respect to the education of the beneficiary and the job duties to be performed mirror the H-1 requirements 8 CFR § 214.2(h)(4)(iv).

No petition is required to be filed for an E-3 visa. The application is made directly at the consulate, similar to other nonimmigrant classifications such as the B-1/B-2 or F-1 classifications. However, a Labor Condition Application that reflects the job offer at the appropriate prevailing wage rate is required as part of the E-3 application.

The term for admission for E-3 beneficiaries is the same as for E-1s and E-2s, in that the initial period of admission is two years. E-3s will receive two-year extensions indefinitely so long as they otherwise continue to qualify for the E-3 classification.

Spouses of E-3 principal beneficiaries are not required to be Australian nationals and are eligible to apply for work authorization in the United States. Such spousal employment may be in a position other than a specialty occupation INA § 214(e)(6).

The forms required and documents are the same as those required for an H1B with the exception of not requiring an I129 petition.

IV. The L Visa

The L visa is for a temporary worker who is coming to work at a subsidiary of a foreign company. L-1A is for a manager or executive. L1-B is for someone with specialized knowledge. L2 is the accompanying visa that spouses and children under 21 years old receive with the worker. The petitioner must be a U.S. company. The U.S. company must be the subsidiary or the affiliate of the foreign company. The foreign parent company must hold at least 51 percent of the U.S. company or one shareholder must hold at least 51 percent of the ownership of both a foreign company and a U.S. company, in such case the U.S. company is the subsidiary of the foreign company. Affiliation exists between legal entities where an identical group of individuals own and control both businesses in basically the same proportion or percentage.

Both types of L worker visas are issued for one year when the business enterprise is less than one year old. The visa will be extended after the initial issuance in two- and three-year increments for a maximum of six years. INA § 101(a)(15)(L), 8 USC § 1101(a)(15)(L); 8 CFR § 214.2(l)(1).

A. The L-1A Visa—Intracompany Transferee

This visa allows an intracompany executive or manager to come to the United States to establish a new business. After the first year that this company has been in business, an immigrant visa may be requested (Multinational Executive/Manager EB-1 visa) as long as the company in the country where the petitioner is originally from is still in business. This type of visa is recommended for people who wish to immigrate with their families in the future. INA § 101(a)(15)(L)(i)(a).

1. Definition:

    a. Executive capacity is:

    An assignment within an organization in which the employee primarily: (i) directs the management of the organization of a major component or functioning organization; (ii) establishes the goals and policies of the organization, component or function; (iii) exercises wide latitude in discretionary decision-making; and (iv) receives only general supervision or direction from higher level executives, directors or stockholders of the organization.

    b. Managerial capacity is:

    An assignment within an organization in which the employee primarily: (i) manages the organization, a department, subdivision, function or organization (ii) supervises and controls the work of other supervisory, professional or employees, or manages an essential function within the organization, a department or subdivision of the organization; (iii) has the authority to fire or recommend those as well as other personnel actions (such as promotion), if another employee or other employees are directly supervised or functions at a senior level and the organizational hierarchy or with respect to the function managed, if no other employee is directly supervised; and (iv) exercises direction over the day-to-day operations of the activity or function.

2. Forms Required:

    The Forms I-129, I-129 Supplement L and G-28 and Forms I-539 and G-28 (for the spouse and accompanying children) must be submitted to the USCIS Service Center.

3. Documents Required:

    a. Previous educational degrees and certificates;

    b. Résumé and/or experience letters reflecting the ability of the individual to direct the enterprise;

    c. Documents of the U.S. company:

        1. Occupational license/permits to operate in the U.S., as well as the company's lease/deed for U.S. premises;

        2. Employer's wage and tax report and photocopy of quarterly income tax return for U.S. location;

        3. Federal Employer Identification Number (new office);

        4. Stock certificate and/or documentary evidence showing that the foreign corporation or the majority shareholder of the foreign corporation own 51 percent or more of the shares of the U.S. company (if an affiliate, establish the claimed affiliation);

        5. Bank letter (evidence showing authorization and/or transfer of funds to the U.S. from the foreign branch, including dollar amount of deposit) or bank statements;

        6. Articles of Incorporation and State Charter Number;

        7. Current financial statement;

        8. Contracts, sale and purchase receipts, budget projections, photographs, brochures, advertising, yellow pages directory, etc.

    d. Documents pertaining to the foreign company:

1. Photocopy of the memorandum and Articles of Association of the foreign company;

2. Notarized statement by the secretary and/or accountant of the foreign company as to the officers, directors, shareholders and percentage of shares held by each and the number of employees by the Chamber of Commerce;

3. Photocopy of the latest financial statement of the foreign company;

4. Evidence that the foreign company has been operating for the prior year, together with evidence that it is still operating: current invoices, bills of sale, payroll records of employees, lease for the preceding year and purchase orders;

5. The latest income tax return for the foreign corporation;

6. Bank letter for the foreign corporation, indicating present balance and the status of account for the preceding year;

7. If available, a copy of foreign corporation's payroll records showing the beneficiary on the payroll for the immediate year and/or personal tax return of the beneficiary;

8. Photocopies of any current licenses required for the operation of the foreign company;

9. Photographs of the premises of the company (both inside and outside);

10. Organizational chart of the company;

11. List of employee's duties; and

12. Utility bills.

e. Passport of the applicant; and

f. Form I-94.

B. The L-1B Visa—Specialized Knowledge Employee

This type of visa allows a person with specialized knowledge to come to the United States to work for the qualifying U.S. company. It has to be demonstrated that said specialty is difficult to be performed by other people and necessary for the operation of the development of the business in the United States. INA § 101(a)(15)(L); 8 C.F.R. § 214.2(l).

1. Forms Required:

The Forms I-129, Supplement L and G-28 and Forms I-539 and G-28 (for the spouse and accompanying children) must be submitted to the USCIS Service Center.

2. Documents Required:

a. Previous educational degrees and certificates;

b. Résumé and/or experience letters reflecting the ability of the individual to direct the enterprise;

c. Documents of the U.S. company:

1. Occupational license/permits to operate in the U.S., as well as the company's lease/deed for U.S. premises;

2. Employer's wage and tax report and photocopy of quarterly income tax return for U.S. location;

3. Federal Employer Identification Number (new office or Form IRS SS-4);

4. Stock certificate and/or documentary evidence showing the exact ownership of the U.S. and foreign company and evidence establishing the claimed affiliation;

5. Bank letter (evidence showing authorization and/or transfer of funds to the U.S. from the foreign branch, including dollar amount of deposit) or bank statements);

6. Articles of Incorporation and State Charter Number;

7. Current financial statement;

8. Contracts, sale and purchase receipts, budget projections, photographs, brochures, advertising, yellow pages directory, etc.

  d. Documents pertaining to the foreign company:

1. Photocopy of the memorandum and Articles of Association of the foreign company;

2. Notarized statement by the secretary and/or accountant of the foreign company as to the officers, directors, shareholders and percentage of shares held by each and the number of employees by the Chamber of Commerce;

3. Photocopy of the latest financial statement of the foreign company;

4. Evidence that the foreign company has been operating for the prior year, together with evidence that it is still operating: current invoices, bills of sale, payroll records of employees, lease for the preceding year and purchase orders;

5. The latest income tax return for the foreign corporation;

6. Bank letter for the foreign corporation, indicating present balance and the status of account for the preceding year;

7. If available, a copy of foreign corporation's payroll records showing the beneficiary on the payroll for the immediate year and/or personal tax return of the beneficiary;

8. Photocopies of any current licenses required for the operation of the foreign company;

9. Photographs of the premises of the company (both inside and outside);

10. Organizational chart of the company;

11. List of employee's duties; and

12. Utility bills.

  e. Passport of the applicant; and

  f. Form I-94.

Appendix

1. Employer/Employee Questionnaire
2. Form I-129, Supplement E
3. E-2 Petition Letter
4. Form G-28
5. Form I-129 and Supplement H
6. H-1B Petition Letter
7. Form G-28
8. Form I-129 and Supplement L
9. L-1 Petition Letter
10. Form G-28

Employer Questionnaire

A. Information Concerning Employer/Petitioner

1. Company name: _____

2. Address: _____

3. Telephone number(s): _____

4. Fax number: _____

5. E-mail address: _____

6. Internet website (www.): _____

7. If employee will work at a different address than above, please state: _____

   _____

8. Date established: _____

9. Employer tax ID #: _____

10. Number of total employees: _____

11. Number of employees on H-1B1 visa: _____

12. Approximate *gross* annual income for current year:

   $ _____

13. Approximate *net* annual income for current year:

   $ _____

14. Please give a detailed description of business:

   _____

   _____

> *Please attach all available information concerning the petitioner (e.g., brochures, advertising material, catalogues, published articles, references, etc).*

15. Full name of company representative who will sign petitioning documents:

_____

16. Which position does the representative hold with the company (e.g., president, vice president, manager of

human resources)? _____

_____

17. Name of contact person at petitioning company, if different from above: _____

_____

B. Information Concerning the Position offered

1. Job title: _____

2. Detailed description of duties to be performed:

_____

_____

_____

3. Hours per week: _____

4. Wages per week: _____

5. Would there be additional compensation? If so, please explain: _____

_____

6. If so, what would that compensation be valued at? _____

_____

7. How long do you intend to employ the beneficiary? _____

_____

Employee Questionnaire

1. Full Name: _____
   Last   First   Middle

2. Address abroad: _____

   _____

   _____

3. Place of Birth: _____
   City/State/Province   Country

4. Date of birth: _____
   Month   Day   Year

5. Country of Citizenship: _____

   Profession/Occupation: _____

6. Do you have a university/college degree?   Yes { }   No { }

   Major/primary field of study: _____

   Degree obtained: _____

   When and where? _____

7. How many years did you spend at college/university? _____

8. Social Security Number: SSN# _____

9. Alien Registration Number: A# _____

10. Address in the U.S. where you will reside: _____

    _____

    _____

11. Gender: Male { }   Female { }

12. Marital status: Married { }   Divorced { } Single { }   Widowed { }

    Spouse's Name: _____
    Last   First   Middle

    Date of birth: _____
    Month   Day   Year

    Place of Birth: _____
    City/State/Province   Country

13. Do you have any children?   Yes { }   No { }

    Child's Name: _____
    Last   First   Middle

    Date of Birth: _____
    Month   Day   Year

    Place of Birth: _____
    City/State/Province   Country

    Country of Citizenship: _____

Form I-129

OMB No. 1615-0009; Expires 07/31/2010

Department of Homeland Security
U.S. Citizenship and Immigration Services

I-129, Petition for a
Nonimmigrant Worker

START HERE - Type or print in black ink.	**For USCIS Use Only**

Part 1. Information about the employer filing this petition *(If the employer is an individual, complete **Number 1**. Organizations should complete **Number 2**.)*

1. Family Name *(Last Name)*   Given Name *(First Name)*

Full Middle Name   Telephone No. w/Area Code
( )

2. Company or Organization Name   Telephone No. w/Area Code
JOHN DOE, INC.   ( )

Mailing Address: *(Street Number and Name)*   Suite #
123 S.W. 27th Avenue

C/O: *(In Care Of)*

City	State/Province
Miami	Forida

Country	Zip/Postal Code	E-Mail Address *(If Any)*
USA	33135	johndoeinc@johndoeinc.c

Federal Employer Identification #	U.S. Social Security #	Individual Tax #
12-34567890	N/A	None

For USCIS Use Only

Returned	Receipt
Date	
Date	
Resubmitted	
Date	
Date	
Reloc Sent	
Date	
Date	
Reloc Rec'd	
Date	
Date	

☐ Petitioner Interviewed on ____

☐ Beneficiary Interviewed on ____

Class: _____
\# of Workers: _____
Priority Number: _____
Validity Dates: _____
From: _____
To: _____

Part 2. Information about this petition *(See instructions for fee information.)*

1. Requested Nonimmigrant Classification. *(Write classification symbol):* E2

2. Basis for Classification *(Check one):*

   a. ☒ New employment (including new employer filing H-1B extension).

   b. ☐ Continuation of previously approved employment without change with the same employer.

   c. ☐ Change in previously approved employment.

   d. ☐ New concurrent employment.

   e. ☐ Change of employer.

   f. ☐ Amended petition.

3. If you checked **Box 2b, 2c, 2d, 2e,** or **2f**, give the petition receipt number.
N/A

4. Prior Petition. If the beneficiary is in the U.S. as a nonimmigrant and is applying to change and/or extend his or her status, give the prior petition or application receipt #:
N/A

5. Requested Action *(Check one):*

   a. ☐ Notify the office in **Part 4** so the person(s) can obtain a visa or be admitted. (**NOTE:** *a petition is not required for an E-1 or E-2 visa*).

   b. ☒ Change the person(s)' status and extend their stay since the person(s) are all now in the U.S. in another status *(see instructions for limitations)*. This is available only where you check "New Employment" in **Item 2**, above.

   c. ☐ Extend the stay of the person(s) since they now hold this status.

☐ **Classification Approved**
   ☐ Consulate/POE/PFI Notified
   At _____
   ☐ Extension Granted
   ☐ COS/Extension Granted

Partial Approval *(explain)*

Action Block

To Be Completed by
Attorney or Representative, if any.

☐ Fill in box if G-28 is attached to represent the applicant.

ATTY State License # _____

Form I-129

Part 2. Information about this petition *(See instructions for fee information.) (Continued)*

   d. ☐ Amend the stay of the person(s) since they now hold this status.

   e. ☐ Extend the status of a nonimmigrant classification based on a Free Trade Agreement. *(See Free Trade Supplement for TN and H1B1 to Form I-129).*

   f. ☐ Change status to a nonimmigrant classification based on a Free Trade Agreement. *(See Free Trade Supplement for TN and H1B1 to Form I-129).*

6. Total number of workers in petition *(See instructions relating to when more than one worker can be included):*

    1

Part 3. Information about the person(s) you are filing for *Complete the blocks below. Use the continuation sheet to name each person included in this petition.*

1. If an Entertainment Group, Give the Group Name

N/A

Family Name *(Last Name)*	Given Name *(First Name)*	Full Middle Name
DOE	John	

All Other Names Used *(include maiden name and names from all previous marriages)*

None		

Date of Birth *(mm/dd/yyyy)*	U.S. Social Security Number *(if any)*	A number *(if any)*
05/15/1960	None	None

Country of Birth	Province of Birth	Country of Citizenship
Poland		Poland

2. If in the United States, Complete the Following:

Date of Last Arrival *(mm/dd/yyyy)*	I-94 Number *(Arrival/Departure Document)*	Current Nonimmigrant Status
12/20/2006	123456789 00	B2

Date Status Expires *(mm/dd/yyyy)*	Passport Number	Date Passport Issued *(mm/dd/yyyy)*	Date Passport Expires *(mm/dd/yyyy)*
05/19/2007	543789	10/11/2006	10/10/2010

Current U.S. Address

8325 SW 72nd Ave, Miami FL 33143

Part 4. Processing Information

1. If the person named in **Part 3** is outside the United States or a requested extension of stay or change of status cannot be granted, give the U.S. consulate or inspection facility you want notified if this petition is approved.

Type of Office *(Check one):* ☒ Consulate   ☐ Pre-flight inspection   ☐ Port of Entry

Office Address *(City)*	U.S. State or Foreign Country
Warsaw	Poland

Person's Foreign Address

Alien's foreign address

Form I-129

Part 4. Processing Information *(Continued)*

2. Does each person in this petition have a valid passport?

    ☐ Not required to have passport   ☐ No - explain on separate paper   ☒ Yes

3. Are you filing any other petitions with this one?   ☒ No   ☐ Yes - How many? [   ]

4. Are applications for replacement/initial I-94s being filed with this petition?   ☒ No   ☐ Yes - How many? [   ]

5. Are applications by dependents being filed with this petition?   ☒ No   ☐ Yes - How many? [   ]

6. Is any person in this petition in removal proceedings?   ☒ No   ☐ Yes - explain on separate paper

7. Have you ever filed an immigrant petition for any person in this petition?   ☒ No   ☐ Yes - explain on separate paper

8. If you indicated you were filing a new petition in **Part 2**, within the past seven years has any person in this petition:

    a. Ever been given the classification you are now requesting?   ☒ No   ☐ Yes - explain on separate paper

    b. Ever been denied the classification you are now requesting?   ☒ No   ☐ Yes - explain on separate paper

9. Have you ever previously filed a petition for this person?   ☒ No   ☐ Yes - explain on separate paper

10. If you are filing for an entertainment group, has any person in this petition not been with the group for at least one year?   ☒ No   ☐ Yes - explain on separate paper

---

Part 5. Basic information about the proposed employment and employer *(Attach the supplement relating to the classification you are requesting.)*

1. Job Title

    President/Executive

2. Nontechnical Job Description

    (Please see attached petition letter)

3. LCA Case Number

    [   ]

4. NAICS Code

    123456

5. Address where the person(s) will work if different from address in **Part 1**. *(Street number and name, city/town, state, zip code)*

    [   ]

6. Is this a full-time position?

    ☐ No - Hours per week: [   ]   ☒ Yes - Wages per week or per year: $750.00 per week

7. Other Compensation *(Explain)*

    None

8. Dates of intended employment *(mm/dd/yyyy)*:

    From: Approval   To: 3 years

Form I-129

Part 5. Basic information about the proposed employment and employer (*Attach the supplement relating to the classification you are requesting.*) *(Continued)*

9. Type of Petitioner - *Check one*:

   ☐ U.S. citizen or permanent resident   ☒ Organization   ☐ Other - explain on separate paper

10. Type of Business

    | Export and Import of Tires for Automobiles and Trucks |

11. Year Established

    | 2003 |

12. Current Number of Employees

    | 8 |

13. Gross Annual Income

14. Net Annual Income

Part 6. Signature *Read the information on penalties in the instructions before completing this section.*

I certify, under penalty of perjury under the laws of the United States of America, that this petition and the evidence submitted with it is all true and correct. If filing this on behalf of an organization, I certify that I am empowered to do so by that organization. If this petition is to extend a prior petition, I certify that the proposed employment is under the same terms and conditions as stated in the prior approved petition. I authorize the release of any information from my records, or from the petitioning organization's records that U.S. Citizenship and Immigration Services needs to determine eligibility for the benefit being sought.

Signature

Daytime Phone Number *(Area/Country Code)*

| (123) 123-1234 |

Print Name

| John Doe, President |

Date *(mm/dd/yyyy)*

NOTE: If you do not completely fill out this form and the required supplement, or fail to submit required documents listed in the instructions, the person(s) filed for may not be found eligible for the requested benefit and this petition may be denied.

Part 7. Signature of person preparing form, if other than above

I declare that I prepared this petition at the request of the above person and it is based on all information of which I have any knowledge.

Signature

Daytime Phone Number *(Area/Country Code)*

| (123) 987-6543 |

Print Name

| Blank Attorney, P.A. |

Date *(mm/dd/yyyy)*

Firm Name and Address

| 2655 LeJeune Road Suite 1001, Miami FL 33134 |

Supplement E

OMB No. 1615-0009; Expires 07/31/2010

Department of Homeland Security
U.S. Citizenship and Immigration Services

E Classification Supplement
to Form I-129

1. Name of person or organization filing petition:

JOHN DOE, INC.

2. Name of person for whom you are filing:

DOE, John

3. Classification sought *(Check one)*:

☐ E-1 Treaty trader   ☒ E-2 Treaty investor

4. Name of country signatory to treaty with U.S.:

POLAND

Section 1.   Information about the employer outside the United States (if any)

Employer's Name

Total Number of Employees

Employer's Address *(Street number and name, city/town, state/province, zip/postal code)*

Principal Product, Merchandise or Service

Employee's Position - Title, duties and number of years employed

---

Section 2.   Additional information about the U.S. Employer

1. The U.S. company is to the company outside the United States *(Check one)*:

☐ Parent   ☐ Branch   ☐ Subsidiary   ☐ Affiliate   ☐ Joint Venture

2. Date and Place of Incorporation or Establishment in the United States

4/30/2003 Miami, Florida

3. Nationality of Ownership *(Individual or Corporate)*

Name *(First/Middle/Last)*	Nationality	Immigration Status	% Ownership
John Doe	Polish	B1	50%
Jessica Doe	Polish	US Resident	50%

4. Assets

250,000.00

5. Net Worth

250,000.00

6. Total Annual Income

250,000.00

Supplement E

Section 2.   Additional information about the U.S. Employer

---

7. Staff in the United States

    a. How many executive and/or managerial employees does petitioner have who are nationals of the treaty country in either E or L status?

    b. How many specialized qualifications or knowledge persons does the petitioner have who are nationals of the treaty country in either E or L status?

    c. Provide the total number of employees in executive or managerial positions in the United States.

    d. Provide the total number of specialized qualifications or knowledge persons positions in the United States.

8. Total number of employees the alien would supervise; or describe the nature of the specialized skills essential to the U.S. company.

```
Start-up phase
```

Section 3.   Complete if filing for an E-1 Treaty Trader

1. Total Annual Gross Trade/Business of the U.S. company

2. For Year Ending *(yyyy)*

3. Percent of total gross trade between the United States and the country of which the treaty trader organization is a national.

Section 4.   Complete if filing for an E-2 Treaty Investor

Total Investment:

Cash	Equipment	Other
250,000.00		

Inventory	Premises	Total
		250,000.00

E-2 Petition Letter

John Doe, Inc.
123 S.W. 77th Avenue
Miami, Florida 33135
Telephone (305) 778-5309

July 20, 2007

RE: Type of Case: E-2 Treaty Investor Application
       Employer: John Doe, Inc.
       Beneficiary: John Doe

Dear Sir or Madam:

This letter is submitted in support of the application for an E-2 Treaty Investor Visa for Mr. John Doe, a Polish National, who resides in Poland. The E-2 Treaty Investor Visa is based upon his 50% ownership and controlled investment of a United States Corporation, John Doe, Inc., incorporated under the laws of the State of Florida. There is a Treaty in effect between the United States and Poland under which nonimmigrant classification pursuant to INA Section 101(a)(15)(E) may be accorded. 9 F.A.M. 41.51.N1. The present application is made pursuant to said treaty. The business enterprise, John Doe, Inc., bears the nationality of a treaty country: Poland.

The information which follows reviews the original investment by Mr. John Doe and gives an update on current and projected operations of John Doe, Inc. The business enterprise was incorporated for the express purpose of engaging in the business of importing, and exporting tires for automobiles and trucks. John Doe, Inc., plans to distribute Cooper Tires, which are made in the United States and Jinglung Tires, which are made in China. The distribution plans include targeting first to the South Florida market, with in-house trained sales force and later on expanding to the entire State of Florida.

The capital used to fund this enterprise is the **substantial amount** of $250,000 U.S. dollars. This investment came directly from Mr. John Doe and the money was deposited directly in cash from funds that were in his possession and control. The amount predominantly came from his business revenues in Poland. Mr. John Doe is the 50% investor for the corporation as is demonstrated in the attached stock certificates.

Also, attached is the accountant's report showing initial capitalization of the company.

Under the current Business Plan and projections statement, as a starting point, Mr. John Doe will distribute Cooper Tires and Jinglung Tires all throughout the South Florida market. In order to achieve this, John Doe, Inc., will have in-house trained sales force that will visit each retail outlet, provide them with a credit application and arrange for product delivery. Thus, the projected business will require the hiring of individuals and create jobs for the United States and consequently help the South Florida economy.

Mr. John Doe intends to work for John Doe, Inc., as the President/Executive and will be in charge in a **supervisory and executive capacity.** He will **direct and develop** the business enterprise by virtue of his 50% ownership and control of the stock, as well as by virtue of his position. As President/Executive of the company he will oversee the import and export of the automobile and truck tire industry as well as monitor the trends of the tire industry in South Florida. This job entails responsibility for establishing the company, planning and developing the U.S. investment as well as running all the financial aspects of the company, setting policies and devising projected rate of expansion. Furthermore, he will review activity reports and financial statements to determine progress and status in attaining objectives.

A detailed description of the President's/Executive's responsibilities in the company are as follows :

President : directs and develop the company, plans develops and establishes policies and objectives and corporation charter: confers with company officials to plan business objectives, to develop organizational policies to coordinate functions and operations between divisions and departments, and to establish responsibilities and procedures for attaining objectives. Reviews activity reports and financial statements to determine progress and status attaining objectives and revises objectives and plans in accordance with current conditions. Directs and coordinates formulation of financial programs to provide funding for new or continuing operations to maximize returns on investments, and to increase productivity. Plans and develops industrial, labor and public relations policies designed to improve the company's image and relations with customer, employees, stockholders, and public. Evaluates performance of executives for compliance with established policies and objectives of firm and contributions in attaining objectives. May preside over board of directors. May serve as chairman of committees, such as management, executive, engineering, and sales.

This job requires unique experience essential to the operation of the enterprise.

Mr. John Doe's qualifications are quite impressive. He is a successful entrepreneur who has made an extraordinary contribution to every enterprise which has been fortunate enough to have his talent. He will handle this position, based on his hands-on business experience of more than **forty years** in the tire market industry.

Mr. John Doe has held several managerial positions in different automobile and tire industries and has successfully developed industrial sites for commercial purposes. Due to his expertise, his company in Poland, The AAA Group, bought Firestone and Goodyear and became the exclusive representatives of those very prestigious American brands. Mr. John Doe's vast experience in marketing and strategic planning have provided him with prosperous businesses and he is proud to say that The AAA Group is the largest tire dealer network in Poland. To this end, he will be particularly useful in the proposed position with the U.S. Company, since coordinating and planning a cost effective tire industry involves a sharp business oriented President/Executive.

John Doe, Inc., has made a **substantial investment** of $250,000. These funds are at risk and could be lost, but Mr. John Doe has other funds to support him and his family in case the investment was to fail. As further evidence that this is a **substantial investment**, documents have been presented to demonstrate that Mr. John Doe has his own source of funds. A successful executive and entrepreneur for many years, Mr. John Doe has other income-generating investments assets, which provide him and his family with a comfortable lifestyle.

This is clear from his personal tax returns.

The investment is not marginal because, as stated above, the company will need to hire an in-house sales force which will provide employment for U.S. workers to continue the expansion of the company throughout the entire state of Florida.

Based on the foregoing facts, Mr. John Doe is fully qualified to be accorded treaty investor status in order to serve in the United States in this supervisory and executive capacity. He will be assigned temporarily to the United States at an initial weekly salary of $750.00 and intends to depart when the E-2 status terminates.

In addition to this letter, we are attaching Form I-129 and the E Supplement and the following documents:

<u>DOCUMENTS RELATING TO INVESTMENT</u>

I. <u>DOCUMENTS ENCLOSED:</u>

In addition, the supporting documentation that follows gives an update on current and projected operations and plans for the U.S. investment.

1. Business Plan and Projections;
2. Evidence of Investment in United States:
   • Cash Investment;
   • Lease agreement;

3. Certificate of Incorporation, Articles of Incorporation;
4. Stock Certificate evidencing 50% ownership;
5. Bank Letters.

II. DOCUMENTS FOR APPLICANT/INVESTOR

1. Curriculum Vitae;
2. Copy of Passport/I-94;
3. Personal Financial Statement.

III. DOCUMENTS OF SPOUSE

1. Marriage Certificate;
2. Passport/I-94.

CONCLUSION

Your kind review and consideration of this petition will be greatly appreciated.

Sincerely,

John Doe, Inc.

John Doe, President

Form G-28

OMB No. 1615-0105; Expires 04/30/2012

G-28, Notice of Entry of Appearance as Attorney or Accredited Representative

Department of Homeland Security

Part 1. Notice of Appearance as Attorney or Accredited Representative

A. This appearance is in regard to immigration matters before:

[x] USCIS - List the form number(s): I-129/E

[ ] CBP - List the specific matter in which appearance is entered:

[ ] ICE - List the specific matter in which appearance is entered:

B. I hereby enter my appearance as attorney or accredited representative at the request of:

List Petitioner, Applicant, or Respondent. **NOTE:** Provide the mailing address of Petitioner, Applicant, or Respondent being represented, and **not** the address of the attorney or accredited representative, except when filed under VAWA.

Principal Petitioner, Applicant, or Respondent	A Number or Receipt Number, if any	
Name: Last First Middle		[x] Petitioner
John Doe Inc.	None	[ ] Applicant
		[ ] Respondent

Address: Street Number and Street Name	Apt. No.	City	State	Zip Code
Petitioner's Address				

Pursuant to the Privacy Act of 1974 and DHS policy, I hereby consent to the disclosure to the named Attorney or Accredited Representative of any record pertaining to me that appears in any system of records of USCIS, USCBP, or USICE.

Signature of Petitioner, Applicant, or Respondent	Date
	11/08/2009

Part 2. Information about Attorney or Accredited Representative *(Check applicable items(s) below)*

A. [x] I am an attorney and a member in good standing of the bar of the highest court(s) of the following State(s), possession(s), territory(ies), commonwealth(s), or the District of Columbia: State of _____ Supreme Court

I am not [x] **or** [ ] **am subject to any order of any court or administrative agency disbarring, suspending, enjoining, restraining, or otherwise restricting me in the practice of law (If you are subject to any order(s), explain fully on reverse side).**

B. [ ] I am an accredited representative of the following qualified non-profit religious, charitable, social service, or similar organization established in the United States, so recognized by the Department of Justice, Board of Immigration Appeals pursuant to 8 CFR 1292.2. Provide name of organization and expiration date of accreditation:

C. [ ] I am associated with _____ .

The attorney or accredited representative of record previously filed Form G-28 in this case, and my appearance as an attorney or accredited representative is at his or her request *(If you check this item, also complete item A or B above in **Part 2**, whichever is appropriate).*

Part 3. Name and Signature of Attorney or Accredited Representative

I have read and understand the regulations and conditions contained in 8 CFR 103.2 and 292 governing appearances and representation before the Department of Homeland Security. I declare under penalty of perjury under the laws of the United States that the information I have provided on this form is true and correct.

Name of Attorney or Accredited Representative	Attorney Bar Number(s), if any
Attorney or Accredited Representative's Name	
Signature of Attorney or Accredited Representative	Date 11/08/2009

Complete Address of Attorney or Organization of Accredited Representative (Street Number and Street Name, Suite No., City, State, Zip Code)

Attorney or Accredited Representative's Address

Phone Number *(Include area code)*	Fax Number, if any *(Include area code)*	E-Mail Address, if any
(305) 442-1322	(305) 444-7578	Valid E-mail Address

Form G-28 (Rev. 04/22/09)N

Form I-129

OMB No. 1615-0009; Expires 07/31/2010

Department of Homeland Security
U.S. Citizenship and Immigration Services

I-129, Petition for a
Nonimmigrant Worker

START HERE - Type or print in black ink.

For USCIS Use Only

Part 1. Information about the employer filing this petition *(If the employer is an individual, complete Number 1. Organizations should complete Number 2.)*

1. Family Name *(Last Name)*   **Given Name** *(First Name)*

Full Middle Name   Telephone No. w/Area Code

(   )

2. Company or Organization Name   Telephone No. w/Area Code

DOE AND ASSOCIATES   (305) 987-6543

Mailing Address: *(Street Number and Name)*   Suite #

2655 LeJeune Road   1001

C/O: *(In Care Of)*

c/o Attorney's Name

City   State/Province

Coral Gables   Florida

Country   Zip/Postal Code   E-Mail Address *(If Any)*

USA   33134   da@associates.com

Federal Employer Identification #   U.S. Social Security #   Individual Tax #

12-1234567   N/A   None

For USCIS Use Only

Returned	Receipt
Date	
Date	
Resubmitted	
Date	
Date	
Reloc Sent	
Date	
Date	
Reloc Rec'd	
Date	
Date	

☐ Petitioner Interviewed on ____

☐ Beneficiary Interviewed on ____

Part 2. Information about this petition *(See instructions for fee information.)*

1. Requested Nonimmigrant Classification. *(Write classification symbol):* H-1B

2. Basis for Classification *(Check one):*

a. ☒ New employment (including new employer filing H-1B extension).

b. ☐ Continuation of previously approved employment without change with the same employer.

c. ☐ Change in previously approved employment.

d. ☐ New concurrent employment.

e. ☐ Change of employer.

f. ☐ Amended petition.

3. If you checked **Box 2b, 2c, 2d, 2e,** or **2f,** give the petition receipt number.

N/A

4. Prior Petition. If the beneficiary is in the U.S. as a nonimmigrant and is applying to change and/or extend his or her status, give the prior petition or application receipt #:

N/A

5. Requested Action *(Check one):*

a. ☐ Notify the office in **Part 4** so the person(s) can obtain a visa or be admitted. (**NOTE:** *a petition is not required for an E-1 or E-2 visa*).

b. ☒ Change the person(s)' status and extend their stay since the person(s) are all now in the U.S. in another status *(see instructions for limitations)*. This is available only where you check "New Employment" in **Item 2,** above.

c. ☐ Extend the stay of the person(s) since they now hold this status.

Class: ____
# of Workers: ____
Priority Number: ____
Validity Dates: ____
From: ____
To: ____

☐ **Classification Approved**
  ☐ Consulate/POE/PFI Notified
    At ____
  ☐ Extension Granted
  ☐ COS/Extension Granted

Partial Approval *(explain)*

Action Block

To Be Completed by
Attorney or Representative, if any.

☐ Fill in box if G-28 is attached to represent the applicant.

ATTY State License #

Form I-129

Part 2. Information about this petition *(See instructions for fee information.) (Continued)*

    d. ☐ Amend the stay of the person(s) since they now hold this status.

    e. ☐ Extend the status of a nonimmigrant classification based on a Free Trade Agreement. *(See Free Trade Supplement for TN and H1B1 to Form I-129).*

    f. ☐ Change status to a nonimmigrant classification based on a Free Trade Agreement. *(See Free Trade Supplement for TN and H1B1 to Form I-129).*

6. Total number of workers in petition *(See instructions relating to when more than one worker can be included):*

> 1

Part 3. Information about the person(s) you are filing for *Complete the blocks below. Use the continuation sheet to name each person included in this petition.*

1. If an Entertainment Group, Give the Group Name

Family Name *(Last Name)*	Given Name *(First Name)*	Full Middle Name
DOE	John	

All Other Names Used *(include maiden name and names from all previous marriages)*

None		

Date of Birth *(mm/dd/yyyy)*	U.S. Social Security Number *(if any)*	A number *(if any)*
05/15/1960	None	None

Country of Birth	Province of Birth	Country of Citizenship
United Kingdom		United Kingdom

2. If in the United States, Complete the Following:

Date of Last Arrival *(mm/dd/yyyy)*	I-94 Number *(Arrival/Departure Document)*	Current Nonimmigrant Status
12/20/2006	123456789 00	B2

Date Status Expires *(mm/dd/yyyy)*	Passport Number	Date Passport Issued *(mm/dd/yyyy)*	Date Passport Expires *(mm/dd/yyyy)*
05/19/2007	543789	10/11/2006	10/10/2010

Current U.S. Address

8325 SW 72nd Ave, Miami FL 33143

Part 4. Processing Information

1. If the person named in **Part 3** is outside the United States or a requested extension of stay or change of status cannot be granted, give the U.S. consulate or inspection facility you want notified if this petition is approved.

Type of Office *(Check one):* ☒ Consulate   ☐ Pre-flight inspection   ☐ Port of Entry

Office Address *(City)*	U.S. State or Foreign Country
London	United Kingdom

Person's Foreign Address

Alien's foreign address

Form I-129

Part 4. Processing Information *(Continued)*

2. Does each person in this petition have a valid passport?

☐ Not required to have passport   ☐ No - explain on separate paper   ☒ Yes

3. Are you filing any other petitions with this one?   ☒ No   ☐ Yes - How many? [   ]

4. Are applications for replacement/initial I-94s being filed with this petition?   ☒ No   ☐ Yes - How many? [   ]

5. Are applications by dependents being filed with this petition?   ☒ No   ☐ Yes - How many? [   ]

6. Is any person in this petition in removal proceedings?   ☒ No   ☐ Yes - explain on separate paper

7. Have you ever filed an immigrant petition for any person in this petition?   ☒ No   ☐ Yes - explain on separate paper

8. If you indicated you were filing a new petition in **Part 2**, within the past seven years has any person in this petition:

  a. Ever been given the classification you are now requesting?   ☒ No   ☐ Yes - explain on separate paper

  b. Ever been denied the classification you are now requesting?   ☒ No   ☐ Yes - explain on separate paper

9. Have you ever previously filed a petition for this person?   ☒ No   ☐ Yes - explain on separate paper

10. If you are filing for an entertainment group, has any person in this petition not been with the group for at least one year?   ☒ No   ☐ Yes - explain on separate paper

Part 5. Basic information about the proposed employment and employer *(Attach the supplement relating to the classification you are requesting.)*

1. Job Title

Marketing Manager

2. Nontechnical Job Description

See attached petition letter.

3. LCA Case Number

I-10088-3311559

4. NAICS Code

123456

5. Address where the person(s) will work if different from address in **Part 1.** *(Street number and name, city/town, state, zip code)*

5525 SW 50 Terrace Suite #250, Miami FL 33166

6. Is this a full-time position?

☐ No -Hours per week: [   ]   ☒ Yes - Wages per week or per year: $600.00 per week

7. Other Compensation *(Explain)*

None

8. Dates of intended employment *(mm/dd/yyyy)*:

From: Approval   To: 3 years

Form I-129

Part 5. Basic information about the proposed employment and employer (*Attach the supplement relating to the classification you are requesting.*) *(Continued)*

9. Type of Petitioner - *Check one*:

☐ U.S. citizen or permanent resident   ☒ Organization   ☐ Other - explain on separate paper

10. Type of Business

Financial Advisement Services

11. Year Established

1995

12. Current Number of Employees

20

13. Gross Annual Income

500,000.00

14. Net Annual Income

100,000.00

Part 6. Signature *Read the information on penalties in the instructions before completing this section.*

I certify, under penalty of perjury under the laws of the United States of America, that this petition and the evidence submitted with it is all true and correct. If filing this on behalf of an organization, I certify that I am empowered to do so by that organization. If this petition is to extend a prior petition, I certify that the proposed employment is under the same terms and conditions as stated in the prior approved petition. I authorize the release of any information from my records, or from the petitioning organization's records that U.S. Citizenship and Immigration Services needs to determine eligibility for the benefit being sought.

Signature

Daytime Phone Number *(Area/Country Code)*

(305) 123-1234

Print Name

Pedro Diaz, President

Date *(mm/dd/yyyy)*

NOTE: If you do not completely fill out this form and the required supplement, or fail to submit required documents listed in the instructions, the person(s) filed for may not be found eligible for the requested benefit and this petition may be denied.

Part 7. Signature of person preparing form, if other than above

I declare that I prepared this petition at the request of the above person and it is based on all information of which I have any knowledge.

Signature

Daytime Phone Number *(Area/Country Code)*

(305) 987-6543

Print Name

Blank Attorney, P.A.

Date *(mm/dd/yyyy)*

Firm Name and Address

2655 LeJeune Road Suite 1001, Miami FL 33134

Form I-129 Supplement H

OMB No.1615-0009; Expires 07/31/2010

**H Classification Supplement
to Form I-129**

Department of Homeland Security
U.S. Citizenship and Immigration Services

1. Name of person or organization filing petition:

DOE AND ASOCIATES

2. Name of person or total number of workers or trainees you are filing for:

DOE, John

3. List each alien's prior periods of stay in H or L classification in the United States for the last six years (aliens requesting H-2A or H-2B classification need only list the last three years). Be sure to only list those periods in which each alien was actually in the United States in an H or L classification. Do not include periods in which the alien was in a dependent status, for example, H-4 or L-2 status.

NOTE: Submit photocopies of Forms I-94, I-797, and/or other USCIS issued documents noting these periods of stay in the H or L classification. If more space is needed, attach an additional sheet.

Subject's Name	Period of Stay *(mm/dd/yyyy)*	
	From	To

4. Classification sought *(Check one)*:

[x] H-1B1 Specialty occupation

[ ] H-1B2 Exceptional services relating to a cooperative research and development project administered by the U.S. Department of Defense (DOD)

[ ] H-1B3 Fashion model of national or international acclaim

[ ] H-2A Agricultural worker

[ ] H-2B Non-agricultural worker

[ ] H-3 Trainee

[ ] H-3 Special education exchange visitor program

Section 1. Complete this section if filing for H-1B classification

1. Describe the proposed duties

See attached petition letter

2. Alien's present occupation and summary of prior work experience

See attached petition letter

Form I-129 Supplement H

Section 1. Complete this section if filing for H-1B classification *(Continued)*

Statement for H-1B specialty occupations only:

By filing this petition, I agree to the terms of the labor condition application for the duration of the alien's authorized period of stay for H-1B employment.

Petitioner's Signature	Print or Type Name	Date *(mm/dd/yyyy)*
	Pedro Diaz, President	

Statement for H-1B specialty occupations and U.S. Department of Defense projects:

As an authorized official of the employer, I certify that the employer will be liable for the reasonable costs of return transportation of the alien abroad if the alien is dismissed from employment by the employer before the end of the period of authorized stay.

Signature of Authorized Official of Employer	Print or Type Name	Date *(mm/dd/yyyy)*
	Pedro Diaz, President	

Statement for H-1B U.S. Department of Defense projects only:

I certify that the alien will be working on a cooperative research and development project or a co-production project under a reciprocal government-to-government agreement administered by the U.S. Department of Defense.

DOD Project Manager's Signature	Print or Type Name	Date *(mm/dd/yyyy)*

Section 2. Complete this section if filing for H-2A or H-2B classification

1. Employment is: *(Check one)*

  a. ☐ Seasonal   **c.** ☐ Intermittent

  b. ☐ Peak Load   **d.** ☐ One-time occurence

2. Temporary need is: *(Check one)*

  a. ☐ Unpredictable   **c.** ☐ Recurrent annually

  b. ☐ Periodic

3. Explain your temporary need for the alien's services *(attach a separate sheet if additional space is needed.)*

Form I-129 Supplement H

Section 2. Complete this section if filing for H-2A or H-2B classification *(Continued)*

---

4. List the country(ies) of citizenship of the H-2A/H-2B worker(s) you plan to hire.

Name of country(ies):

[ ]

5. If the H-2A or H-2B workers you plan to hire are not from a country that has been designated as a participating country in accordance with 8 CFR 214.2(h)(5)(i)(F)(1) or 214.2(h)(6)(i)(E)(1), you must provide all the information requested below. See **www.uscis.gov** website for the list of participating countries. (Attach a separate sheet if additional space is needed)

Family Name (Last Name):

Given Name (First Name):

Full Middle Name:

Date of Birth *(mm/dd/yyyy)*

All Other Names Used:

Country of Birth:

Country of Citizenship:

6. **a.** Have any of the workers listed in Number 5 above ever been admitted to the United States previously in H-2A/H-2B status ?   ☐ Yes ☐ No

Visa Classification (H-2A or H-2B):

b. If you answered question **6 a.** "Yes," did they comply with the terms of their status?   ☐ Yes ☐ No

If you answered question **6 b.** "Yes," attach evidence of the workers' compliance.

c. If the H-2A or H-2B worker(s) you plan to hire are from a country not on the list of eligible countries, and you want the petition to be considered for approval, you must also provide evidence that: (1) a worker with the required skills is not available from a country on the list of eligible countries; (2) there is no potential for abuse, fraud, or other harm to the integrity of the H-2A/H-2B visa program through the potential admission of these worker(s) that you plan to hire; and (3) there are other factors that would serve the U.S. interest (if any).

7. Did you or do you plan to use a staffing, recruiting, or similar placement service or agent to locate the H-2A/H-2B workers that you intend to hire by filing this petition?   ☐ Yes ☐ No

If "Yes," list the name and address of service used.

Name:

Address:

8. Did any of the H-2A/H-2B workers that you have located or plan to hire pay you, the above service, or any service or agent, any form of compensation as a condition of the employment or do they have an agreement to pay you or the service at a later date? (Do not include reasonable travel expenses, government visa fees, or other reasonable fees for which the worker is responsible.) See 8 CFR 214.2(h)(5)(xi)(A) or 214.2(h)(6)(i)(B).   ☐ Yes ☐ No

Form I-129 Supplement H

Section 2. Complete this section if filing for H-2A or H-2B classification *(Continued)*

If the workers paid a fee, have they been reimbursed for such fees or compensation, or if the workers had an agreement to pay a fee that has not been paid, has that agreement been terminated before being paid by the workers?   ☐ Yes   ☐ No

(Attach evidence of termination or reimbursement to this petition.)

9. Have you ever had an H-2A/H-2B petition denied or revoked because an employee paid a job placement fee or other similar compensation as a condition of the job offer?   ☐ Yes   ☐ No

If "Yes,"

When? _____

Receipt Number: _____

Was the worker(s) reimbursed for such fees or compensation?   ☐ Yes   ☐ No

(Attach evidence of reimbursement.)

If you answered "No" because of failure to locate the worker, attach evidence of the efforts to locate the worker.

10. If you are an H-2A petitioner, are you a participant in the E-Verify program?   ☐ Yes   ☐ No

If "Yes," E-Verify Company ID or Client Company ID: _____

The H-2A/H-2B petitioner and each employer consent to allow government access to the site where the labor is being performed for the purpose of determining compliance with H-2A/H-2B requirements. The petitioner further agrees to notify DHS beginning on a date and in a manner specified in a notice published in the Federal Register within 2 workdays if: an H-2A/H-2B worker fails to report for work within 5 workdays after the employment start date stated on the petition or, applicable to H-2A petitioners only, within 5 workdays of the start date established by the petitioner, whichever is later; the agricultural labor or services for which H-2A/H-2B workers were hired is completed more than 30 days early; or the H-2A/H-2B worker absconds from the worksite or is terminated prior to the completion of agricultural labor or services for which he or she was hired. The petitioner agrees to retain evidence of such notification and make it available for inspection by DHS officers for a one-year period. "Workday" means the period between the time on any particular day when such employee commences his or her principal activity and the time on that day at which he or she ceases such principle activity or activities.

For H-2A petitioners only: The petitioner agrees to pay $10 in liquidated damages for each instance where it cannot demonstrate it is in compliance with the notification requirement.

The petitioner must execute **Part A**. If the petitioner is the employer's agent, the employer must execute **Part B**. If there are joint employers, they must each execute **Part C**.

Part A. Petitioner:

By filing this petition, I agree to the conditions of H-2A/H-2B employment and agree to the notification requirements. For H-2A petitioners: I also agree to the liquidated damages requirements defined in 8 CFR 214.2(h)(5)(vi)(B)(3).

Petitioner's Signature	**Print or Type Name**	**Date** *(mm/dd/yyyy)*

Form I-129 Supplement H

Part B. Employer who is not the petitioner:

I certify that I have authorized the party filing this petition to act as my agent in this regard. I assume full responsibility for all representations made by this agent on my behalf and agree to the conditions of H-2A/H-2B eligibility.

Employer's Signature	Print or Type Name	Date *(mm/dd/yyyy)*

Part C. Joint Employers:

I agree to the conditions of H-2A eligibility.

Joint Employer's Signature(s)	Print or Type Name	Date *(mm/dd/yyyy)*
Joint Employer's Signature(s)	Print or Type Name	Date *(mm/dd/yyyy)*
Joint Employer's Signature(s)	Print or Type Name	Date *(mm/dd/yyyy)*
Joint Employer's Signature(s)	Print or Type Name	Date *(mm/dd/yyyy)*

Section 3. Complete this section if filing for H-3 classification

1. If you answer "yes" to any of the following questions, attach a full explanation.

   a. Is the training you intend to provide, or similar training, available in the alien's country? ☐ No ☐ Yes

   b. Will the training benefit the alien in pursuing a career abroad? ☐ No ☐ Yes

   c. Does the training involve productive employment incidental to training? ☐ No ☐ Yes

   d. Does the alien already have skills related to the training? ☐ No ☐ Yes

   e. Is this training an effort to overcome a labor shortage? ☐ No ☐ Yes

   f. Do you intend to employ the alien abroad at the end of this training? ☐ No ☐ Yes

2. If you do not intend to employ this person abroad at the end of this training, explain why you wish to incur the cost of providing this training and your expected return from this training.

Form I-129 Supplement H

Department of Homeland Security
U.S. Citizenship and Immigration Services

H-1B Data Collection and Filing Fee Exemption Supplement

Petitioner's Full Name

Part A.   General Information

1. **Employer Information** - *(check all items that apply)*

   a. Is the petitioner a dependent employer? ☐ No ☐ Yes

   b. Has the petitioner ever been found to be a willful violator? ☐ No ☐ Yes

   c. Is the beneficiary an exempt H-1B nonimmigrant? ☐ No ☐ Yes

      1. If yes, is it because the beneficiary's annual rate of pay is equal to at least $60,000? ☐ No ☐ Yes

      2. Or is it because the beneficiary has a master's or higher degree in a speciality related to the employment? ☐ No ☐ Yes

   d. Has the petitioner received TARP funding? ☐ No ☐ Yes

2. Beneficiary' s Last Name   First Name   Middle Name

   Attention To or In Care Of   Current Residential Address - Street Number and Name   Apt. #

   City   State   Zip/Postal Code

   U.S. Social Security # *(If Any)*   I-94 # *(Arrival/Departure Document)*   Previous Receipt # *(If Any)*

3. **Beneficiary's Highest Level of Education**   (Check one box below)

   ☐ NO DIPLOMA

   ☐ HIGH SCHOOL GRADUATE - high school DIPLOMA or the equivalent (example: GED)

   ☐ Some college credit, but less than one year

   ☐ One or more years of college, no degree

   ☐ Associate's degree *(for example: AA, AS)*

   ☐ Bachelor's degree *(for example: BA, AB, BS)*

   ☐ Master's degree *(for example: MA, MS, MEng, MEd, MSW, MBA)*

   ☐ Professional degree *(for example: MD, DDS, DVM, LLB, JD)*

   ☐ Doctorate degree *(for example: PhD, EdD)*

4. Major/Primary Field of Study

5. Has the beneficiary of this petition earned a master's or higher degree from a U.S. institution of higher education as defined in 20 U.S.C. section 1001(a)?

   ☐ No   ☐ Yes (If "Yes" provide the following information):

   Name of the U.S. institution of higher education

   Date Degree Awarded   Type of U.S. Degree

   Address of the U.S. institution of higher education

6. Rate of Pay Per Year   7. LCA Code   8. NAICS Code

Form I-129 Supplement H

Part B. Fee Exemption and/or Determination

In order for USCIS to determine if you must pay the additional **$1,500** or **$750** fee, answer all of the following questions:

1. ☐ Yes ☐ No Are you an institution of higher education as defined in the Higher Education Act of 1965, section 101 (a), 20 U.S.C. section 1001(a)?

2. ☐ Yes ☐ No Are you a nonprofit organization or entity related to or affiliated with an institution of higher education, as such institutions of higher education are defined in the Higher Education Act of 1965, section 101 (a), 20 U.S.C. section 1001(a)?

3. ☐ Yes ☐ No Are you a nonprofit research organization or a governmental research organization, as defined in 8 CFR 214.2(h)(19)(iii)(C)?

4. ☐ Yes ☐ No Is this the second or subsequent request for an extension of stay that you have filed for this alien?

5. ☐ Yes ☐ No Is this an amended petition that does not contain any request for extensions of stay?

6. ☐ Yes ☐ No Are you filing this petition in order to correct a USCIS error?

7. ☐ Yes ☐ No Is the petitioner a primary or secondary education institution?

8. ☐ Yes ☐ No Is the petitioner a non-profit entity that engages in an established curriculum-related clinical training of students registered at such an institution?

If you answered "Yes" to any of the questions above, then you are required to submit the fee for your H-1B Form I-129 petition, which is $320. If you answered "No" to all questions, please answer Question 9.

9. ☐ Yes ☐ No Do you currently employ a total of no more than 25 full-time equivalent employees in the United States, including any affiliate or subsidiary of your company?

If you answered "Yes" to Question 9 above, then you are required to pay an additional fee of $750. If you answered "No", then you are required to pay an additional fee of $1,500.

NOTE: On or after March 8, 2005, a U.S. employer seeking initial approval of H-1B or L nonimmigrant status for a beneficiary, or seeking approval to employ an H-1B or L nonimmigrant currently working for another U.S. employer, must submit an additional $500 fee. This additional $500 Fraud Prevention and Detection fee was mandated by the provisions of the H-1B Visa Reform Act of 2004. **There is no exemption from this fee.**

Part C. Numerical Limitation Exemption Information

1. ☐ Yes ☐ No Are you an institution of higher education as defined in the Higher Education Act of 1965, section 101 (a), 20 U.S.C. section 1001(a)?

2. ☐ Yes ☐ No Are you a nonprofit organization or entity related to or affiliated with an institution of higher education, as such institutions of higher education as defined in the Higher Education Act of 1965, section 101(a), 20 U.S.C. section 1001(a)?

3. ☐ Yes ☐ No Are you a nonprofit research organization or a governmental research organization, as defined in 8 CFR 214.2(h)(19)(iii)(C)?

4. ☐ Yes ☐ No Is the beneficiary of this petition a J-1 nonimmigrant alien who received a waiver of the two-year foreign residency requirement described in section 214 (l)(1)(B) or (C) of the Act?

5. ☐ Yes ☐ No Has the beneficiary of this petition been previously granted status as an H-1B nonimmigrant in the past 6 years and not left the United States for more than one year after attaining such status?

6. ☐ Yes ☐ No If the petition is to request a change of employer, did the beneficiary previously work as an H-1B for an institution of higher education, an entity related to or affiliated with an institution of higher education, or a nonprofit research organization or governmental research institution defined in questions 1, 2 and 3 of Part C of this form?

Form I-129 Supplement H

Part C. Numerical Limitation Exemption Information   *(Continued)*

7.   ☐ Yes   ☐ No   Has the beneficiary of this petition earned a master's or higher degree from a U.S. institution of higher education, as defined in the Higher Education Act of 1965, section 101(a), 20 U.S.C. section 1001(a)?

I certify under penalty of perjury, under the laws of the United States of America, that this attachment and the evidence submitted with it is true and correct. If filing this on behalf of an organization or entity, I certify that I am empowered to do so by that organization or entity. I authorize the release of any information from my records, or from the petitioning organization or entity's records, that U.S. Citizenship and Immigration Services may need to determine eligibility for the exemption being sought.

Certification

Signature

Date *(mm/dd/yyyy)*

Print Name

Title

H-1B Petition Letter

DOE AND ASSOCIATES

5525 S.W. 50 TERRACE, SUITE# 250, MIAMI, FLORIDA 33166

December 4, 2007

U.S. Department of Homeland Security
U.S. Citizenship and Immigration Service
Texas Service Center
P.O. Box 852211
Mesquite, TX 75185-2211

Re: **I-129H1B1 Petition of DOE AND ASSOCIATES**
      On Behalf of Mr. John Doe

Dear Sir or Madam:

This letter is submitted in support of the H-1B extension petition of **DOE AND ASSOCIATES** to classify Mr. John Doe, an English national, as an H-1B1 nonimmigrant in a specialty occupation. He will serve as Marketing Manager for a three year period. To this end, we take the liberty of detailing below the nature of our business as well as the professional position, which Mr. Doe will hold and his qualifications for the same.

The Petitioner

DOE AND ASSOCIATES was founded in 1995 with a profound commitment to excellence. Our philosophy has been to provide our clients with the best financial advisement service that is second to none. Our staff consists of twenty (20) effective and efficient individuals who are carefully selected to match proper experience and adequacy. Our team members are selected based on the strength of their experience and must have an excellent track record. **DOE AND ASSOCIATES** was established to provide financial advisement services to multi-million dollar companies.

The Position Offered

At this time, we wish to employ Mr. John Doe in the professional capacity as Marketing Manager. In this capacity Mr. Doe will perform the following duties: be responsible for developing and implementing marketing objectives, strategies, and programs designed to increase and improve the company's business services; supervise the implementation of marketing programs, assuring their timely, effective, and efficient execution in the marketplace; directing the company's advertising strategies, ensuring quality performance in the workplace, promotions, and other creative work.

Upon further expansion in our company, he will hire and train the Marketing Department personnel, in order to achieve above standard performance in the areas of advertising, promotion, service development, marketing, and public relations.

He will also be responsible for trainees by directing staffing, training, and performance evaluations to develop and control the service program of our company. Mr. Doe will coordinate services by establishing territories and goals. His duties in the position of Marketing Manager will also include meeting personally with our clients to explain and research advertising and sales techniques. Mr. Doe will review market analyses to determine client/customer need, volume potential, price schedules, and discount rates. He will also be responsible for the development of sales campaigns to accommodate the goals of **DOE AND ASSOCIATES** and further consolidate its position in the marketplace.

A. Specialty Occupation—In General

The **Immigration and Nationality Act** (INA) provides nonimmigrant status to an alien coming to work temporarily in a "specialty occupation," INA § 101(a)(15)(H)(i)(b). A "Specialty Occupation" is one that normally requires theoretical and practical application of a body of highly specialized knowledge and attainment of a bachelor's or higher degree in the specific specialty (or the equivalent of such degree) as a minimum for entry into the occupation in the United States, 8 CFR § 214(i)(1). In addition, the worker must be qualified to fill the position, through completion of the degree for the occupation or through work experience equivalent to the degree. The worker must also possess a valid state driver's license if such is required.

These requirements are essentially the same as the requirements for a "profession" under the INA before it was amended in 1990. The INA lists several occupations as professions but recognizes that its list is not all-inclusive. INA § 101(a)(32). The Service, through regulation and precedent decision, has recognized that other occupations are professions, and thus, specialty occupations.

> On the **regulatory side**, the Service's position is that "[i]f a job's duties are so complex that theory, knowledge, and skills normally gained by attainment of a baccalaureate or higher degree in certain occupational specialties are required, then the Service would conclude that the position is a profession." *Summary of Regulations*, 55 Fed. Reg. 2610, January 26, 1990. And, where "the nature of the specific duties are so specialized and complex that knowledge required to perform the duties is usually associated with the attainment of a baccalaureate or higher degree; and the position's level of responsibility and authority are commensurate with professional standing," the position is a specialty occupation, 8 CFR §§ 214.2(h)(3)(A)(4), (5). The I.N.S. regulations state that "business specialties" are specialty occupations, 8 C.F.R. § 214.2(h)(4)(1996).

Through **precedent decisions**, the Service has recognized occupations as specialty occupations by evaluating the responsibilities, duties, tasks, demands, and actual requirements of the position. *In Re X*, LIN93 245 51412, 12 Imm. Rptr. B2-200 (AAU, Int. Dec. March 28, 1994). Indeed, it has been held that "[a] position may be considered a profession based on the complexity of the duties alone." *Hong Kong T.V. Video Program, LLC v. Ilchert*, 685 F. Supp 712 (N.D. Ca. 1988).

Although the attainment of a bachelor's or higher degree in the specified occupation is ordinarily required, on occasion, the Service has also recognized that at times, certain occupations develop faster than educational institutions can develop degree programs. These occupations have been found to be professions or specialty occupations in transition. *Matter of Caron International, LLC*, Int. Dec. 3085 (BIA October 22, 1988).

B. Position of Marketing Manager is a Specialty Occupation

As contemplated by the law and **regulations**, the job offered in this case requires a unique combination of complex skills and knowledge relating to marketing. This is so on account of the particular nature of the enterprise and the petitioner's venturing into new markets. The nature of the specific duties that the beneficiary would be performing as outlined above are sufficiently specialized and complex that knowledge required to perform the duties is usually associated with the attainment of a baccalaureate degree.

In the areas of responsibility of this position, there have been **precedent decisions**, including the following:

AAU WAC 95 010 50835 WSC (LOS), April 13, 1995. In these proceedings, the duties of the position are dispositive and not the job title. The proffered position appears to be that of a **market research analyst**. In view of the foregoing, it is concluded that the petitioner has demonstrated that the proffered position is a specialty occupation within the meaning of regulations. In view of the foregoing, it is concluded that the grounds for denial have been overcome. Consequently, the appeal will be sustained and the petition will be approved. **The AAO ruled that the petition be approved. The appeal is sustained. The decision of the director is withdrawn and the petition is approved.**

AAU EAC 94 214 50527 ESC (MIA), Feb. 3, 1995. The director determined that the petitioner, which is a small and new firm, has not established that it requires the services of a **market research analyst**. However, in these proceedings, a petitioner's size, scope, and newness of operation are not dispositive. In view of the foregoing, it is concluded that the grounds for denial have been overcome. **Consequently, the appeal will be sustained and the petition will be approved. The director's decision is withdrawn and the petition is approved.**

AAU EAC 94 234 51571, 1995 WL 1796712 (INS). In these proceedings, the duties are dispositive and not the job title. While the proffered position appears to be that of a **marketing manager**, its principal duties appear to be those of a **market research analyst. In view of the foregoing, it is concluded that the grounds for denial have been overcome. As a consequence, the appeal will be sustained and the petition be approved. The appeal is sustained. The director's decision is withdrawn and the petition is approved.**

Note that we have attached herein copy of the above stated AAU cases as proof that the cited cases do state that the position of Marketing Manager is a specialty occupation.

The AAO as quoted above determined that the duties of a Hispanic Market Research Associate parallel those of a social scientist, market analyst, or industrial psychologist, all of which are H-1B level occupations. The **Occupational Outlook Handbook** (OOH) section for "Economists and Marketing Research Analysts" points out the type of duties carried out by marketing professionals. While the title of the position in this petition is Hispanic Market Research Associate, it has been the policy that the emphasis is on the actual duties of the position and not the title itself. As a Market Research Associate the duties of implementing marketing strategy and objectives and programs designed to increase/improve the company's business services involved in this case are basically those found in the OOH for a Marketing Analyst.

The Beneficiary

Work Experience:

1996–2002	SACOS EVARISTO S.A.
	<u>Position Held:</u>
	Administrative and Financial Manager
1990–1996	CASCI S.A.
	<u>Position Held:</u> **Marketing Manager**

Moreover, Mr. Doe has experience in the fields of administration, sales, marketing, and advertising. His educational and professional background required him to be responsible for administration of company properties, accounts receivable, expanding client bases, maintaining good public relations with clientele, coordination of events and setting up and revising accounts.

The beneficiary's professional experience, education, and background would make him a great asset to our company. A large part of our clientele is Spanish speaking, therefore Mr. Doe's bilingual ability makes him especially suited for this position.

Terms of Employment

We currently intend to continue to employ Mr. Doe for an additional three-year period, as of the date of approval. We understand the temporary scope of his employment with us therefore no written contract has been entered into with Mr. Doe. His proposed entry-level weekly salary is $600.00. However, upon determining that company goals and targets have been reached or surpassed, a review of his salary will be made and the appropriate changes will be made.

Very truly yours,

DOE AND ASSOCIATES

_____

Mr. Pedro Diaz
President

Form G-28

OMB No. 1615-0105; Expires 04/30/2012

G-28, Notice of Entry of Appearance as Attorney or Accredited Representative

Department of Homeland Security

Part 1. Notice of Appearance as Attorney or Accredited Representative

A. This appearance is in regard to immigration matters before:

[X] USCIS - List the form number(s): I-129/H   [ ] CBP - List the specific matter in which appearance is entered:

[ ] ICE - List the specific matter in which appearance is entered: _____

B. I hereby enter my appearance as attorney or accredited representative at the request of:

List Petitioner, Applicant, or Respondent. **NOTE:** Provide the mailing address of Petitioner, Applicant, or Respondent being represented, and **not** the address of the attorney or accredited representative, except when filed under VAWA.

Principal Petitioner, Applicant, or Respondent	A Number or Receipt Number, if any	[X] Petitioner
Name: Last First Middle DOE AND ASOCIATES	None	[ ] Applicant [ ] Respondent

Address: Street Number and Street Name	Apt. No.	City	State	Zip Code
Petitioner's Address				

Pursuant to the Privacy Act of 1974 and DHS policy, I hereby consent to the disclosure to the named Attorney or Accredited Representative of any record pertaining to me that appears in any system of records of USCIS, USCBP, or USICE.

Signature of Petitioner, Applicant, or Respondent	Date
	11/08/2009

Part 2. Information about Attorney or Accredited Representative *(Check applicable items(s) below)*

A. [X] I am an attorney and a member in good standing of the bar of the highest court(s) of the following State(s), possession(s), territory(ies), commonwealth(s), or the District of Columbia: State of _____ Supreme Court

I am not [X] or [ ] **am subject to any order of any court or administrative agency disbarring, suspending, enjoining, restraining, or otherwise restricting me in the practice of law (If you are subject to any order(s), explain fully on reverse side).**

B. [ ] I am an accredited representative of the following qualified non-profit religious, charitable, social service, or similar organization established in the United States, so recognized by the Department of Justice, Board of Immigration Appeals pursuant to 8 CFR 1292.2. Provide name of organization and expiration date of accreditation: _____

C. [ ] I am associated with _____ .

The attorney or accredited representative of record previously filed Form G-28 in this case, and my appearance as an attorney or accredited representative is at his or her request *(If you check this item, also complete item A or B above in **Part 2**, whichever is appropriate).*

Part 3. Name and Signature of Attorney or Accredited Representative

I have read and understand the regulations and conditions contained in 8 CFR 103.2 and 292 governing appearances and representation before the Department of Homeland Security. I declare under penalty of perjury under the laws of the United States that the information I have provided on this form is true and correct.

Name of Attorney or Accredited Representative	Attorney Bar Number(s), if any
Attorney or Accredited Representative's Name	

Signature of Attorney or Accredited Representative	Date
	11/08/2009

Complete Address of Attorney or Organization of Accredited Representative (Street Number and Street Name, Suite No., City, State, Zip Code)

Attorney or Accredited Representative's Address

Phone Number *(Include area code)*	Fax Number, if any *(Include area code)*	E-Mail Address, if any
(305) 442-1322	(305) 444-7578	Valid E-mail Address

Form G-28 (Rev. 04/22/09)N

Form I-129

OMB No. 1615-0009; Expires 07/31/2010

Department of Homeland Security
U.S. Citizenship and Immigration Services

I-129, Petition for a
Nonimmigrant Worker

START HERE - Type or print in black ink.

For USCIS Use Only

Part 1. Information about the employer filing this petition *(If the employer is an individual, complete **Number 1**. Organizations should complete **Number 2**.)*

1. Family Name *(Last Name)*   Given Name *(First Name)*

   Full Middle Name   Telephone No. w/Area Code

   (   )

2. Company or Organization Name   Telephone No. w/Area Code

   DOE AND ASSOCIATES   (305) 123-1234

   Mailing Address: *(Street Number and Name)*   Suite #

   2655 LeJeune Road   1001

   C/O: *(In Care Of)*

   c/o Attorney's Name

   City   State/Province

   Coral Gables   Florida

   Country   Zip/Postal Code   E-Mail Address *(If Any)*

   USA   33134   da@associates.com

   Federal Employer Identification #   U.S. Social Security #   Individual Tax #

   12-1234567   N/A   None

For USCIS Use Only	
Returned	Receipt
Date	
Date	
Resubmitted	
Date	
Date	
Reloc Sent	
Date	
Date	
Reloc Rec'd	
Date	
Date	
☐ Petitioner Interviewed on ____	
☐ Beneficiary Interviewed on ____	

Part 2. Information about this petition *(See instructions for fee information.)*

1. **Requested Nonimmigrant Classification.** *(Write classification symbol):* L-1A

2. **Basis for Classification** *(Check one):*
   a. ☒ New employment (including new employer filing H-1B extension).
   b. ☐ Continuation of previously approved employment without change with the same employer.
   c. ☐ Change in previously approved employment.
   d. ☐ New concurrent employment.
   e. ☐ Change of employer.
   f. ☐ Amended petition.

3. If you checked **Box 2b, 2c, 2d, 2e,** or **2f,** give the petition receipt number.
   N/A

4. **Prior Petition.** If the beneficiary is in the U.S. as a nonimmigrant and is applying to change and/or extend his or her status, give the prior petition or application receipt #:
   N/A

5. **Requested Action** *(Check one):*
   a. ☒ Notify the office in **Part 4** so the person(s) can obtain a visa or be admitted. (**NOTE:** *a petition is not required for an E-1 or E-2 visa*).
   b. ☐ Change the person(s)' status and extend their stay since the person(s) are all now in the U.S. in another status *(see instructions for limitations)*. This is available only where you check "New Employment" in **Item 2,** above.
   c. ☐ Extend the stay of the person(s) since they now hold this status.

Class: _____
# of Workers: _____
Priority Number: _____
Validity Dates:
From: _____
To: _____
☐ **Classification Approved**
☐ Consulate/POE/PFI Notified
At _____
☐ Extension Granted
☐ COS/Extension Granted
Partial Approval *(explain)*
Action Block

To Be Completed by
Attorney or Representative, if any.

☐ Fill in box if G-28 is attached to represent the applicant.

ATTY State License #

Form I-129 (Rev. 06/12/09)Y

Form I-129

Part 2. Information about this petition *(See instructions for fee information.) (Continued)*

    d. ☐ Amend the stay of the person(s) since they now hold this status.

    e. ☐ Extend the status of a nonimmigrant classification based on a Free Trade Agreement. *(See Free Trade Supplement for TN and H1B1 to Form I-129).*

    f. ☐ Change status to a nonimmigrant classification based on a Free Trade Agreement. *(See Free Trade Supplement for TN and H1B1 to Form I-129).*

6. Total number of workers in petition *(See instructions relating to when more than one worker can be included):*   `1`

Part 3. Information about the person(s) you are filing for *Complete the blocks below. Use the continuation sheet to name each person included in this petition.*

1. If an Entertainment Group, Give the Group Name

Family Name *(Last Name)*	Given Name *(First Name)*	Full Middle Name
DOE	John	

All Other Names Used *(include maiden name and names from all previous marriages)*

None		

Date of Birth *(mm/dd/yyyy)*	U.S. Social Security Number *(if any)*	A number *(if any)*
05/15/1960	None	None

Country of Birth	Province of Birth	Country of Citizenship
United Kingdom		United Kingdom

2. If in the United States, Complete the Following:

Date of Last Arrival *(mm/dd/yyyy)*	I-94 Number *(Arrival/Departure Document)*	Current Nonimmigrant Status

Date Status Expires *(mm/dd/yyyy)*	Passport Number	Date Passport Issued *(mm/dd/yyyy)*	Date Passport Expires *(mm/dd/yyyy)*

Current U.S. Address

Part 4. Processing Information

1. If the person named in **Part 3** is outside the United States or a requested extension of stay or change of status cannot be granted, give the U.S. consulate or inspection facility you want notified if this petition is approved.

Type of Office *(Check one):*   ☒ Consulate   ☐ Pre-flight inspection   ☐ Port of Entry

Office Address *(City)*	U.S. State or Foreign Country
London	United Kingdom

Person's Foreign Address

Alien's foreign address

Form I-129

Part 4. Processing Information *(Continued)*

2. Does each person in this petition have a valid passport?

   ☐ Not required to have passport   ☐ No - explain on separate paper   ☒ Yes

3. Are you filing any other petitions with this one?   ☒ No   ☐ Yes - How many?

4. Are applications for replacement/initial I-94s being filed with this petition?   ☒ No   ☐ Yes - How many?

5. Are applications by dependents being filed with this petition?   ☒ No   ☐ Yes - How many?

6. Is any person in this petition in removal proceedings?   ☒ No   ☐ Yes - explain on separate pape

7. Have you ever filed an immigrant petition for any person in this petition?   ☒ No   ☐ Yes - explain on separate pape

8. If you indicated you were filing a new petition in **Part 2**, within the past seven years has any person in this petition:

   a. Ever been given the classification you are now requesting?   ☒ No   ☐ Yes - explain on separate pape

   b. Ever been denied the classification you are now requesting?   ☒ No   ☐ Yes - explain on separate pape

9. Have you ever previously filed a petition for this person?   ☒ No   ☐ Yes - explain on separate pape

10. If you are filing for an entertainment group, has any person in this petition not
    been with the group for at least one year?   ☒ No   ☐ Yes - explain on separate pape

---

Part 5. Basic information about the proposed employment and employer *(Attach the supplement relating t classification you are requesting.)*

1. Job Title

   President and Chief Executive Officer

2. Nontechnical Job Description

   See attached addendum

3. LCA Case Number

4. NAICS Code

5. Address where the person(s) will work if different from address in **Part 1**. *(Street number and name, city/town, state, zip co*

   5525 SW 50 Terrace Suite #250, Miami FL 33166

6. Is this a full-time position?

   ☐ No -Hours per week: ☐ Yes - Wages per week or per year: $600.00 per week

7. Other Compensation *(Explain)*

   None

8. Dates of intended employment *(mm/dd/yyyy)*:

   From: Approval   To: 3 years

Form I-129

Part 5. Basic information about the proposed employment and employer *(Attach the supplement relating to tl classification you are requesting.) (Continued)*

9. Type of Petitioner - *Check one*:

    ☐ U.S. citizen or permanent resident   ☒ Organization   ☐ Other - explain on separate paper

10. Type of Business

Financial Advisement Services

11. Year Established

1995

12. Current Number of Employees

20

13. Gross Annual Income

2,500,000.00

14. Net Annual Income

1,000,000.00

Part 6. Signature *Read the information on penalties in the instructions before completing this section.*

I certify, under penalty of perjury under the laws of the United States of America, that this petition and the evidence submitted with is all true and correct. If filing this on behalf of an organization, I certify that I am empowered to do so by that organization. If this petition is to extend a prior petition, I certify that the proposed employment is under the same terms and conditions as stated in the prior approved petition. I authorize the release of any information from my records, or from the petitioning organization's records tl U.S. Citizenship and Immigration Services needs to determine eligibility for the benefit being sought.

Signature

Daytime Phone Number *(Area/Country Code*

(305) 123-1234

Print Name

Pedro Diaz, Manager

Date *(mm/dd/yyyy)*

NOTE: If you do not completely fill out this form and the required supplement, or fail to submit required documents listed in the instructions, the person(s) filed for may not be found eligible for the requested benefit and this petition may be denied.

Part 7. Signature of person preparing form, if other than above

I declare that I prepared this petition at the request of the above person and it is based on all information of which I have any knowledge.

Signature

Daytime Phone Number *(Area/Country Code*

(305) 987-6543

Print Name

Blank Attorney, P.A.

Date *(mm/dd/yyyy)*

Firm Name and Address

Blank Attorney, P.A.
2655 LeJeune Road Suite 1001, Coral Gables FL 33134

Form I-129 Supplement L

OMB No.1615-0009; Expires 07/31/2010

Department of Homeland Security
U.S. Citizenship and Immigration Services

**L Classification Supplement
to Form I-129**

---

1. Name of person or organization filing petition:

> DOE AND ASOCIATES

2. Name of person you are filing for:

> DOE, John

3. This petition is *(Check one)*:

       a. [x] An individual petition   **b.** [ ] A blanket petition

---

Section 1.   Complete this section if filing for an individual petition

1. Classification sought *(Check one)*:

       a. [x] L-1A manager or executive   **b.** [ ] L-1B specialized knowledge

2. List the alien's and any dependent family member's prior periods of stay in an H or L classification in the United States for the last seven years. Be sure to list only those periods in which the alien and/or family members were actually in the U.S. in an H or L classification. **NOTE:** Submit photocopies of Forms I-94, I-797 and/or other USCIS issued documents noting these periods of stay in the H or L classification. If more space is needed, attach an additional sheet(s).

Subject's Name	Period of Stay *(mm/dd/yyyy)*	
None	From:	To:
	From:	To:
	From:	To:
	From:	To:
	From:	To:

3. Name of employer abroad

> DONTI, C.A.

4. Address of employer abroad *(Street number and name, city/town, state/province, zip/postal code)*

> 526 Liberty Road, Suite #50 London, United Kingdom

5. Dates of alien's employment with this employer. Explain any interruptions in employment.

Dates of Employment *(mm/dd/yyyy)*	Explanation of Interruptions
From: 04/20/2002 To: Present	
From: To:	
From: To:	

6. Description of the alien's duties for the past three years.

> See attached petition letter

7. Description of the alien's proposed duties in the United States.

> See attached addendum

8. Summary of the alien's education and work experience.

> See attached petition letter

Form I-129 Supplement L

1. Name of person or organization filing petition:	2. Name of person you are filing for:
DOE AND ASSOCIATES	DOE, John

Section 1.   Complete this section if filing for an individual petition   *(Continued)*

9. The U.S. company is to the company abroad: *(Check one)*

    a. ☐ Parent   **b.** ☐ Branch   **c.** ☒ Subsidiary   **d.** ☐ Affiliate   **e.** ☐ Joint Venture

10. Describe the stock ownership and managerial control of each company. Provide the U.S. Tax Code Number for each company.

Company stock ownership and managerial control of each company	U.S. Tax Code Number
DONTI, C.A. owns 51% of the shares of Doe and Associates	123456789

11. Do the companies currently have the same qualifying relationship as they did during the one-year period of the alien's employment with the company abroad?   ☒ Yes   ☐ No *(Attach explanation)*

12. Is the alien coming to the United States to open a new office?   ☐ Yes *(Attach explanation)*   ☒ No

13. If you are seeking L-1B specialized knowledge status for an individual, answer the following question:

    Will the beneficiary be stationed primarily offsite (at the worksite of an employer other than the petitioner or its affiliate, subsidiary, or parent)?   ☐ Yes   ☐ No

    If you answered "Yes" to the preceding question, describe how and by whom the beneficiary's work will be controlled and supervised. Include a description of the amount of time each supervisor is expected to control and supervise the work. Use an attachment if needed.

    If you answered "Yes" to the preceding question, also describe the reasons why placement at another worksite outside the petitioner, subsidiary or parent is needed. Include a description of how the beneficiary's duties at another worksite relate to the need for the specialized knowledge he or she possesses. Use an attachment if needed.

Section 2.   Complete this section if filing a blanket petition

List all U.S. and foreign parent, branches, subsidiaries and affiliates included in this petition. *(Attach a separate sheet(s) of paper if additional space is needed.)*

Name and Address	Relationship

Section 3.   Fraud Prevention and Detection Fee

As of **March 8, 2005,** a U.S. employer seeking initial approval of L nonimmigrant status for a beneficiary, or seeking approval to employ an L nonimmigrant currently working for another U.S. employer, must submit an additional **$500** fee. This additional **$500.00** Fraud Prevention and Detection fee was mandated by the provisions of the H-1B Visa Reform Act of 2004. **There is no exemption from this fee.** You must include payment of this **$500** fee with your submission of this form. Failure to submit the fee when required will result in rejection or denial of your submission.

L-1 Petition Letter

DOE AND ASSOCIATES

5525 s.w. 50 Terrace, Suite#250
Miami, Florida 33166
Telephone: (305) 222-4444

December 10, 2007

U.S. Department of Homeland Security
Bureau of Immigration and Citizenship Services
Texas Service Center
P.O. Box 852211
Mesquite, Texas 75185-2211

Re: <u>L-1A Petition of Nonimmigrant Worker</u>
<u>Petitioner:</u> DOE AND ASSOCIATE
<u>Beneficiary:</u> DOE, John
Form I-129 with Supplement (L)

Dear Sir or Madam:

This letter is submitted in support of the L-1A petition of **HERALPIN USA, INC.**, on behalf of Mr. John Doe, an English national, and Marketing Manager of our foreign company. We wish to temporarily transfer Mr. Doe to our Florida subsidiary for a one-year period.

THE PETITIONER AND CORPORATE RELATIONSHIP

DOE AND ASSOCIATES was founded in 1995 with a profound commitment to excellence. Our philosophy has been to provide our clients with the best financial advisement service that is second to none. Our staff consists of twenty (20) effective and efficient individuals who are carefully selected to match proper experience and adequacy. Our team members are selected based on the strength of their experience and must have an excellent performance record. **DOE AND ASSOCIATES** was established to provide financial advisement services to multi-million dollar companies.

Our parent company, *DONTI C.A.*, was incorporated in London, England on June 28, 1990. The company is involved in everything related to the field of consulting, in general. *DONTI C.A.*, is located in the heart of London, England at 526 Liberty Road, Suite#50, London, England. During the following tax periods, *DONTI C.A.*, grossed the following net income: (1) In the year 2002, $525,000 was grossed; (2) In 2001, $425,000 was grossed; (3) and in 2000, $300,000 was grossed. Currently our company has a staff of 13 employees. The parent company, *DONTI C.A.*, owns 51% of the shares of **DOE AND ASSOCIATES**.

TRANSFEREE'S QUALIFICATIONS AND POSITION ABROAD

John Doe is the General Manager of our parent company, *DONTI C.A.* Since April 20, 2002, Mr. Doe has been responsible for developing the company's administrative sector. The duties include formulating policies, managing daily operations, and planning the use of materials and human resources, personnel, purchasing, or administrative services. In some instances, he has overlapped the duties of chief executive officers.

THE U.S. POSITION TO BE HELD BY THE TRANSFEREE

We wish to temporarily transfer Mr. Doe to our Florida subsidiary, in the position of President and Chief Executive Officer. Mr. Doe will perform duties as described above in the United States to establish our U.S. operations and ensure that business plans and policies are fully implemented as contemplated by the parent company. His duties include: Planning, developing, and establishing goals, policies, and objectives of the organization in accordance with board directives and the corporation charter; hiring and firing personnel; reviewing activity reports and financial statements to determine progress and status in attaining objectives and revising objectives and plans in accordance with current conditions; directing and coordinating formulation of financial programs to provide and to increase productivity; planning and developing industrial, labor, and public relations policies designed to improve the company's image and relations with customers; evaluating performance of executives for compliance with established policies and objectives of firm and contributions in attaining objectives; presiding over board of directors.

In short, Mr. Doe will have autonomous control over and exercise wide latitude for the successful direction of our United States activities. This is a senior level position and an essential function at our Miami subsidiary. With respect to all matters in his jurisdiction, he will exercise broad discretion over day-to-day operations.

TERMS OF EMPLOYMENT

We currently intend to employ Mr. Doe temporarily at a beginning salary of $600.00 per week. Mr. Doe will work 40 hours per week with overtime as needed.

We respectfully request that the L-1 visa petition on behalf of Mr. John Doe be granted.

Thank you for giving this matter your attention and kind consideration.

Very truly yours,

DOE AND ASSOCIATES

_____

Pedro Diaz
Manager

L1 SAMPLE LETTER

Form G-28

OMB No. 1615-0105; Expires 04/30/2012

G-28, Notice of Entry of Appearance as Attorney or Accredited Representative

Department of Homeland Security

Part 1. Notice of Appearance as Attorney or Accredited Representative

A. This appearance is in regard to immigration matters before:

[x] USCIS - List the form number(s): I-129/L

[ ] CBP - List the specific matter in which appearance is entered:

[ ] ICE - List the specific matter in which appearance is entered:

B. I hereby enter my appearance as attorney or accredited representative at the request of:

List Petitioner, Applicant, or Respondent. **NOTE:** Provide the mailing address of Petitioner, Applicant, or Respondent being represented, and **not** the address of the attorney or accredited representative, except when filed under VAWA.

Principal Petitioner, Applicant, or Respondent	A Number or Receipt Number, if any	
Name: Last First Middle DOE AND ASOCIATES	None	[x] Petitioner [ ] Applicant [ ] Respondent

Address: Street Number and Street Name	Apt. No.	City	State	Zip Code
Petitioner's Address				

Pursuant to the Privacy Act of 1974 and DHS policy, I hereby consent to the disclosure to the named Attorney or Accredited Representative of any record pertaining to me that appears in any system of records of USCIS, USCBP, or USICE.

Signature of Petitioner, Applicant, or Respondent   **Date**
11/08/2009

Part 2. Information about Attorney or Accredited Representative *(Check applicable items(s) below)*

A. [x] I am an attorney and a member in good standing of the bar of the highest court(s) of the following State(s), possession(s), territory(ies), commonwealth(s), or the District of Columbia: State of _____   Supreme Court

I am not [x] or [ ] **am subject to any order of any court or administrative agency disbarring, suspending, enjoining, restraining, or otherwise restricting me in the practice of law (If you are subject to any order(s), explain fully on reverse side).**

B. [ ] I am an accredited representative of the following qualified non-profit religious, charitable, social service, or similar organization established in the United States, so recognized by the Department of Justice, Board of Immigration Appeals pursuant to 8 CFR 1292.2. Provide name of organization and expiration date of accreditation:

C. [ ] I am associated with _____ .
The attorney or accredited representative of record previously filed Form G-28 in this case, and my appearance as an attorney or accredited representative is at his or her request *(If you check this item, also complete item A or B above in **Part 2**, whichever is appropriate).*

Part 3. Name and Signature of Attorney or Accredited Representative

I have read and understand the regulations and conditions contained in 8 CFR 103.2 and 292 governing appearances and representation before the Department of Homeland Security. I declare under penalty of perjury under the laws of the United States that the information I have provided on this form is true and correct.

Name of Attorney or Accredited Representative	Attorney Bar Number(s), if any
Attorney or Accredited Representative's Name	

Signature of Attorney or Accredited Representative	Date 11/08/2009

Complete Address of Attorney or Organization of Accredited Representative (Street Number and Street Name, Suite No., City, State, Zip Code)
Attorney or Accredited Representative's Address

Phone Number *(Include area code)*	Fax Number, if any *(Include area code)*	E-Mail Address, if any
(305) 442-1322	(305) 444-7578	Valid E-mail Address

Form G-28 (Rev. 04/22/09)N

CHAPTER 4

Temporary Visas for Studying

I. Introduction

Individuals are allowed to enter the United States in order to study at an educational institution or to participate in an educational program approved by the Attorney General. The student is the applicant and the organization providing the education or program is termed the educational institution or the sponsoring agency.

II. The F-1 Visa

This type of visa allows the student to study full-time at an academic institution such as a university, private school or language institute. INA §101(a)(15)(F)(i); 8 U.S.C. §1101(a)(15)(F); 8 C.F.R. §214.2 (f).

There are certain key issues that a student must be aware of in order not to violate or "fall out" of his/her student status. Those issues are extensions, reinstatements, grace periods, reporting requirements of the school and employment.

Extension is the manner in which the student maintains status by extending his/her status. If a student wishes to extend his/her program, s/he must do so prior to the end date indicated on his/her Form I-20 (Certificate of Student Eligibility). If s/he does not complete his/her studies and does not ask for an extension, the student is out of status.

Reinstatement is the manner in which an individual tries to regain his/her status after s/he has fallen out of status for a period of time. If a student falls out of status but wants to reinstate his/her student status, s/he must apply for the reinstatement not more than five months after being out of status. For a reinstatement to be approved, the student must show either that (i) the violation of the status relates to a reduction in a student's course load, and that failure to approve the reinstatement would result in extreme hardship to the student or (ii) that the violation of the status resulted from circumstances beyond the student's control (e.g., medical emergencies or financial situations in the country of the sponsor).

Grace period is a period of time given to the student to maintain his/her status after s/he has completed his/her program. Students who have completed their studies and/or training have a 60-day grace period after the expiration of their F-1 status to depart the United States or change their status to another visa. If a student withdraws from school, s/he has a 15-day grace period to either leave the United States or change his/her status.

Employment while the student is in F-1 status is allowed only in certain circumstances. The student may work on campus as long as USCIS approves the employment. A new student is not allowed to begin working sooner than 30 days prior to the actual start date of classes. Transfer students may not work on campus until the school has the students' records on the particular school's SEVIS (Student and Exchange Visitor Information System) program. SEVIS is a reporting and tracking system of students by which all educational institutions must abide. Each semester, the school must report whether the F-1 student has enrolled, the identification of any F-1 student who has dropped below a full course of study without authorization and the current address of the F-1 student. This must be done within three days of the beginning of the semester.

Employment is allowed off campus under a program termed Optional Practical Training (OPT). A student may request a one-year period of OPT, which becomes available after completion of the course requirements. A student may engage in OPT one year after obtaining his/her bachelor's degree, one year after completing his/her master's degree and one year after completing his/her Ph.D. degree. However, before s/he may work, the student must obtain an Employment Authorization Document (EAD). To apply for an EAD, the following documents must be filed with USCIS: Form I-765, proof of completion of studies, a signature card with the signature of the student and two recent passport style photographs to the USCIS Service Center having jurisdiction of the area where the school is located.

1. Forms Required:

   a. Certificate of Eligibility for Nonimmigrant (F-1) Student Status;

   b. Form I-20 A-B/I-20 ID, Certificate of Eligibility for Nonimmigrant (F-1) Student Status For Academic and Language Students, which is issued by a school approved by USCIS for attendance by foreign students;

   c. Form I-20M-N, Certificate of Eligibility for Nonimmigrant (M-1) Student Status for Vocational Students;

   d. Form DS-156, Nonimmigrant Visa Applicant, together with a Form DS-158;

   e. Some applicants will also be required to complete and sign Form DS-157. A separate form is needed for children, even if they are included in a parent's passport; and

   f. Form I-134, Affidavit of Support, from a financial sponsor for the amount indicated on Form I-20, current employment letter and last three years of income tax returns.

2. Documents Required:

   a. A passport valid for at least six months after the alien's proposed date of entry into the United States;

   b. Form I-94;

   c. One recent passport style photograph;

   d. A MRV fee receipt to show payment of the visa application fee, a visa issuance fee if applicable and a separate SEVIS I-901 fee receipt;

   e. Previous educational degrees and certificates;

   f. Résumé;

   g. Transcripts and diplomas from previous institutions attended;

   h. Scores from standardized tests required by the educational institution (i.e., TOEFL, SAT, GRE, GMAT, etc.);

   Applicants with dependents **must** also provide:

   i. Proof of the student's relationship to his/her spouse and/or children (e.g., marriage and birth certificates.);

   j. It is preferred that families apply for F-1 and F-2 visas at the same time, but if the spouse and children must apply separately at a later time, they should bring a copy of the student visa holder's passport and visa, along with all other required documents.

III. The J Visa

This type of visa allows a student intern to work or train with an organization that has been approved for an exchange program under the J visa regulations. These individuals are termed exchange aliens. INA § 101(a)(15)(J); 8 U.S.C. §§ 1101(a)(15)(J); 8 C.F.R. § 214.2(j)(1)(i).

1. Forms Required:

   a. Form DS 2019, Certificate of Eligibility for Exchange Visitor Status, issued by the State Department United States Information Agency to J Program Provider;

    b. Form DS-156, Nonimmigrant Visa Application, completed and signed;

    c. Form DS-157, Supplemental Nonimmigrant Visa Application;

    d. Form DS-158, Contact Information and Work History; and

    e. Form I-134, Affidavit of Support, from a financial sponsor for the amount indicated on Form I-20, current employment letter and last three years of income tax returns.

2. Documents Required:

    a. One recent passport style photograph;

    b. Previous educational degrees and certificates;

    c. Résumé;

    d. A passport valid for at least six months after the alien's proposed date of entry into the United States; and

    e. Form I-94.

IV. The M Visa

This type of visa allows an individual to attend an approved course of study leading to a specific educational or vocational objective and engage in a full course of study. INA § 101(a)(15)(M), 8 U.S.C. § 1101(A)(15)(M); 8 C.F.R. § 214.2(m).

1. Forms Required:

    a. Form I-20A-B, Certificate of Eligibility for Nonimmigrant (F-1) Student Status For Academic and Language Students or Form I-20M-N, Certificate of Eligibility for Nonimmigrant (M-1) Student Status for Vocational Students

    b. Form DS-156, Nonimmigrant Visa Applicant, together with a Form DS-158

    c. Some applicants will also be required to complete and sign Form DS-157. A separate form is needed for children, even if they are included in a parent's passport; and

    d. Form I-134, Affidavit of Support, from a financial sponsor for the amount indicated on Form I-20, current employment letter and last three years of income tax returns.

2. Documents Required:

    a. A passport valid for at least six months after the alien's proposed date of entry into the United States;

    b. Form I-94;

    c. One recent passport style photograph;

    d. A MRV fee receipt to show payment of the visa application fee, a visa issuance fee if applicable and a separate SEVIS I-901 fee receipt;

    e. Previous educational degrees and certificates;

    f. Résumé;

    g. Transcripts and diplomas from previous institutions attended;

    h. Scores from standardized tests required by the educational institution (i.e., TOEFL, SAT, GRE, GMAT, etc.);

    Applicants with dependents **must** also provide:

    i. Proof of the student's relationship to his/her spouse and/or children (e.g., marriage and birth certificates.);

    j. It is preferred that families apply for F-1 and F-2 visas at the same time, but if the spouse and children must apply separately at a later time, they should bring a copy of the student visa holder's passport and visa, along with all other required documents.

Appendix

1. Form I-539, G-28
2. Cover Letter

Form I-539

OMB No. 1615-0003; Expires 02/29/12

Department of Homeland Security
U.S. Citizenship and Immigration Services

**I-539, Application to Extend/
Change Nonimmigrant Status**

START HERE - Please type or print in black ink	For USCIS Use Only	

Part 1.   Information About You

Family Name	Given Name	Middle Name
DOE	John	

Address -
In care of - Blank Attorney, P.A.

Street Number and Name 222 S.W. 27th Drive		Apt. Number

City	State	Zip Code	Daytime Phone Number
Weston	FL	33751	(954) 777-8855

Country of Birth	Country of Citizenship
United Kingdom	United Kingdom

Date of Birth (mm/dd/yyyy) 05/20/1986	U. S. Social Security # (if any) None	A-Number (if any) None

Date of Last Arrival Into the U.S. 12/20/2009	I-94 Number 123456789 00

Current Nonimmigrant Status B2	Expires on (mm/dd/yyyy) 05/19/2010

Part 2.   Application Type *(See instructions for fee)*

1. I am applying for: *(Check one)*

  a. ☐ An extension of stay in my current status.

  b. ☒ A change of status. The new status I am requesting is: F1

  c. ☐ Reinstatement to student status.

2. Number of people included in this application: *(Check one)*

  a. ☒ I am the only applicant.

  b. ☐ Members of my family are filing this application with me.
The total number of people (including me) in the application is:
(Complete the supplement for each co-applicant.) _____

Part 3.   Processing Information

1. I/We request that my/our current or requested status be extended until (mm/dd/yyyy): _____

2. Is this application based on an extension or change of status already granted to your spouse, child, or parent?
☒ No ☐ Yes. USCIS Receipt # _____

3. Is this application based on a separate petition or application to give your spouse, child, or parent an extension or change of status? ☐ No ☐ Yes, filed with this I-539.

☒ Yes, filed previously and pending with USCIS. Receipt #: _____

4. If you answered "Yes" to Question 3, give the name of the petitioner or applicant: _____

If the petition or application is pending with USCIS, also give the following data:

Office filed at	Filed on (mm/dd/yyyy)

Part 4.   Additional Information

1. For applicant #1, provide passport information:
Country of Issuance: United Kingdom

Valid to: (mm/dd/yyyy)
10/10/2012

2. Foreign Address: Street Number and Name
56 Mainstream Drive

Apt. Number
25

City or Town London	State or Province

Country United Kingdom	Zip/Postal Code E15 6PP

For USCIS Use Only

Returned	Receipt
Date	
Resubmitted	
Date	
Reloc Sent	
Date	
Reloc Rec'd	
Date	

☐ Applicant Interviewed on
_____
Date

☐ *Extension Granted to (Date):*
_____

Change of Status/Extension Granted
New Class: From *(Date):* _____
_____ To *(Date):* _____

If Denied:
☐ Still within period of stay
☐ S/D to: _____
☐ Place under docket control

Remarks:

Action Block

To Be Completed by
Attorney or Representative, **if any**

☐ Fill in box if G-28 is attached to represent the applicant.

ATTY State License #

Form I-539 (Rev. 06/12/09)Y

Form I-539

3. Answer the following questions. If you answer "Yes" to any question, describe the circumstances in detail and explain on a separate sheet of paper.

		Yes	No
a.	Are you, or any other person included on the application, an applicant for an immigrant visa?	☐	☒
b.	Has an immigrant petition ever been filed for you or for any other person included in this application?	☐	☒
c.	Has Form I-485, Application to Register Permanent Residence or Adjust Status, ever been filed by you or by any other person included in this application?	☐	☒
d. 1.	Have you, or any other person included in this application, ever been arrested or convicted of any criminal offense since last entering the United States?	☐	☒

d. 2. Have you EVER ordered, incited, called for, commited, assisted, helped with, or otherwise participated in any of the following:

    (a) Acts involving torture or genocide?

    (b) Killing any person?

    (c) Intentionally and severely injuring any person?

    (d) Engaging in any kind of sexual contact or relations with any person who was being forced or threatened?

    (e) Limiting or denying any person's ability to exercise religious beliefs?   ☐ ☒

d. 3. Have you EVER:

    (a) Served in, been a member of, assisted in, or participated in any military unit, paramilitary unit, police unit, self-defense unit, vigilante unit, rebel group, guerrilla group, militia, or insurgent organization?

    (b) Served in any prison, jail, prison camp, detention facility, labor camp, or any other situation that involved detaining persons?   ☐ ☒

d. 4. Have you EVER been a member of, assisted in, or participated in any group, unit, or organization of any kind in which you or other persons used any type of weapon against any person or threatened to do so?   ☐ ☒

d. 5. Have you EVER assisted or participated in selling or providing weapons to any person who to your knowledge used them against another person, or in transporting weapons to any person who to your knowledge used them against another person?   ☐ ☒

d. 6. Have you EVER received any type of military, paramilitary, or weapons training?   ☐ ☒

e.	Have you, or any other person included in this application, done anything that violated the terms of the nonimmigrant status you now hold?	☐	☒
f.	Are you, or any other person included in this application, now in removal proceedings?	☐	☒
g.	Have you, or any other person included in this application, been employed in the United States since last admitted or granted an extension or change of status?	☐	☒

    1. If you answered "Yes" to Question 3f, give the following information concerning the removal proceedings on the attached page entitled **"Part 4. Additional information. Page for answers to 3f and 3g."** Include the name of the person in removal proceedings and information on jurisdiction, date proceedings began, and status of proceedings.

    2. If you answered "No" to Question 3g, fully describe how you are supporting yourself on the attached page entitled **"Part 4. Additional information. Page for answers to 3f and 3g."** Include the source, amount, and basis for any income.

    3. If you answered "Yes" to Question 3g, fully describe the employment on the attached page entitled **"Part 4. Additional information. Page for answers to 3f and 3g."** Include the name of the person employed, name and address of the employer, weekly income, and whether the employment was specifically authorized by USCIS.

Form I-539

		Yes	**No**
h.	Are you currently or have you ever been a J-1 exchange visitor or a J-2 dependent of a J-1 exchange visitor?	☐	☒

If "Yes," you must provide the dates you maintained status as a J-1 exchange visitor or J-2 dependent. Willful failure to disclose this information (or other relevant information) can result in your application being denied. Also, provide proof of your J-1 or J-2 status, such as a copy of Form DS-2019, Certificate of Eligibility for Exchange Visitor Status, or a copy of your passport that includes the J visa stamp.

Part 5. Applicant's Statement and Signature *(Read the information on penalties in the instructions before completing this section. You must file this application while in the United States.)*

Applicant's Statement (Check One):

☒ I can read and understand English, and have read and understand each and every question and instruction on this form, as well as my answer to each question.

☐ Each and every question and instruction on this form, as well as my answer to each question, has been read to me by the person named below in _____, a language in which I am fluent. I understand each and every question and instruction on this form, as well as my answer to each question.

Applicant's Signature

I certify, under penalty of perjury under the laws of the United States of America, that this application and the evidence submitted with it is all true and correct. I authorize the release of any information from my records that U.S. Citizenship and Immigration Services needs to determine eligibility for the benefit I am seeking.

Signature	Print your Name	Date
	John Doe	
Daytime Telephone Number (954) 777-8855	**E-Mail Address**	

NOTE: *If you do not completely fill out this form or fail to submit required documents listed in the instructions, you may not be found eligible for the requested benefit and this application may be denied.*

Part 6. Interpreter's Statement

Language used: _____

I certify that I am fluent in English and the above-mentioned language. I further certify that I have read each and every question and instruction on this form, as well as the answer to each question, to this applicant in the above-mentioned language, and the applicant has understood each and every instruction and question on the form, as well as the answer to each question.

Signature	Print Your Name	Date
Firm Name (if applicable)	**Daytime Telephone Number** *(Area Code and Number)*	
Address	**Fax Number** *(Area Code and Number)*	**E-Mail Address**

Form I-539

Part 7. Signature of Person Preparing Form, if Other Than Above *(Sign Below)*

Signature	Print Your Name	Date
	Blank Attorney, Esq.	

Firm Name (if applicable)	Daytime Telephone Number *(Area Code and Number)* (305) 987-6543	
Address 2655 LeJeune Road Suite 1001 Coral Gables, FL 33134	Fax Number *(Area Code and Number)* (305) 987-5658	E-Mail Address attorney@attorney.com

I declare that I prepared this application at the request of the above person and it is based on all information of which I have knowledge.

Part 4. (Continued) Additional Information. (Page 2 for answers to 3f and 3g.)

If you answered "Yes" to Question 3f in Part 4 on Page 3 of this form, give the following information concerning the removal proceedings. Include the name of the person in removal proceedings and information on jurisdiction, date proceedings began, and status of proceedings.

```
N/A
```

If you answered "No" to Question 3g in Part 4 on Page 3 of this form, fully describe how you are supporting yourself. Include the source, amount and basis for any income.

```
Source: Jane Doe, sister and financial sponsor
Amount: $50,000.00

The applicant's financial sponsor will incur all education costs during his studies at Florida
Atlantic University (see attached letter).

The above stated sponsor currently has a balance of $50,000.00 in his savings account (see attached
blank letter).
```

If you answered "Yes" to Question 3g in Part 4 on Page 3 of this form, fully describe the employment. Include the name of the person employed, name and address of the employer, weekly income, and whether the employment was specifically authorized by USCIS.

```
N/A
```

Form I-539

Supplement -1
Attach to Form I-539 when more than one person is included in the petition or application.
(List each person separately. Do not include the person named in Form I-539.)

Family Name	Given Name	Middle Name	Date of Birth (mm/dd/yyyy)	
Country of Birth	Country of Citizenship	U.S. Social Security # (if any)	A-Number (if any)	
Date of Arrival (mm/dd/yyyy)		I-94 Number		
Current Nonimmigrant Status:		Expires on (mm/dd/yyyy)		
Country Where Passport Issued		Expiration Date (mm/dd/yyyy)		

Family Name	Given Name	Middle Name	Date of Birth (mm/dd/yyyy)	
Country of Birth	Country of Citizenship	U.S. Social Security # (if any)	A-Number (if any)	
Date of Arrival (mm/dd/yyyy)		I-94 Number		
Current Nonimmigrant Status:		Expires on (mm/dd/yyyy)		
Country Where Passport Issued		Expiration Date (mm/dd/yyyy)		

Family Name	Given Name	Middle Name	Date of Birth (mm/dd/yyyy)	
Country of Birth	Country of Citizenship	U.S. Social Security # (if any)	A-Number (if any)	
Date of Arrival (mm/dd/yyyy)		I-94 Number		
Current Nonimmigrant Status:		Expires on (mm/dd/yyyy)		
Country Where Passport Issued		Expiration Date (mm/dd/yyyy)		

Family Name	Given Name	Middle Name	Date of Birth (mm/dd/yyyy)	
Country of Birth	Country of Citizenship	U.S. Social Security # (if any)	A-Number (if any)	
Date of Arrival (mm/dd/yyyy)		I-94 Number		
Current Nonimmigrant Status:		Expires on (mm/dd/yyyy)		
Country Where Passport Issued		Expiration Date (mm/dd/yyyy)		

Family Name	Given Name	Middle Name	Date of Birth (mm/dd/yyyy)	
Country of Birth	Country of Citizenship	U.S. Social Security # (if any)	A-Number (if any)	
Date of Arrival (mm/dd/yyyy)		I-94 Number		
Current Nonimmigrant Status:		Expires on (mm/dd/yyyy)		
Country Where Passport Issued		Expiration Date (mm/dd/yyyy)		

If you need additional space, attach a separate sheet of paper.
Place your name, A-Number, if any, date of birth, form number, and application date at the top of the sheet of paper.

Form I-539 (Rev. 06/12/09)Y Page 5

Form G-28

OMB No. 1615-0105; Expires 04/30/2012

**G-28, Notice of Entry of Appearance
as Attorney or Accredited Representative**

Department of Homeland Security

Part 1. Notice of Appearance as Attorney or Accredited Representative

A. This appearance is in regard to immigration matters before:

[×] USCIS - List the form number(s): I-539 _____   [ ] CBP - List the specific matter in which appearance is entered:

[ ] ICE - List the specific matter in which appearance is entered: _____

_____

B. I hereby enter my appearance as attorney or accredited representative at the request of:

List Petitioner, Applicant, or Respondent. **NOTE:** Provide the mailing address of Petitioner, Applicant, or Respondent being represented, and **not** the address of the attorney or accredited representative, except when filed under VAWA.

Principal Petitioner, Applicant, or Respondent			A Number or Receipt Number, if any	
Name: Last	First	Middle		[ ] Petitioner
DOE	John		None	[×] Applicant
				[ ] Respondent

Address: Street Number and Street Name	Apt. No.	City	State	Zip Code
Applicant's Address				

Pursuant to the Privacy Act of 1974 and DHS policy, I hereby consent to the disclosure to the named Attorney or Accredited Representative of any record pertaining to me that appears in any system of records of USCIS, USCBP, or USICE.

Signature of Petitioner, Applicant, or Respondent	Date
	11/08/2009

Part 2. Information about Attorney or Accredited Representative *(Check applicable items(s) below)*

A. [×] I am an attorney and a member in good standing of the bar of the highest court(s) of the following State(s), possession(s), territory(ies), commonwealth(s), or the District of Columbia: State of _____   Supreme Court _____

I am not [×] **or** [ ] **am subject to any order of any court or administrative agency disbarring, suspending, enjoining, restraining, or otherwise restricting me in the practice of law (If you are subject to any order(s), explain fully on reverse side).**

B. [ ] I am an accredited representative of the following qualified non-profit religious, charitable, social service, or similar organization established in the United States, so recognized by the Department of Justice, Board of Immigration Appeals pursuant to 8 CFR 1292.2. Provide name of organization and expiration date of accreditation:

_____

C. [ ] I am associated with _____ .

The attorney or accredited representative of record previously filed Form G-28 in this case, and my appearance as an attorney or accredited representative is at his or her request *(If you check this item, also complete item A or B above in **Part 2**, whichever is appropriate)*.

Part 3. Name and Signature of Attorney or Accredited Representative

I have read and understand the regulations and conditions contained in 8 CFR 103.2 and 292 governing appearances and representation before the Department of Homeland Security. I declare under penalty of perjury under the laws of the United States that the information I have provided on this form is true and correct.

Name of Attorney or Accredited Representative	Attorney Bar Number(s), if any
Attorney or Accredited Representative's Name	

Signature of Attorney or Accredited Representative	Date
	11/08/2009

Complete Address of Attorney or Organization of Accredited Representative (Street Number and Street Name, Suite No., City, State, Zip Code)
Attorney or Accredited Representative's Address

Phone Number *(Include area code)*	Fax Number, if any *(Include area code)*	E-Mail Address, if any
(305) 442-1322	(305) 444-7578	Valid E-mail Address

Form G-28 (Rev. 04/22/09)N

Cover Letter

November 13, 2007

CERTIFIED RETURN RECEIPT

U.S. Department of Homeland Security
U.S. Citizenship and Immigration Services
Texas Service Center
P.O. Box 851182
Mesquite, Texas 75185-1182

Re: I-539—Application to Extend/Change Nonimmigrant Status
APPLICANT:

Dear Sir or Madam:

Enclosed herein are the following documents for processing:

1. Form I-539/Filing Fee/Form G-28;
2. Passport/Form I-94; 3. Copy of plane ticket, of applicant;
4. Copy of bank statements, of applicant as proof of income; and
5. Invitation letter.

I would appreciate your attention to this matter.

Very truly yours,

_____

I539LTR (SAMPLE)

CHAPTER 5

Temporary Visas for Particular Occupations—O, P, Q and R Visas

I. Introduction

Individuals who seek employment in particular occupations may qualify for certain temporary visas. Some examples are: O-1 visa for an extraordinary culinary chef, P-1 for a folk singing group, Q-1 for an Irish river dancer, O-1 for an extraordinary muralist and R-1 for an evangelist.

II. The O Visas—Extraordinary Ability Artists/Entertainers, Business People, Scientists, Educators and Athletes

The O-1 applies to foreign nationals of extraordinary or high achievement in the sciences, arts, education, business or athletics as demonstrated by sustained national or international acclaim, or, with regard to motion picture and television productions, a demonstrated record of extraordinary achievement, which have been recognized in the field through extensive documentation. Once in the United States, they must continue to work solely in the area of extraordinary ability. The arts include, but are not limited to, culinary arts, fine arts, visual arts and performing arts and apply to, among others, designers, choreographers, composers/conductors, language and voice coaches, arrangers, musical supervisors, costume designers, makeup artists, stage technicians and urban planners. INA §101(a)(15)(O), 8 U.S.C. §1101(a)(15)(O); 8 C.F.R. §214.2(o)(ii)(A)(1) and (2).

A. The O-1 Visa—Science, Education, Business and Athletics

In science, education, business and athletics, the alien must be one of a small percentage who has reached the top of his/her field or has received a major award such as a Nobel Prize.

B. Artists

In the arts, the alien must demonstrate distinction in his/her field. Distinction means a high level of achievement, one who is renowned, leading or well known or having won a major award such as an Academy Award. This is a less rigorous standard.

C. Star in Motion Pictures and Television

In the motion pictures and television industry, the alien must demonstrate a record of a very high level of achievement and must be recognized as outstanding, notable or leading in the motion picture or television field.

1. Forms Required:

   The Petition for Nonimmigrant Worker (Form I-129) Supplement O, Form G-28 and Forms I-539 and G-28 (for the spouse and accompanying children) must be submitted to the USCIS Service Center.

2. Documents Required:

   a. Résumé;

   b. Receipt of prizes or major internationally recognized awards such as a Nobel Prize; or

   c. At least three of the following evidentiary proof:

      1. Documentation of the alien's receipt of nationally or internationally recognized prizes or awards for excellence in his/her field;

      2. Membership in associations in the field that require outstanding achievement as judged by international or recognized experts;

      3. Published materials in major publications or media;

      4. Participation in a panel where the alien judged the work of others in the field of specialization;

      5. Original scientific, scholarly or business-related contributions of major significance;

      6. Authorship of scholarly article in professional journals or other major media;

      7. Employment in an organization that has a distinguished reputation;

      8. Proof of commanding a high salary presently or in the past; and

      9. Other comparable evidence;

   d. The evidentiary proof for individuals in the arts:

      1. Performing a lead or starring role in a production or event of distinguished reputation, publicity release, contracts and publications. (**Note:** Opera singers can sing in the chorus.);

      2. National or international recognition reviews in major newspapers, magazines or trade journals;

      3. Performing a lead or starring role in organizations or establishments of distinguished reputation evidenced by media articles or testimonials;

      4. Record of major commercial or critically acclaimed success;

      5. Significant recognition from organizations, critics, government agencies, governments or experts;

      6. Proof of commanding a high salary or remuneration; and

      7. Other comparable evidence.

   e. The evidentiary proof for artists and entertainers performing in motion pictures or television is the same as in "d," however, it will be weighed differently; a higher standard will be applied to artists and entertainers in the motion picture and television industry.

D. The O-2 Visa — Support Staff of Artists and Athletes

The O-2 visa is for an alien entering (1) for a specific event or events; (2) who is an integral part of such actual performance; (3) (a) has critical skills and experience with the principal alien that are not of a general nature or cannot be performed by other individuals or, (b) in the case of a motion picture or television production, has skills and experience with the O-1 alien that are not of a general nature and are critical and essential to the successful completion of the production; and (4) has a foreign residence which the alien has no intention of abandoning. INA § 101(a) (15)(O)(ii) (1), 8 U.S.C. § 1101(a)(15)(O) (ii).

E. Peer Group Consultation

For the O-1 and O-2 visas, a labor union or peer group must provide, in writing, a consultation on the abilities or achievements of the alien. The person or organization receiving the request has 15 days to respond with either an opinion or "no objection" letter. After the 15 days, USCIS must adjudicate the petition within 14 days.

No advisory opinion is required if petitioner proves no peer group exists. A labor union may respond with just a "no objection" letter. The union's objection must contain a specific statement of facts supporting the conclusion reached. A non-specific or conclusionary statement is the same as a "no objection letter" according to the regulations.

The regulations state that consultations are not binding on USCIS whether favorable or unfavorable.

In case of an unfavorable decision, the regulations allow the employer to rebut the adverse determination by submitting an opinion from an expert in the field particularly when the advisory opinion fails to elaborate reasons for the unfavorable recommendation.

F. Self-Employment

If the alien will be self-employed or working for more than one employer or foreign employer, an agent is required and the alien must provide an agency contract or summary of an oral contract and the itinerary of events.

The O-1 beneficiary may not petition for him/herself. However, a person of extraordinary ability in the sciences, arts, education, business or athletics may qualify for permanent residency under the Employment-Based First Preference (EB-1) mentioned in Chapter 7 and may be self-employed and petition for himself.

The O visa cannot be used for freelancing. It will be approved for working at the employer's workplace or for events or projects for more than one employer.

III. The P Visas

This visa applies to an internationally recognized athlete performing at a major athletic event as an individual athlete or as part of a group or team and for an artist or member of internationally recognized entertainment group. These individuals do not qualify for the O category.

A. The P-1 Visa—Athletes, Athletic Teams and Entertainment Groups

This category covers an internationally recognized athlete performing at a specific athletic competition as an individual athlete or part of a group or team at an internationally recognized level of performance or as a member of internationally recognized entertainment group who has had a sustained and substantial relationship with the group (in most cases, for one year or more) and provides functions that are integral to the group's performance in the United States. INA § 101(a)(15)(P)(i), 8 USC § 1101(a)(15)(P), 8 C.F.R. § 214.2(p)(i).

B. The P-2 Visa—Artists and Entertainer Reciprocal Exchange

This category covers an artist or entertainer under a reciprocal exchange program between the United States and foreign organization(s) providing for temporary exchange of artists and entertainers (including groups). INA § 101(P)(ii)(1), 8 C.F.R. § 214.2(p)(B).

C. The P-3 Visa—Artists and Entertainers Integral to Performance

This category covers an artist or entertainer whose performance, teaching or coaching is integral to the performance of a group performing under a commercial or non-commercial program that is culturally unique. INA §101(A)(15)(P)(iii)(1), 8 C.F.R. §214.2(p)(i)(C).

1. Forms Required:

   The Petition for Non-Immigrant Worker, Form I-129, Supplement P, Form G-28 and Forms I-539 and G-28 (for the spouse and accompanying children) must be submitted to the USCIS Service Center.

2. Documents Required:

   P-1 athlete, at least two of the following:

   a. Significant participation in prior season in major leagues;

   b. Participation in international competition with a national team;

   c. Significant participation in prior season in college, university or intercollegiate competition;

   d. U.S. sports official's written statement regarding individual's or team's international recognition;

   e. Experts or sports media statement regarding individual's or team's international recognition;

   f. Ranking of individual or team; and

   g. Significant honors or awards in the sport.

   P-2 entertainer, at least three of the following:

   a. Star or lead performance with a distinguished reputation;

   b. Reviews in major publications;

   c. Star or lead performance for organization with distinguished reputation;

   d. Major commercial or critically acclaimed success;

   e. Testimonials regarding significant recognition of the group; and

   f. Group commands high salary.

   P-2 artists and entertainers in reciprocal exchange program, at least two of the following:

   a. Reciprocal or exchange agreement;

   b. Statement from sponsoring organization regarding exchange;

   c. Appropriate U.S. labor organization negotiated or involved with the reciprocal program; and

   d. All exchange artists or entertainers have comparable skills and terms employment.

   P-3 artist and entertainer integral to performance, at least two of the following:

   a. Affidavits, letters or testimonials from recognized experts attesting to authenticity of alien's or group's skills in performing, presenting, coaching or teaching the unique or traditional art form, including credentials of sources; and

   b. Performance is culturally unique, as evidenced by published reviews.

   c. Description of beneficiary's essentiality, critical skills and experience with principal alien(s); and

   d. Contract or summary of terms of oral agreement with employer.

D. Peer Group Consultation

Consultation with an appropriate peer or labor organization should address the following, depending upon the classification:

P-1: Advisory opinion regarding individual's or group's ability, the degree of international recognition and whether the U.S. activities will be appropriate for an internationally recognized athlete or entertainment group.

P-2: Advisory opinion regarding the bona fide nature of the reciprocal program and whether it meets P-2 standards.

P-3: Advisory opinion regarding the cultural uniqueness of the beneficiary's skills, whether the U.S. events will be predominantly cultural in nature and whether the proposed U.S. activities meet P-3 standards.

No advisory opinion is required if petitioner proves no peer group exists. A labor union may respond with just a "no objection" letter. The union's objection must contain a specific statement of facts supporting the conclusion reached. A non-specific or conclusionary statement is the same as a "no objection letter" according to the regulations.

The regulations state that consultations are not binding on USCIS whether favorable or unfavorable.

In case of an unfavorable decision, the regulations allow the employer to rebut the adverse determination by submitting an opinion from an expert on the field particularly when the advisory opinion fails to elaborate reasons for the unfavorable recommendation.

IV. The Q-1 Visa

The Q-1 applies to a foreign national entering the United States for the purpose of obtaining practical training, employment and the sharing of history, culture, philosophy and tradition of the alien's home country.

The foreign national must have a residence in a foreign country that s/he has no intention of abandoning and coming to the United States temporarily (for a period not to exceed 15 months) as a participant in an international cultural exchange program approved by the Attorney General for the purpose of providing practical training, employment and the sharing of the history, culture and traditions of the country of the alien's nationality and who will be employed under the same wages and working conditions as U.S. workers. INA 101(a)(15)(Q)(i), 8 U.S.C. §1101 (a) (15) (Q); 8 C.F.R. §214.2 (q).

1. Forms Required:

   The Petition for Nonimmigrant Worker, Form I-129, Supplement Q, Form G-28 and Forms I-539 and G-28 (for the spouse and accompanying children) must be submitted to the USCIS Service Center.

2. Documents Required:

   a. Provide proof that the program will take place in school, museum, business or place with access to the American public;

   b. Provide proof of shared common cultural intent;

   c. Obtain employer information about cultural exchange (e.g., custom, heritage, philosophy or tradition of alien's home country and how cultural component will be presented);

   d. Résumé; and

   e. Brochures or other documents about employer, if any.

V. The R-1 Visa

R-1 visa is for a foreign national with a religious profession, occupation or vocation (e.g., minister, professional holding degree or foreign equivalent degree, cantor, monk, evangelist or nun).

This visa applies to a foreign national who: (1) for the two years immediately preceding the time of application for admission, has been a member of a religious denomination having a bona fide not-for-profit religious organization in the United States and (2) seeks to enter the United States for a period not to exceed five years solely to carry on the vocation of a minister of the religious denomination to work for the religious organization at the request of the organization in a professional capacity or to work for the organization in a religious vocation or occupation. INA §101 (a) (15) (R), 8 U.S.C. §1101 (a) (15) (R); 22 C.F.R. §41.58; 8 C.F.R. §214.2 (r).

1. Forms Required:

    The Petition for Nonimmigrant Worker, Form I-129, Supplement R, Form G-28 and Forms I-539 and G-28 (for the spouse and accompanying children) must be submitted to the USCIS Service Center.

2. Documents Required:

    a. Evidence that petitioner is a not-for-profit organization exempt from taxation in accordance with Section 501(c) (3) of the Internal Revenue Code,

    b. Letter from an authorized official of the religious organization in the United States establishing the following:

        1. that immediately prior to the filing of the petition, the alien had the required two years of membership in the denomination and the required two years of experience in the religious vocation, religious work or other religious work (**Note:** Professionals need not prove two years experience.); and

        2. that if the alien is a minister, s/he has authorization to conduct religious worship and perform other duties usually performed by authorized members of the clergy, including a detailed description of such authorized duties (in appropriate cases, the certificate of ordination or authorization may be requested); or

        3. that if the alien is a religious professional, s/he has at least a U.S. baccalaureate or its foreign equivalent required for entry into the religious profession. In all professional cases, an official academic record showing that the alien has the required degree must be submitted; or

        4. that if the alien is to work in another religious vocation or occupation, s/he is qualified in the religious vocation or occupation. Evidence of such qualifications may include, but need not be limited to, evidence establishing that the alien is a nun, monk or religious brother or that the type of work to be done relates to a traditional religious function;

        5. that the letter must also describe the job offer. The authorized official of the religious organization in the United States must state how the alien will be solely carrying on the vocation of a minister, including any terms of payment for services or other remuneration or how the alien will be paid or remunerated if the alien will work in a professional religious capacity or in other religious work. The documentation should clearly indicate that the alien will not be solely dependent on supplemental employment or solicitation of funds for support.

    c. Current financial statement of the organization;

    d. Church membership figures; and

    e. If a professional position, résumé and copy of degree(s).

Appendix

1. Employer Questionnaire
2. Employee Questionnaire
3. O-1 Visa Petition Letter
4. Form I-129 and Supplement O/P
5. Form G-28
6. P-3 Visa Petition Letter
7. Form I-129 P-3 and Supplement O/P
8. Form G-28

Employer Questionnaire

A. Information Concerning Employer/Petitioner

1. Company name: _____

2. Address: _____

3. Telephone number(s): _____

4. Fax number: _____

5. E-mail address: _____

6. Internet website (www.): _____

7. If employee will work at a different address than above, please state: _____

_____

8. Date established: _____

9. Employer tax ID #: _____

10. Number of total employees: _____

11. Number of employees on H-1B1 visa: _____

12. Approximate *gross* annual income for current year:

    $ _____

13. Approximate *net* annual income for current year:

    $ _____

14. Please give a detailed description of business:

_____

_____

> *Please attach all available information concerning the petitioner (e.g., brochures, advertising material, catalogues, published articles, references, etc).*

15. Full name of company representative who will sign petitioning documents:

_____

16. Which position does the representative hold with the company (e.g., president, vice president, manager of

human resources)? _____

_____

17. Name of contact person at petitioning company, if different from above: _____

_____

B. Information Concerning the Position offered

1. Job title: _____

2. Detailed description of duties to be performed:

_____

_____

_____

3. Hours per week: _____

4. Wages per week: _____

5. Would there be additional compensation? If so, please explain: _____

_____

6. If so, what would that compensation be valued at? _____

_____

7. How long do you intend to employ the beneficiary? _____

_____

Employee Questionnaire

1. Full Name: _____
   Last   First   Middle

2. Address abroad: _____

   _____

   _____

3. Place of Birth: _____
   City/State/Province   Country

4. Date of birth: _____
   Month   Day   Year

5. Country of Citizenship: _____

   Profession/Occupation: _____

6. Do you have a university/college degree?   Yes {   }   No {   }

   Major/primary field of study: _____

   Degree obtained: _____

   When and where? _____

7. How many years did you spend at college/university? _____

8. Social Security Number: SSN# _____

9. Alien Registration Number: A# _____

10. Address in the U.S. where you will reside: _____

    _____

    _____

11. Gender: Male {   }   Female {   }

12. Marital status: Married {   }   Divorced {   }   Single {   }   Widowed {   }

    Spouse's Name: _____
    Last   First   Middle

    Date of birth: _____
    Month   Day   Year

    Place of Birth: _____
    City/State/Province   Country

13. Do you have any children?   Yes {   }   No {   }

    Child's Name: _____
    Last   First   Middle

    Date of Birth: _____
    Month   Day   Year

    Place of Birth: _____
    City/State/Province   Country

    Country of Citizenship: _____

T.V. PRODUCTIONS, INC.

October 4, 2007

Via Express Mail

U.S. Citizenship and Immigration Services
Texas Service Center
P.O. Box 852211
Mesquite, TX 75185-2211

RE: **O-1 VISA PETITION FOR A NONIMMIGRANT WORKER.**
    PETITIONER: TV PRODUCTIONS, INC.
    BENEFICIARY: DOE, John.
    Form I-129/O

Dear Sir or Madam:

This letter is in support of non-immigrant (O-1) classification for John Doe, a Mexican national of extraordinary ability and demonstrated record of achievement on radio and television entertainer in his home country and abroad with an international distinction in the field of broadcasting. Mr. Doe has a level of expertise indicating that he is one of a small percentage who has risen to the very top of his field.

There are three (3) standards to prove qualifications for an O-1 visa:

(1) In the sciences, education, business and athletics the alien must be one of a small percentage that has reached the top of his field or has received a major award such as a Nobel Prize. 8 CFR 214.20(3)(iii).

(2) **In the arts extraordinary is distinction. Distinction means a high level of achievement one who is renowned leading or well known, or who has won a major award such as Academy Award. This is a less rigorous standard. 8 CFR 214.02(3)(iv).**

(3) Extraordinary ability in the T.V. and Motion Picture Industry. Here, the test is the alien's distinction, but s/he must meet a higher standard. 8 CFR 214.2(0)(3)(v).

The second is a less rigorous standard. In this case Mr. Doe, who is a member of the arts, falls into the "distinction" standard.

THE PETITIONER

TV PRODUCTIONS, INC., is an entertainment company founded in 2003 in Miami, Fla. This company is primarily engaged in radio and television production and broadcasting, assistance, promotion, enhancement, and representation of artists in contractual matters.

POSITION REQUIRING A PERSON OF EXTRAORDINARY ABILITY

Mr. Doe is an internationally renowned radio and television announcer with vast experience in radio and television broadcasting. He has been offered a high level position as a radio and television announcer and "anchor voice" as more fully discussed below. In this position, Mr. Doe will perform the following duties: He will work in

26XX NW 27 Ave. Miami, FL 3319X
Phone (305) XXX-XXXX Fax (305) XXX-XXXX
Email: tvproductions@tvproductions.com
Webpage: www.tvproductions.com

T.V. PRODUCTIONS, INC.

the entertainment field which is his primary source of earned income. He will be involved in production activities, such as announcing radio and television programs to audiences; memorize script, read, or ad-lib to identify station, introduce and close shows, announce station breaks, commercials, or public service information, and read news flashes to keep audience informed of important events.

Mr. Doe, as radio and television announcer, will announce program transmission over network and affiliated stations and be designated Network Announcer, and will announce in foreign languages for international broadcasts.

THE EXTRAORDINARY ABILITY OF THE ALIEN

Mr. John Doe is a Mexican individual with proven extraordinary ability in the arts, who possesses a high level of expertise in the entertainment and broadcasting industry.

Since August 17, 1978 Mr. John Doe has been affiliated with the Professional Syndication of Workers in Radio, Theater, Movie, Television, and Similar of The District Capital in Mexico. *(Please see Exhibit "_")*

Mr. John Doe began his career as a radio announcer in 1980, in one of the leading stations, MEXICAN RADIO 1099 AM, and after producing various programs, he joined the team as one of the founders of FASHION STATION in 1988.

Mr. Doe also developed an important career in television. Among the programs that stand out is: "XXXXXXX," broadcasted by TELEVISION MEXICANA in 1986. While working in this station, he also performed promotional voice-overs from 1986–1990.

Because of Mr. Doe's outstanding labor in the media, he has been awarded with the "Gold Voice Award" as Best Radio and Television Announcer from 1991 to 1994, and Best Disc-jockey in 1991 by the "Mexican Artists Association." Similarly, he was recognized as the Best Latin American Announcer by the Embassy of Venezuela in our country in the year 1997.

It is important to point out that the Gold Voice Award is conferred by popular votes in opinion polls that are carried out by the national circulation and prestigious "Mexico Today" Newspaper.

In addition, the "National Artist Award" received by Mr. Doe from the Mexican Artist Association Foundation is annually conferred to the most outstanding professional in the business. *(Please see Exhibit "_")*

Due to Mr. Doe's outstanding success, acclaim, and extraordinary artistic ability, his work has received national and international recognition from well-known personalities and experts in the field, including:

Mrs. Gabriela Sanchez, BCI LATINA On-Air Manager, who stated:

*"I have known Mr. **JOHN DOE** since I began working in this company. His experience as announcer has set him apart him as the **official voice of BCI LATINA** in all of Latin America, a signal that has been reaching 23 territories for more than 11 years. Since then, we have made a united and proactive team. I consider him to be a*

26XX NW 27 Ave. Miami, FL 3319X
Phone (305) XXX-XXXX Fax (305) XXX-XXXX
Email: tvproductions@tvproductions.com
Webpage: www.tvproductions.com

T.V. PRODUCTIONS, INC.

talented and dedicated professional, always ready to assume new challenges and succeeding in reaching all the goals he puts forth."

Mrs. Monic M. Bellorin, Administration Manager of FASHION RADIO, who stated:

"Since he began working here, Mr. Doe has performed as a Professional Announcer, in a continuous manner, not only on the air, but in promotions, currently being the voice that identifies our spots 'Exitos' and 'Fashion Radio Noticias'" (Hits and News spots). In addition to his activity in our new circuit, Mr. Doe has developed a prolific career as promotional voice-over, being one of the most requested voices in Mexico."

Mr. Jhon Larrain, General Manager of Radio Mexicana, dated May 12, 2003, who stated:

"I certify that Mr. Doe works as our official announcer in Mexicana FM station.

We are extremely proud to have Mr. Doe as our official announcer because his voice is well recognized among listeners all over our country and he gives our station a distinctive hallmark on the FM band."

(See Exhibit "_." The Alien has received significant recognition for achievements from organizations, critics, government agencies or other recognized experts in the field in which he is engaged.)

Currently, Mr. Doe is one of the most recognized voices, not only in Mexico, but also in Latin America and important cities in North America. Additionally, he works as an announcer in various stations in Mexico such as: TV OLE for all Latin American; KQ 99.9 FM in New York; Salsa 1930 AM in Orlando; Grupo Super Mega Communications in Washington, Boston, and Philadelphia; Tropicalisima FM in Philadelphia; Bravisima FM in Connecticut; Super Mania 92.9 FM in the Dominican Republic; 188.9 FM in Bogotá of CQ Super Estación in Colombia; and Universal 83.7 in Santiago, Chile.

Moreover, Mr. John Doe has demonstrated a record of achievement in radio and television shows as announcer and entertainer with more than 23 years of experience in his home country and abroad. Mr. Doe has been the leading voice that identifies many recognized and distinguished brands, products and institutions such as: Disney On Ice; Mi Mesa Flour; Aceite Vatel of Cargill de Mexico; Ariel of Protec & Gamble; Evempro; Water Brother Production; Ketazolino of Vargas Laboratories; Rayban Glasses; Lois Pants; Plumrose; Ingeve; Milani; Union Radio; Fusion; Lowering Texas; Gillette de Venezuela; Ford Motor de Venezuela; Banco de Mexico; Leaders Entertainment Group (Mexico); Radio Hief (Santo Domingo); Cadena Super (Colombia); Universo 93.7 FM (Chile); and many others in Venezuela and worldwide.

(Please see Exhibit "8.")

In addition, Mr. John Doe has offered his voice-over services for promotions and presentations of various events of national importance presented in Mexico such as The Classics (2001); David Copperfield (2000); Juan Gabriel (2001); Eric Clapton, (2002); Gustavo Ceratti (2002); the Backstreet Boys (2001); and a festival that counted with the participation of such performers as Sting, Sheryl Crow, Maná, Ruben Blades, Roberto Blades, Oasis, Papa Roach, Korn, Christina Aguilera, No Noubt, La Ley and Paulina Rubio, among others.

26XX NW 27 Ave. Miami, FL 3319X
Phone (305) XXX-XXXX Fax (305) XXX-XXXX
Email: tvproductions@tvproductions.com
Webpage: www.tvproductions.com

T.V. PRODUCTIONS, INC.

(Please see Exhibit "8" The alien has performed a lead, starring, or critical role for organizations and establishments that have a distinguished reputation.)

CONCLUSION

To establish the alien's distinction, the rules require that the alien must be recognized as being prominent in his/her field as demonstrated by at least three of the following forms of documentation:

Has or will perform a lead or starring role in production or events that have a distinguished reputation;

Has achieved national or international recognition for achievements as evidenced by critical reviews or other published materials by or about the individuals in major newspapers, trade journals, magazines or other publications;

Has performed a lead, starring or critical role for organizations and establishments that have a distinguished reputation;

Has a record of major commercial or critically acclaimed successes;

Has received significant recognition for achievements from organizations, critics, government agencies or other recognized experts in the field in which the alien is engaged;

Has commanded or now commands a high salary or other substantial remuneration for services in relation to others in the field; or

Other comparable evidence.

As proof that Mr. Doe's extraordinary ability in entertainment is internationally recognized, we enclosed herewith the following exhibits:

Exhibit "1"   Résumé & Overview;

Exhibit "2"   Copy of Letter Asking for Advisory Opinion Letter to The American Federation of Television and Radio Artists;

Exhibit "3"   Certificate of Announcer;

Exhibit "4"   Certificate of Membership in the Professional Syndication;

Exhibit "5"   The Alien has achieved national or international recognition and awards for his achievements;

Exhibit "6"   International recognitions for achievements from organizations, critics, government agencies or other recognized experts in the field in which the alien is engaged;

26XX NW 27 Ave. Miami, FL 3319X
Phone (305) XXX-XXXX Fax (305) XXX-XXXX
Email: tvproductions@tvproductions.com
Webpage: www.tvproductions.com

T.V. PRODUCTIONS, INC.

Exhibit "7"   The alien has performance in a lead, starring or critical role for artist productions;

Exhibit "8"   The alien has a record of major commercial or critically acclaimed successes (occupational achievements reported in trade journals, major newspapers or other publications).

From the exhibits included herein, the following is apparent regarding Mr. Doe's extraordinary ability:

He is the recipient of national and internationally recognized prizes and awards;

He is responsible for artistic contributions of major significance in the field of entertainment and broadcasting;

His work is internationally displayed on radio and television;

He has performed and will perform in leading or critical roles for establishments that have a distinguished reputation;

He will command a high salary for his work;

He is at the top of his field.

TERMS OF EMPLOYMENT

We proposed to employ Mr. John Doe for a temporary period of three years at a salary of $700.00 per week. He will work 40 hours a week. We understand the temporary nature of this agreement and have informed Mr. Doe of this condition.

We respectfully request that the O-1 petition on behalf of Mr. John Doe be granted.

Thank you for giving this matter your attention and kind consideration.

Very truly yours,

TV PRODUCTIONS, INC.

_____

John Smith

Director

26XX NW 27 Ave. Miami, FL 3319X
Phone (305) XXX-XXXX Fax (305) XXX-XXXX
Email: tvproductions@tvproductions.com
Webpage: www.tvproductions.com

Form I-129

OMB No. 1615-0009; Expires 07/31/2010

Department of Homeland Security
U.S. Citizenship and Immigration Services

**I-129, Petition for a
Nonimmigrant Worker**

START HERE - Type or print in black ink.

For USCIS Use Only

Part 1. Information about the employer filing this petition *(If the employer is an individual, complete **Number 1**. Organizations should complete **Number 2**.)*

1. Family Name *(Last Name)*

Given Name *(First Name)*

Full Middle Name

Telephone No. w/Area Code
( )

2. Company or Organization Name
T.V. PRODUCTIONS, INC.

Telephone No. w/Area Code
(305) 123-1234

Mailing Address: *(Street Number and Name)*
2655 LeJeune Road

Suite #
1001

C/O: *(In Care Of)*
c/o Attorney's Name

City
Coral Gables

State/Province
Florida

Country
USA

Zip/Postal Code
33134

E-Mail Address *(If Any)*
main@tvprod.com

Federal Employer Identification #
12-1234567

U.S. Social Security #
N/A

Individual Tax #
None

For USCIS Use Only	
Returned	Receipt
Date	
Date	
Resubmitted	
Date	
Date	
Reloc Sent	
Date	
Date	
Reloc Rec'd	
Date	
Date	

☐ Petitioner
Interviewed
on _____

☐ Beneficiary
Interviewed
on _____

Part 2. Information about this petition *(See instructions for fee information.)*

1. Requested Nonimmigrant Classification. *(Write classification symbol):* O-1

2. Basis for Classification *(Check one):*

   a. ☒ New employment (including new employer filing H-1B extension).

   b. ☐ Continuation of previously approved employment without change with the same employer.

   c. ☐ Change in previously approved employment.

   d. ☐ New concurrent employment.

   e. ☐ Change of employer.

   f. ☐ Amended petition.

3. If you checked **Box 2b, 2c, 2d, 2e,** or **2f,** give the petition receipt number.

N/A

4. Prior Petition. If the beneficiary is in the U.S. as a nonimmigrant and is applying to change and/or extend his or her status, give the prior petition or application receipt #:

N/A

5. Requested Action *(Check one):*

   a. ☐ Notify the office in **Part 4** so the person(s) can obtain a visa or be admitted. (**NOTE:** *a petition is not required for an E-1 or E-2 visa*).

   b. ☒ Change the person(s)' status and extend their stay since the person(s) are all now in the U.S. in another status *(see instructions for limitations)*. This is available only where you check "New Employment" in **Item 2**, above.

   c. ☐ Extend the stay of the person(s) since they now hold this status.

Class: _____
# of Workers: _____
Priority Number: _____
Validity Dates: _____
From: _____
To: _____

☐ **Classification Approved**
   ☐ Consulate/POE/PFI Notified
     At _____
   ☐ Extension Granted
   ☐ COS/Extension Granted

Partial Approval *(explain)*

Action Block

To Be Completed by
Attorney or Representative, if any.

☐ Fill in box if G-28 is attached to represent the applicant.

ATTY State License #

Form I-129

Part 2. Information about this petition *(See instructions for fee information.) (Continued)*

   d. ☐ Amend the stay of the person(s) since they now hold this status.

   e. ☐ Extend the status of a nonimmigrant classification based on a Free Trade Agreement. *(See Free Trade Supplement for TN and H1B1 to Form I-129).*

   f. ☐ Change status to a nonimmigrant classification based on a Free Trade Agreement. *(See Free Trade Supplement for TN and H1B1 to Form I-129).*

6. Total number of workers in petition *(See instructions relating to when more than one worker can be included):*   `1`

Part 3. Information about the person(s) you are filing for *Complete the blocks below. Use the continuation sheet to name each person included in this petition.*

1. If an Entertainment Group, Give the Group Name

Family Name *(Last Name)*	Given Name *(First Name)*	Full Middle Name
DOE	John	

All Other Names Used *(include maiden name and names from all previous marriages)*

None		

Date of Birth *(mm/dd/yyyy)*	U.S. Social Security Number *(if any)*	A number *(if any)*
05/15/1960	N/A	None

Country of Birth	Province of Birth	Country of Citizenship
United Kingdom		United Kingdom

2. If in the United States, Complete the Following:

Date of Last Arrival *(mm/dd/yyyy)*	I-94 Number *(Arrival/Departure Document)*	Current Nonimmigrant Status
12/20/2009	123456789 00	B2

Date Status Expires *(mm/dd/yyyy)*	Passport Number	Date Passport Issued *(mm/dd/yyyy)*	Date Passport Expires *(mm/dd/yyyy)*
05/19/2010	543789	10/11/2006	10/10/2012

Current U.S. Address

8325 SW 72nd Ave, Miami FL 33143

Part 4. Processing Information

1. If the person named in **Part 3** is outside the United States or a requested extension of stay or change of status cannot be granted, give the U.S. consulate or inspection facility you want notified if this petition is approved.

Type of Office *(Check one):* ☒ Consulate   ☐ Pre-flight inspection   ☐ Port of Entry

Office Address *(City)*	U.S. State or Foreign Country
London	United Kingdom

Person's Foreign Address

Alien's foreign address

Form I-129

Part 4. Processing Information *(Continued)*

2. Does each person in this petition have a valid passport?

☐ Not required to have passport   ☐ No - explain on separate paper   ☒ Yes

3. Are you filing any other petitions with this one?   ☒ No   ☐ Yes - How many? [　　　]

4. Are applications for replacement/initial I-94s being filed with this petition?   ☒ No   ☐ Yes - How many? [　　　]

5. Are applications by dependents being filed with this petition?   ☒ No   ☐ Yes - How many? [　　　]

6. Is any person in this petition in removal proceedings?   ☒ No   ☐ Yes - explain on separate paper

7. Have you ever filed an immigrant petition for any person in this petition?   ☒ No   ☐ Yes - explain on separate paper

8. If you indicated you were filing a new petition in **Part 2**, within the past seven years has any person in this petition:

    a. Ever been given the classification you are now requesting?   ☒ No   ☐ Yes - explain on separate paper

    b. Ever been denied the classification you are now requesting?   ☒ No   ☐ Yes - explain on separate paper

9. Have you ever previously filed a petition for this person?   ☒ No   ☐ Yes - explain on separate paper

10. If you are filing for an entertainment group, has any person in this petition not been with the group for at least one year?   ☒ No   ☐ Yes - explain on separate paper

---

Part 5. Basic information about the proposed employment and employer *(Attach the supplement relating to the classification you are requesting.)*

1. Job Title

> Radio and Television Announcer and "Anchor Voice"

2. Nontechnical Job Description

> Announce radio and television programs.

3. LCA Case Number

> [　　　]

4. NAICS Code

> [　　　]

5. Address where the person(s) will work if different from address in **Part 1.** *(Street number and name, city/town, state, zip code)*

> T.V. Productions Inc. 123 S.W. 77th Avenue Miami FL 33135 USA

6. Is this a full-time position?

☐ No - Hours per week: [　　　]   ☒ Yes - Wages per week or per year: $700.00 per week

7. Other Compensation *(Explain)*

> None

8. Dates of intended employment *(mm/dd/yyyy):*

From: Approval   To: 3 years

Form I-129

Part 5.   Basic information about the proposed employment and employer (*Attach the supplement relating to the classification you are requesting.*) *(Continued)*

---

9. Type of Petitioner - *Check one*:

☐ U.S. citizen or permanent resident   ☒ Organization   ☐ Other - explain on separate paper

10. Type of Business

Radio and television production and broadcasting, promotion and representation

11. Year Established

2003

12. Current Number of Employees

8

13. Gross Annual Income

500,000.00

14. Net Annual Income

175,000.00

Part 6.   Signature *Read the information on penalties in the instructions before completing this section.*

I certify, under penalty of perjury under the laws of the United States of America, that this petition and the evidence submitted with it is all true and correct. If filing this on behalf of an organization, I certify that I am empowered to do so by that organization. If this petition is to extend a prior petition, I certify that the proposed employment is under the same terms and conditions as stated in the prior approved petition. I authorize the release of any information from my records, or from the petitioning organization's records that U.S. Citizenship and Immigration Services needs to determine eligibility for the benefit being sought.

Signature

Daytime Phone Number *(Area/Country Code)*

(305) 123-1234

Print Name

John Smith, Director

Date *(mm/dd/yyyy)*

NOTE: If you do not completely fill out this form and the required supplement, or fail to submit required documents listed in the instructions, the person(s) filed for may not be found eligible for the requested benefit and this petition may be denied.

Part 7.   Signature of person preparing form, if other than above

---

I declare that I prepared this petition at the request of the above person and it is based on all information of which I have any knowledge.

Signature

Daytime Phone Number *(Area/Country Code)*

(305) 987-6543

Print Name

Blank Attorney, P.A.

Date *(mm/dd/yyyy)*

.

Firm Name and Address

2655 LeJeune Road Suite 1001, Coral Gables FL 33134

Form I-129 Supplement O/P

Department of Homeland Security
U.S. Citizenship and Immigration Services

O and P Classifications
Supplement to Form I-129

1. **Name of person or organization filing petition:**

   T.V. PRODUCTIONS, INC.

2. **Name of person or group or total number of workers you are filing for:**

   Doe, John

3. **Classification sought** *(Check one)*:

   a. ☐ O-1A Alien of extraordinary ability in sciences, education, business or athletics (not including the arts, motion picture or television industry.)

   b. ☒ O-1B Alien of extraordinary ability in the arts or extraordinary achievement in the motion picture or television industry.

   c. ☐ O-2 Accompanying alien who is coming to the U.S. to assist in the performance of the O-1.

   d. ☐ P-1 Athletic/Entertainment group.

   e. ☐ P-1S Essential Support Personnel for P-1.

   f. ☐ P-2 Artist or entertainer for reciprocal exchange program.

   g. ☐ P-2S Essential Support Personnel for P-2.

   h. ☐ P-3 Artist/Entertainer coming to the United States to perform, teach or coach under a program that is culturally unique.

   i. ☐ P-3S Essential Support Personnel for P-3.

4. **Explain the nature of the event**

   Radio and Television Announcer

5. **Describe the duties to be performed**

   See attached petition letter.

6. **If filing for an O-2 or P support alien, list dates of the alien's prior experience with the O-1 or P alien**

   N/A

7. **Have you obtained the required written consultation(s)?**   ☐ Yes - Attached   ☒ No - Copy of request attached

   If not, give the following information about the organization(s) to which you have sent a duplicate of this petition.

   O-1 Extraordinary Ability

Name of Recognized Peer Group	Daytime Telephone # *(Area/Country Code)*
AFTRA New York	(212) 532-0800
Complete Address	Date Sent *(mm/dd/yyyy)*
260 Madison Avenue, 7th Floor New York, NY 10016	

   O-1 Extraordinary achievement in motion pictures or television

Name of Labor Organization	Daytime Telephone # *(Area/Country Code)*
	( )
Complete Address	Date Sent *(mm/dd/yyyy)*
Name of Management Organization	Daytime Telephone # *(Area/Country Code)*
	( )
Complete Address	Date sent *(mm/dd/yyyy)*

   O-2 or P alien

Name of Labor Organization	Daytime Telephone # *(Area/Country Code)*
	( )
Complete Address	Date Sent *(mm/dd/yyyy)*

Form G-28

OMB No. 1615-0105; Expires 04/30/2012

G-28, Notice of Entry of Appearance as Attorney or Accredited Representative

Department of Homeland Security

Part 1. Notice of Appearance as Attorney or Accredited Representative

A. This appearance is in regard to immigration matters before:

[x] USCIS - List the form number(s): I-129/O

[ ] CBP - List the specific matter in which appearance is entered:

[ ] ICE - List the specific matter in which appearance is entered:

B. I hereby enter my appearance as attorney or accredited representative at the request of:

List Petitioner, Applicant, or Respondent. **NOTE:** Provide the mailing address of Petitioner, Applicant, or Respondent being represented, and **not** the address of the attorney or accredited representative, except when filed under VAWA.

Principal Petitioner, Applicant, or Respondent			A Number or Receipt Number, if any	[x] Petitioner
Name: Last First Middle				[ ] Applicant
T.V. PRODUCTIONS, INC.			None	[ ] Respondent

Address: Street Number and Street Name	Apt. No.	City	State	Zip Code
Petitioner's Address				

Pursuant to the Privacy Act of 1974 and DHS policy, I hereby consent to the disclosure to the named Attorney or Accredited Representative of any record pertaining to me that appears in any system of records of USCIS, USCBP, or USICE.

Signature of Petitioner, Applicant, or Respondent

Date
11/08/2009

Part 2. Information about Attorney or Accredited Representative *(Check applicable items(s) below)*

A. [x] I am an attorney and a member in good standing of the bar of the highest court(s) of the following State(s), possession(s), territory(ies), commonwealth(s), or the District of Columbia: State of _____   Supreme Court

I am not [x] or [ ] am subject to any order of any court or administrative agency disbarring, suspending, enjoining, restraining, or otherwise restricting me in the practice of law (If you are subject to any order(s), explain fully on reverse side).

B. [ ] I am an accredited representative of the following qualified non-profit religious, charitable, social service, or similar organization established in the United States, so recognized by the Department of Justice, Board of Immigration Appeals pursuant to 8 CFR 1292.2. Provide name of organization and expiration date of accreditation:

C. [ ] I am associated with _____ .

The attorney or accredited representative of record previously filed Form G-28 in this case, and my appearance as an attorney or accredited representative is at his or her request *(If you check this item, also complete item A or B above in Part 2, whichever is appropriate).*

Part 3. Name and Signature of Attorney or Accredited Representative

I have read and understand the regulations and conditions contained in 8 CFR 103.2 and 292 governing appearances and representation before the Department of Homeland Security. I declare under penalty of perjury under the laws of the United States that the information I have provided on this form is true and correct.

Name of Attorney or Accredited Representative	Attorney Bar Number(s), if any
Attorney or Accredited Representative's Name	
Signature of Attorney or Accredited Representative	Date 11/08/2009

Complete Address of Attorney or Organization of Accredited Representative (Street Number and Street Name, Suite No., City, State, Zip Code)
Attorney or Accredited Representative's Address

Phone Number *(Include area code)*	Fax Number, if any *(Include area code)*	E-Mail Address, if any
(305) 442-1322	(305) 444-7578	Valid E-mail Address

Form G-28 (Rev. 04/22/09)N

ARTWORKS, INC.
XXXX ALHAMBRA CIRCLE
MIAMI, FLORIDA 34134

October 23, 2007

U.S. Citizenship and Immigration Services
Texas Service Center
P.O. Box 852211
Mesquite, TX 75185-2211

Re: **I-129/P-3 Petition of ARTWORKS, INC.**
       On Behalf of John Doe.

Dear Sir or Madam:

I write in support of the P-3 petition of ARTWORKS, INC., on behalf of Mr. John Doe, a Mexican national. Mr. John Doe is a renowned master painter, with emphasis in fine artistry, with extraordinary ability and a demonstrated record of achievement. Based on his expertise and credentials, we are inviting him to work on several projects in the United States. Accordingly, we request an approval of our P-3 petition on his behalf.

THE PETITIONER

ARTWORKS, INC., is involved in the fulfillment of commissions of corporations for fine artworks, commemorative art objects, trophies and other related art projects.

ARTWORKS, INC., is also involved in the sale of fine art on consignment through commercial art galleries in Miami, Fla., and throughout the U.S. and South America.

CONSULTATION

Under INS Rule Section 214c(6)(1), Petitioner may submit an advisory opinion from a peer group if no labor organization exists. Please see attached advisory opinion by Professor Richard Lytle, director of Graduate Studies, Painting at Yale School of Art.

THE POSITION OFFERED

Mr. John Doe is being offered temporary employment in the position of Creative Producer and Master Artist for our corporation. The position involves design and creation. Additional responsibilities include marketing and promotion of services and products through custom designed, high quality artwork and other promotional materials, as well as communication with clients regarding design, form, style and other aspects of fine art creations. As a master artist and experienced marketer and promoter of fine art, Mr. John Doe will establish and recommend to management, objectives and policies regarding the commission of artworks by the company for corporations.

Mr. John Doe is a master artist and has the required experience. Mr. Doe a gallery owner, administrator and art dealer, which will enable our company to expand our operations by the delivery of fine art objects to multi-national clientele.

THE BENEFICIARY

Mr. John Doe has extensive professional work experience since 1988.

From 1988–2000, he has been exhibiting his artwork in Mexico at numerous collective exhibitions. From 1992–1999, he has been awarded distinctions for his artwork such as scholarships, awards and merits of honor. And from 1996–1999 he has been involved in activities related to his field of work experience.

At the gallery, in addition to major exhibitions, he provided courses in painting, linoleum block, printing, mix print and engraving, woodcut print, lithography, metal etching and screen print. Mr. Doe uses a technique of design repetition within his work to create "ensembles" rather than multiples of the same process. Each etching is unique and original using techniques of etching dating back to the Middle Ages.

Mr. Doe has been reviewed in several publications for his sculptures. See enclosed exhibits.

To attest to his culturally unique style of artistic expression and methodology we also enclose the following:

Exhibit "1":   Résumé

Exhibit "2":   Artwork completed

Exhibit "3":   Publications by Mr. John Doe

Exhibit "4":   Prizes and Recognitions

Exhibit "5":   Exhibitions

Exhibit "6":   Newspaper articles

Exhibit "7":   Letters from educational and art institutions

Exhibit "8":   Advisory Opinion by Professor Richard Lytle, director of Graduate Studies, Painting at Yale School of Art.

CULTURALLY UNIQUE

"Culturally unique" means a style of artistic expression, methodology or medium, which is unique to a particular county, nation, class, society, religion or other group of persons. 8 CFR Section 214.2(P)(3).

The expert that has evaluated his work, Professor Richard Lytle, director of Graduate Studies, Painting at Yale School of Art, had this to say: *"The use of Baroque theatrics to depict observations of current cultural phenomena, especially in a highly rendered style not usually associated with Mexican art, seems original and strong in a challenging and unexpected way that is provocative. The artist looks to be most skillful, thoughtful and knowledgeable, and yes, original enough, to say that his potential contribution is individually unique ..."* Please see expert opinion (Exhibit "8").

Mr. John Doe is one of the young Mexican painters with more projection and future along with talent and creativity, including his unique personality portrayed in his artwork. The power and expression of the colorful texture and composition in his portraits makes him an artist that is out of this world. Mr. Doe also uses free brush in acrylic and oil, which he incorporates in his artwork. His style is highly influenced by the classical school, especially the "Flamenco" by Pablo Rubens and the "Romantics" of the XIX century, even though he does put his seal of contemporary characteristics and incorporates various elements from this century.

The paintings of John Doe are the revisions of a society in decomposed stage; word games, revisions, repeated images of a city according to its habitants lost in dignity and hope, allowing itself to be led by degeneration as a result of misery, material and morality of the people.

Mr. John Doe is well known for the style dubbed "gore naturalism," where he depicts blood and monsters in his artwork with paintings that deal with reality, in an obscure, terrorizing manner similar to North American horror films. After three years of pictorial experimentation, and from his stay in communities for artists in Massachusetts and New York, he changed his work and inclines towards perspective.

TERMS OF EMPLOYMENT

We currently intend to employ Mr. John Doe for a one-year engagement period. We understand the temporary scope of Mr. John Doe employment with us. No written contract has been entered into with Mr. John Doe. He will receive a weekly salary of $600.00 as compensation with bonuses based on production.

Very truly yours,

ARTWORKS, INC.

_____

John Smith
Director
/rdmp 129-5551

Form I-129 P-3

OMB No. 1615-0009; Expires 07/31/2010

Department of Homeland Security
U.S. Citizenship and Immigration Services

**I-129, Petition for a
Nonimmigrant Worker**

START HERE - Type or print in black ink.

	For USCIS Use Only

Part 1. Information about the employer filing this petition (*If the employer is an individual, complete Number 1. Organizations should complete Number 2.*)

1. Family Name *(Last Name)*   Given Name *(First Name)*

Full Middle Name   Telephone No. w/Area Code
(   )

2. Company or Organization Name   Telephone No. w/Area Code
ARTWORKS, INC.   (305) 123-1234

Mailing Address: *(Street Number and Name)*   Suite #
2655 LeJeune Road   1001

C/O: *(In Care Of)*
c/o Attorney's Name

City   State/Province
Coral Gables   Florida

Country   Zip/Postal Code   E-Mail Address *(If Any)*
USA   33134

Federal Employer Identification #   U.S. Social Security #   Individual Tax #
12-1234567   N/A   None

For USCIS Use Only

Returned	Receipt
Date	
Date	
Resubmitted	
Date	
Date	
Reloc Sent	
Date	
Date	
Reloc Rec'd	
Date	
Date	

☐ Petitioner Interviewed on _____

☐ Beneficiary Interviewed on _____

Part 2. Information about this petition *(See instructions for fee information.)*

1. **Requested Nonimmigrant Classification.** *(Write classification symbol):* P-3

2. **Basis for Classification** *(Check one):*
   a. ☒ New employment (including new employer filing H-1B extension).
   b. ☐ Continuation of previously approved employment without change with the same employer.
   c. ☐ Change in previously approved employment.
   d. ☐ New concurrent employment.
   e. ☐ Change of employer.
   f. ☐ Amended petition.

3. If you checked **Box 2b, 2c, 2d, 2e,** or **2f,** give the petition receipt number.
   N/A

4. **Prior Petition.** If the beneficiary is in the U.S. as a nonimmigrant and is applying to change and/or extend his or her status, give the prior petition or application receipt #:
   N/A

5. **Requested Action** *(Check one):*
   a. ☒ Notify the office in **Part 4** so the person(s) can obtain a visa or be admitted. (**NOTE:** *a petition is not required for an E-1 or E-2 visa*).
   b. ☐ Change the person(s)' status and extend their stay since the person(s) are all now in the U.S. in another status *(see instructions for limitations).* This is available only where you check "New Employment" in **Item 2,** above.
   c. ☐ Extend the stay of the person(s) since they now hold this status.

| Class: _____ |
| # of Workers: _____ |
| Priority Number: _____ |
| Validity Dates: _____ |
| From: _____ |
| To: _____ |

☐ **Classification Approved**
  ☐ Consulate/POE/PFI Notified
    At _____
  ☐ Extension Granted
  ☐ COS/Extension Granted

Partial Approval *(explain)*

Action Block

To Be Completed by
Attorney or Representative, if any.

☐ Fill in box if G-28 is attached to represent the applicant.

ATTY State License # _____

Form I-129 P-3

Part 2. Information about this petition *(See instructions for fee information.) (Continued)*

    d. ☐ Amend the stay of the person(s) since they now hold this status.

    e. ☐ Extend the status of a nonimmigrant classification based on a Free Trade Agreement. *(See Free Trade Supplement for TN and H1B1 to Form I-129).*

    f. ☐ Change status to a nonimmigrant classification based on a Free Trade Agreement. *(See Free Trade Supplement for TN and H1B1 to Form I-129).*

6. Total number of workers in petition *(See instructions relating to when more than one worker can be included):* | 1

Part 3. Information about the person(s) you are filing for *Complete the blocks below. Use the continuation sheet to name each person included in this petition.*

1. If an Entertainment Group, Give the Group Name

> N/A

Family Name *(Last Name)*	Given Name *(First Name)*	Full Middle Name
DOE	John	

All Other Names Used *(include maiden name and names from all previous marriages)*

None		

Date of Birth *(mm/dd/yyyy)*	U.S. Social Security Number *(if any)*	A number *(if any)*
05/15/1960	N/A	None

Country of Birth	Province of Birth	Country of Citizenship
United Kingdom		United Kingdom

2. If in the United States, Complete the Following:

Date of Last Arrival *(mm/dd/yyyy)*	I-94 Number *(Arrival/Departure Document)*	Current Nonimmigrant Status

Date Status Expires *(mm/dd/yyyy)*	Passport Number	Date Passport Issued *(mm/dd/yyyy)*	Date Passport Expires *(mm/dd/yyyy)*

Current U.S. Address

Part 4. Processing Information

1. If the person named in **Part 3** is outside the United States or a requested extension of stay or change of status cannot be granted, give the U.S. consulate or inspection facility you want notified if this petition is approved.

Type of Office *(Check one)*: ☒ Consulate   ☐ Pre-flight inspection   ☐ Port of Entry

Office Address *(City)*	U.S. State or Foreign Country
London	United Kingdom

Person's Foreign Address

Alien's foreign address

Form I-129 P-3

Part 4. Processing Information *(Continued)*

2. Does each person in this petition have a valid passport?

   ☐ Not required to have passport   ☐ No - explain on separate paper   ☒ Yes

3. Are you filing any other petitions with this one?   ☒ No   ☐ Yes - How many? [   ]

4. Are applications for replacement/initial I-94s being filed with this petition?   ☒ No   ☐ Yes - How many? [   ]

5. Are applications by dependents being filed with this petition?   ☒ No   ☐ Yes - How many? [   ]

6. Is any person in this petition in removal proceedings?   ☒ No   ☐ Yes - explain on separate paper

7. Have you ever filed an immigrant petition for any person in this petition?   ☒ No   ☐ Yes - explain on separate paper

8. If you indicated you were filing a new petition in **Part 2**, within the past seven years has any person in this petition:

   a. Ever been given the classification you are now requesting?   ☒ No   ☐ Yes - explain on separate paper

   b. Ever been denied the classification you are now requesting?   ☒ No   ☐ Yes - explain on separate paper

9. Have you ever previously filed a petition for this person?   ☒ No   ☐ Yes - explain on separate paper

10. If you are filing for an entertainment group, has any person in this petition not been with the group for at least one year?   ☒ No   ☐ Yes - explain on separate paper

---

Part 5. Basic information about the proposed employment and employer *(Attach the supplement relating to the classification you are requesting.)*

1. Job Title

   Music Producer

2. Nontechnical Job Description

   Please see attached petition letter

3. LCA Case Number

   N/A

4. NAICS Code

   123456

5. Address where the person(s) will work if different from address in **Part 1**. *(Street number and name, city/town, state, zip code)*

   123 S.W. 77th Avenue, Miami FL 33135 USA

6. Is this a full-time position?

   ☐ No - Hours per week: [   ]   ☒ Yes - Wages per week or per year: $750.00 per week

7. Other Compensation *(Explain)*

   None

8. Dates of intended employment *(mm/dd/yyyy)*:

   From: 05/15/2010   To: 05/14/2011

Form I-129 P-3

Part 5. Basic information about the proposed employment and employer *(Attach the supplement relating to the classification you are requesting.) (Continued)*

---

9. Type of Petitioner - *Check one*:

☐ U.S. citizen or permanent resident   ☒ Organization   ☐ Other - explain on separate paper

10. Type of Business

Music and video production

11. Year Established

2003

12. Current Number of Employees

3

13. Gross Annual Income

0.00

14. Net Annual Income

0.00

Part 6. Signature *Read the information on penalties in the instructions before completing this section.*

I certify, under penalty of perjury under the laws of the United States of America, that this petition and the evidence submitted with it is all true and correct. If filing this on behalf of an organization, I certify that I am empowered to do so by that organization. If this petition is to extend a prior petition, I certify that the proposed employment is under the same terms and conditions as stated in the prior approved petition. I authorize the release of any information from my records, or from the petitioning organization's records that U.S. Citizenship and Immigration Services needs to determine eligibility for the benefit being sought.

Signature

Daytime Phone Number *(Area/Country Code)*

(305) 123-1234

Print Name

Gerardo Jimenez, Director

Date *(mm/dd/yyyy)*

NOTE: If you do not completely fill out this form and the required supplement, or fail to submit required documents listed in the instructions, the person(s) filed for may not be found eligible for the requested benefit and this petition may be denied.

Part 7. Signature of person preparing form, if other than above

---

I declare that I prepared this petition at the request of the above person and it is based on all information of which I have any knowledge.

Signature

Daytime Phone Number *(Area/Country Code)*

(305) 987-6543

Print Name

Blank Attorney, P.A.

Date *(mm/dd/yyyy)*

Firm Name and Address

Blank Attorney, P.A.
2655 LeJeune Road Suite 1001, Coral Gables FL 33134

Form I-129 (Rev. 06/12/09)Y Page 4

Form I-129 Supplement O/P

OMB No.1615-0009; Expires 07/31/2010

Department of Homeland Security
U.S. Citizenship and Immigration Services

O and P Classifications
Supplement to Form I-129

1. Name of person or organization filing petition:

ARTWORKS, INC.

2. Name of person or group or total number of workers you are filing for:

DOE, John

3. Classification sought *(Check one):*

a. ☐ O-1A Alien of extraordinary ability in sciences, education, business or athletics (not including the arts, motion picture or television industry.)

b. ☐ O-1B Alien of extraordinary ability in the arts or extraordinary achievement in the motion picture or television industry.

c. ☐ O-2 Accompanying alien who is coming to the U.S. to assist in the performance of the O-1.

d. ☐ P-1 Athletic/Entertainment group.

e. ☐ P-1S Essential Support Personnel for P-1.

f. ☐ P-2 Artist or entertainer for reciprocal exchange program.

g. ☐ P-2S Essential Support Personnel for P-2.

h. ☒ P-3 Artist/Entertainer coming to the United States to perform, teach or coach under a program that is culturally unique.

i. ☐ P-3S Essential Support Personnel for P-3.

4. Explain the nature of the event

Music Production

5. Describe the duties to be performed

The position involves writing musical compositions and creating musical ideas using unique Afro-Venezuelan rhythms and percussion. See petition letter.

6. If filing for an O-2 or P support alien, list dates of the alien's prior experience with the O-1 or P alien

N/A

7. Have you obtained the required written consultation(s)?   ☐ Yes - Attached   ☒ No - Copy of request attached

If not, give the following information about the organization(s) to which you have sent a duplicate of this petition.

O-1 Extraordinary Ability

Name of Recognized Peer Group	Daytime Telephone # *(Area/Country Code)*
	( )
Complete Address	Date Sent *(mm/dd/yyyy)*

O-1 Extraordinary achievement in motion pictures or television

Name of Labor Organization	Daytime Telephone # *(Area/Country Code)*
	( )
Complete Address	Date Sent *(mm/dd/yyyy)*
Name of Management Organization	Daytime Telephone # *(Area/Country Code)*
	( )
Complete Address	Date sent *(mm/dd/yyyy)*

O-2 or P alien

Name of Labor Organization	Daytime Telephone # *(Area/Country Code)*
American Federation of Musicians of the US and Canada	(345) 128-4598
Complete Address	Date Sent *(mm/dd/yyyy)*
1501 Broadway, Suite 600 New YOrk, NY 10036	02/08/2007

Form G-28

OMB No. 1615-0105; Expires 04/30/2012

**G-28, Notice of Entry of Appearance
as Attorney or Accredited Representative**

Department of Homeland Security

Part 1. Notice of Appearance as Attorney or Accredited Representative

A. This appearance is in regard to immigration matters before:

[X] USCIS - List the form number(s): I-129/P   ☐ CBP - List the specific matter in which appearance is entered:

☐ ICE - List the specific matter in which appearance is entered: _____

B. I hereby enter my appearance as attorney or accredited representative at the request of:

List Petitioner, Applicant, or Respondent. **NOTE:** Provide the mailing address of Petitioner, Applicant, or Respondent being represented, and **not** the address of the attorney or accredited representative, except when filed under VAWA.

Principal Petitioner, Applicant, or Respondent			A Number or Receipt Number, if any	
Name: Last	First	Middle		[X] Petitioner
ARTWORKS, INC.			None	☐ Applicant
				☐ Respondent

Address: Street Number and Street Name	Apt. No.	City	State	Zip Code
Petitioner's Address				

Pursuant to the Privacy Act of 1974 and DHS policy, I hereby consent to the disclosure to the named Attorney or Accredited Representative of any record pertaining to me that appears in any system of records of USCIS, USCBP, or USICE.

Signature of Petitioner, Applicant, or Respondent

Date
11/08/2009

Part 2. Information about Attorney or Accredited Representative *(Check applicable items(s) below)*

A. [X] I am an attorney and a member in good standing of the bar of the highest court(s) of the following State(s), possession(s), territory(ies), commonwealth(s), or the District of Columbia: State of _____   Supreme Court

I am not [X] or ☐ **am subject to any order of any court or administrative agency disbarring, suspending, enjoining, restraining, or otherwise restricting me in the practice of law (If you are subject to any order(s), explain fully on reverse side).**

B. ☐ I am an accredited representative of the following qualified non-profit religious, charitable, social service, or similar organization established in the United States, so recognized by the Department of Justice, Board of Immigration Appeals pursuant to 8 CFR 1292.2. Provide name of organization and expiration date of accreditation: _____

C. ☐ I am associated with _____ .
The attorney or accredited representative of record previously filed Form G-28 in this case, and my appearance as an attorney or accredited representative is at his or her request *(If you check this item, also complete item A or B above in **Part 2**, whichever is appropriate).*

Part 3. Name and Signature of Attorney or Accredited Representative

I have read and understand the regulations and conditions contained in 8 CFR 103.2 and 292 governing appearances and representation before the Department of Homeland Security. I declare under penalty of perjury under the laws of the United States that the information I have provided on this form is true and correct.

Name of Attorney or Accredited Representative	Attorney Bar Number(s), if any
Attorney or Accredited Representative's Name	
Signature of Attorney or Accredited Representative	Date 11/08/2009

Complete Address of Attorney or Organization of Accredited Representative (Street Number and Street Name, Suite No., City, State, Zip Code)
Attorney or Accredited Representative's Address

Phone Number *(Include area code)*	Fax Number, if any *(Include area code)*	E-Mail Address, if any
(305) 442-1322	(305) 444-7578	Valid E-mail Address

Form G-28 (Rev. 04/22/09)N

CHAPTER 6

Temporary and Permanent Visas for Victims—T and U Visas

I. Introduction

Individuals in the United States who are victimized may be eligible for visas that afford them legal status in the United States along with work permission. The status may also lead to legal permanent residence. The laws allowing these visas were enacted not only for the protection of the victims, but also for the providing of assistance to law enforcement agencies in the prosecution of the abusers or those engaged in criminal activity. There are two types of visas available. There is the T visa for victims of trafficking and the U visa for victims of criminal activity. INA § 101(a)(15)T and INA 101 (a)(15)(u) 8 C.F. R. § 214.11.

II. T Visa

The T nonimmigrant status is available to admissible aliens who are "victims of severe forms of trafficking in persons who have complied with any reasonable request for assistance in the investigation or prosecution of acts of trafficking in persons and who can demonstrate that they would suffer extreme hardship involving unusual and severe harm if they were removed from the United States." (8 C.F.R. § 103) If a law enforcement endorsement is not available (which is primary evidence of the assistance), the Service will accept secondary evidence. Those that are under 15 years old do not have to show that they complied with any reasonable request to assist law enforcement agencies.

A. Nonimmigrant Visa

The cap for these types of cases is 5,000 per year. (The T status is separate and distinct from the provision of "continued presence" pursuant to 28 CFR 1100.35 which allows for the Service, in cooperation and/or at the request of law enforcement agencies to arrange for the presence of the victim in the United States as needed for law enforcement purposes.) The T status is for 3 years. The victim must show that he/she is a victim of trafficking in persons, that he/she is physically present in the United States or its underlying possessions or port of entry on account of the trafficking, that he/she has complied with the reasonable request for assistance if over 15 years of age, and that he/she would suffer extreme hardship involving unusual and severe harm if removed from the United States. The victim must also show that they are admissible or obtain a waiver for inadmissibility from USCIS. In order to be a victim, the alien must show that he/she was recruited, harbored, transported for labor services or commercial sex act. But, there must be some form of force, coercion or fraud in cases of commercial sex acts, unless the alien is under 18 years of age.

1. Forms Required:

   The Form I-914 includes two supplements, Supplement A, Application for Immediate Family Members and Supplement B, Declaration of Law Enforcement Officer for Victim of Trafficking in Persons

2. Documents Required:

   a. Three current photographs

   b. Statement of the victim (indicating that he or she is a victim of a severe form of trafficking in persons; credible evidence of victimization and cooperation, describing what the alien has done to report the crime to a law enforcement agency; and a statement indicating whether similar records for the time and place of the crime are available)

   c. Proof of victimization (proof of being harbored, transported, recruited, for labor or services or a commercial sex act)

   d. Evidence if there is no declaration of law enforcement officer—trial transcripts, court documents, police reports, news articles and copies of reimbursement forms for travel to and from court and affidavits from witnesses.

   e. Evidence that the applicant would suffer extreme hardships involving unusual and severe harm if removed from the United States—affidavits of possible harm, country reports, police reports, etc.

B. Immigrant Visa

The victim must file an application for residency within the 90 day window before their status expires. In order to be eligible, the victim must show that he/she is admissible, has been physically present in the U. S. for a continuous period of at least 3 years since the date of admission with T-1 nonimmigrant status, has been a person of good moral character, establish that during the period has complied with the reasonable request for assistance or that they would suffer extreme hardship involving unusual and severe harm upon removal from the U. S. Qualifying family members include: spouse and children if the victim is over 21 years old, or spouse, children, parent, and siblings under 18 if the victim is under 21 years old.

1. Forms Required:

   The Forms I-485 and G-28, together with Form G325A and proof of T status (Form I-797), and I-765. In addition, if a waiver of admissibility is required, Form I-192—Application for Advance Permission to Enter as a Nonimmigrant, must be submitted.

2. Documents Required:

   a. Taxes and other proof of good moral character

   b. Proof of assistance with law enforcement agency—trial transcripts, court documents, police reports, news articles and copies of reimbursement forms for travel to and from court and affidavits from witnesses or

   c. Evidence that the applicant would suffer extreme hardship involving unusual and severe harm if removed from the United States—affidavits of possible harm, country reports, police reports, etc.

III. U Visa

The U nonimmigrant status is available to alien victims of criminal activity who have suffered substantial mental and/or physical abuse because of the activity and who also are willing to assist law enforcement agencies or government officials in the investigation of such activity. Qualifying criminal activity includes one or more of the following:

Abduction, abusive sexual conduct, blackmail, domestic violence, extortion, false imprisonment, felonious assault, female genital mutilation, hostage, incest, involuntary servitude, kidnapping, manslaughter, murder, obstruction of justice, peonage, perjury, prostitution, rape, sexual assault, sexual exploitation, slave trade, torture, trafficking, unlawful criminal restraint, witness tampering and other related crimes. INA § 101(a)(15)U, 8 C.F.R § 214.11.

The abuser does not need to be a U.S. Citizen or Lawful Permanent Resident and the alien does not need to be married to the abuser. Furthermore, the alien is not required to be physically present in the U.S. and can apply while abroad as long as criminal activity violated U.S. law or occurred in U.S. territories.

The alien must provide at time of filing a certification from a federal, state or local law enforcement official that (a) the alien has been a victim of the qualifying criminal activity; the alien possesses information about the qualifying criminal activity; and the alien has been, is being or is likely to be helpful to the investigation and/or prosecution of that qualifying criminal activity. This certification must be completed by the certifying agency within six months immediately preceding the alien's submission of Petition for U Nonimmigrant Status (Form I-918) on the U Nonimmigrant Status Certification (Form I-918, Supplement B).

A. Non-Immigrant Visa

The cap for these types of visa is 10,000 per year and the limit only applies to principal aliens and does not include derivatives such as: spouse, children or parents (if alien under twenty one years of age) of the applicant. The alien is eligible for work authorization and USCIS officers are instructed to protect the alien from removal through parole, deferred action, stays of removal and continuances. Persons granted U-1 status can remain in the U.S. for up to four years with extensions under certain circumstances. After three years of U status, alien and immediate family members may apply adjustment of status or lawful permanent residence.

1. Forms Required:

   The Form I-918, Petition for U Nonimmigrant Status, I-918, Supplement A and Supplement B, U Nonimmigrant Status Certification, and Form I-929, Petition for Qualifying Family Members and Form G-28 (for each petition).

2. Documents Required:

   a. evidence to support criminal activity mentioned in Supplement B such as trial transcript, court documents, police report, news article, affidavits and order of protection;

   b. evidence of physical or mental abuse such as reports from medical personnel, school officials, clergy, and social workers;

   c. photos of visible injuries;

   d. affidavits from witnesses, such as family members and friends who have personal knowledge of the facts of the criminal activity;

   e. personal statement (narrative) of petitioner's victimization;

   f. waiver or grounds of inadmissibility, Form I-192, Application for Advance Permission to Enter as a Nonimmigrant.

   g. proof of family relationship; and

   h. filing fees: See USCIS.gov for current fees, if any.

B. Immigrant Visa

The U visa holder is eligible to adjust status to lawful permanent resident unless the Secretary of the Department of Homeland Security has proof that the U visa holder refused to assist in the criminal investigation or prosecution. Once the U visa is approved, the qualifying family members may apply for adjustment of status or consular processing. Qualifying family members include: child, parent and spouse.

1. Forms Required:

The Forms I-485 and G-28, together with Form G325A and proof of U status (Form I-797), and I-765. In addition, if a waiver of admissibility is required, Form I-192—Application for Advance Permission to Enter as a Nonimmigrant, must be submitted.

2. Documents Required:

   a. Birth Certificates for all applicants

   b. Marriage Certificate (certified copy)

   c. Divorce Decree, if any (certified copy)

Appendix

1. Form I-914, Supplement A & B

2. Sample Memorandum of T Request

3. Form 918, Supplement A & B

4. Form I-929

5. Form I-192

6. Form I-485

7. Form G-325

8. Form I-765

Form I-914

Department of Homeland Security
U.S. Citizenship and Immigration Services

OMB No. 1615-0099; Expires 03/31/11

I-914, Application for T Nonimmigrant Status

	For USCIS Use Only

START HERE – Type or print. *Use black ink. See Instructions for information about eligibility and how to complete and file this application.*

For USCIS Use Only	
Returned	Receipt
Date	
Date	
Resubmitted	
Date	
Date	
Reloc Sent	
Date	
Date	
Reloc Rec'd	
Date	
Date	

PART A. Purpose for Filing the Application

Check all that apply:

- [✓] I am filing an application for T-1 nonimmigrant status, and have not previously filed for such status.
- [ ] I have a T-1 application pending. EAC #: _____
- [ ] I have received T-1 status.
- [ ] I am applying to bring family member(s) to the United States.

PART B. General Information About You *(Person filing this form as a victim)*

Family Name *(Last Name)*
Doe

Given Name *(First Name)*
Jane

Middle Name *(if any)*

Other Names Used *(Include maiden name/nickname)*
None

Home Address - Street Number and Name
123 Main Drive

Apt. #

City
Weston

State/Province
Florida

Zip/Postal Code
33484

Safe Mailing Address (if other than above) - Street Number and Name

Apt. #

C/O *(in care of):*

City

State/Province

Zip/Postal Code

Home Telephone # *(with area code)*

Safe Daytime Phone # *(with area code)*
(954) 777-8855

E-Mail Address *(optional)*

A # (if any)
None

U.S. Social Security # (if any)
N/A

Gender
[✓] Male   [ ] Female

Marital Status:
[✓] Married   [ ] Single/Never Married   [ ] Divorced   [ ] Widowed

Date of Birth *(mm/dd/yyyy)*
05/20/1986

Country of Birth
United Kingdom

Country of Citizenship
United Kingdom

Passport #
123456

Place of Issuance
London

Date of Issue *(mm/dd/yyyy)*
10/11/2008

Place of Last Entry
Miami, FL

Date of Last Entry *(mm/dd/yyyy)*
07/20/2002

I-94 # *(Arrival/Departure Document)*
123456789 00

Current Immigration Status
B-2

Validity Dates
From: _____
To: _____

Remarks

Conditional Approval
Stamp #   Date

Action Block

To Be Completed by
Attorney or Representative, if any
[ ] Fill in box if G-28 is attached to represent the applicant.

ATTY State License #

Form I-914 (Rev. 03/30/09) N

Form I-914

PART C.   Additional Information

Answers to the following questions about your claim require explanation and supporting documentation. You should attach documents in support of your claim that you are a victim of a severe form of trafficking in persons and the specific facts on which you are relying to support your claim. It is strongly encouraged that you attach a personal narrative statement describing the trafficking. If you are only applying for T derivative status for a family member subsequent to your (the principal applicant) initial filing, evidence supporting the original application is not required to be resubmitted with the new Form I-914.

Attach additional sheets of paper as needed. Write your name and Alien Registration Number (A-Number), if any, at the top of each sheet and indicate the number of the item that you are answering. Include the Part and letter or number relating to the additional information you provided (example: Part C, 3).

1. I **am** or have been a victim of a severe form of trafficking in persons. *(Attach evidence to support your claim.)*   ☑ Yes   ☐ No

2. I **am** submitting a law enforcement agency (LEA) declaration on Form I-914, Supplement B, Declaration of Law Enforcement Officer for Victim of Trafficking in Persons. *(If "No," explain why you are not submitting the LEA Certification.)*   ☑ Yes   ☐ No

3. I **am** physically present in the United States, American Samoa, or the Commonwealth of the Northern Mariana Islands, or at a port of entry, **on account of trafficking.** *(If "Yes," explain in detail and attach evidence and documents supporting this claim.)*   ☑ Yes   ☐ No

4. I fear that I will suffer extreme hardship involving unusual and severe harm upon removal. *(If "Yes," explain in detail and attach evidence and documents supporting this claim.)*   ☑ Yes   ☐ No

5. I have reported the crime of which I am claiming to be a victim. *(If "Yes," indicate to which law enforcement agency and office you have made the report, the address and phone number of that office, and the case number assigned, if any. If "No," explain the circumstances.)*   ☑ Yes   ☐ No

Law Enforcement Agency and Office	Address	Phone Number	Case Number
Name of the Agency			02020202
Circumstances:			
[DESCRIBE IN DETAIL]			

6. I am under *the age of 18 years. (If "Yes," proceed to Question 8.)*   ☐ Yes   ☑ No

7. I have complied with requests from Federal, State, or local law enforcement authorities for assistance in the investigation or prosecution of acts of trafficking. *(If "No," explain the circumstances.)*   ☑ Yes   ☐ No

8. This is the first time I have entered the United States. *(If "No," list each date, place of entry, and under which status you entered the United States for the past five years, and explain the circumstances of your most recent arrival.)*   ☑ Yes   ☐ No

Date of Entry	Place of Entry	Status

Form I-914

9. My most recent entry was on account of the trafficking that forms the basis for my claim. *(Explain the circumstances of your most recent arrival.)*   ☑ Yes ☐ No

10. I want an Employment Authorization Document.   ☑ Yes ☐ No

11. **I am** now applying for one or more eligible family members. *(If "Yes," complete and include a Form I-914, Supplement A, Application for Immediate Family Member of T-1 Recipient, for each family member for whom you are now applying. You may also apply to bring eligible family members to the United States at a later date.)*   ☑ Yes ☐ No

PART D.   Processing Information

Answer the following questions about yourself. For purposes of this application, if applicable, you must answer "Yes" to the following questions, even if your records were sealed or otherwise cleared or if anyone, including a judge, law enforcement officer, or attorney, told you that you no longer have a record. *(If your answer is "Yes" to any one of these questions, explain on a separate sheet of paper. Additionally, explain if any of the acts or circumstances below are related to you having been a victim of a severe form of trafficking. Answering "Yes" does not necessarily mean that you will be denied T nonimmigrant status or are not entitled to adjust your status or register for permanent residence.)*

1. Have you **EVER**:

   a. Committed a crime or offense for which you have not been arrested?   ☐ Yes ☑ No

   b. Been arrested, cited, or detained by any law enforcement officer (including DHS, former INS, and military officers) for any reason?   ☐ Yes ☑ No

   c. Been charged with committing any crime or offense?   ☐ Yes ☑ No

   d. Been convicted of a crime or offense (even if violation was subsequently expunged or pardoned)?   ☐ Yes ☑ No

   e. Been placed in an alternative sentencing or a rehabilitative program (for example: diversion, deferred prosecution, withheld adjudication, deferred adjudication)?   ☐ Yes ☑ No

   f. Received a suspended sentence, been placed on probation, or been paroled?   ☐ Yes ☑ No

   g. Been in jail or prison?   ☐ Yes ☑ No

   h. Been the beneficiary of a pardon, amnesty, rehabilitation, or other act of clemency or similar action?   ☐ Yes ☑ No

   i. Exercised diplomatic immunity to avoid prosecution for a criminal offense in the United States?   ☐ Yes ☑ No

If you answered "Yes" to any of the above questions, complete the following table. If you need more space, use a separate sheet of paper to give the same information.

Why were you arrested, cited, detained, or charged?	Date of arrest, citation, detention, charge *(mm/dd/yyyy)*	Where were you arrested, cited, detained, or charged? *(City, State, Country)*	Outcome or disposition *(e.g., no charges filed, charges dismissed, jail, probation, etc.)*

Form I-914

2. Have you EVER received public assistance in the United States from any source, including the U.S. Government or any State, county, city or other municipality (other than emergency medical treatment), or are you likely to receive public assistance in the future?   ☐ Yes ☑ No

3. Have you:

    a. Engaged in prostitution or procurement of prostitution or do you intend to engage in prostitution or procurement of prostitution?   ☐ Yes ☑ No

    b. EVER engaged in any unlawful commercialized vice, including, but not limited to illegal gambling?   ☐ Yes ☑ No

    c. EVER knowingly encouraged, induced, assisted, abetted, or aided any alien to try to enter the United States illegally?   ☐ Yes ☑ No

    d. EVER illicitly trafficked in any controlled substance, or knowingly assisted, abetted, or colluded in the illicit trafficking of any controlled substance?   ☐ Yes ☑ No

4. Have you EVER committed, planned or prepared, participated in, threatened to, attempted to, or conspired to commit, gathered information for, or solicited funds for any of the following:

    a. Hijacking or sabotage of any conveyance (including an aircraft, vessel, or vehicle)?   ☐ Yes ☑ No

    b. Seizing or detaining, and threatening to kill, injure, or continue to detain, another individual in order to compel a third person (including a governmental organization) to do or abstain from doing any act as an explicit or implicit condition for the release of the individual seized or detained?   ☐ Yes ☑ No

    c. Assassination?   ☐ Yes ☑ No

    d. The use of any firearm with intent to endanger, directly or indirectly, the safety of one or more individual or to cause substantial damage to property?   ☐ Yes ☑ No

    e. The use of any biological agent; chemical agent; or nuclear weapon or device; explosive; or other weapon or dangerous device, with intent to endanger, directly or indirectly, the safety of one or more individuals or to cause substantial damage to property?   ☐ Yes ☑ No

5. Have you EVER been a member of, solicited money or members for, provided support for, attended military training (as defined in section 2339D(c)(1) of title 18, United States Code) by or on behalf of, or been associated with an organization that is:

    a. Designated as a terrorist organization under section 219 of the Immigration and Nationality Act?   ☐ Yes ☑ No

    b. Any other group of two or more individuals, whether organized or not, which has engaged in or has a subgroup which has engaged in:

        1. Hijacking or sabotage of any conveyance (including an aircraft, vessel, or vehicle)?   ☐ Yes ☑ No

        2. Seizing or detaining, and threatening to kill, injure, or continue to detain another individual in order to compel a third person (including a governmental organization) to do or abstain from doing any act as an explicit or implicit condition for the release of the individual seized or detained?   ☐ Yes ☑ No

        3. Assassination?   ☐ Yes ☑ No

        4. The use of any firearm with intent to endanger, directly or indirectly, the safety of one or more individual or to cause substantial damage to property?   ☐ Yes ☑ No

        5. Soliciting money or members or otherwise providing material support to a terrorist organization?   ☐ Yes ☑ No

Form I-914

---

6. The use of any biological agent; chemical agent; or nuclear weapon or device; explosive, or other weapon or dangerous device, with intent to endanger, directly or indirectly, the safety of one or more individuals or to cause substantial damage to property? ☐ Yes ☑ No

---

6. Do you intend to engage in the United States in:

   a. Espionage? ☐ Yes ☑ No

   b. Any unlawful activity, or any activity the purpose of which is in opposition, to control, or overthrow of the government of the United States? ☐ Yes ☑ No

   c. Solely, principally, or incidentally in any activity related to espionage or sabotage or to violate any law involving the export of goods, technology, or sensitive information? ☐ Yes ☑ No

---

7. Have you ever been or do you continue to be a member of the Communist or other totalitarian party, except when membership was involuntary? ☐ Yes ☑ No

---

8. Have you, during the period of March 23, 1933, to May 8, 1945, in association with either the Nazi Government of Germany or any organization or government associated or allied with the Nazi Government of Germany, ever ordered, incited, assisted, or otherwise participated in the persecution of any person because of race, religion, nationality, membership in a particular social group, or political opinion? ☐ Yes ☑ No

---

9. Have you EVER been present or nearby when any person was:

   a. Intentionally killed, tortured, beaten, or injured? ☐ Yes ☑ No

   b. Displaced or moved from his or her residence by force, compulsion, or duress? ☐ Yes ☑ No

   c. In any way compelled or forced to engage in any kind of sexual contact or relations? ☐ Yes ☑ No

---

10. a. Are removal, exclusion, rescission, or deportation proceedings pending against you? ☐ Yes ☑ No

    b. Have removal, exclusion, rescission, or deportation proceedings EVER been initiated against you? ☐ Yes ☑ No

    c. Have you EVER been removed, excluded, or deported from the United States? ☐ Yes ☑ No

    d. Have you EVER been ordered to be removed, excluded, or deported from the United States? ☐ Yes ☑ No

    e. Have you EVER been denied a visa or denied admission to the United States? *(If a visa was denied, explain why on a separate sheet of paper.)* ☐ Yes ☑ No

    f. Have you EVER been granted voluntary departure by an immigration officer or an immigration judge and failed to depart within the allotted time? ☐ Yes ☑ No

---

11. Have you EVER ordered, incited, called for, committed, assisted, helped with, or otherwise participated in any of the following:

    a. Acts involving torture or genocide? ☐ Yes ☑ No

    b. Killing any person? ☐ Yes ☑ No

    c. Intentionally and severely injuring any person? ☐ Yes ☑ No

    d. Engaging in any kind of sexual contact or relations with any person who was being forced or threatened? ☐ Yes ☑ No

    e. Limiting or denying any person's ability to exercise religious beliefs? ☐ Yes ☑ No

---

Form I-914

12. Have you EVER:

    a. Served in, been a member of, assisted in, or participated in any military unit, paramilitary unit, police unit, self-defense unit, vigilante unit, rebel group, guerrilla group, militia, or insurgent organization? ☐ Yes ☑ No

    b. Served in any prison, jail, prison camp, detention facility, labor camp, or any other situation that involved detaining persons? ☐ Yes ☑ No

13. Have you EVER been a member of, assisted in, or participated in any group, unit, or organization of any kind in which you or other persons used any type of weapon against any person or threatened to do so? ☐ Yes ☑ No

14. Have you EVER assisted or participated in selling or providing weapons to any person who to your knowledge used them against another person, or in transporting weapons to any person who to your knowledge used them against another person? ☐ Yes ☑ No

15. Have you EVER received any type of military, paramilitary, or weapons training? ☐ Yes ☑ No

16. Are you under a final order or civil penalty for violating section 274C (producing and/or using false documentation to unlawfully satisfy a requirement of the Immigration and Nationality Act)? ☐ Yes ☑ No

17. Have you EVER, by fraud or willful misrepresentation of a material fact, sought to procure, or procured, a visa or other documentation, for entry into the United States or any immigration benefit? ☐ Yes ☑ No

18. Have you EVER left the United States to avoid being drafted into the U.S. Armed Forces? ☐ Yes ☑ No

19. Have you EVER been a J nonimmigrant exchange visitor who was subject to the two-year foreign residence requirement and not yet complied with that requirement or obtained a waiver of such? ☐ Yes ☑ No

20. Have you EVER detained, retained, or withheld the custody of a child, having a lawful claim to U.S. citizenship, outside the United States from a U.S. citizen granted custody? ☐ Yes ☑ No

21. Do you plan to practice polygamy in the United States? ☐ Yes ☑ No

22. Have you entered the United States as a stowaway? ☐ Yes ☑ No

23. **a.** Do you have a communicable disease of public health significance? ☐ Yes ☑ No

    b. Do you have or have you had a physical or mental disorder and behavior (or a history of behavior that is likely to recur) associated with the disorder which has posed or may pose a threat to the property, safety, or welfare of yourself or others? ☐ Yes ☑ No

    c. Are you now or have you been a drug abuser or drug addict? ☐ Yes ☑ No

Form I-914

PART E. Information About Your Family Members

Provide the following information about your spouse and all of your sons and daughters. If you need more space, attach an additional sheet of paper.

1. ☑ Spouse

Family Name *(Last Name)*	Given Name *(First Name)*	Middle Name *(if any)*	Date of Birth *(mm/dd/yyyy)*
Doe	John		01/07/1986

Country of Birth		Current Location	
United Kingdom		United Kingdom	

2. ☐ Children

a.

Family Name *(Last Name)*	Given Name *(First Name)*	Middle Name *(if any)*	Date of Birth *(mm/dd/yyyy)*

Country of Birth	Relationship	Current Location

b.

Family Name *(Last Name)*	Given Name *(First Name)*	Middle Name *(if any)*	Date of Birth *(mm/dd/yyyy)*

Country of Birth	Relationship	Current Location

c.

Family Name *(Last Name)*	Given Name *(First Name)*	Middle Name *(if any)*	Date of Birth *(mm/dd/yyyy)*

Country of Birth	Relationship	Current Location

Complete Form I-914, Supplement A, Application for Immediate Family Member of T-1 Recipient, for each family member listed above for whom you are now applying to have join you in the United States, and attach it to this application.

PART F. Attestation, Release, and Signature

After reading the information regarding penalties in the instructions, complete and sign below. If someone helped you prepare this application, he or she must complete Part G.

I have read, or had read to me, this form, the information provided on it and the evidence provided with it, and I certify, under penalty of perjury under the laws of the United States of America, that all of the information in this entire application package, including the documentary evidence submitted with it, is true and correct.

I authorize the release of any information from my record that U.S. Citizenship and Immigration Services (USCIS) needs to determine eligibility for the benefit I am seeking, to investigate my claim, and to investigate fraudulent claims. I further authorize USCIS to release information to law enforcement agencies and prosecutors investigating or prosecuting crimes of trafficking or related crimes. I further authorize USCIS to release information to Federal, State, and local public and private agencies providing benefits, to be used solely in making determinations of eligibility for benefits pursuant to 8 USC 1641(c).

Form I-914

PART F. Attestation, Release, and Signature   *(Continued)*

Applicant's Statement *(Check one)*:

[✓] I can read and understand English, and I have read and understand each and every question and instruction on this form, as well as my answer to each question.

[ ] Each and every question and instruction on this form, as well as my answer to each question, has been read to me in the _____ language, a language in which I am fluent, by the person named in **Interpreter's Statement and Signature.** I understand each and every question and instruction on this form, as well as my answer to each question.

I certify, under penalty of perjury under the laws of the United States of America, that the information provided with this application is all true and correct. I certify also that I have not withheld any information that would affect the outcome of this application.

Signature of Applicant *(the Person in Part A)*

Date *(mm/dd/yyyy)*

PART G. Preparer and/or Interpreter Certification *(To be completed and signed if form is prepared by a person other than the applicant)*

Preparer's Statement and Signature *(if applicable)*

I declare that I prepared this application at the request of the above person, and it is based on all information of which I have knowledge. I have not knowingly withheld any material information that would affect the outcome of this application.

Attorney or Representative: In the event of a Request for Evidence, may USCIS contact you by fax or e-mail?   [ ] Yes   [ ] No

Preparer's Signature

Date *(mm/dd/yyyy)*

Preparer's Printed Name

Preparer's Firm Name *(if applicable)*

Blank Attorney, P.A.

Preparer's Address

2655 Le Jeune Road Suite 1001, Coral Gables FL 33134

Daytime Phone Number *(with area code)*	**Fax Number** *(if any)*	**E-Mail Address** *(if any)*
(123) 456-7890		Doe@server.com

Interpreter's Statement and Signature *(if applicable)*

I certify that I am fluent in English and the below-mentioned language.

Language Used *(language in which applicant is fluent)*:

I further certify that I have read each and every question and instruction on this form, as well as the answer to each question, to this applicant in the above-mentioned language, and the applicant has understood each and every instruction and question on the form, as well as the answer to each question.

Interpreter's Signature

Date *(mm/dd/yyyy)*

Printed Name

Telephone Number *(with area code)*

Form I-914 (Rev. 03/30/09) N Page 8

Form I-914

PART H. Checklist

☑ I completely filled out and signed the form.

☑ I have attached evidence that:

    a. I am or have been a victim of a severe form of trafficking;

    b. I am physically present in the United States, American Samoa, or the Commonwealth of the Northern Mariana Islands, or at a port of entry, on account of trafficking;

    c. I am cooperating with Federal, State, or local law enforcement authorities in the investigation or prosecution of the traffickers (unless under age 18); and

    d. I would suffer extreme hardship involving unusual and severe harm upon removal from the United States.

☑ I have included three photographs of myself.

If I am applying for one or more family members:

    ☑ I have completed Form I-914, Supplement A for each member for whom I am now applying and, if he or she is in the United States, each family member has signed that Form I-914, Supplement A.

    ☑ I have submitted the required evidence, including evidence of:

        a. My relationship to the family member for whom I am applying;

        b. My age, if I am applying for my parent or unmarried sibling under the age of 18;

        c. My child's age, if I am applying for my child; and

        d. My sibling's age, if I am applying for my unmarried sibling; and

☑ I have included three photographs of each family member for whom I am now applying.

☑ I have included Form I-765, Application for Employment Authorization, if I am requesting employment authorization for my family member, along with fee or request for fee waiver.

WARNING: **Applicants who are in the United States illegally are subject to removal if their claims are not granted. Any information provided in completing this application may be used as a basis for the institution of, or as evidence in, removal proceedings even if the application is later withdrawn.**

Form I-914, Supplement A

Department of Homeland Security
U.S. Citizenship and Immigration Services

**I-914, Supplement A, Application for
Immediate Family Member of T-1 Recipient**

| START HERE - Type or print. *Use black ink. See Instructions for information about eligibility and how to complete and file this application. The recipient of the T nonimmigrant classification is referred to as the principal applicant. His or her family member(s) is referred to as a derivative applicant. Form I-914, Supplement A, is to be completed by the principal applicant.* | For USCIS Use Only |

For USCIS Use Only

Returned	Receipt
Date	
Date	
Resubmitted	
Date	
Date	
Reloc Sent	
Date	
Date	
Reloc Rec'd	
Date	
Date	

PART A. Family Member Relationship to You *(the principal)*

The family member that I am filing for is my: *(Check one)*

[✓] Husband/Wife [ ] Child [ ] Parent [ ] Unmarried Sibling Under Age 18

PART B. General Information About You *(the principal)*

Family Name *(Last Name)*	Given Name *(First Name)*	Middle Name *(if any)*
Doe	Jane	

Date of Birth *(mm/dd/yyyy)*	A # *(if any)*
05/20/1986	None

Status of your Form I-914, Application for T Nonimmigrant Status: *(Check one)*

[✓] Filing this Form I-914, Supplement A, concurrently
[ ] Pending   [ ] Approved

PART C. Information About Your Family Member *(the derivative)*

Family Name *(Last Name)*	Given Name *(First Name)*	Middle Name *(if any)*
Doe	John	

Validity Dates
From:
To:

Remarks

Other Names Used *(include maiden name/nickname)*

Date of Birth *(mm/dd/yyyy)*	Country of Birth	Country of Citizenship
01/07/1986	United Kingdom	United Kingdom

Residence or Intended Residence in the U.S. - Street Number and Name   Apt. #
123 Main Drive

City	State	Zip Code
Weston	Florida	33484

Conditional Approval
Stamp #   Date

Safe Mailing Address *(if other than above)* - Street Number and Name   Apt. #

Action Block

C/O *(in care of)*:

City	State/Province	Zip/Postal Code

Home Telephone # *(with area code)*	Safe Daytime Phone # *(with area code)*	I-94 # *(Arrival-Departure Document)*
(123) 456-7890		

To Be Completed by
Attorney or Representative, if any

[ ] Fill in box if G-28 is attached to represent the applicant.

A # *(if any)*	U.S. Social Security # *(if any)*	Gender
None	N/A	[ ] Male [✓] Female

ATTY State License #

Marital Status:
[✓] Married [ ] Single/Never Married [ ] Divorced [ ] Widowed

Form I-914, Supplement A (Rev. 03/30/09) N

Form I-914, Supplement A

PART C. Information About Your Family Member   *(Continued)*

1. Give the following information about your family member if he or she is currently in the United States.

Place of Last Entry	Date of Last Entry *(mm/dd/yyyy)*	Current Immigration Status
Miami, Florida	07/20/2002	B-2

Passport #	Place of Issuance	Date of Issue *(mm/dd/yyyy)*
012345	London	10/11/2008

2. Give the following information about your family member if he or she has previously traveled to the United States.

Place of Entry	Date of Entry *(mm/dd/yyyy)*	Date Authorized Stay Expired *(mm/dd/yyyy)*	Immigration Status
N/A			

3. If your family member was previously married, list names of prior spouses and dates of termination of marriage. Documents such as divorce decrees or death certificates must be attached.

Name of Former Spouse(s)	Date Marriage Ended *(mm/dd/yyyy)*	Where and How Marriage Ended
N/A		

4. If your family member is outside the United States, indicate the U.S. consulate or inspection facility you want notified if this application is approved.

Type of Office *(Check one):* ☑ Consulate   ☐ Pre-Flight Inspection   ☐ Port of Entry

Office Address *(City)*	U.S. State or Foreign Country
London, England	

Foreign Address Where You Want Notification Sent

123 London Road, London, United Kingdom

5. Has your family member ever been in immigration proceedings?   ☐ Yes ☑ No

If "Yes," what type of proceedings? *(Check all that apply)*

☐ Removal Date *(mm/dd/yyyy)*	☐ Exclusion Date *(mm/dd/yyyy)*	☐ Deportation Date *(mm/dd/yyyy)*	☐ Rescission Date *(mm/dd/yyyy)*	☐ Judicial Date *(mm/dd/yyyy)*

Form I-914, Supplement A

6. Is your family member requesting an Employment Authorization Document? *(If "Yes," submit Form I-765, Application for Employment Authorization Document, separately.)*   ☑ Yes ☐ No

NOTE: *If your family member is living outside the United States, he or she is not eligible to receive employment authorization until he or she is lawfully admitted to the United States. Do not file Form I-765 for a family member living outside the United States.*

PART D. Processing Information

Answer the following questions about your family member. For the purposes of this application, if applicable, you must answer "Yes" to the following questions even if the records were sealed or otherwise cleared or if anyone, including a judge, law enforcement officer, or attorney, told you that your family member no longer has a record. *(If your answer is "Yes" to any one of these questions, explain on a separate sheet of paper. Answering "Yes" does not necessarily mean that your family member will be denied T nonimmigrant status.)*

1. Has the family member for whom you are filing **EVER**:

    a. Committed a crime or offense for which he or she has not been arrested?   ☐ Yes ☑ No

    b. Been arrested, cited, or detained by any law enforcement officer (including DHS, former INS, and military officers) for any reason?   ☐ Yes ☑ No

    c. Been charged with committing any crime or offense?   ☐ Yes ☑ No

    d. Been convicted of a crime or offense (even if violation was subsequently expunged or pardoned)?   ☐ Yes ☑ No

    e. Been placed in an alternative sentencing or a rehabilitative program (for example: diversion, deferred prosecution, withheld adjudication, deferred adjudication)?   ☐ Yes ☑ No

    f. Received a suspended sentence, been placed on probation, or been paroled?   ☐ Yes ☑ No

    g. Been in jail or prison?   ☐ Yes ☑ No

    h. Been the beneficiary of a pardon, amnesty, rehabilitation, or other act of clemency or similar action?   ☐ Yes ☑ No

    i. Exercised diplomatic immunity to avoid prosecution for a criminal offense in the United States?   ☐ Yes ☑ No

If the answer is "Yes" to any of the above questions, complete the following table. If you need more space, use a separate sheet of paper.

Why was the family member for whom you are filing arrested, cited, detained, or charged?	Date of arrest, citation, detention, charge *(mm/dd/yyyy)*	Where was the family member for whom you are filing arrested, cited, detained, or charged? *(City, State, Country)*	Outcome or disposition *(e.g., no charges filed, charges dismissed, jail, probation, etc.)*
N/A			

Form I-914, Supplement A

2. Has the family member for whom you are filing EVER received public assistance in the United States from any source, including the U.S. Government or any State, county, city or other municipality (other than emergency medical treatment), or is he or she likely to receive public assistance in the future?   ☐ Yes ☑ No

3. Has the family member for whom you are filing:

a. Engaged in prostitution or procurement of prostitution or does he or she intend to engage in prostitution or procurement of prostitution?   ☐ Yes ☑ No

b. EVER engaged in any unlawful commercialized vice, including but not limited to illegal gambling?   ☐ Yes ☑ No

c. EVER knowingly encouraged, induced, assisted, abetted, or aided any alien to try to enter the United States illegally?   ☐ Yes ☑ No

d. EVER illicitly trafficked in any controlled substance, or knowingly assisted, abetted, or colluded in the illicit trafficking of any controlled substance?   ☐ Yes ☑ No

4. Has the family member for whom you are filing EVER committed, planned or prepared, participated in, threatened to, attempted to, or conspired to commit, gathered information for, or solicited funds for any of the following:

a. Hijacking or sabotage of any conveyance (including an aircraft, vessel, or vehicle)?   ☐ Yes ☑ No

b. Seizing or detaining, and threatening to kill, injure, or continue to detain, another individual in order to compel a third person (including a governmental organization) to do or abstain from doing any act as an explicit or implicit condition for the release of the individual seized or detained?   ☐ Yes ☑ No

c. Assassination?   ☐ Yes ☑ No

d. The use of any firearm with intent to endanger, directly or indirectly, the safety of one or more individual or to cause substantial damage to property?   ☐ Yes ☑ No

e. The use of any biological agent; chemical agent; or nuclear weapon or device; explosive; or other weapon or dangerous device, with intent to endanger, directly or indirectly, the safety of one or more individuals or to cause substantial damage to property?   ☐ Yes ☑ No

5. Has the family member for whom you are filing EVER been a member of, solicited money or members for, provided support for, attended military training (as defined in section 2339D(c)(1) of title 18, United States Code) by or on behalf of, or been associated with an organization that is:

a. Designated as a terrorist organization under section 219 of the Immigration and Nationality Act?   ☐ Yes ☑ No

b. Any other group of two or more individuals, whether organized or not, which has engaged in or has a subgroup which has engaged in:

1. Hijacking or sabotage of any conveyance (including an aircraft, vessel, or vehicle)?   ☐ Yes ☑ No

2. Seizing or detaining, and threatening to kill, injure, or continue to detain another individual in order to compel a third person (including a governmental organization) to do or abstain from doing any act as an explicit or implicit condition for the release of the individual seized or detained?   ☐ Yes ☑ No

3. Assassination?   ☐ Yes ☑ No

4. The use of any firearm with intent to endanger, directly or indirectly, the safety of one or more individual or to cause substantial damage to property?   ☐ Yes ☑ No

Form I-914, Supplement A

    5. Soliciting money or members or otherwise providing material support to a terrorist organization? ☐ Yes ☑ No

    6. The use of any biological agent; chemical agent; or nuclear weapon or device; explosive; or other weapon or dangerous device, with intent to endanger, directly or indirectly, the safety of one or more individuals or to cause substantial damage to property? ☐ Yes ☑ No

6. Does the family member for whom you are filing intend to engage in the United States in:

    a. Espionage? ☐ Yes ☑ No

    b. Any unlawful activity, or any activity the purpose of which is in opposition, to control or overthrow of the Government of the United States? ☐ Yes ☑ No

    c. Solely, principally, or incidentally in any activity related to espionage or sabotage or to violate any law involving the export of goods, technology, or sensitive information? ☐ Yes ☑ No

7. Has the family member for whom you are filing EVER been or does he or she continue to be a member of the Communist or other totalitarian party, except when membership was involuntary? ☐ Yes ☑ No

8. Has the family member for whom you are filing, during the period of March 23, 1933, to May 8, 1945, in association with either the Nazi Government of Germany or any organization or government associated or allied with the Nazi Government of Germany, ever ordered, incited, assisted, or otherwise participated in the persecution of any person because of race, religion, nationality, membership in a particular social group, or political opinion? ☐ Yes ☑ No

9. Has the family member for whom you are filing EVER been present or nearby when any person was:

    a. Intentionally killed, tortured, beaten, or injured? ☐ Yes ☑ No

    b. Displaced or moved from his or her residence by force, compulsion, or duress? ☐ Yes ☑ No

    c. In any way compelled or forced to engage in any kind of sexual contact or relations? ☐ Yes ☑ No

10. a. Are removal, exclusion, rescission, or deportation proceedings pending against the family member for whom your are filing? ☐ Yes ☑ No

    b. Have removal, exclusion, rescission, or deportation proceedings EVER been initiated against the family member for whom your are filing? ☐ Yes ☑ No

    c. Has the family member for whom your are filing EVER been removed, excluded, or deported from the United States? ☐ Yes ☑ No

    d. Has the family member for whom your are filing EVER been ordered to be removed, excluded, or deported from the United States? ☐ Yes ☑ No

    e. Has the family member for whom your are filing EVER been denied a visa or denied admission to the United States? *(If a visa was denied, explain why on a separate sheet of paper.)* ☐ Yes ☑ No

    f. Has the family member for whom your are filing EVER been granted voluntary departure by an immigration officer or an immigration judge and failed to depart within the allotted time? ☐ Yes ☑ No

Form I-914, Supplement A

11. Has the family member for whom you are filing (or has any member of his or her family) EVER ordered, incited, called for, committed, assisted, helped with, or otherwise participated in any of the following:

    a. Acts involving torture or genocide? ☐ Yes ☑ No

    b. Killing any person? ☐ Yes ☑ No

    c. Intentionally and severely injuring any person? ☐ Yes ☑ No

    d. Engaging in any kind of sexual contact or relations with any person who was being forced or threatened? ☐ Yes ☑ No

    e. Limiting or denying any person's ability to exercise religious beliefs? ☐ Yes ☑ No

12. Has the family member for whom you are filing EVER:

    a. Served in, been a member of, assisted in, or participated in any military unit, paramilitary unit, police unit, self-defense unit, vigilante unit, rebel group, guerrilla group, militia, or insurgent organization? ☐ Yes ☑ No

    b. Served in any prison, jail, prison camp, detention facility, labor camp, or any other situation that involved detaining persons? ☐ Yes ☑ No

13. Has the family member for whom you are filing EVER been a member of, assisted in, or participated in any group, unit, or organization of any kind in which he or she or any other persons used any type of weapon against any person or threatened to do so? ☐ Yes ☑ No

14. Has the family member for whom you are filing EVER assisted or participated in selling or providing weapons to any person who to his or her knowledge used them against another person, or in transporting weapons to any person who to his or her knowledge used them against another person? ☐ Yes ☑ No

15. Has the family member for whom you are filing EVER received any type of military, paramilitary, or weapons training? ☐ Yes ☑ No

16. Is the family member for whom you are filing under a final order or civil penalty for violating section 274C (producing and/or using false documentation to unlawfully satisfy a requirement of the Immigration and Nationality Act)? ☐ Yes ☑ No

17. Has the family member for whom you are filing EVER, by fraud or willful misrepresentation of a material fact, sought to procure, or procured, a visa or other documentation, for entry into the United States or any immigration benefit? ☐ Yes ☑ No

18. Has the family member for whom you are filing EVER left the United States to avoid being drafted into the U.S. Armed Forces? ☐ Yes ☑ No

19. Has the family member for whom you are filing EVER been a J nonimmigrant exchange visitor who was subject to the two-year foreign residence requirement and not yet complied with that requirement or obtained a waiver of such? ☐ Yes ☑ No

20. Has the family member for whom you are filing EVER detained, retained, or withheld the custody of a child, having a lawful claim to U.S. citizenship, outside the United States from a U.S. citizen granted custody? ☐ Yes ☑ No

Form I-914, Supplement A

21. Does the family member for whom you are filing plan to practice polygamy in the United States?   ☐ Yes   ☑ No

22. Did the family member for whom you are filing enter the United States as a stowaway?   ☐ Yes   ☑ No

23. a. Does the family member for whom you are filing have a communicable disease of public health significance?   ☐ Yes   ☑ No

    b. Does the family member for whom you are filing have or has he or she you had a physical or mental disorder and behavior (or a history of behavior that is likely to recur) associated with the disorder which has posed or may pose a threat to the property, safety, or welfare of themselves or others?   ☐ Yes   ☑ No

    c. Is the family member for whom you are filing now or has he or she been a drug abuser or drug addict?   ☐ Yes   ☑ No

PART E. Attestation, Release, and Signature

After reading the information regarding penalties in the instructions, you, the principal, must sign below. Your family member for whom you are applying must also sign below if he or she is presently in the United States. If someone helped you prepare this supplementary application, he or she must complete Part F.

I have read, or had read to me, this form, the information provided on it, and the evidence provided with it.

I authorize the release of any information from my record that U.S. Citizenship and Immigration Services (USCIS) needs to determine eligibility for the benefit I am seeking for the family member for whom I am applying, to investigate my claim, and to investigate fraudulent claims. I further authorize USCIS to release information to law enforcement agencies and prosecutors investigating or prosecuting crimes of trafficking or related crimes. I further authorize USCIS to release information to Federal, State, and local public and private agencies providing benefits, to be used solely in making determinations of eligibility for benefits pursuant to 8 USC 1641(c).

Principal Applicant's Statement and Signature *(Choose one of the following)*:

☑ I can read and understand English, and I have read and understand each and every question and instruction on this form, as well as my answer to each question.

☐ Each and every question and instruction on this form, as well as my answer to each question, has been read to me in the _____ language, a language in which I am fluent, by the person named in **Interpreter's Statement and Signature.** I understand each and every question and instruction on this form, as well as my answer to each question.

Principal Applicant's Signature *(you)*   **Date** *(mm/dd/yyyy)*

Signature of Derivative *(your family member if physically present in the United States)*   **Date** *(mm/dd/yyyy)*

Form I-914, Supplement A

PART F. Preparer and/or Interpreter Certification and Signature

To be completed and signed if form is prepared by a person other than the applicant.

Preparer's Statement and Signature *(if applicable)*

I declare that I prepared this application at the request of the above person, and it is based on all information of which I have knowledge. I have not knowingly withheld any material information that would affect the outcome of this application.

Attorney or Representative: In the event of a Request for Evidence, may USCIS contact you by fax or e-mail? ☑ Yes ☐ No

Preparer's Signature

Date *(mm/dd/yyyy)*

Preparer's Printed Name

Preparer's Firm Name *(if applicable)*

Blank Attorney, P.A.

Preparer's Address

2655 Le.Jeune Road Suite 1001 Coral Gables FL 33134

Daytime Phone Number *(with area code)*

(123) 456-7890

Fax Number *(if any)*

E-Mail Address *(if any)*

Interpreter's Statement and Signature *(if applicable)*

I certify that I am fluent in English and the below-mentioned language.

Language used *(language in which applicant is fluent):*

I further certify that I have read each and every question and instruction on this form, as well as the answer to each question, to this applicant in the above-mentioned language, and the applicant has understood each and every instruction and question on the form, as well as the answer to each question.

Interpreter's Signature

Date *(mm/dd/yyyy)*

Printed Name

Telephone Number *(with area code)*

WARNING: Applicants who are in the United States illegally are subject to removal if their claims are not granted. Any information provided in completing this application may be used as a basis for the institution of, or as evidence in, removal proceedings even if the application is later withdrawn.

Form I-914, Supplement B

| Department of Homeland Security U.S. Citizenship and Immigration Services | Form I-914, Supplement B, Declaration of Law Enforcement Officer for Victim of Trafficking in Persons |

START HERE - Type or print in blank ink. This form should be completed by Federal, State, or local law enforcement authorities for victims under the Victims of Trafficking and Violence Protection Act, Public Law 106-386, as amended.

For USCIS Use Only

	Returned	Receipt
	Date	

PART A. Victim Information

Family Name *(Last Name)*	Given Name *(First Name)*	Middle Name *(if any)*
Doe	Jane	

Date	
Date Resubmitted	

Other Names Used *(include maiden name/nickname)*

None

Date	

Date of Birth *(mm/dd/yyyy)*   **Gender**

05/20/1986   ☑ Male ☐ Female

Date	
Reloc Sent	

A # (if known)   **Social Security # (if known)**

None   N/A

Date	
Date	
Reloc Rec'd	

Part B.   Agency Information

Name of Certifying Agency

Agency Name

Date	

Name of Certifying Official   **Title and Division/Office of Certifying Official**

Date	

Agency Address - Street Number and Name   **Suite #**

Remarks

City   **State/Province**   **Zip/Postal Code**

Daytime Phone # *(area code and/or extension)*   **Fax #** *(with area code)*

Agency Type
☐ Federal   ☑ State   ☐ Local

Case Status
☑ On-going   ☐ Completed   ☐ Local _____

Certifying Agency Category
☐ Judge   ☑ Law Enforcement   ☐ Prosecutor   ☐ Other _____

Case Number   **FBI # or SID #** *(if applicable)*

02020202   N/A

Part C. Statement of Claim

1. The applicant is or has been a victim of a severe form of trafficking in persons. Specifically, he or she is a victim of: *(Check all that apply. Base your analysis on the practices to which the victim was subjected rather than on the specific violations charged, the counts on which convictions were obtained, or whether any prosecution resulted in convictions. Note that the definitions that control this analysis are not the elements of criminal offenses, but are those set forth at 8 CFR 214.11(a).)*

   ☐ Sex trafficking in which a commercial sex act was induced by force, fraud, or coercion. Sex trafficking means the recruitment, harboring, transportation, provision, or obtaining of a person for the purpose of a commercial sex act.

   ☐ Sex trafficking and the victim is under the age of 18.

Form I-914, Supplement B (Rev. 03/30/09) N

Form I-914, Supplement B

☑ The recruitment, harboring, transportation, provision, or obtaining of a person for labor or services through the use of force, fraud, or coercion for subjection to involuntary servitude, peonage, debt bondage, or slavery.

☐ Not applicable.

☐ Other, specify on attached additional sheets.

2. Please describe the victimization upon which the applicant's claim is based and identify the relationship between that victimization and the crime under investigation/prosecution. Attach the results of any name or database inquiry performed in the investigation of the case, as well as any relevant reports and findings. Include relevant dates, etc. Attach additional sheets, if necessary.

> See Memorandum

3. Has the applicant expressed any fear of retaliation or revenge if removed from the United States? If yes, explain. Attach additional sheets, if necessary.

> See Memorandum

4. Provide the date(s) on which the acts of trafficking occurred.

Date *(mm/dd/yyyy)*	Date *(mm/dd/yyyy)*	Date *(mm/dd/yyyy)*	Date *(mm/dd/yyyy)*
[DATE]			

5. List the statutory citation(s) for the acts of trafficking being investigated or prosecuted, or that were investigated or prosecuted.

6. Provide the date on which the investigation or prosecution was initiated.

Date *(mm/dd/yyyy)*

7. Provide the date on which the investigation or prosecution was completed *(if any)*.

Date *(mm/dd/yyyy)*

Form I-914, Supplement B

Part D. Cooperation of Victim *(Attach additional sheets, if necessary)*

The applicant:

☐ Has complied with requests for assistance in the investigation/prosecution of the crime of trafficking. *(Explain below.)*

☐ Has failed to comply with requests to assist in the investigation/prosecution of the crime of trafficking. *(Explain below.)*

☐ Has not been requested to assist in the investigation/prosecution of any crime of trafficking.

☐ Has not yet attained the age of 18.

☐ Other, specify on attached additional sheets.

[DESCRIBE]

Part E. Family Members Implicated In Trafficking

☐ Yes ☑ No Are any of the applicant's family members believed to have been involved in his or her trafficking to the United States? If "Yes," list the relative(s) and describe the involvement. Attach additional sheets if necessary.

Full Name	Relationship	Involvement

Part F. Attestation

Based upon investigation of the facts, I certify, under penalty of perjury, that the above noted individual is or has been a victim of a severe form of trafficking in persons as defined by the VTVPA. I certify that the above information is true and correct to the best of my knowledge, and that I have made, and will make, no promises regarding the above victim's ability to obtain a visa from U.S. Citizenship and Immigration Services, based upon this certification. I further certify that if the victim unreasonably refuses to assist in the investigation or prosecution of the acts of trafficking of which he/she is a victim, I will notify USCIS.

Signature of Law Enforcement Officer *(identified in Part B)*

Date *(mm/dd/yyyy)*

Signature of Supervisor of Certifying Officer

Date *(mm/dd/yyyy)*

Printed Name of Supervisor

Sample Memorandum of T Request

UNITED STATES DEPARTMENT OF HOMELAND SECURITY
U.S. CITIZENSHIP AND IMMIGRATION SERVICES
-- x
                                                                          :
IN THE MATTER OF APPLICATION FOR T   :
NONIMMIGRANT STATUS OF   :
                                                                          :
-- x

MEMORANDUM OF LAW IN SUPPORT OF APPLICATION FOR T NONIMMIGRANT STATUS OF

This memorandum of law is submitted on behalf of _____(Name), in support of

her application for T Nonimmigrant status, pursuant to the Trafficking Victims Protection

Act of 2000 ("TVPA" or "the Act"), 22 U.S.C.A. § 7101, et. seq.

INTRODUCTION

Name, a 20 year-old Guatemalan national, was brought to the United States

through false promises that she would find work and a better life. Upon her arrival, she

was held captive and abused for several days before being transported to Los Angeles,

where she was forced to work as a prostitute in several brothels for a group of people

who were later charged with forty (40) criminal counts ranging from kidnapping to rape,

and convicted of promoting prostitution. See Indictment in the case of ..... She and the

other women with whom she was held were threatened with severe physical force which

included punching, kicking and choking as well as rape when they refused to cooperate

fully in the prostitution scheme, their lives were monitored twenty four hours a day,

prohibiting them from any contact beyond were they were kept, and the money that was

paid for their services as prostitutes was kept by the men holding them captive.

She was able to escape her captors and went to the Los Angeles Police Department to aid

in the investigation, capture and prosecution of her captors. See Affidavit of _____. In

Sample Memorandum of T Request

fact, she was granted "Continued Presence" from USCIS to facilitate her cooperation with law enforcement, and certified by the Department of Health and Human Services for federal benefits under Section 107(b) of the Trafficking Victims Protection Act. According to 8 CFR 214.11(f)(2), documentation from the Service granting continued presence is considered <u>primary</u> evidence that the applicant has been the victim of a severe form of trafficking. Her victimization and cooperation with law enforcement is further corroborated by newspaper articles reporting the case, a letter from the District Attorney's office, and an attorney affirmation. Accordingly, Name respectfully requests that U.S. Citizenship and Immigration Services (USCIS) approve her petition for T-status.

STATEMENT OF FACTS

She arrived in the United States on _____.   She was induced into coming to the United States by a friend, who promised he would help her continue her studies as a doctor and get her a good job to help support her family in Guatemala. Upon her entry to the United States, she was held captive in an abandoned construction site in the California desert for several days. During that time, she was repeatedly abused and brutalized. She later learned that her "job" was going to be to be sent to Los Angeles to work as a prostitute. In Guatemala, she had attended college.

In Los Angeles, she was forced to work in several brothels for fourteen to sixteen hours per day. She suffered through this existence for about one month, during which time she was routinely beaten and abused by her captors who controlled her in every

Sample Memorandum of T Request

respect, and forced her to prostitute herself without seeing any money. Her desperation was shared by the two other women who were brought from Mexico.

After about a month, around _____, she and one of the other women, Maria, escaped from one of the brothels despite the risk that their captors would find them and hurt them and/or their families in Guatemala and Mexico. They met a waitress at a coffee diner, who felt sorry for them and took them to the police station. They provided the police with vital information which led to the apprehension, arrest, and prosecution of their captors. They placed themselves in danger by setting a trap for their captors.

The captors were subsequently prosecuted for several counts of kidnapping, counts of unlawful imprisonment, counts of rape, counts of sexual abuse, counts of sodomy, counts of assault, counts of promoting prostitution, and counts of sexual misconduct. <u>See</u> Indictment of _____. In _____, she testified as a key witness in the government's case against her captors.(See newspaper clippings....) As a result, the captors were found guilty and sentenced to five (5) to fourteen (14) years of imprisonment in _____. <u>See</u> Certificate of Disposition Indictment in the case of......

<u>ARGUMENT</u>

She is eligible for a grant of T status. To be eligible for such a visa, she must show that she: (1) is physically present in the United States, American Samoa or the Commonwealth of the Northern Mariana Islands as a result of trafficking; (2) is a victim of a severe form of trafficking in persons; (3) would suffer extreme hardship involving unusual and severe harm upon removal; and (4) has complied with any reasonable

Sample Memorandum of T Request

request for assistance in the investigation and prosecution of acts of trafficking in persons. <u>See</u> 8 CFR §214.11(b)(1) - (4).

To establish that she was a victim of a severe form of trafficking in persons, she must demonstrate that she was brought to the United States either: (1) for the purpose of a commercial sex act, which act was either induced by force, fraud, coercion, or occurred when the applicant had not reached 18 years of age, or (2) for the purpose of labor or services induced by force, fraud, or coercion for the purpose of subjecting the applicant to involuntary servitude, peonage, debt bondage or slavery. <u>Id</u>.

As more fully set forth below, she meets the required criteria and her application for T-1 status should be granted.

I. Is Physically Present in the United States.

As demonstrated, she is present in the United States as a result of trafficking. She is currently living in Miami, Florida, satisfying the residency prong of the requirements for a T-1 Visa. She has not departed the United States since being trafficked in. Indeed, she was issued "continued presence" to assist in the prosecution of her trafficker. <u>See</u> Form I-797A, Notice of Action (attached).

II. Is a Victim Of A Severe Form of Trafficking.

She is a victim of a severe form of trafficking, which includes "sex trafficking in which a commercial sex act is induced by force, fraud or coercion…". 8 CFR §214.11(a). A commercial sex act is defined as any sex for which anything of value is given to or received by any person. <u>Id.</u> She was repeatedly forced to engage in sexual acts with men for which her captor collected money. To force her cooperation in performing commercial sex acts, she was repeatedly beaten and abused. In addition, she was held

Sample Memorandum of T Request

captive in the brothels under constant supervision. She was never permitted to leave without one of the captors, and was moved from location to location, preventing her from becoming well-oriented to her surroundings. Her captors took all of her money and would beat her if they suspected that she had money she was not giving them. Thus, she was induced by force into commercial sex acts, thereby establishing that she is a victim of a severe form of trafficking.

II. Has Cooperated With Law Enforcement.

After escaping from one of the brothels, she went to the Los Angeles city police to press charges against her captors. Despite her own fear and risks to herself, she agreed to help the police capture her captors. It was through her reports to the police and active cooperation in a "sting", that the police were able to arrest them and compile the evidence necessary to prosecute them. She was granted continued presence in order to assist law enforcement in the arrest and prosecution of the captors. <u>See</u> Form I-797A, Notice of Action (attached).

With her help, the state of California subsequently brought charges against the captors for kidnapping, rape, sodomy, assault, unlawful imprisonment, sexual abuse, sexual misconduct and promoting prostitution. Her cooperation with the Los Angeles Police Department, her constant willingness to make herself available both in person and by telephone, and the key information she provided, allowed the Office of the District Attorney to indict and prosecute her captors. <u>See</u> Letters from ……. She is named as the victim in over half of the forty (40) counts charged against her captors. <u>See</u> Indictment in the case of ……. Her captors' case went to trial in _____, and judgment was entered in _____. <u>See</u> Certificate of Disposition Indictment in the case of ……..

Sample Memorandum of T Request

She agreed to testify against her captors, serving as a key witness for the government. <u>See newspaper clippings.</u>

Her cooperation led to a conviction for promoting prostitution which holds a potential sentence of fifteen (15) years imprisonment. Her captors were sentenced to five (5) to fourteen (14) years imprisonment. <u>See</u> Certificate of Disposition Indictment in the case of _____.

Her cooperation with law enforcement was facilitated by the grant of continued presence, which serves as primary evidence that she has been the victim of a severe form of trafficking. 8 CFR 214.11(f)(2). While the captors were prosecuted and convicted under California State law, her continued presence was renewed as of _____ pursuant to the continued possibility of the federal prosecution of her captors in the District of California. Moreover, her cooperation with law enforcement is further corroborated by letters from the State Attorney's office and three news articles and the attached attorney affirmation.

IV. Would Suffer Extreme Hardship Upon Removal.

She would suffer extreme hardship if forced to leave the United States. In the United States, she has access to counseling and social services to help her deal with the trauma that she suffered. Such services would not be readily available to her in Guatemala. Moreover, cultural mores against pre-marital sex and the protection of abused women in Guatemala would impede her from discussing her ordeal with friends and family, as she fears she would be subject to rejection and humiliation. She also fears

Sample Memorandum of T Request

returning to Guatemala because her captors have influential family members in Guatemala and they may choose to seek revenge against her.

Over the last years in the U.S., she has grown particularly dependent upon the services and support provided by her local community social services. She has established a community of friends through this organization who are understanding of her past. She also met her husband through this organization; it is very special to her and a big part of her life. The organization would be unavailable to her in Guatemala and the absence of the counseling and inability to access its support would negatively impact her already fragile mental state and cause her to severely regress in her healing process.

In the years since she escaped from her captors, she has consistently cooperated with law enforcement. While present in the U.S. for this purpose, she has also established a life for herself in this country. She is currently living with her husband in Miami, Florida. She has made many friends in the United States and enjoys living near her adopted family and is expecting her first child. She has made great efforts to put this tragic incident behind her, and would suffer hardship, not only from being forced to give up the life she has worked so hard to create in the United States, but also because she needs the counseling she has access to in the United States.

In addition, she has not lived in Guatemala for almost three (3) years. Her education was interrupted when she was trafficked into the U.S., and as a result, she has no job prospects in that country. In addition, returning her to Guatemala would put her at risk of being 're-trafficked.' While the laws in Central and South America prohibit trafficking in persons, trafficking still remains a serious problem, and the U.S. Department of State has documented "credible reports that police, immigration, and

Sample Memorandum of T Request

customs officials were involved in the trafficking of such persons." <u>See</u> United States Department of State, <u>Guatemala: Country Reports on Human Rights Practices 2003,</u> (hereinafter "Human Rights Report"). Mexico is a transit point for primarily Mexican and Central American migrants traveling to the United States, some of who are trafficked or at risk of being trafficked for labor or sexual exploitation. The laws of Mexico would not protect her either if she were "re-trafficked" See U.S. Department of State, <u>Trafficking in Persons </u>Report, at 17 (June 11, 2003) (hereinafter "Trafficking Report"). Baja California is a major transit point for illegal migrants of all types, and smuggling for purposes of prostitution continued throughout 2002. <u>Human Rights Report</u> at 30.

Moreover, the Governments of Guatemala and Mexico do not fully comply with the minimum standards for the elimination of trafficking; although it has made efforts to interdict illicit migration, efforts to assist victims and punish traffickers, especially those that sexually exploit minors, are still limited. <u>Trafficking Report</u> at 17. These individuals remain the most common victims of human trafficking and trafficking in women for the purpose of sexual exploitation, in particular, is a problem. <u>Human Rights Report</u> at 21. The threat of being trafficked again is therefore very real to her, and in the United States she remains safe from such a thing ever happening to her again.

Thus, under the prevailing standards, she has met the criteria necessary to establish her claim, and the Department of Homeland Security should grant her T-Visa status.

<u>CONCLUSION</u>

Sample Memorandum of T Request

For the reasons stated above, Name respectfully requests that the Department of

Homeland Security grant her application for T status.

Dated: _____
    Miami, Florida

                                        _____

Form I-918

OMB No. 1615-0104; Expires 08/31/2010

Department of Homeland Security
U.S. Citizenship and Immigration Services

I-918, Petition for U Nonimmigrant Status

START HERE - Please type or print in black ink.

Part 1.   Information about you. *(Person filing this petition as a victim)*

Family Name	Given Name	Middle Name
DOE	John	

Other Names Use (Include maiden name/nickname)

Home Address - Street Number and Name | Apt. #
123 Main Drive

City	State/Province	Zip/Postal Code
Weston	Florida	33484

Safe Mailing Address (if other than above) - Street Number and Name   Apt. #

C/O (*in care of*):

City	State/Province	Zip/Postal Code

Home Telephone # *(with area code)*	Safe Daytime Phone # *(with area code)*	E-Mail Address *(optional)*
(123) 456-7890		m

A # *(if any)*	U.S. Social Security # *(if any)*	Gender
None	N/A	☑ Male ☑ Female

Marital Status
☐ Single   ☑ Married   ☐ Divorced   ☐ Widowed

Date of Birth *(mm/dd/yyyy)*	Country of Birth
05/20/1986	United Kingdom

Country of Citizenship	Passport #
United Kingdom	543789

Place of Issuance	Date of Issue *(mm/dd/yyyy)*
London	10/11/2008

Place of Last Entry	Date of Last Entry *(mm/dd/yyyy)*
Miami, Florida	07/20/2002

I-94 # *(Arrival/Departure Document)*	Current Immigration Status
123456789 00	B-2

For USCIS Use Only.

Returned	Receipt
Date	
Date	
Resubmitted	
Date	
Date	
Reloc Sent	
Date	
Date	
Reloc Rec'd	
Date	
Date	

U.S. Embassy/Consulate:

Validity Dates
From: _____
To: _____

Remarks

Conditional Approval

Stamp #: _____   Date

Action Block

To Be Completed by
Attorney or Representative, if any.

☐ Fill in box if G-28 is attached to represent the applicant.

ATTY State License #

Form I-918

Part 2. Additional information.

Answers to the questions below require explanations and supporting documentation. Attach relevant documents in support of your claims that you are a victim of criminal activity listed in the Immigration and Nationality Act (INA), section 101(a)(15)(U). You must also attach a personal narrative statement describing the criminal activity of which you were the victim. If you are only petitioning for U derivative status for a qualifying family member(s) subsequent to your (the principal petitioner) initial filing, evidence supporting the original petition is not required to be submitted with the new Form I-918.

Attach additional sheets of paper as needed. Write your name and Alien Registration Number (A #), if any, at the top of each sheet and indicate the number of the item that refers to your answer. Include the Part and letter or number relating to the additional information you provided (example: Part 2, Z).

Check either "Yes" or "No" as appropriate to each of the following questions.

1. I am a victim of criminal activity listed in the INA at section 101(a)(15)(U).   ☑ Yes   ☐ No

2. I have suffered substantial physical or mental abuse as a result of having been a victim of this criminal activity.   ☑ Yes   ☐ No

3. I possess information concerning the criminal activity of which I was a victim.   ☑ Yes   ☐ No

4. I am submitting a certification from a certifying official on Form I-918 Supplement B, U Nonimmigrant Status Certification.   ☑ Yes   ☐ No

5. The crime of which I am a victim occurred in the United States including Indian country and military installations) or violated the laws of the United States.   ☑ Yes   ☐ No

6. I am under the age of 16 years.   ☐ Yes   ☑ No

7. I want an Employment Authorization Document.   ☑ Yes   ☐ No

8. Have you ever been in immigration proceedings?   ☐ Yes   ☑ No

   If "Yes," what type of proceedings? *(Check all that apply.)*

   ☐ Removal Date *(mm/dd/yyyy)*   ☐ Exclusion Date *(mm/dd/yyyy)*   ☐ Deportation Date *(mm/dd/yyyy)*   ☐ Recission Date *(mm/dd/yyyy)*   ☐ Judicial Date *(mm/dd/yyyy)*

9. List each date, place of entry and status under which you entered the United States during the five years preceding the filing of this petition.

Date of Entry *(mm/dd/yyyy)*	Place of Entry	Status at Entry
07/20/2002	Miami, Florida	B-2

Form I-918

Part 2. Additional information.   *(Continued.)*

10. If you are outside the United States, give the U.S. consulate or inspection facility you want notified if this petition is approved.

Type of Office *(Check one)*: ☐ Consulate   ☐ Pre-flight inspection   ☐ Port of Entry

Office Address *(City)*   U.S. State or Foreign Country

Safe Foreign Address Where You Want Notification Sent - Street Number and Name   Apt. #

City   State/Province   Country   Zip/Postal Code

Part 3. Processing information.

Please answer the following questions about yourself. For the purposes of this petition, you must answer "Yes" to the following questions, if applicable, even if your records were sealed or otherwise cleared or if anyone, including a judge, law enforcement officer or attorney, told you that you no longer have a record. *(Answering "Yes" does not necessarily mean that you will be denied U nonimmigrant status.)*

1. Have you **EVER**:

   a. Committed a crime or offense for which you have not been arrested? ☐ Yes ☑ No

   b. Been arrested, cited or detained by any law enforcement officer (including DHS, former INS and military officers) for any reason? ☐ Yes ☑ No

   c. Been charged with committing any crime or offense? ☐ Yes ☑ No

   d. Been convicted of a crime or offense (even if violation was subsequently expunged or pardoned)? ☐ Yes ☑ No

   e. Been placed in an alternative sentencing or a rehabilitative program (for example: diversion, deferred prosecution, withheld adjudication, deferred adjudication)? ☐ Yes ☑ No

   f. Received a suspended sentence, been placed on probation or been paroled? ☐ Yes ☑ No

   g. Been in jail or prison? ☐ Yes ☑ No

   h. Been the beneficiary of a pardon, amnesty, rehabilitation, or other act of clemency or similar action? ☐ Yes ☑ No

   i. Exercised diplomatic immunity to avoid prosecution for a criminal offense in the United States? ☐ Yes ☑ No

If you answered "Yes" to any of the above questions, complete the following table. If you need more space, use a separate sheet of paper to give the same information.

Why were you arrested, cited, detained or charged?	Date of arrest, citation, detention, charge. *(mm/dd/yyyy)*	Where were you arrested, cited, detained or charged? *(City, State, Country)*	Outcome or disposition. *(e.g., no charges filed, charges dismissed, jail, probation, etc.)*

Form I-918

2. Have you ever received public assistance in the United States from any source, including the U.S. government or any State, county, city or other municipality (other than emergency medical treatment), or are you likely to receive public assistance in the future?   ☐ Yes ☑ No

3. Have you:

    a. Engaged in prostitution or procurement of prostitution or do you intend to engage in prostitution or procurement of prostitution?   ☐ Yes ☑ No

    b. Ever engaged in any unlawful commercialized vice, including, but not limited to illegal gambling?   ☐ Yes ☑ No

    c. Ever knowingly encouraged, induced, assisted, abetted or aided any alien to try to enter the United States illegally?   ☐ Yes ☑ No

    d. Ever illicitly trafficked in any controlled substance, or knowingly assisted, abetted or colluded in the illicit trafficking of any controlled substance?   ☐ Yes ☑ No

4. Have you ever committed, planned or prepared, participated in, threatened to, attempted to, or conspired to commit, gathered information for, solicited funds for any of the following:

    a. Highjacking or sabotage of any conveyance (including an aircraft, vessel, or vehicle?   ☐ Yes ☑ No

    b. Seizing or detaining, and threatening to kill, injure, or continue to detain, another individual in order to compel a third person (including a governmental organization) to do or abstain from doing any act as an explicit or implicit condition for the release of the individual seized or detained?   ☐ Yes ☑ No

    c. Assassination?   ☐ Yes ☑ No

    d. The use of any firearm with intent to endanger, directly or indirectly, the safety of one or more individual or to cause substantial damage to property?   ☐ Yes ☑ No

    e. The use of any biological agent, chemical agent, or nuclear weapon or device, or explosive, or other weapon or dangerous device, with intent to endanger, directly or indirectly, the safety of one or more individuals or to cause substantial damage to property?   ☐ Yes ☑ No

5. Have you ever been a member of, solicited money or members for, provided support for, attended military training (as defined in section 2339D(c)(1) of title 18, United States Code) by or on behalf of, or been associated with an organization that is:

    a. Designated as a terrorist organization under section 219 of the Immigration and Nationality Act?   ☐ Yes ☑ No

    b. Any other group of two or more individuals, whether organized or not, which has engaged in or has a subgroup which has engaged in: ☐ Yes ☑ No

    c. Highjacking or sabotage of any conveyance (including an aircraft, vessel, or vehicle?   ☐ Yes ☑ No

    d. Seizing or detaining, and threatening to kill, injure, or continue to detain, another individual in order to compel a third person (including a governmental organization) to do or abstain from doing any act as an explicit or implicit condition for the release of the individual seized or detained?   ☐ Yes ☑ No

    e. Assassination?   ☐ Yes ☑ No

    f. The use of any firearm with intent to endanger, directly or indirectly, the safety of one or more individual or to cause substantial damage to property?   ☐ Yes ☑ No

Form I-918

g. The use of any biological agent, chemical agent, or nuclear weapon or device, or explosive, or other weapon or dangerous device, with intent to endanger, directly or indirectly, the safety of one or more individuals or to cause substantial damage to property?   ☐ Yes ☑ No

h. Soliciting money or members or otherwise providing material support to a terrorist organization?   ☐ Yes ☑ No

6. Do you intend to engage in the United States in:

 a. Espionage?   ☐ Yes ☑ No

 b. Any unlawful activity, or any activity the purpose of which is in opposition to, or the control or overthrow of the government of the United States?   ☐ Yes ☑ No

 c. Solely, principally, or incidentally in any activity related to espionage or sabotage or to violate any law involving the export of goods, technology, or sensitive information?   ☐ Yes ☑ No

7. Have you ever been or do you continue to be a member of the Communist or other totalitarian party, except when membership was involuntary?   ☐ Yes ☑ No

8. Have you, during the period of March 23, 1933 to May 8, 1945, in association with either the Nazi Government of Germany or any organization or government associated or allied with the Nazi Government of Germany, ever ordered, incited, assisted or otherwise participated in the persecution of any person because of race, religion, nationality, membership in a particular social group or political opinion?   ☐ Yes ☑ No

9. Have you EVER ordered, committed, assisted, helped with, or otherwise participated in any act that involved:

 a. Torture or genocide?   ☐ Yes ☑ No

 b. Killing, beating, or injuring any person?   ☐ Yes ☑ No

 c. Displacing or moving any persons from their residence by force, threat of force, compulsion, or duress?   ☐ Yes ☑ No

 d. Engaging in any kind of sexual contact or relations with any person who was being subjected to force, threat of force, compulsion, or duress?   ☐ Yes ☑ No

 e. Limiting or denying any person's ability to exercise religious beliefs?   ☐ Yes ☑ No

 f. The persecution of any person because of race, religion, national origin, membership in a particular social group, or political opinion?   ☐ Yes ☑ No

 If you answer "Yes," please describe the circumstances on a separate sheet(s) of paper.

10. Have you EVER advocated that another person commit any of the acts described in the preceding question, urged, or encouraged another person, to commit such acts? (If you answer "Yes," describe the circumstances on a separate sheet(s) of paper.)   ☐ Yes ☑ No

Form I-918

11. Have you EVER been present or nearby when any person was:

    a. Intentionally killed, tortured, beaten, or injured? ☐ Yes ☑ No

    b. Displaced or moved from his or her residence by force, compulsion or duress? ☐ Yes ☑ No

    c. In any way compelled or forced to engage in any kind of sexual contact or relations? ☐ Yes ☑ No

    If you answer "Yes," please describe the circumstances on a separate sheet(s) of paper.

12. Have you (or has any member of your family) EVER served in, been a member of, or been involved in any way with:

    a. Any military unit, paramilitary unit, police unit, self-defense unit, vigilante unit, rebel group, guerrilla group, or insurgent organization? ☐ Yes ☑ No

    b. Any prison, jail, prison camp, detention camp, labor camp, or any other situation that involved guarding prisoners? ☐ Yes ☑ No

    c. Any group, unit, or organization of any kind in which you or other persons possessed, transported, or used any type of weapon? ☐ Yes ☑ No

    If you answer "Yes," please describe the circumstances on a separate sheet(s) of paper.

13. Have your EVER received any type of military, paramilitary or weapons training? (If you answer "Yes," please describe the circumstances on a separate sheet(s) of paper.) ☐ Yes ☑ No

14. a. Are removal, exclusion, rescission or deportation proceedings pending against you? ☐ Yes ☑ No

    b. Have removal, exclusion, rescission or deportation proceedings EVER been initiated against you? ☐ Yes ☑ No

    c. Have you EVER been removed, excluded or deported from the United States? ☐ Yes ☑ No

    d. Have you EVER been ordered to be removed, excluded or deported from the United States? ☐ Yes ☑ No

    e. Have you EVER been denied a visa or denied admission to the United States? *(If a visa was denied, explain why on a seperate sheet of paper.)* ☐ Yes ☑ No

    f. Have you EVER been granted voluntary departure by an immigration officer or an immigration judge and failed to depart within the allotted time? ☐ Yes ☑ No

15. Are you under a final order or civil penalty for violating section 274C (producing and/or using false documentation to unlawfully satisfy a requirement of the Immigration and Nationality Act)? ☐ Yes ☑ No

16. Have you ever, by fraud or willful misrepresentation of a material fact, sought to procure, or procured, a visa or other documentation, for entry into the United States or any immigration benefit? ☐ Yes ☑ No

17. Have you ever left the United States to avoid being drafted into the U.S. Armed Forces? ☐ Yes ☑ No

Form I-918

18. Have you ever been a J nonimmigrant exchange visitor who was subject to the two-year foreign residence requirement and not yet complied with that requirement or obtained a waiver of such?   ☐ Yes   ☑ No

19. Have you ever detained, retained, or withheld the custody of a child, having a lawful claim to United States citizenship, outside the United States from a United States citizen granted custody?   ☐ Yes   ☑ No

20. Do you plan to practice polygamy in the United States?   ☐ Yes   ☑ No

21. Have you entered the United States as a stowaway?   ☐ Yes   ☑ No

22. a.   Do you have a communicable disease of public health significance?   ☐ Yes   ☑ No

    b.   Do you have or have you had a physical or mental disorder and behavior (or a history of behavior that is likely to recur) associated with the disorder which has posed or may pose a threat to the property, safety, or welfare of yourself or others?   ☐ Yes   ☑ No

    c.   Are you now or have you been a drug abuser or drug addict?   ☐ Yes   ☑ No

1. ☑ Spouse

Family Name	Given Name	Middle Name
Doe	Jane	

Date of Birth *(mm/dd/yyyy)*	Country of Birth	Relationship	Current Location
01/07/1986	United Kingdom	Wife	United Kingdom

2. ☐ Children

Family Name	Given Name	Middle Name

Date of Birth *(mm/dd/yyyy)*	Country of Birth	Relationship	Current Location

Family Name	Given Name	Middle Name

Date of Birth *(mm/dd/yyyy)*	Country of Birth	Relationship	Current Location

(If more space is needed, attach additional sheet(s) of paper.)

Form I-918

Part 5.   Filing on behalf of family members.

I am now petitioning for one or more qualifying family member(s). *(If "Yes," complete and include Form I-918, Supplement A and Supplement B, for each family member for whom you are petitioning.)*   ☑ Yes   ☐ No

Part 6. Attestation, release and signature. *(Read information on penalties in the instructions before completing this part.)*

I certify, under penalty of perjury under the laws of the United States of America, that the information provided with this petition is all true and correct. I certify also that I have not withheld any information that would affect the outcome of this petition.

Signature

Date *(mm/dd/yyyy)*

NOTE: *If you do not completely fill out this form or fail to submit required documents listed in the instructions, you may not be found eligible for the benefit sought and this petition will be denied.*

Part 7. Signature of person preparing form, if other than above. *(Sign below.)*

I declare that I prepared this petition at the request of the above person, and it is based on all information of which I have knowledge. I have not knowingly withheld any material information that would affect the outcome of this petition.

Attorney or Representative: In the event of a Request for Evidence, may USCIS contact you by Fax or E-Mail? ☐ Yes ☐ No

Preparer's Signature

Date *(mm/dd/yyyy)*

Preparer's Printed Name

Preparer's Firm Name *(if applicable)*

Blank Attorney, P.A.

Preparer's Address

2655 LeJeune Road Suite 1001, Coral Gables FL 33134

Daytime Phone Number *(with area code)*

(123) 456-7890

Fax Number *(if any)*

E-Mail Address *(if any)*

Form I-918, Supplement A

OMB No. 1615-0104: Expires 08/31/2010

Department of Homeland Security

U.S. Citizenship and Immigration Services

I-918 Supplement A, Petition for Qualifying Family Member of U-1 Recipient

START HERE - Please type or print in black ink.	**For USCIS Use Only.**

(The recipient of the U-1 nonimmigrant classification is referred to as the "principal." His or her family member(s) is referred to as a "derivative." Form I-918, Supplement A is to be completed by the principal.)

Part 1.   Family member(s) relationship to you (the principal).

The family member that I am filing for is my:

[✓] Spouse   [ ] Child

[ ] Parent   [ ] Unmarried sibling under 18 years of age

Part 2.   Information about you.

Family Name	Given Name	Middle Name
DOE	John	

Date of Birth *(mm/dd/yyyy)*	A # *(if any)*
05/20/1986	None

Status of your Form I-918, Petition for U Nonimmigrant Status.

[ ] Pending   [ ] Approved

Part 3.   Information about your family member (the derivative).

Family Name	Given Name	Middle Name
Doe	Jane	

Other Names Used (Include maiden name/nickname)

None

Date of Birth *(mm/dd/yyyy)*	Country of Birth	Country of Citizenship
01/07/1986	United Kingdom	United Kingdom

Residence or Intended Residence in the U.S. - Street Number and Name   Apt. #

123 Main Drive

City	State/Province	Zip/Postal Code
Weston	FL	33484

Safe Mailing Address (if other than above) - Street Number and Name   Apt. #

C/O (*in care of*):

City	State/Province	Zip/Postal Code

A # *(if any)*	U.S. Social Security # *(if any)*	I-94 # *(if any)*
None	N/A	123456789 00

Home Phone # *(with area code)*	Safe Daytime Phone # *(with area code)*
(123) 456-7890	

Marital Status   Gender

[ ] Single   [✓] Married   [ ] Male

[ ] Divorced [ ] Widowed   [✓] Female

For USCIS Use Only.

Returned	Receipt
Date	
Date	
Resubmitted	
Date	
Date	
Date	
Reloc Sent	
Date	
Date	
Reloc Rec'd	
Date	
Date	

U.S. Embassy/Consulate:

Validity Dates

From: _____

To: _____

Remarks

Conditional Approval

Stamp #: _____   Date

Action Block

To Be Completed by
Attorney or Representative, if any.

[ ] Fill in box if G-28 is attached to represent the applicant.

ATTY State License #

Form I-918, Supplement A

Part 4. Additional information about your family member.

1. Give the following information about your family member if he or she is currently in the United States.

Place of Last Entry	Date of Last Entry	Current Immigration Status
Miami, Florida	07/20/2002	B-2

Passport #	Place of Issuance	Date of Issue *(mm/dd/yyyy)*
0502061	London	10/11/2008

2. Give the following information about your family member if he or she has previously traveled to the United States.

Place of Entry	Date of Entry *(mm/dd/yyyy)*	Date Authorized Stay Expired *(mm/dd/yyyy)*	Immigration Status
N/A			

3. If your relative was previously married, list names of prior spouses and dates of termination of marriage. Documents such as divorce decrees or death certificates must be attached.

Name of Former Spouse(s)	Date Mariage Ended *(mm/dd/yyyy)*	Where and How Marriage Ended
N/A		

4. If your relative is outside the United States give the U.S. consulate or inspection facility you want notified if this petition is approved.

Type of Office *(Check one):* ☐ Consulate ☐ Pre-flight inspection ☐ Port of Entry

Office Address *(City)*	U.S. State or Foreign Country

Foreign Address Where You Want Notification Sent.

5. Has your family member ever been in immigration proceedings? ☐ Yes ☑ No

If "Yes," what type of proceedings? *(Check all that apply.)*

☐ Removal Date *(mm/dd/yyyy)*	☐ Exclusion Date *(mm/dd/yyyy)*	☐ Deportation Date *(mm/dd/yyyy)*	☐ Recission Date *(mm/dd/yyyy)*	☐ Judicial Date *(mm/dd/yyyy)*

6. Is your family member requesting an Employment Authorization Document? (If "Yes," submit Form I-765, Application for Employment Authorization Document, separately.) ☑ Yes ☐ No

NOTE: *If your family member is living outside the United States, he or she is not eligible to receive employment authorization until he or she is lawfully admitted to the United States. Do not file an I-765 for a family member living outside the United States.*

7. List your family member's spouse and children. *(Attach additional sheet(s) of paper if necessary.)*

Full Name	Date of Birth *(mm/dd/yyyy)*	Country of Birth	Relationship
None			

Form I-918, Supplement A

Part 4. Additional information about your family member. *(Continued.)*

Please answer the following questions about your family member. For the purposes of this petition, you must answer "Yes" to the following questions, if applicable, even if the records were sealed or otherwise cleared or if anyone, including a judge, law enforcement officer, or attorney, told you that your family member no longer has a record. *(Answering "Yes" does not necessarily mean that your family member will be denied U nonimmigrant status.)*

8. Has the family member for whom you are filing **EVER**:

   a. Committed a crime or offense for which he or she has not been arrested? ☐ Yes ☑ No

   b. Been arrested, cited, or detained by any law enforcement officer (including DHS (former INS) and military officers) for any reason? ☐ Yes ☑ No

   c. Been charged with committing any crime or offense? ☐ Yes ☑ No

   d. Been convicted of a crime or offense (even if violation was subsequently expunged or pardoned)? ☐ Yes ☑ No

   e. Been placed in an alternative sentencing or a rehabilitative program (for example: diversion, deferred prosecution, withheld adjudication, deferred adjudication)? ☐ Yes ☑ No

   f. Received a suspended sentence, been placed on probation, or been paroled? ☐ Yes ☑ No

   g. Been in jail or prison? ☐ Yes ☑ No

   h. Been the beneficiary of a pardon, amnesty, rehabilitation, or other act of clemency or similar action? ☐ Yes ☑ No

   i. Exercised diplomatic immunity to avoid prosecution for a criminal offense in the United States? ☐ Yes ☑ No

If the answer is "Yes" to any of the above questions, complete the following table. If you need more space, use a separate sheet(s) of paper.

Why was the family member for whom you are filing arrested, cited, detained or charged?	Date of arrest, citation, detention, charge. *(mm/dd/yyyy)*	Where was the family member for whom you are filing arrested, cited, detained or charged? *(City, State, Country)*	Outcome or disposition. *(e.g., no charges filed, charges dismissed, jail, probation, etc.)*

9. Has the family member for whom you are filing ever received public assistance in the United States from any source, including the U.S. government or any State, county, city or other municipality (other than emergency medical treatment), or is he or she likely to receive public assistance in the future? ☐ Yes ☑ No

Form I-918, Supplement A

10. Has the family member for whom you are filing:

a. Engaged in prostitution or procurement of prostitution or does he or she intend to engage in prostitution or procurement of prostitution? ☐ Yes ☑ No

b. Ever engaged in any unlawful commercialized vice, including, but not limited to illegal gambling? ☐ Yes ☑ No

c. Ever knowingly encouraged, induced, assisted, abetted or aided any alien to try to enter the United States illegally? ☐ Yes ☑ No

d. Ever illicitly trafficked in any controlled substance, or knowingly assisted, abetted or colluded in the illicit trafficking of any controlled substance? ☐ Yes ☑ No

11. Has the family member for whom you are filing ever committed, planned or prepared, participated in, threatened to, attempted to, or conspired to commit, gathered information for, solicited funds for any of the following:

a. Highjacking or sabotage of any conveyance (including an aircraft, vessel, or vehicle? ☐ Yes ☑ No

b. Seizing or detaining, and threatening to kill, injure, or continue to detain, another individual in order to compel a third person (including a governmental organization) to do or abstain from doing any act as an explicit or implicit condition for the release of the individual seized or detained? ☐ Yes ☑ No

c. Assassination? ☐ Yes ☑ No

d. The use of any firearm with intent to endanger, directly or indirectly, the safety of one or more individual or to cause substantial damage to property? ☐ Yes ☑ No

e. The use of any biological agent, chemical agent, or nuclear weapon or device, or explosive, or other weapon or dangerous device, with intent to endanger, directly or indirectly, the safety of one or more individuals or to cause substantial damage to property? ☐ Yes ☑ No

12. Has the family member for whom you are filing ever been a member of, solicited money or members for, provided support for, attended military training (as defined in section 2339D(c)(1) of title 18, United States Code) by or on behalf of, or been associated with an organization that is:

a. Designated as a terrorist organization under section 219 of the Immigration and Nationality Act? ☐ Yes ☑ No

b. Any other group of two or more individuals, whether organized or not, which has engaged in or has a subgroup which has engaged in: ☐ Yes ☑ No

1. Highjacking or sabotage of any conveyance (including an aircraft, vessel, or vehicle? ☐ Yes ☑ No

2. Seizing or detaining, and threatening to kill, injure, or continue to detain, another individual in order to compel a third person (including a governmental organization) to do or abstain from doing any act as an explicit or implicit condition for the release of the individual seized or detained? ☐ Yes ☑ No

3. Assassination? ☐ Yes ☑ No

Form I-918, Supplement A

4. The use of any firearm with intent to endanger, directly or indirectly, the safety of one or more individual or to cause substantial damage to property?   ☐ Yes   ☑ No

5. The use of any biological agent, chemical agent, or nuclear weapon or device, or explosive, or other weapon or dangerous device, with intent to endanger, directly or indirectly, the safety of one or more individuals or to cause substantial damage to property?   ☐ Yes   ☑ No

6. Soliciting money or members or otherwise providing material support to a terrorist organization?   ☐ Yes   ☑ No

13. Does the family member for whom you are filing intend to engage in the United States in:

   a. Espionage?   ☐ Yes   ☑ No

   b. Any unlawful activity, or any activity the purpose of which is in opposition to, or the control or overthrow of the government of the United States?   ☐ Yes   ☑ No

   c. Solely, principally, or incidentally in any activity related to espionage or sabotage or to violate any law involving the export of goods, technology, or sensitive information?   ☐ Yes   ☑ No

14. Has the family member for whom you are filing ever been or does her or she continue to be a member of the Communist or other totalitarian party, except when membership was involuntary?   ☐ Yes   ☑ No

15. Has the family member for whom you are filing, during the period of March 23, 1933 to May 8, 1945, in association with either the Nazi Government of Germany or any organization or government associated or allied with the Nazi Government of Germany, ever ordered, incited, assisted or otherwise participated in the persecution of any person because of race, religion, nationality, membership in a particular social group or political opinion?   ☐ Yes   ☑ No

16. Has the family member for whom you are filing EVER ordered, committed, assisted, helped with, or otherwise participated in any act that involved:

   a. Torture or genocide?   ☐ Yes   ☑ No

   b. Killing, beating, or injuring any person?   ☐ Yes   ☑ No

   c. Displacing or moving any persons from their residence by force, threat of force, compulsion, or duress?   ☐ Yes   ☑ No

   d. Engaging in any kind of sexual contact or relations with any person who was being subjected to force, threat of force, compulsion, or duress?   ☐ Yes   ☑ No

   e. Limiting or denying any person's ability to exercise religious beliefs?   ☐ Yes   ☑ No

   f. The persecution of any person because of race, religion, national origin, membership in a particular social group, or political opinion?   ☐ Yes   ☑ No

If the answer is "Yes," please describe the circumstances on a separate sheet(s) of paper.

Form I-918, Supplement A

17. Has the family member for whom you are filing EVER advocated that another person commit any of the acts described in the preceding question, urged, or encouraged another person, to commit such acts? (If the answer is "Yes," describe the circumstances on a separate sheet(s) of paper.) ☐ Yes ☑ No

18. Has the family member for whom you are filing EVER been present or nearby when any person was:

a. Intentionally killed, tortured, beaten, or injured? ☐ Yes ☑ No

b. Displaced or moved from his or her residence by force, compulsion or duress? ☐ Yes ☑ No

c. In any way compelled or forced to engage in any kind of sexual contact or relations? ☐ Yes ☑ No

If the answer is "Yes," please describe the circumstances on a separate sheet(s) of paper.

19. Has the family member for whom you are filing (or has any member of his or her family) EVER served in, been a member of, or been involved in any way with:

a. Any military unit, paramilitary unit, police unit, self-defense unit, vigilante unit, rebel group, guerrilla group, or insurgent organization? ☐ Yes ☑ No

b. Any prison, jail, prison camp, detention camp, labor camp, or any other situation that involved guarding prisoners? ☐ Yes ☑ No

c. Any group, unit, or organization of any kind in which you or other persons possessed, transported, or used any type of weapon? ☐ Yes ☑ No

If the answer is "Yes," please describe the circumstances on a separate sheet(s) of paper.

20. Has the family member for whom you are filing EVER received any type of military, paramilitary or weapons training? (If the answer ia "Yes," please describe the circumstances on a separate sheet(s) of paper.) ☐ Yes ☑ No

21. a. Are removal, exclusion, rescission or deportation proceedings pending against the family member for whom you are filing? ☐ Yes ☑ No

b. Have removal, exclusion, rescission or deportation proceedings EVER been initiated against the family member for whom you are filing? ☐ Yes ☑ No

c. Has the family member for whom you are filing EVER been removed, excluded or deported from the United States? ☐ Yes ☑ No

d. Has the family member for whom you are filing EVER been ordered to be removed, excluded or deported from the United States? ☐ Yes ☑ No

Form I-918, Supplement A

    e. Has the family member for whom you are filing **EVER** been denied a visa or denied admission to the United States? *(If a visa was denied, explain why on a seperate sheet of paper.)* ☐ Yes ☑ No

    f. Has the family member for whom you are filing **EVER** been granted voluntary departure by an immigration officer or an immigration judge and failed to depart within the allotted time? ☐ Yes ☑ No

22. Is the family member for whom you are filing under a final order or civil penalty for violating section 274C (producing and/or using false documentation to unlawfully satisfy a requirement of the Immigration and Nationality Act)? ☐ Yes ☑ No

23. Has the family member for whom you are filing ever, by fraud or willful misrepresentation of a material fact, sought to procure, or procured, a visa or other documentation, for entry into the United States or any immigration benefit? ☐ Yes ☑ No

24. Has the family member for whom you are filing ever left the United States to avoid being drafted into the U.S. Armed Forces? ☐ Yes ☑ No

25. Has the family member for whom you are filing ever been a J nonimmigrant exchange visitor who was subject to the two-year foreign residence requirement and not yet complied with that requirement or obtained a waiver of such? ☐ Yes ☑ No

26. Has the family member for whom you are filing ever detained, retained, or withheld the custody of a child, having a lawful claim to United States citizenship, outside the United States from a United States citizen granted custody? ☐ Yes ☑ No

27. Does the family member for whom you are filing plan to practice polygamy in the United States? ☐ Yes ☑ No

21. Have you entered the United States as a stowaway? ☐ Yes ☑ No

22. a. Do you have a communicable disease of public health significance? ☐ Yes ☑ No

    b. Do you have or have you had a physical or mental disorder and behavior (or a history of behavior that is likely to recur) associated with the disorder which has posed or may pose a threat to the property, safety, or welfare of yourself or others? ☐ Yes ☑ No

    c. Are you now or have you been a drug abuser or drug addict? ☐ Yes ☑ No

Form I-918, Supplement A

Part 5. Attestation, release and signature. *(Read information on penalties in the instructions before completing this part.)*

I certify, under penalty of perjury under the laws of the United States of America, that the information provided with this petition is all true and correct. I certify also that I have not withheld any information that would affect the outcome of this petition.

Signature of Principal *(you)*

Date *(mm/dd/yyyy)*

Please Note: Your qualifying family member for whom you are filing must sign if he or she is present in the United States.

Signature of Qualifying Family Member if in the United States

Date *(mm/dd/yyyy)*

WARNING: Petitioners who are in the United States illegally are subject to removal if their claims are not granted. Any information provided while completing this supplementary petition may be used as a basis for the institution of, or as evidence in, removal proceedings even if the petition is withdrawn.

Part 6. Signature of person preparing form, if other than above. *(Sign below.)*

I declare that I prepared this petition at the request of the above person, and it is based on all information of which I have knowledge. I have not knowingly withheld any material information that would affect the outcome of this petition.

Attorney or Representative: In the event of a Request for Evidence, may USCIS contact you by Fax or E-Mail? ☑ Yes ☐ No

Preparer's Signature

Date *(mm/dd/yyyy)*

Preparer's Printed Name

Preparer's Firm Name *(if applicable)*

Blank Attorney, P.A.

Preparer's Address

2655 LeJeune Road Suite 1001 Coral Gables FL 33134

Daytime Phone Number *(with area code)*

(123) 456-7890

Fax Number *(if any)*

E-Mail Address *(if any)*

Form I-918, Supplement B

OMB No. 1615-0104: Expires 08/31/2010

Department of Homeland Security

U.S. Citizenship and Immigration Services

I-918 Supplement B,
U Nonimmigrant Status Certification

START HERE - Please type or print in black ink.

	For USCIS Use Only.

Part 1.   Victim information.

	Returned	Receipt

Family Name

Doe

Given Name

John

Middle Name

Date	

Other Names Used *(Include maiden name/nickname)*

None

| Date | |
| Resubmitted | |

Date of Birth *(mm/dd/yyyy)*

05/20/1986

Gender

☑ Male   ☐ Female

Date	
Date	
Reloc Sent	

Part 2.   Agency information.

Name of Certifying Agency

Date	

Name of Certifying Official   Title and Division/Office of Certifying Official

| Date | |
| Reloc Rec'd | |

Name of Head of Certifying Agency

Date	

Agency Address - Street Number and Name   Suite #

Date	
Remarks	

City   State/Province   Zip/Postal Code

Daytime Phone # *(with area code and/or extension)*   Fax # *(with area code)*

Agency Type

☐ Federal   ☑ State   ☐ Local

Case Status

☑ On-going   ☐ Completed   ☐ Other

Certifying Agency Category

☐ Judge ☑ Law Enforcement ☐ Prosecutor ☐ Other

Case Number

02020202

FBI # or SID # *(if applicable)*

N/A

Part 3. Criminal acts.

1. The applicant is a victim of criminal activity involving or similar to violations of one of the following Federal, State or local criminal offenses. *(Check all that apply.)*

☐ Abduction	☐ Female Genital Mutilation	☐ Obstruction of Justice	☐ Slave Trade
☐ Abusive Sexual Contact	☐ Hostage	☐ Peonage	☐ Torture
☐ Blackmail	☐ Incest	☐ Perjury	☐ Trafficking
☐ Domestic Violence	☑ Involuntary Servitude	☐ Prostitution	☐ Unlawful Criminal Restraint
☐ Extortion	☐ Kidnapping	☐ Rape	☐ Witness Tampering
☐ False Imprisonment	☐ Manslaughter	☐ Sexual Assault	☐ Related Crime(s)
☐ Felonious Assault	☐ Murder	☐ Sexual Exploitation	☐ Other: *(If more space needed, attach seperate sheet of paper.)*
☐ Attempt to commit any of the named crimes	☑ Conspiracy to commit any of the named crimes	☐ Solicitation to commit any of the named crimes	

Form I-918, Supplement B

Part 3. Criminal acts.   *(Continued.)*

2. Provide the date(s) on which the criminal activity occurred.

Date *(mm/dd/yyyy)*   Date *(mm/dd/yyyy)*   Date *(mm/dd/yyyy)*   Date *(mm/dd/yyyy)*

[DATE]

3. List the statutory citation(s) for the criminal activity being investigated or prosecuted, or that was investigated or prosecuted.

4. Did the criminal activity occur in the United States, including Indian country and military installations, or the territories or possessions of the United States?   ☑ Yes   ☐ No

   a. Did the criminal activity violate a Federal extraterritorial jurisdiction statute?   ☐ Yes   ☑ No

   b. If "Yes," provide the statutory citation providing the authority for extraterritorial jurisdiction.

   c. Where did the criminal activity occur?

5. Briefly describe the criminal activity being investigated and/or prosecuted and the involvement of the individual named in Part 1. Attach copies of all relevant reports and findings.

   [DESCRIBE]

6. Provide a description of any known or documented injury to the victim. Attach copies of all relevant reports and findings.

   [DESCRIBE]

Part 4. Helpfulness of the victim.

The victim (or parent, guardian or next friend, if the victim is under the age of 16, incompetent or incapacitated.):

1. Possesses information concerning the criminal activity listed in **Part 3**.   ☑ Yes   ☐ No

2. Has been, is being or is likely to be helpful in the investigation and/or prosecution of the criminal activity detailed above. *(Attach an explanation briefly detailing the assistance the victim has provided.)*   ☑ Yes   ☐ No

3. Has not been requested to provide further assistance in the investigation and/or prosecution. *(Example: prosecution is barred by the statute of limitation.) (Attach an explanation.)*   ☑ Yes   ☐ No

4. Has unreasonably refused to provide assistance in a criminal investigation and/or prosecution of the crime detailed above. *(Attach an explanation.)*   ☐ Yes   ☑ No

Form I-918, Supplement B

Part 4. Helpfulness of the victim.   *(Continued.)*

5. Other, please specify.

[DESCRIBE]

Part 5. Family members implicated in criminal activity.

1. Are any of the victim's family members believed to have been involved in the criminal activity of which he or she is a victim?   ☐ Yes   ☑ No

2. If "Yes," list relative(s) and criminal involvement. *(Attach extra reports or extra sheet(s) of paper if necessary.)*

Full Name	Relationship	Involvement
Jane Doe	Wife	None

Part 6. Certification.

I am the head of the agency listed in **Part 2** or I am the person in the agency who has been specifically designated by the head of the agency to issue U nonimmigrant status certification on behalf of the agency. Based upon investigation of the facts, I certify, under penalty of perjury, that the individual noted in **Part 1** is or has been a victim of one or more of the crimes listed in **Part 3**. I certify that the above information is true and correct to the best of my knowledge, and that I have made, and will make no promises regarding the above victim's ability to obtain a visa from the U.S. Citizenship and Immigration Services, based upon this certification. I further certify that if the victim unreasonably refuses to assist in the investigation or prosecution of the qualifying criminal activity of which he/she is a victim, I will notify USCIS.

Signature of Certifying Official Identified in Part 2.

Date *(mm/dd/yyyy)*

Form I-929

OMB No. 1615-0106; Expires 06/30/10

Form I-929, Petition for Qualifying Family Member of a U-1 Nonimmigrant

Department of Homeland Security
U.S. Citizenship and Immigration Services

DO NOT WRITE IN THIS BLOCK— FOR USCIS USE ONLY

		Action Block	Bar Code (USCIS Use only)
Bene. A-file reviewed	☐ Yes ☐ No		
U-1 A-file reviewed	☐ Yes ☐ No		
Bene. filed I-485	☐ Yes ☐ No		Remarks
U-1 adjusted	☐ Yes ☐ No		
U-1 I-485 pending	☐ Yes ☐ No		

START HERE – TYPE OR PRINT LEGIBLY USING BLACK INK

I am filing for my: (Check one)

☑ Spouse   Child: ☐ Biological Child   Parent: ☐ Biological Parent
                         ☐ Stepchild   ☐ Stepparent
                         ☐ Adopted Child   ☐ Parent who adopted me

Part 1. Information About You	Part 2. Information About Your Alien Relative
Last Name (Family Name)	**Last Name (Family Name)**
Doe	Doe
First Name (Given Name)	**First Name (Given Name)**
John	Jane
Middle Name	**Middle Name**

Current Address

Street Number and Name	Apt. Number	Street Number and Name	Apt. Number
123 Main Drive		123 Main Drive	

City	State	Zip Code	City	State/Province
Weston	FL	33484	Weston	Florida

			Country	Postal/Zip Code
			USA	33484

Safe Mailing Address If Other Than Above   **Mailing Address If Other Than Above**

Street Number and Name	Apt. Number

City	State	Zip Code

Date of Birth	A-Number	Date of Birth	A-Number
05/20/1986	None	01/07/1986	None

Form I-929 (Rev. 07/15/09) Y

Form I-929

Part 1. Information About You (Cont'd)

Country of Birth	Social Security Number
United Kingdom	N/A

Country of Citizenship/Nationality

United Kingdom

Gender: (Check one)   ☑ Male   ☐ Female

If you ever used other names, provide them below:

Last Name (Family Name)	First Name (Given Name)
N/A	

Middle Name

Last Name (Family Name)	First Name (Given Name)

Middle Name

Last Name (Family Name)	First Name (Given Name)

Middle Name

Marital Status: (Check one)
☐ Single (Never Married)   ☑ Married
☐ Divorced   ☐ Widowed

Spouse's Name:

Last Name (Family Name)	First Name (Given Name)
Doe	Jane

Middle Name ·

Place of Marriage

United Kingdom

Part 2. Information About Your Alien Relative (Cont'd)

Country of Birth	Social Security Number
United Kingdom	N/A

Country of Citizenship/Nationality

United Kingdom

Gender: (Check one)   ☐ Male   ☑ Female

If alien relative ever used other names, provide them below:

Last Name (Family Name)	First Name (Given Name)
N/A	

Middle Name

Last Name (Family Name)	First Name (Given Name)

Middle Name

Last Name (Family Name)	First Name (Given Name)

Middle Name

Marital Status: (Check one)
☐ Single (Never Married)   ☑ Married
☐ Divorced   ☐ Widowed

Spouse's Name:

Last Name (Family Name)	First Name (Given Name)
Doe	John

Middle Name

Place of Marriage

United Kingdom

Form I-929

Part 1. Information About You (Cont'd)

Number of marriages including current marriage: | 01

List any previous marriage(s) beginning with the most recent. If you need more space, attach an additional sheet of paper.

Prior Spouse's Name:

Last Name (Family Name)	First Name (Given Name)
N/A	

Middle Name	Date of Marriage

Place of Marriage

Date of Termination	Place of Termination

Reason for Termination:

☐ Divorce   ☐ Death   ☐ Annulment

☐ Other _____

Prior Spouse's Name:

Last Name (Family Name)	First Name (Given Name)

Middle Name	Date of Marriage

Place of Marriage

Date of Termination	Place of Termination

Reason for Termination:

☐ Divorce   ☐ Death   ☐ Annulment

☐ Other _____

Part 2. Information About Your Alien Relative (Cont'd)

Number of marriages including current marriage: | 01

List any previous marriage(s) beginning with the most recent. If you need more space, attach an additional sheet of paper.

Prior Spouse's Name:

Last Name (Family Name)	First Name (Given Name)
N/A	

Middle Name	Date of Marriage

Place of Marriage

Date of Termination	Place of Termination

Reason for Termination:

☐ Divorce   ☐ Death   ☐ Annulment

☐ Other _____

Prior Spouse's Name:

Last Name (Family Name)	First Name (Given Name)

Middle Name	Date of Marriage

Place of Marriage

Date of Termination	Place of Termination

Reason for Termination:

☐ Divorce   ☐ Death   ☐ Annulment

☐ Other _____

Form I-929

Part 1. Information About You (Cont'd)

Prior Spouse's Name:

Last Name (Family Name)	First Name (Given Name)

Middle Name	Date of Marriage

Place of Marriage

Date of Termination	Place of Termination

Reason for Termination:

☐ Divorce   ☐ Death   ☐ Annulment

☐ Other _____

(Check One):

☐ I am a Lawful Permanent Resident

I obtained my Lawful
Permanent Residence on: _____

☐ My Form I-485 is currently pending

Receipt Number

Part 2. Information About Your Alien Relative (Cont'd)

Prior Spouse's Name:

Last Name (Family Name)	First Name (Given Name)

Middle Name	Date of Marriage

Place of Marriage

Date of Termination	Place of Termination

Reason for Termination:

☐ Divorce   ☐ Death   ☐ Annulment

☐ Other _____

Complete if your relative is in the United States

Date of Admission	Place of Admission
07/20/2002	Miami, Florida

Class of Admission	Date Authorized to Stay
B-2	

Part 3. Information About Your Alien Relative's Children

Last Name (Family Name)	First Name (Given Name)	Middle Name
None		

Date of Birth	Place of Birth	

☐ Biological Child   ☐ Stepchild   ☐ Adopted Child

Gender: (Check one)   ☐ Male   ☐ Female

Street Number and Name	Apt. Number	City	State/Province

Country	Postal/Zip Code	A-Number	Country of Birth

Name of Mother

Last Name (Family Name)	First Name (Given Name)	Middle Name

Name of Father

Last Name (Family Name)	First Name (Given Name)	Middle Name

Form I-929

Part 3. Information About Your Alien Relative's Children (Cont'd)

Last Name (Family Name)	First Name (Given Name)	Middle Name

Date of Birth   Place of Birth   ☐ Biological Child ☐ Stepchild ☐ Adopted Child

Gender: (Check one) ☐ Male ☐ Female

Street Number and Name	Apt. Number	City	State/Province

Country	Postal/Zip Code	A-Number	Country of Birth

Name of Mother

Last Name (Family Name)	First Name (Given Name)	Middle Name

Name of Father

Last Name (Family Name)	First Name (Given Name)	Middle Name

Last Name (Family Name)	First Name (Given Name)	Middle Name

Date of Birth   Place of Birth   ☐ Biological Child ☐ Stepchild ☐ Adopted Child

Gender: (Check one) ☐ Male ☐ Female

Street Number and Name	Apt. Number	City	State/Province

Country	Postal/Zip Code	A-Number	Country of Birth

Name of Mother

Last Name (Family Name)	First Name (Given Name)	Middle Name

Name of Father

Last Name (Family Name)	First Name (Given Name)	Middle Name

Last Name (Family Name)	First Name (Given Name)	Middle Name

Date of Birth   Place of Birth   ☐ Biological Child ☐ Stepchild ☐ Adopted Child

Gender: (Check one) ☐ Male ☐ Female

Form I-929

Part 3. Information About Your Alien Relative's Children (Cont'd)

Street Number and Name	Apt. Number	City	State/Province

Country	Postal/Zip Code	A-Number	Country of Birth

Name of Mother

Last Name (Family Name)	First Name (Given Name)	Middle Name

Name of Father

Last Name (Family Name)	First Name (Given Name)	Middle Name

Last Name (Family Name)	First Name (Given Name)	Middle Name

Date of Birth	Place of Birth	☐ Biological Child ☐ Stepchild ☐ Adopted Child
		Gender: (Check one) ☐ Male ☐ Female

Street Number and Name	Apt. Number	City	State/Province

Country	Postal/Zip Code	A-Number	Country of Birth

Name of Mother

Last Name (Family Name)	First Name (Given Name)	Middle Name

Name of Father

Last Name (Family Name)	First Name (Given Name)	Middle Name

Name and address of your alien relative in the language written in the country where he/she currently resides.

Last Name (Family Name)	First Name (Given Name)	Middle Name

C/O: (In Care Of)	Street Number and Name	Apt. Number

City/State or Province	Country	Postal/Zip Code

Form I-929

Part 4. Processing Information

1. Check one:

a. ☑ The person named in **Part 2** is now in the United States

b. ☐ The person named in **Part 2** is now outside the United States. (Indicate below at which U.S. Embassy or consulate your relative will apply for a visa.)

U.S. Embassy or consulate at: _____

City and Country

2. Is the person named in **Part 2** or has this person ever been in deportation or removal proceedings in the United States?

a. ☑ No

b. ☐ Yes (Indicate when and where): _____

Part 6. Signature

I certify, or if outside the United States, I swear or affirm, under penalty of perjury under the laws of the United States of America, that this petition and the evidence submitted with it, is all true and correct. I authorize the release of any information from my record that U.S. Citizenship and Immigration Services needs to determine eligibility for the benefit I am seeking.

Signature	Print Your Full Name	Date
	John Doe	

Part 7. Preparer's Information, If Other Than Person Signing Above

I declare that I prepared this petition at the request of the above person, and it is based on all the information that I have knowledge.

Signature	Print Your Full Name	Date
	Attorney	

Firm Name	Street Number and Name	Suite Number
Blank Attorney, P.A.	2655 Le Jeune Road	Suite 1001

City/State or Province	Postal/Zip Code	Telephone Number
Coral Gables /FL	33134	954-777-8855

Form I-192

OMB No. 1615-0017; Expires 11/30/09

**I-192, Application for Advance
Permission to Enter as Nonimmigrant**
[Pursuant to Section 212(d)(3)(A)(ii) of the INA]

Department of Homeland Security
U.S. Citizenship and Immigration Services

(Read instructions to the form.)
Type or Print in Black Ink

Fee Stamp

File No. A- None

I hereby apply to the Secretary of Homeland Security for permission to enter the United States temporarily under the provisions of section 212(d)(3)(A)(ii) of the Immigration and Nationality Act (INA).

1. Full Name	2. Date of Birth (mm/dd/yyyy)
John Doe	05/20/1986

3. Place of Birth (City-Town, State/Province, Country)	4. Present Citizenship/Nationality
London, England, United Kingdom	United Kingdom

5. Present Address, Telephone Number, and E-Mail address
123 Main Street Weston, Florida, 33484

6. All addresses at which I have resided during the past five years (Use a separate sheet of paper, if necessary.)

7. Desired Port of Entry into the United States	8. Means of Transportation
Miami, Florida	Airplane

9. Proposed Date of Entry	10. Approximate Length of Stay in the United States
	[UNDER TERMS OF VISA]

11. My purpose for entering the United States is: (Explain fully)

[DESCRIBE]

12. I believe that I may be inadmissible to the United States for the following reason(s) and no others:

[DESCRIBE]

13. I ☐ have ☑ have not previously filed an application for advance permission to enter as a nonimmigrant

on _____ , _____ , at _____ .

If you are an applicant for T and U nonimmigrant status, you do not need to answer questions 14 through 17.

14. Have you ever been in the United States for a period of six months or more? If yes, when, for how long, and in what immigration status?

N/A

Form I-192 (Rev. 03/23/09)Y

Form I-192

15. Have you ever filed an application or petition for immigration benefits with the U.S. Government, or has one ever been filed on your behalf? If yes, list the applications and/or petitions, the filing locations, and describe the outcome of each application/petition (for example: denied, approved, pending).

N/A

16. Have you ever been denied or refused an immigration benefit by the U.S. Government, or had a benefit revoked or terminated (including but not limited to visas)? Describe in detail.

N/A

17. Have you ever, in or outside the United States, been arrested, cited, charged, indicted, fined, or imprisoned for breaking or violating any law or ordinance, excluding minor traffic violations? Describe in detail. Include all offenses where impaired driving may have been an issue.

N/A

18. Applicant's Signature and Certification

I understand that the information herein contained may be used in any proceedings (including civil, criminal, immigration, or any other judicial proceeding) hereafter instituted against me.

I certify that the statements above and all attachments hereto are true and correct to the best of my knowledge and belief.

_____   _____
(Signature of Applicant)   (Date)

Signature of the Applicant/Signature of Guardian or Family Member (if Applicant is unable to sign)

19. Preparer's Signature and Certification

I declare that this document was prepared by me at the request of the applicant or qualified relative/legal guardian of the applicant, and it is based on all information of which I have knowledge and/or was provided to me by the above named person in response to the exact questions contained on this form. I have not knowingly withheld any information.

_____   (Address)   (Date)
(Signature)

RECEIVED	TRANS. IN	RET'D TRANS. OUT	COMPLETED

Form I-485

OMB No. 1615-0023; Expires 11/30/2011

Department of Homeland Security
U.S. Citizenship and Immigration Services

**I-485, Application to Register
Permanent Residence or Adjust Status**

START HERE - Type or print in black ink.

Part 1.   Information About You

	For USCIS Use Only	
Returned		Receipt

Family Name DOE	Given Name John	Middle Name

Address- C/O
Blank Attorney, P.A.

Street Number and Name 222 SW 27th Drive	Apt. #

City

Weston

State Florida	Zip Code 33751

Date of Birth *(mm/dd/yyyy)* 05/20/1986	Country of Birth: United Kingdom
	Country of Citizenship/Nationality: United Kingdom

U.S. Social Security # N/A	A # *(if any)* None

Date of Last Arrival *(mm/dd/yyyy)* 07/20/2002	I-94 # 123456789 00

Current USCIS Status B2	Expires on *(mm/dd/yyyy)* 01/19/2003

For USCIS Use Only

Returned

Resubmitted

Reloc Sent

Reloc Rec'd

Applicant Interviewed

Receipt

Part 2.   Application Type   *(Check one)*

I am applying for an adjustment to permanent resident status because:

a. ☒ An immigrant petition giving me an immediately available immigrant visa number that has been approved. (Attach a copy of the approval notice, or a relative, special immigrant juvenile, or special immigrant military visa petition filed with this application that will give you an immediately available visa number, if approved.)

b. ☐ My spouse or parent applied for adjustment of status or was granted lawful permanent residence in an immigrant visa category that allows derivative status for spouses and children.

c. ☐ I entered as a K-1 fiancé(e) of a U.S. citizen whom I married within 90 days of entry, or I am the K-2 child of such a fiancé(e). (Attach a copy of the fiancé(e) petition approval notice and the marriage certificate).

d. ☐ I was granted asylum or derivative asylum status as the spouse or child of a person granted asylum and am eligible for adjustment.

e. ☐ I am a native or citizen of Cuba admitted or paroled into the United States after January 1, 1959, and thereafter have been physically present in the United States for at least one year.

f. ☐ I am the husband, wife, or minor unmarried child of a Cuban described above in **(e)**, and I am residing with that person, and was admitted or paroled into the United States after January 1, 1959, and thereafter have been physically present in the United States for at least one year.

g. ☐ I have continuously resided in the United States since before January 1, 1972.

h. ☐ Other basis of eligibility. Explain (for example, I was admitted as a refugee, my status has not been terminated, and I have been physically present in the United States for one year after admission). If additional space is needed, use a separate piece of paper.

I am already a permanent resident and am applying to have the date I was granted permanent residence adjusted to the date I originally arrived in the United States as a nonimmigrant or parolee, or as of May 2, 1964, whichever date is later, and: *(Check one)*

i. ☐ I am a native or citizen of Cuba and meet the description in **(e)** above.

j. ☐ I am the husband, wife, or minor unmarried child of a Cuban and meet the description in **(f)** above.

Section of Law

☐ Sec. 209(b), INA
☐ Sec. 13, Act of 9/11/57
☐ Sec. 245, INA
☐ Sec. 249, INA
☐ Sec. 1 Act of 11/2/66
☐ Sec. 2 Act of 11/2/66
☐ Other

Country Chargeable

Eligibility Under Sec. 245

☐ Approved Visa Petition
☐ Dependent of Principal Alien
☐ Special Immigrant
☐ Other

Preference

Action Block

To be Completed by
Attorney or Representative, **if any**
☐ Fill in box if G-28 is attached to represent the applicant.

VOLAG #

ATTY State License #

Form I-485 (Rev. 12/16/08)Y

a. Birth certificate of the petitioner, certificate of U.S. citizenship, U.S. passport or photocopy of Permanent Resident Card (in cases where the LPR is the petitioner;

b. Marriage certificate between the petitioner and alien; divorce decrees, if any;

c. Marriage certificate between the parents of the petitioner and alien if the petition is for a brother/sister;

d. Birth certificate of alien with English translations;

e. One recent photograph of the alien (passport type);

f. One recent photograph of the petitioner (passport type);

B. Adjustment of Status

The adjustment of status to permanent residence is the second step in filing for a family member for cases of categories other than immediate relative, and for cases of immediate relative when the beneficiary is not in the United States. This step is performed when the priority date has been reached or concurrently with the petition process when the beneficiary is an immediate relative and is in the United States.

1. Forms Required:

   The forms required on behalf of the beneficiary are I-485, G-325A, I-765 (for work authorization), I-131 (for travel authorization) and G-28 on behalf of the beneficiary. The forms required on behalf of the petitioner are I-864 and G-28. (See below for requisites and evidence required with the submission of Form I-864.)

2. Documents Required:

   a. Passport of alien;

   b. Form I-94;

   c. Medical exam of the alien from a designated medical clinic/doctor;

   d. Eight recent photographs of the alien (passport type);

   e. Affidavit of support (Form I-864) including Form W-2, current form 1040 income tax returned and current employment letter.

      If there is an eligible spouse or child, submit a complete packet which includes all the forms and documents mentioned above for each applicant. The petition must also include the marriage certificate to include the spouse.

3. The Marriage Interview

   If the beneficiary is the spouse of the petitioner, s/he will be required to be interviewed by a USCIS officer to determine whether the marriage was not entered solely for the purposes of obtaining legal permanent residence.

   At the interview the couple should present evidence of the sharing of assets or responsibilities.

   Examples of Evidence of Viability of the Marriage:

   i.   Deeds of jointly owned real estate property and/or lease of residence property;

   ii. Automobile registration of jointly owned vehicles;

   iii. Receipts or contracts for purchases jointly owned;

   iv. Joint bank statements;

   v.   Contracts for services for the wedding;

   vi. Insurance contracts benefiting both or each party;

   vii. Photographs of vacations or events; and

   viii. Photocopies of jointly filed income tax returns;

   ix. Photographs of wedding or engagement party;

   x.   Airline tickets and/or hotel accommodation receipts of vacations taken together.

C. Consular Processing

The consular processing for an immigrant visa is the second step in filing for a family member for cases of the preference categories and immediate relatives outside the United States. This step is performed when the priority date has been reached or immediately after the approval of the I-130 beneficiary if an immediate relative.

1. Forms Required:

   The forms required on behalf of the beneficiary are Forms DS-230 Part I and Part II. Once the petition has been approved or the priority date has been reached, the applicant will receive Forms DS-230 from the National Visa Center. The forms required on behalf of the petitioner are I-864 and G-28. (See below for requisites and evidence required with the submission of Form I-864.) Follow the instructions from the National Visa Center on when and where to submit Form I-864 with accompanying evidence.

2. Documents Required at the Consular Interview:

   a. Birth certificate of the petitioner, passport or certificate of citizenship or photocopy of Permanent Resident Card;

   b. Marriage certificate between the petitioner and alien; divorce decrees, if any;

   c. Marriage certificate between the parents of the petitioner and alien, if the petition is for a brother/sister;

   d. Birth certificate of alien;

   e. One recent photograph of the alien (passport type);

   f. Passport of alien;

   g. Form I-94;

   h. Medical exam of the alien from a designated medical clinic/doctor;

   i. Police clearance letter;

   j. Military history;

   i. Removal/Deporation information.

D. Preparing Forms I-864 and I-864(a)—Affidavit of Support

The purpose of the Affidavit of Support is to show that the intending immigrant has adequate means of financial support and is not likely to become a public charge.

1. Evidence of current employment or self-employment:

   a. Individual tax returns for the most recent year from the petitioner or joint sponsor;

   b. W-2 Forms;

   c. IRS Form 1099;

   d. Deed to properties; and

   e. Portfolio of stocks and other assets.

2. Evidence of assets of beneficiary

   Assets of the beneficiary may also be used as long as they have a cash value that equals at least five times the difference between the sponsor's total household income and the amount reflected in the poverty guideline for the household's size.

3. Co-Sponsor

   If the petitioner does not meet the requirements for sponsorship, the beneficiary may obtain a second co-sponsor. The co-sponsor must submit the same information as is required of a petitioner.

V. Conditional Residence

Individuals who have been married fewer than two years to the U.S. citizen or a LPR spouse at the time of the issuance of the residency will receive permanent residency status for two years only. The applicant must file Form I-751 to "remove the condition." If s/he is still married, the alien files jointly with the spouse. If s/he is divorced, the alien may file the form to remove the condition by him/herself. S/he must submit Form I-751 with proof that the relationship continued after the approval of the residency. INA § 216, 8 USC § 1186a., 8 C.F.R. § 235.11(b)

1. Forms Required:

   Forms I-751 and G-28, along with the above documents, must be submitted to the USCIS Service Center.

2. Documents Required:

   a. Photocopy of Alien Resident Card (Form I-551);

   b. Two recent photographs of the applicant;

   c. Deeds of jointly owned real estate property and/or lease of residential property;

   d. Automobile registration of jointly owned vehicles;

   e. Receipts or contracts for purchases jointly owned;

   f. Joint bank statements;

   g. Contracts for services for the wedding;

   h. Insurance contracts benefiting both or each party;

   i. Photographs of vacations or events; and

   j. Photocopies of jointly filed income tax returns;

   k. Photographs of wedding or engagement party;

   l. Airline tickets and/or hotel accommodation receipts of vacations taken together;

   m. Birth certificates of children.

VI. The K-1 Visa

This visa allows fiancées of U.S. citizens to enter the United States for the purposes of marrying the U.S. citizen and processing their legal permanent residence status. INA § 101(a)(15)(K)(i), 8 USC § 1101, 8 C.F.R. § 214.2(k)

A. Evidence Required

1. Forms Required:

   The Forms I-129F, G-325A for both petitioner and beneficiary and G-28 must be submitted to the USCIS Service Center.

2. Documents Required:

   a. A signed statement from both parties showing that they plan to marry within 90 days;

   b. Evidence of petitioner's U.S. citizenship;

   c. Proof of legal termination of all prior marriages;

   d. Once recent photograph (passport type) for each party;

   e. Copies of evidence showing that the parties have personally met within the last two years, such as:

      i. Photographs;

      ii. Airline tickets;

      iii. Stamps of entry/exit on passport of each; and

      iv. Telephone bills.

If the petitioner and the beneficiary have not met each other, provide a detailed explanation of evidence of the extreme hardship or customary, cultural or social practices prohibiting their meeting before the marriage such as:

a. Photographs of the engagement party; and

b. Contract for dowry.

B. Application for Residency

The couple must marry within 90 days of the applicant's entry into the United States. The applicant will then process his/her legal permanent residency through the adjustment of status process outlined previously.

VII. The K-3 Visa

This type of visa allows a spouse of a U.S. citizen to enter the United States. Once the spouse of the U.S. citizen has arrived in the United States, s/he can immediately file for a change of status to legal permanent residence. This visa is for those relatives whose process will take too long if they wait for the approval of an I-130 petition while they are outside of the United States. INA § 101(a)(15)(K)(ii), 8 USC 1101, 8 C.F.R. § 214.2.

A. Evidence Required

1. Forms Required:

   The forms for the petitioning process mentioned above must be filed with the USCIS Service Center. Once the I-130 receipt is received, Forms I-129F and G-28 must be submitted to the USCIS Service Center.

2. Documents Required:

   a. Proof of U.S. citizenship of petitioning U.S. citizen;

   b. Proof of termination of prior marriages;

   c. Marriage certificate and birth certificate of children; and

   d. Photocopy of receipt of I-130.

B. Application for Residency

The applicant will then process his/her legal permanent residency through the adjustment of status process outlined previously in this chapter.

VIII. The V Visa

This type of visa allows the beneficiary of an LPR, who has an approved petition but has not received a visa because of USCIS backlogs, to enter the United States. The spouse receives a V-1 visa and the minor child of the resident receives a V-2 visa. The petition must have been filed prior to December 21, 2000, and have been pending for at least three or more years. INA § 101(a)(15)(v), 8 USC § 1101.

A. Evidence Required

1. Forms Required:

   The forms for the petitioning process mentioned above must be filed with the USCIS Service Center. Once the I-130 has been pending for three years after December 21, 2000, submit Form I-539 with Supplement A to the USCIS Regional Service Center with jurisdiction.

2. Documents Required:

   a. Photocopy of LPR Card of petitioner;

   b. Marriage certificate, if the petition is for a spouse, or birth certificate, if for child;

   c. Photocopy of receipt of I-130 petition (Form I-797C) filed prior to December 21, 2000; and

   d. Form I-693 completed by a certified civil surgeon. The vaccination supplement should not be submitted;

   e. Photocopy of I-130 receipt.

B. Application for Residency

Once the priority date is reached, the applicant will then process his/her legal permanent residency through the adjustment of status process outlined above.

Appendix

1. Form I-130
2. Form G-28 for I-130 Petition
3. Cover Letter for Form I-131
4. Form I-131
5. Form G-28 for I-131 Application
6. Form I-485
7. Form G-28 for I-485 Application
8. Form I-765
9. Form G-28 for I-765 Application
10. Form I-864
11. Form G-325A

Form I-130

DO NOT WRITE IN THIS BLOCK - FOR USCIS OFFICE ONLY		
A#	Action Stamp	Fee Stamp

Section of Law/Visa Category
- [ ] 201(b) Spouse - IR-1/CR-1
- [ ] 201(b) Child - IR-2/CR-2
- [ ] 201(b) Parent - IR-5
- [ ] 203(a)(1) Unm. S or D - F1-1
- [ ] 203(a)(2)(A)Spouse - F2-1
- [ ] 203(a)(2)(A) Child - F2-2
- [ ] 203(a)(2)(B) Unm. S or D - F2-4
- [ ] 203(a)(3) Married S or D - F3-1
- [ ] 203(a)(4) Brother/Sister - F4-1

Petition was filed on: _____ (priority date)
- [ ] Personal Interview
- [ ] Pet. [ ] Ben. " A" File Reviewed
- [ ] Field Investigation
- [ ] 203(a)(2)(A) Resolved
- [ ] Previously Forwarded
- [ ] I-485 Filed Simultaneously
- [ ] 204(g) Resolved
- [ ] 203(g) Resolved

Remarks:

A. Relationship   You are the petitioner.   Your relative is the beneficiary.

1. I am filing this petition for my:
[ ] Husband/Wife [ ] Parent [ ] Brother/Sister [×] Child

2. Are you related by adoption?
[ ] Yes [×] No

3. Did you gain permanent residence through adoption?
[ ] Yes [×] No

B. Information about you

1. Name (Family name in CAPS)   (First)   (Middle)
DI   Elena

2. Address (Number and Street)   (Apt. No.)
222 SW 27th Drive

(Town or City)   (State/Country)   (Zip/Postal Code)
Weston   Florida USA   33134

3. Place of Birth (Town or City)   (State/Country)
London   United Kingdom

4. Date of Birth   **5. Gender**   **6. Marital Status**
09/01/1949
[ ] Male [×] Female
[ ] Married [ ] Single [ ] Widowed [ ] Divorced

7. Other Names Used (including maiden name)
None

8. Date and Place of Present Marriage (if married)
01/10/1999   London, United Kingdom

9. U.S. Social Security Number (If any)   **10. Alien Registration Number**
555-22-8888   None

11. Name(s) of Prior Husband(s)/Wive(s)   **12. Date(s) Marriage(s) Ended**

13. If you are a U.S. citizen, complete the following:
My citizenship was acquired through (check one):
- [ ] Birth in the U.S.
- [×] Naturalization. Give certificate number and date and place of issuance.
  8899456   2003-10-01   Miami, Florida
- [ ] Parents. Have you obtained a certificate of citizenship in your own name?
  - [ ] Yes. Give certificate number, date and place of issuance. [ ] No

14. If you are a lawful permanent resident alien, complete the following:
Date and place of admission for or adjustment to lawful permanent residence and class of admission.

14b. Did you gain permanent resident status through marriage to a U.S. citizen or lawful permanent resident?
[ ] Yes [×] No

C. Information about your relative

1. Name (Family name in CAPS)   (First)   (Middle)
DOE   John

2. Address (Number and Street)   (Apt. No.)
56 Mainstream Drive Apt. 25

(Town or City)   (State/Country)   (Zip/Postal Code)
London   United Kingdom

3. Place of Birth (Town or City)   (State/Country)
London   United Kingdom

4. Date of Birth   **5. Gender**   **6. Marital Status**
05/20/1986
[×] Male [ ] Female
[ ] Married [×] Single [ ] Widowed [ ] Divorced

7. Other Names Used (including maiden name)
None

8. Date and Place of Present Marriage (if married)
None

9. U.S. Social Security Number (If any)   **10. Alien Registration Number**
None   None

11. Name(s) of Prior Husband(s)/Wive(s)   **12. Date(s) Marriage(s) Ended**

13. Has your relative ever been in the U.S.?   [ ] Yes [ ] No

14. If your relative is currently in the U.S., complete the following:
He or she arrived as a:
(visitor, student, stowaway, without inspection, etc.) B2

Arrival/Departure Record (I-94)   Date arrived
| 1 | 2 | 3 | ■ | 4 | 5 | 6 | 7 | 8 | 9 | 0 | 0 | 07/20/2002

Date authorized stay expired, or will expire, as shown on Form I-94 or I-95   01/19/2003

15. Name and address of present employer (if any)
None

Date this employment began

16. Has your relative ever been under immigration proceedings?
[ ] No [ ] Yes Where _____ When _____
[ ] Removal [ ] Exclusion/Deportation [ ] Rescission [ ] Judicial Proceedings

INITIAL RECEIPT   RESUBMITTED   RELOCATED: Rec'd   Sent   COMPLETED: Appv'd   Denied   Ret'd

Form I-130 (Rev. 05/27/08)Y

Form I-130

C. Information about your alien relative (continued)

17. List husband/wife and all children of your relative.

(Name)	(Relationship)	(Date of Birth)	(Country of Birth)

18. Address in the United States where your relative intends to live.

(Street Address)	(Town or City)	(State)
222 SW 27th Drive	Weston	Florida

19. Your relative's address abroad. (Include street, city, province and country)   Phone Number (if any)

56 Mainstream Dr, London, United Kingdom

20. If your relative's native alphabet is other than Roman letters, write his or her name and foreign address in the native alphabet.

(Name)   Address (Include street, city, province and country):

None

21. If filing for your husband/wife, give last address at which you lived together. (Include street, city, province, if any, and country):

From: To:

22. Complete the information below if your relative is in the United States and will apply for adjustment of status.

Your relative is in the United States and will apply for adjustment of status to that of a lawful permanent resident at the USCIS office in:

If your relative is not eligible for adjustment of status, he or she will apply for a visa abroad at the American consular post in:

Miami Beach	Florida		
(City)	(State)	(City)	(Country

NOTE: Designation of a U.S. embassy or consulate outside the country of your relative's last residence does not guarantee acceptance for processing by that post. Acceptance is at the discretion of the designated embassy or consulate.

D. Other information

1. If separate petitions are also being submitted for other relatives, give names of each and relationship.

2. Have you ever before filed a petition for this or any other alien? ☐ Yes ☒ No

If "Yes," give name, place and date of filing and result.

WARNING: USCIS investigates claimed relationships and verifies the validity of documents. USCIS seeks criminal prosecutions when family relationships are falsified to obtain visas.

PENALTIES: By law, you may be imprisoned for not more than five years or fined $250,000, or both, for entering into a marriage contract for the purpose of evading any provision of the immigration laws. In addition, you may be fined up to $10,000 and imprisoned for up to five years, or both, for knowingly and willfully falsifying or concealing a material fact or using any false document in submitting this petition.

YOUR CERTIFICATION: I certify, under penalty of perjury under the laws of the United States of America, that the foregoing is true and correct. Furthermore, I authorize the release of any information from my records that U.S. Citizenship and Immigration Services needs to determine eligiblity for the benefit that I am seeking.

E. Signature of petitioner.

Date   Phone Number (954) 777-8855

F. Signature of person preparing this form, if other than the petitioner.

I declare that I prepared this document at the request of the person above and that it is based on all information of which I have any knowledge.

Print Name	Blank Attorney, P.A.	Signature		Date
Address	222 SW 27th Drive		G-28 ID or VOLAG Number, if any.	370

Form G-28 for I-130 Petition

OMB No. 1615-0105; Expires 04/30/2012

G-28, Notice of Entry of Appearance
as Attorney or Accredited Representative

Department of Homeland Security

Part 1. Notice of Appearance as Attorney or Accredited Representative

A. This appearance is in regard to immigration matters before:

[x] USCIS - List the form number(s): I-130   [ ] CBP - List the specific matter in which appearance is entered:

[ ] ICE - List the specific matter in which appearance is entered:

B. I hereby enter my appearance as attorney or accredited representative at the request of:

List Petitioner, Applicant, or Respondent. **NOTE:** Provide the mailing address of Petitioner, Applicant, or Respondent being represented, and **not** the address of the attorney or accredited representative, except when filed under VAWA.

Principal Petitioner, Applicant, or Respondent			A Number or Receipt Number, if any	[x] Petitioner
Name: Last	First	Middle		[ ] Applicant
DI	Elena		None	[ ] Respondent

Address: Street Number and Street Name   Apt. No.   City   State   Zip Code

Petitioner's Address

Pursuant to the Privacy Act of 1974 and DHS policy, I hereby consent to the disclosure to the named Attorney or Accredited Representative of any record pertaining to me that appears in any system of records of USCIS, USCBP, or USICE.

Signature of Petitioner, Applicant, or Respondent

Date
11/08/2009

Part 2. Information about Attorney or Accredited Representative *(Check applicable items(s) below)*

A. [x] I am an attorney and a member in good standing of the bar of the highest court(s) of the following State(s), possession(s), territory(ies), commonwealth(s), or the District of Columbia: State of _____   Supreme Court

I am not [x] or [ ] am subject to any order of any court or administrative agency disbarring, suspending, enjoining, restraining, or otherwise restricting me in the practice of law (If you are subject to any order(s), explain fully on reverse side).

B. [ ] I am an accredited representative of the following qualified non-profit religious, charitable, social service, or similar organization established in the United States, so recognized by the Department of Justice, Board of Immigration Appeals pursuant to 8 CFR 1292.2. Provide name of organization and expiration date of accreditation:

C. [ ] I am associated with _____.

The attorney or accredited representative of record previously filed Form G-28 in this case, and my appearance as an attorney or accredited representative is at his or her request (If you check this item, also complete item A or B above in **Part 2**, whichever is appropriate).

Part 3. Name and Signature of Attorney or Accredited Representative

I have read and understand the regulations and conditions contained in 8 CFR 103.2 and 292 governing appearances and representation before the Department of Homeland Security. I declare under penalty of perjury under the laws of the United States that the information I have provided on this form is true and correct.

Name of Attorney or Accredited Representative	Attorney Bar Number(s), if any
Attorney or Accredited Representative's Name	
Signature of Attorney or Accredited Representative	Date 11/08/2009

Complete Address of Attorney or Organization of Accredited Representative (Street Number and Street Name, Suite No., City, State, Zip Code)

Attorney or Accredited Representative's Address

Phone Number *(Include area code)*	Fax Number, if any *(Include area code)*	E-Mail Address, if any
(305) 442-1322	(305) 444-7578	Valid E-mail Address

Cover Letter for Form I-131

September 2, 2007

U.S. Citizenship and Immigration Services
Miami District Office
Miami, Florida 33138

Dear Sir or Madam:

I, John Doe, am in the process of Adjustment of Status to obtain the residency in the United States. It will be necessary for me to travel to attend family and personal matters on the following dates:

Destination	Purpose of Trip	From	To
England	Family	10/01/2003	11/02/2003
England	Pleasure	02/03/2004	03/07/2004
England	Family	09/01/2004	09/30/2004

I would appreciate your prompt attention to this matter.

Very truly yours,

_____

John Doe   TRAVELLTR (Sample)

Form I-131

Department of Homeland Security
U. S. Citizenship and Immigration Services

OMB No. 1615-0013; Expires 03/31/12

I-131, Application for Travel Document

DO NOT WRITE IN THIS BLOCK		FOR USCIS USE ONLY (except G-28 block below)
Document Issued ☐ Reentry Permit ☐ Refugee Travel Document ☐ Single Advance Parole ☐ Multiple Advance Parole Valid to: _____	**Action Block**	**Receipt**
If Reentry Permit or Refugee Travel Document, mail to: ☐ Address in Part 1 ☐ U.S. Embassy/consulate at: _____ ☐ Overseas DHS office at: _____		☐ Document Hand Delivered On _____ By _____
		To be completed by Attorney/Representative, if any. Attorney State License # _____ ☐ Check box if G-28 is attached.

Part 1. **Information About You** *(Type or print in black ink)*

1. A Number	2. Date of Birth *(mm/dd/yyyy)*	3. Class of Admission	4. Gender
None	1986-20-05	B2	☒Male ☐Female

5. Name *(Family name in capital letters)*	*(First)*	*(Middle)*
DOE	John	

6. Address *(Number and Street)*		Apt. Number
222 SW 27th Drive		

City	State or Province	Zip/Postal Code	Country
Weston	Florida	33751	USA

7. Country of Birth	8. Country of Citizenship	9. Social Security # *(if any)*
United Kingdom	United Kingdom	None

Part 2. **Application Type** *(Check one)*

a. ☐ I am a permanent resident or conditional resident of the United States, and I am applying for a reentry permit.

b. ☐ I now hold U.S. refugee or asylee status, and I am applying for a Refugee Travel Document.

c. ☐ I am a permanent resident as a direct result of refugee or asylee status, and I am applying for a Refugee Travel Document.

d. ☒ I am applying for an advance parole document to allow me to return to the United States after temporary foreign travel.

e. ☐ I am outside the United States, and I am applying for an Advance Parole Document.

f. ☐ I am applying for an Advance Parole Document for a person who is outside the United States. *If you checked box "f," provide the following information about that person:*

1. Name *(Family name in capital letters)*   *(First)*   *(Middle)*

2. Date of Birth *(mm/dd/yyyy)*   3. Country of Birth   4. Country of Citizenship

5. Address *(Number and Street)*   Apt. #   Daytime Telephone # *(area/country code)*

City   State or Province   Zip/Postal Code   Country

Form I-131 (Rev. 07/14/09)Y

Form I-131

Part 3. Processing Information

1. Date of Intended Departure *(mm/dd/yyyy)*	**2.** Expected Length of Trip
12/10/2004	Multiple trips

3. Are you, or any person included in this application, now in exclusion, deportation, removal, or rescission proceedings?   ☐ Yes ☒ No   *(Name of DHS office):* [   ]

If you are applying for an Advance Parole Document, skip to Part 7.

4. Have you ever before been issued a reentry permit or Refugee Travel Document?
☐ No ☐ Yes   *(If "Yes," give the following information for the last document issued to you):*

Date Issued *(mm/dd/yyyy)*: [   ]   Disposition *(attached, lost, etc.):* [   ]

5. Where do you want this travel document sent? *(Check one)*

a. ☐ To the U.S. address shown in **Part 1** on the first page of this form.

b. ☐ To a U.S. Embassy or consulate at: City: [   ]   Country: [   ]

c. ☐ To a DHS office overseas at: City: [   ]   Country: [   ]

d. If you checked "b" or "c," where should the notice to pick up the travel document be sent?

☐ To the address shown in **Part 2** on the first page of this form.

☐ To the address shown below:

Address *(Number and Street)*	Apt. #	Daytime Telephone # *(area/country code)*

City	State or Province	Zip/Postal Code	Country

Part 4. Information About Your Proposed Travel

Purpose of trip. *(If you need more room, continue on a separate sheet of paper.)*	List the countries you intend to visit.

Part 5. Complete Only If Applying for a Reentry Permit

Since becoming a permanent resident of the United States (or during the past five years, whichever is less) how much total time have you spent outside the United States?

☐ less than six months   ☐ two to three years
☐ six months to one year   ☐ three to four years
☐ one to two years   ☐ more than four years

Since you became a permanent resident of the United States, have you ever filed a Federal income tax return as a nonresident or failed to file a Federal income tax return because you considered yourself to be a nonresident? *(If "Yes," give details on a separate sheet of paper.)*   ☐ Yes   ☐ No

Part 6. Complete Only If Applying for a Refugee Travel Document

1. Country from which you are a refugee or asylee: [   ]

If you answer "Yes" to any of the following questions, you must explain on a separate sheet of paper.

2. Do you plan to travel to the country named above?   ☐ Yes   ☐ No

3. Since you were accorded refugee/asylee status, have you ever:
   a. Returned to the country named above?   ☐ Yes   ☐ No
   b. Applied for and/or obtained a national passport, passport renewal, or entry permit of that country?   ☐ Yes   ☐ No
   c. Applied for and/or received any benefit from such country (for example, health insurance benefits).   ☐ Yes   ☐ No

4. Since you were accorded refugee/asylee status, have you, by any legal procedure or voluntary act:
   a. Reacquired the nationality of the country named above?   ☐ Yes   ☐ No
   b. Acquired a new nationality?   ☐ Yes   ☐ No
   c. Been granted refugee or asylee status in any other country?   ☐ Yes   ☐ No

Form I-131

Part 7. Complete Only If Applying for Advance Parole

On a separate sheet of paper, explain how you qualify for an Advance Parole Document, and what circumstances warrant issuance of advance parole. Include copies of any documents you wish considered. *(See instructions.)*

1. How many trips do you intend to use this document? ☐ One Trip ☒ More than one trip

2. If the person intended to receive an Advance Parole Document is outside the United States, provide the location (city and country) of the U.S. Embassy or consulate or the DHS overseas office that you want us to notify.

City

Country

3. If the travel document will be delivered to an overseas office, where should the notice to pick up the document be sent?:

☐ To the address shown in **Part 2** on the first page of this form.

☐ To the address shown below:

Address *(Number and Street)*

Apt. #

Daytime Telephone # *(area/country code)*

City

State or Province

Zip/Postal Code

Country

Part 8. Signature

Read the information on penalties in the instructions before completing this section. If you are filing for a reentry permit or Refugee Travel Document, you must be in the United States to file this application.

I certify, under penalty of perjury under the laws of the United States of America, that this application and the evidence submitted with it are all true and correct. I authorize the release of any information from my records that U.S. Citizenship and Immigration Services needs to determine eligibility for the benefit I am seeking.

Signature

Date *(mm/dd/yyyy)*

Daytime Telephone Number *(with area code)*

(954) 777-8855

Note: If you do not completely fill out this form or fail to submit required documents listed in the instructions, you may not be found eligible for the requested document and this application may be denied.

Part 9. Signature of Person Preparing Form, If Other Than the Applicant *(Sign below)*

I declare that I prepared this application at the request of the applicant, and it is based on all information of which I have knowledge.

Signature

Print or Type Your Name

Blank Attorney, P.A.

Firm Name and Address

Blank Attorney, P.A.
2655 LeJeune Road Suite 1001
Coral Gables FL 33134

Daytime Telephone Number *(with area code)*

(954) 777-8855

Fax Number *(if any)*

(954) 777-8856

Date *(mm/dd/yyyy)*

Form G-28 for I-131 Application

OMB No. 1615-0105; Expires 04/30/2012

G-28, Notice of Entry of Appearance as Attorney or Accredited Representative

Department of Homeland Security

Part 1. Notice of Appearance as Attorney or Accredited Representative

A. This appearance is in regard to immigration matters before:

☒ USCIS - List the form number(s): I-131   ☐ CBP - List the specific matter in which appearance is entered:

☐ ICE - List the specific matter in which appearance is entered: _____

B. I hereby enter my appearance as attorney or accredited representative at the request of:

List Petitioner, Applicant, or Respondent. **NOTE:** Provide the mailing address of Petitioner, Applicant, or Respondent being represented, and **not** the address of the attorney or accredited representative, except when filed under VAWA.

Principal Petitioner, Applicant, or Respondent			A Number or Receipt Number, if any	☐ Petitioner
Name: Last	First	Middle		☒ Applicant
DOE	John		None	☐ Respondent

Address: Street Number and Street Name	Apt. No.	City	State	Zip Code
Applicant's Address				

Pursuant to the Privacy Act of 1974 and DHS policy, I hereby consent to the disclosure to the named Attorney or Accredited Representative of any record pertaining to me that appears in any system of records of USCIS, USCBP, or USICE.

Signature of Petitioner, Applicant, or Respondent   **Date** 11/08/2009

Part 2. Information about Attorney or Accredited Representative *(Check applicable items(s) below)*

A. ☒ I am an attorney and a member in good standing of the bar of the highest court(s) of the following State(s), possession(s), territory(ies), commonwealth(s), or the District of Columbia: State of _____ Supreme Court

I am not ☒ or ☐ **am subject to any order of any court or administrative agency disbarring, suspending, enjoining, restraining, or otherwise restricting me in the practice of law (If you are subject to any order(s), explain fully on reverse side).**

B. ☐ I am an accredited representative of the following qualified non-profit religious, charitable, social service, or similar organization established in the United States, so recognized by the Department of Justice, Board of Immigration Appeals pursuant to 8 CFR 1292.2. Provide name of organization and expiration date of accreditation:

C. ☐ I am associated with _____ .

The attorney or accredited representative of record previously filed Form G-28 in this case, and my appearance as an attorney or accredited representative is at his or her request *(If you check this item, also complete item A or B above in **Part 2**, whichever is appropriate).*

Part 3. Name and Signature of Attorney or Accredited Representative

I have read and understand the regulations and conditions contained in 8 CFR 103.2 and 292 governing appearances and representation before the Department of Homeland Security. I declare under penalty of perjury under the laws of the United States that the information I have provided on this form is true and correct.

Name of Attorney or Accredited Representative	Attorney Bar Number(s), if any
Attorney or Accredited Representative's Name	
Signature of Attorney or Accredited Representative	Date 11/08/2009

Complete Address of Attorney or Organization of Accredited Representative (Street Number and Street Name, Suite No., City, State, Zip Code)
Attorney or Accredited Representative's Address

Phone Number *(Include area code)*	Fax Number, if any *(Include area code)*	E-Mail Address, if any
(305) 442-1322	(305) 444-7578	Valid E-mail Address

Form G-28 (Rev. 04/22/09)N

Form I-485

OMB No. 1615-0023; Expires 11/30/2011

Department of Homeland Security
U.S. Citizenship and Immigration Services

I-485, Application to Register
Permanent Residence or Adjust Status

START HERE - Type or print in black ink.

Part 1.   Information About You

Family Name	Given Name	Middle Name
DOE	John	

Address- C/O
Blank Attorney, P.A.

Street Number and Name		Apt. #
222 SW 27th Drive		

City
Weston

State	Zip Code
Florida	33751

Date of Birth *(mm/dd/yyyy)*	Country of Birth: United Kingdom
05/20/1986	Country of Citizenship/Nationality: United Kingdom

U.S. Social Security #	A # *(if any)*
N/A	None

Date of Last Arrival *(mm/dd/yyyy)*	I-94 #
07/20/2002	123456789 00

Current USCIS Status	Expires on *(mm/dd/yyyy)*
B2	01/19/2003

For USCIS Use Only

Returned	Receipt

Resubmitted

Reloc Sent

Reloc Rec'd

Applicant Interviewed

Part 2.   Application Type *(Check one)*

I am applying for an adjustment to permanent resident status because:

a. ☒ An immigrant petition giving me an immediately available immigrant visa number that has been approved. (Attach a copy of the approval notice, or a relative, special immigrant juvenile, or special immigrant military visa petition filed with this application that will give you an immediately available visa number, if approved.)

b. ☐ My spouse or parent applied for adjustment of status or was granted lawful permanent residence in an immigrant visa category that allows derivative status for spouses and children.

c. ☐ I entered as a K-1 fiancé(e) of a U.S. citizen whom I married within 90 days of entry, or I am the K-2 child of such a fiancé(e). (Attach a copy of the fiancé(e) petition approval notice and the marriage certificate).

d. ☐ I was granted asylum or derivative asylum status as the spouse or child of a person granted asylum and am eligible for adjustment.

e. ☐ I am a native or citizen of Cuba admitted or paroled into the United States after January 1, 1959, and thereafter have been physically present in the United States for at least one year.

f. ☐ I am the husband, wife, or minor unmarried child of a Cuban described above in **(e)**, and I am residing with that person, and was admitted or paroled into the United States after January 1, 1959, and thereafter have been physically present in the United States for at least one year.

g. ☐ I have continuously resided in the United States since before January 1, 1972.

h. ☐ Other basis of eligibility. Explain (for example, I was admitted as a refugee, my status has not been terminated, and I have been physically present in the United States for one year after admission). If additional space is needed, use a separate piece of paper.

I am already a permanent resident and am applying to have the date I was granted permanent residence adjusted to the date I originally arrived in the United States as a nonimmigrant or parolee, or as of May 2, 1964, whichever date is later, and: *(Check one)*

i. ☐ I am a native or citizen of Cuba and meet the description in **(e)** above.

j. ☐ I am the husband, wife, or minor unmarried child of a Cuban and meet the description in **(f)** above.

Section of Law

☐ Sec. 209(b), INA
☐ Sec. 13, Act of 9/11/57
☐ Sec. 245, INA
☐ Sec. 249, INA
☐ Sec. 1 Act of 11/2/66
☐ Sec. 2 Act of 11/2/66
☐ Other

Country Chargeable

Eligibility Under Sec. 245

☐ Approved Visa Petition
☐ Dependent of Principal Alien
☐ Special Immigrant
☐ Other

Preference

Action Block

To be Completed by
Attorney or Representative, **if any**
☐ Fill in box if G-28 is attached to represent the applicant.

VOLAG #

ATTY State License #

Form I-485 (Rev. 12/16/08)Y

Form I-864

Part 5. Sponsor's household size.

	For Government Use Only

21. Your Household Size - <u>DO NOT COUNT ANYONE TWICE</u>

Persons you are sponsoring in this affidavit:

  a. Enter the number you entered on line 10.   ☐ `1`

Persons NOT sponsored in this affidavit:

  b. Yourself.   **1**

  c. If you are currently married, enter "1" for your spouse.   ☐ `1`

  d. If you have dependent children, enter the number here.   ☐☐

  e. If you have any other dependents, enter the number here.   ☐☐

  f. If you have sponsored any other persons on an I-864 or I-864 EZ who are now lawful permanent residents, enter the number here.   ☐☐

  g. OPTIONAL: If you have <u>siblings, parents, or adult children</u> with the same principal residence who are combining their income with yours by submitting Form I-864A, enter the number here.   ☐☐

  h. Add together lines and enter the number here. **Household Size:**   ☐ `3`

Part 6. Sponsor's income and employment.

22. I am currently:

  a.   ☒ Employed as a/an   `Project Manager`   .

  Name of Employer #1 *(if applicable)*   `Heinz Corporation`   .

  Name of Employer #2 *(if applicable)*   _____   .

  b.   ☐ Self-employed as a/an   _____   .

  c.   ☐ Retired from _____ since _____   .
  (Company Name)   *(Date)*

  d.   ☐ Unemployed since _____   .
                                (Date)

23. **My current individual annual income is:** $ `66,000.00`
                                                  (See Step-by-Step Instructions)

Form I-864

	For Government Use Only

24. My current annual household income:

a. List your income from line 23 of this form. $ 66,000.00

b. Income you are using from any other person who was counted in your household size, including, in certain conditions, the intending immigrant. (See step-by-step instructions.) Please indicate name, relationship and income.

Name	Relationship	Current Income
DOE, John	Child	$
		$
		$
		$

Household Size =

_____

Poverty line for year

_____ is:

$ _____

c. Total Household Income: $ 66,000.00

(Total all lines from 24a and 24b. Will be Compared to Poverty Guidelines -- See Form I-864P.)

d. ☐ The persons listed above have completed Form I-864A. I am filing along with this form all necessary Forms I-864A completed by these persons.

e. ☐ The person listed above, _John Doe_____ does not need to
                                        (Name)
complete Form I-864A because he/she is the intending immigrant and has no accompanying dependents.

25. Federal income tax return information.

☒ I have filed a Federal tax return for each of the three most recent tax years. I have attached the required photocopy or transcript of my Federal tax return for only the most recent tax year.

My total income (adjusted gross income on IRS Form 1040EZ) as reported on my Federal tax returns for the most recent three years was:

Tax Year		Total Income
2009	*(most recent)*	$ 66,000.00
2008	*(2nd most recent)*	$ 66,000.00
2007	*(3rd most recent)*	$ 66,000.00

☒ *(Optional)* I have attached photocopies or transcripts of my Federal tax returns for my second and third most recent tax years.

Form I-864

	For Government Use Only
Part 7. Use of assets to supplement income. *(Optional)*	
If your income, or the total income for you and your household, from line 24c exceeds the Federal Poverty Guidelines for your household size, YOU ARE NOT REQUIRED to complete this Part. Skip to Part 8.	Household Size = _____
26. Your assets *(Optional)*	
a. Enter the balance of all savings and checking accounts. $ _____	Poverty line for year
b. Enter the net cash value of real-estate holdings. (Net means current assessed value minus mortgage debt.) $ _____	_____ is:
c. Enter the net cash value of all stocks, bonds, certificates of deposit, and any other assets not already included in lines 26 (a) or (b). $ _____	$ _____
d. Add together lines 26 a, b and c and enter the number here. TOTAL: $ _____	
27. Your household member's assets from Form I-864A. *(Optional)*	
Assets from Form I-864A, line 12d for $ _____ _____ *(Name of Relative)*	
28. Assets of the principal sponsored immigrant. *(Optional)*	
The principal sponsored immigrant is the person listed in line 2.	
a. Enter the balance of the sponsored immigrant's savings and checking accounts. $ _____	
b. Enter the net cash value of all the sponsored immigrant's real estate holdings. (Net means investment value minus mortgage debt.) $ _____	
c. Enter the current cash value of the sponsored immigrant's stocks, bonds, certificates of deposit, and other assets not included on line a or b. $ _____	The total value of all assests, line 29, must equal 5 times (3 times for spouses and children of USCs, or 1 time for orphans to be formally adopted in the U.S.) the difference between the poverty guidelines and the sponsor's household income, line 24c.
d. Add together lines 28a, b, and c, and enter the number here. $ _____	
29. Total value of assets.	
Add together lines 26d, 27 and 28d and enter the number here. TOTAL: $ _____	

Form I-864

Part 8. Sponsor's Contract.

Please note that, by signing this Form I-864, you agree to assume certain specific obligations under the Immigration and Nationality Act and other Federal laws. The following paragraphs describe those obligations. Please read the following information carefully before you sign the Form I-864. If you do not understand the obligations, you may wish to consult an attorney or accredited representative.

What is the Legal Effect of My Signing a Form I-864?

If you sign a Form I-864 on behalf of any person (called the "intending immigrant") who is applying for an immigrant visa or for adjustment of status to a permanent resident, and that intending immigrant submits the Form I-864 to the U.S. Government with his or her application for an immigrant visa or adjustment of status, under section 213A of the Immigration and Nationality Act these actions create a contract between you and the U. S. Government. The intending immigrant's becoming a permanent resident is the "consideration" for the contract.

Under this contract, you agree that, in deciding whether the intending immigrant can establish that he or she is not inadmissible to the United States as an alien likely to become a public charge, the U.S. Government can consider your income and assets to be available for the support of the intending immigrant.

What If I choose Not to Sign a Form I-864?

You cannot be made to sign a Form I-864 if you do not want to do so. But if you do not sign the Form I-864, the intending immigrant may not be able to become a permanent resident in the United States.

What Does Signing the Form I-864 Require Me to do?

If an intending immigrant becomes a permanent resident in the United States based on a Form I-864 that you have signed, then, until your obligations under the Form I-864 terminate, you must:

-- Provide the intending immigrant any support necessary to maintain him or her at an income that is at least 125 percent of the Federal Poverty Guidelines for his or her household size (100 percent if you are the petitioning sponsor and are on active duty in the U.S. Armed Forces and the person is your husband, wife, unmarried child under 21 years old.)

-- Notify USCIS of any change in your address, within 30 days of the change, by filing Form I-865.

What Other Consequences Are There?

If an intending immigrant becomes a permanent resident in the United States based on a Form I-864 that you have signed, then until your obligations under the Form I-864 terminate, your income and assets may be considered ("deemed") to be available to that person, in determining whether he or she is eligible for certain Federal means-tested public benefits and also for State or local means-tested public benefits, if the State or local government's rules provide for consideration ("deeming") of your income and assets as available to the person.

This provision does **not** apply to public benefits specified in section 403(c) of the Welfare Reform Act such as, but not limited to, emergency Medicaid, short-term, non-cash emergency relief; services provided under the National School Lunch and Child Nutrition Acts; immunizations and testing and treatment for communicable diseases; and means-tested programs under the Elementary and Secondary Education Act.

Contract continued on following page.

Form I-864

What If I Do Not Fulfill My Obligations?

If you do not provide sufficient support to the person who becomes a permanent resident based on the Form I-864 that you signed, that person may sue you for this support.

If a Federal, State or local agency, or a private agency provides any covered means-tested public benefit to the person who becomes a permanent resident based on the Form I-864 that you signed, the agency may ask you to reimburse them for the amount of the benefits they provided. If you do not make the reimbursement, the agency may sue you for the amount that the agency believes you owe.

If you are sued, and the court enters a judgment against you, the person or agency that sued you may use any legally permitted procedures for enforcing or collecting the judgment. You may also be required to pay the costs of collection, including attorney fees.

If you do not file a properly completed Form I-865 within 30 days of any change of address, USCIS may impose a civil fine for your failing to do so.

When Will These Obligations End?

Your obligations under a Form I-864 will end if the person who becomes a permanent resident based on a Form I-864 that you signed:

- Becomes a U.S. citizen;
- Has worked, or can be credited with, 40 quarters of coverage under the Social Security Act;
- No longer has lawful permanent resident status, and has departed the United States;
- Becomes subject to removal, but applies for and obtains in removal proceedings a new grant of adjustment of status, based on a new affidavit of support, if one is required; or
- Dies.

Note that divorce **does not** terminate your obligations under this Form I-864.

Your obligations under a Form I-864 also end if you die. Therefore, if you die, your Estate will not be required to take responsibility for the person's support after your death. Your Estate may, however, be responsible for any support that you owed before you died.

30. I, _Elena Di_____ ,

(Print Sponsor's Name)

certify under penalty of perjury under the laws of the United States that:

a. I know the contents of this affidavit of support that I signed.

b. All the factual statements in this affidavit of support are true and correct.

c. I have read and I understand each of the obligations described in Part 8, and I agree, freely and without any mental reservation or purpose of evasion, to accept each of those obligations in order to make it possible for the immigrants indicated in Part 3 to become permanent residents of the United States;

d. I agree to submit to the personal jurisdiction of any Federal or State court that has subject matter jurisdiction of a lawsuit against me to enforce my obligations under this Form I-864;

e. Each of the Federal income tax returns submitted in support of this affidavit are true copies, or are unaltered tax transcripts, of the tax returns I filed with the U.S. Internal Revenue Service; and

Sign on following page.

Form I-864

f. I authorize the Social Security Administration to release information about me in its records to the Department of State and U.S. Citizenship and Immigration Services.

g. Any and all other evidence submitted is true and correct.

31. _____   _____
                    (Sponsor's Signature)   *(Date-- mm/dd/yyyy)*

Part 9. Information on Preparer, if prepared by someone other than the sponsor.

I certify under penalty of perjury under the laws of the United States that I prepared this affidavit of support at the sponsor's request and that this affidavit of support is based on all information of which I have knowledge.

Signature: _____   **Date:** _____

                                                                              (mm/dd/yyyy)

Printed Name: Blank Attorney, P.A.

Firm Name: Blank Attorney, P.A.

Address: 222 SW 27th Drive, Weston FL 33751

Telephone Number: (954) 777-4444

E-Mail Address :   attorney@attorney.com

Business State ID # *(if any)* 123456789

Form G-325A

Department of Homeland Security
U.S. Citizenship and Immigration Services

OMB No. 1615-0008; Expires 06/30/2011

G-325, Biographic Information

(Family Name)	(First Name)	(Middle Name)	☒ Male ☐ Female	Date of Birth (mm/dd/yyyy)	Citizenship/Nationality	File Number
DOE	John			05/20/1986	British	A 000-000-000

All Other Names Used (include names by previous marriages)	City and Country of Birth	U.S. Social Security # (if any)
None	London, United Kingdom	000-00-0000

	Family Name	First Name	Date of Birth (mm/dd/yyyy)	City, and Country of Birth (if known)	City and Country of Residence
Father	Doe	Eric	10/10/1950	London, United Kingdom	London, United Kingdom
Mother (Maiden Name)	Di	Elena	09/01/1949	London, United Kingdom	Weston, FL, USA

Current Husband or Wife (If none, so state) Family Name (For wife, give maiden name)	First Name	Date of Birth (mm/dd/yyyy)	City and Country of Birth	Date of Marriage	Place of Marriage
None					

Former Husbands or Wives (If none, so state) Family Name (For wife, give maiden name)	First Name	Date of Birth (mm/dd/yyyy)	City and Country of Birth	Date of Termination of Marriage	Place of Termination of Marriage
None					

Applicant's residence last five years. List present address first.

Street and Number	City	Province or State	Country	From Month	From Year	To Month	To Year
222 SW 27th Drive	Weston	Florida	USA	7	2007	Present Time	
56 Mainstream Drive	London	London	United Kingdom	5	1986	7	2007

Applicant's last address outside the United States of more than one year.

Street and Number	City	Province or State	Country	From Month	From Year	To Month	To Year
56 Mainstream Drive	London	England	United Kingdom	5	1986	7	2007

Applicant's employment last five years. (If none, so state.) List present employment first.

Full Name and Address of Employer	Occupation (Specify)	From Month	From Year	To Month	To Year
None	Student	8	1991	Present Time	

Last occupation abroad if not shown above. (Include all information requested above.)

This form is submitted in connection with an application for:	Signature of Applicant	Date
☐ Naturalization ☐ Other (Specify): ☒ Status as Permanent Resident		

If your native alphabet is in other than Roman letters, write your name in your native alphabet below:

Penalties: Severe penalties are provided by law for knowingly and willfully falsifying or concealing a material fact.

Applicant: Print your name and Alien Registration Number in the box outlined by heavy border below.

Complete This Box (Family Name)	(Given Name)	(Middle Name)	(Alien Registration Number)
DOE	John		A 000-000-000

Form G-325 (Rev. 06/12/09)Y

CHAPTER 8

Employment-Based and Investor Immigrant Preferences

I. Introduction

Employment based immigration for lawful permanent residence falls under five preferences categories: (1) priority workers: persons of extraordinary ability, outstanding professors or researchers and intracompany transfers of executives or managers; (2) Labor Certification: professionals with advanced degrees or persons of exceptional ability and waiver in the national interest; (3) Labor Certification—PERM: skilled workers, professionals and other workers and Schedule A; (4) special immigrants, including ministers and religious workers; and (5) investors with the potential to hire 10 U.S. workers. The employing entity is called the petitioner and the employee seeking the benefit is called the beneficiary.

II. First Preference—EB-1—Priority Workers

A. Extraordinary Ability in the Sciences, Arts, Education, Business or Athletics

1. This category includes aliens with extraordinary ability in sciences, art, education, business or athletics as proven by sustained international or national acclaim. The alien may self-petition; thus, no job offer is required as in some of the other preference categories. INA § 203(b)(1)(A), 8 U.S.C. § 1153(b)(1)(A); 8 C.F.R. § 204.5(h)(2).

2. The applicant must demonstrate receipt of a major award (e.g., Nobel Prize), or three of the following criteria with supporting evidence (8 C.F.R. § 204.5(h)(3)(i-x):

    a. Receipt of lesser nationally or internationally recognized prizes or awards;

    b. Membership in associations that require outstanding achievement;

    c. Published material in professional or major trade publications;

    d. Evidence of participation on a panel or individually as a judge of the work of others in the same or an allied field;

    e. Original scientific, scholarly, artistic, athletic or business-related contributions of major significance in the field;

    f. Authorship of scholarly articles in the field;

    g. Display of the alien's work;

    h. Proof of performance in a leading or critical role for organizations or establishments with a distinguished reputation;

    i. Proof of having commanded a high salary;

j. Commercial success in the performing arts; and

k. Other comparable evidence.

3. Also required is a consultation from a peer group, labor and/or management organization attesting to the alien's extraordinary ability or qualifications.

B. Outstanding Professors and Researchers

1. This category includes outstanding professors and researchers who are recognized internationally for their outstanding academic achievements in a particular field. INA § 203(b)(1)(B), 8 U.S.C. § 1153(b)(1)(B); 8 C.F.R. § 204.5.

2. The professor or researcher must:

   a. Be recognized internationally as outstanding in a specific academic field;

   b. Possess at least three years of experience in teaching or research in the academic field;

   c. Seek to enter the United States for a tenured, tenure-track teaching or research position at a university, or a comparable research position with a private employer, if the employer has at least three full-time researchers and documented accomplishments in the research field.

3. Two of the following six criteria must be met with supporting evidence [8 C.F.R. § 204.5(i)(i-x)]:

   a. Receipt of major prizes or awards for outstanding achievement;

   b. Membership in associations that require members to demonstrate outstanding achievements;

   c. Published material in professional publications written by others about the alien's work in the academic field;

   d. Participation, either on a panel or individually, as a judge of the work of others in the same or allied academic field;

   e. Original scientific or scholarly research contributions in the field;

   f. Authorship of scholarly books or articles (in scholarly journals with international circulation) in the field;

   g. Any grants;

   h. Any trademark or patent applications; and

   i. Any other comparable evidence.

4. A labor certification is not required; however, the alien must have a job offer.

C. International Executives and Managers

1. This category applies to executives, managers and employees of foreign companies or affiliates who are transferred to the United States. To qualify for this category the alien must have been employed for at least one year prior to filing the application by the petitioning firm or corporation, other legal entity, an affiliate or subsidiary thereof, in the three years preceding the time of his or her application for classification and admission into the United States, and the alien must seek to enter the United States in order to continue to render services to the same employer, subsidiary or affiliate in a managerial or executive capacity. INA § 203(b)(1)(C), 8 U.S.C. § 1153(b)(1) (C) 8 C.F.R. § 204.5(j)(2).

   a. Executive capacity is:

   An assignment within an organization in which the employee primarily: (i) directs the management of the organization of a major component or functioning organization; (ii) establishes the goals and policies of the organization, component or function; (iii) exercises wide latitude in discretionary decision-making; and (iv) receives only general supervision or direction from higher level executives, directors, or stockholders of the organization.

b. Managerial capacity is:

An assignment within an organization in which the employee primarily: (i) manages the organization, a department, subdivision, function or organization (ii) supervises and controls the work of other supervisory or professional employees or manages an essential function within the organization, department or subdivision of the organization; (iii) has the authority to fire or recommend those as well as other personnel actions (such as promotion) if another employee or other employees are directly supervised or functions at a senior level and the organizational hierarchy or with respect to the function managed, if no other employee is directly supervised; and (iv) exercises direction over the day-to-day operations of the activity or function.

2. Evidence required from U.S. entity:

a. Licenses or permits to operate a U.S. company;

b. Lease or deed for U.S. premises;

c. Employer's wage and tax report and copy of quarterly income tax return;

d. Stock certificate (documentary evidence showing the exact ownership of the U.S. and foreign company and evidence establishing the claimed affiliation). The foreign parent company must own more than 51 percent of the U.S. corporation. This can be demonstrated by issuance of a stock certificate to foreign entity. A 50/50 joint venture qualifies;

e. Bank statements for at least one year of operations;

f. Articles of incorporation, including certificate under seal with state charter number;

g. Current financial statements; and

h. Proof of business such as, invoices, brochures, contract, photographs or list of customers.

3. Evidence required from foreign entity:

a. Proof of foreign national employed at least one year in the past three years for foreign enterprise. This proof can be individual foreign tax return or accountant's letter;

b. Current corporate tax returns;

c. Documentary evidence showing number of employees at the foreign location;

d. Documentary evidence showing address of foreign company (letterhead);

e. Articles of incorporation;

f. Current corporate financial statements;

g. Bank letter and/or bank statements (evidence to show that the foreign company is present in operation and viable);

h. Proof of business such as invoices, brochures, contract or photographs of business; and

i. Detailed description of company's activities in the home country and in the United States and of the employee's and the transferee's duties abroad and in the United States.

III. Second Preference—EB-2—Professionals with Advanced Degrees or Exceptional Ability

This classification includes aliens who are members of the professions holding advanced degrees or their equivalent or aliens of exceptional ability. It also includes individuals who are members of the professions with advanced degrees (any degree above a baccalaureate degree or a baccalaureate degree and at least five years of progressive experience in the professions). This group requires the filing of a Labor Certification Application with Department of Labor called PERM. Aliens with exceptional ability are exempt from the job offer requirement and labor certification is waived if the position is in the national interest of the United States. INA §203(b)(2)(B), 8 U.S.C. 1153(b)(2); 8 C.F.R. §204.5k:

The foreign national must be a member of the profession holding an advanced degree or its equivalent or who, because of their exceptional ability in the sciences, arts or business, will substantially and prospectively benefit the national economy, cultural or educational interests or welfare of the United States and whose services in the sciences, arts, professions or business are sought by an employer in the United States.

Advanced degree means any United States academic or professional degree or a foreign equivalent degree above that of a baccalaureate. A U.S. baccalaureate degree or foreign equivalent degree followed by at least five years of progressive experience in the specialty shall be considered the equivalent of a master's degree. If a doctorate is customarily required by the specialty, the alien must have a U.S. doctoral degree or a foreign equivalent degree.

Exceptional ability in the sciences, arts or business means a degree of expertise significantly above that ordinarily encountered in the sciences, arts, or business.

In addition, the alien must (i) seek work in an area of "substantial merit," (ii) the work must have a benefit which "will be national in scope," and (iii) the beneficiary must serve the national interest to a substantially greater degree than would an available U.S. worker having the same minimum qualifications.

Any three of the following is required:

1. Official academic record showing the alien has a university or college degree relating to area of exceptional ability;

2. Letters from current or former employer(s) demonstrating that the alien has at least 10 years of full time experience in the occupation;

3. License to practice the profession;

4. Evidence that the alien has commanded a salary which demonstrates exceptional ability;

5. Evidence of membership in professional organizations;

6. Evidence of recognition for achievements and significant contributions to the industry or field by peers, governmental entities or professional or business organizations; and

7. Other comparable evidence.

IV. Third Preference—EB-3—Labor Certification—PERM-Skilled Workers, Professionals and Other Workers; Schedule A; Visa Retrogression

A. Labor Certification—PERM-Skilled Workers, Professionals and Other Workers

This category covers skilled workers, professionals and other workers. The labor certification is a "certification" by the U.S. Department of Labor (DOL) that there are no able, willing, qualified and available U.S. workers for the position offered. This is proven through a recruitment campaign, which includes placing advertisements in newspapers of general circulation or professional journals, the Internet, employment agencies and on-the-job posting.

The employer must provide proof that it has tested the labor market by the above mentioned recruitment campaign to verify that there are no minimally qualified U.S. workers. INA §203(b)(3), 8 U.S.C. §1153(b)(3); 8 C.F.R. §204.5(l).

Professional, skilled worker and other worker are defined a follows:

> Professional: an alien who holds at least a U.S. baccalaureate degree or a foreign equivalent degree and who is a member of the profession. Though this category belongs to the EB2 category, it requires the same process for a PERM as the EB3 and the OW.

Skilled Worker: an alien who is capable, at the time of petitioning for this classification, of performing skilled labor (requiring at least two years training or experience), not of a temporary or seasonal nature, for which qualified workers are not available in the United States.

Other Worker: an alien who is capable, at the time of petitioning for this classification, of performing unskilled labor (requiring less than two years training or experience), not of a temporary or seasonal nature, for which qualified workers are not available in the United States.

All labor certifications must be filed under the PERM regulations. The Program Electronic Review Management—PERM—process requires recruitment prior to filing the application for Labor Employment Certification, ETA Form 9089. The form may be filed electronically or by mail. However, the Department of Labor recommends that the employer file electronically for a speedier process.

Pending labor certifications at the backlog centers may be converted to the PERM process to maintain the old priority. However, careful investigation and analysis must be done before a conversion is chosen. The conditions of employment must be identical. This means that the job position, duties and address of employment must be identical. The wage, however, may be different.

The initial step is to choose the position from O*NET (http://online.onetcenter.org). Once the position has been determined, the employer or its agent must request the prevailing wage for the position. Obtaining the prevailing wage can be done through the portal of the Department of Labor website through form ETA 9141, http://icert.doleta.gov or by mailing the ETA 9141 Form to the National Prevailing Wage and Help Desk Center (NPWHDC) in Washington DC.

1. Recruitment must be conducted not less than 30 days and not more than 180 days prior to filing the Form ETA 9089. The recruitment process begins with the placement of the job order on the website of the Workforce Center (in Florida is https://www.employflorida.com). The job order must be placed for at least 30 days. This information may be found at http://www.doleta.gov/usworkforce/onestop/onestopmap.cfm. The Form ETA 9089 may not be filed until 30 days more have elapsed since the closing of the job order. This period is called the "clean" period. Additionally, a Notice of Filing must be posted at the job site for 10 consecutive business days.

The rest of the recruitment process varies according to whether the position is a professional or non-professional position and whether the position is for a physical therapist, nurse or college/university professor. A professional position is a position that requires at least a bachelor's degree to perform the duties of the position or a position which is listed in Appendix A to the preamble of the PERM regulations 20 CFR § 656.17 (e).

For non-professional positions there must be two Sunday advertisements placed in a newspaper of general circulation. The advertisements may be placed for two consecutive Sundays. The advertisement must state the name of the employer and provide contact information of the employer and a description of the position. Any additional information to be placed in the advertisement is at the discretion of the employer. The more information placed in the advertisement, the easier it is to disqualify unqualified applicants.

For professional positions, there must be three additional recruitment steps followed. In this case, the employer may substitute a professional journal advertisement for one of the Sunday advertisements mentioned above. The employer may choose from the following types of recruitment:

Job Fair: In order to substantiate this type of recruitment, the employer should submit brochures advertising the fair and newspaper advertisements in which the employer is named as a participant in the job fair;

Employer's website: Dated copies of pages from the site that advertised the occupation.

Job search website other than employer's: Dated copies of pages from one or more websites that advertised the position (e.g., Monster.com);

On-campus recruiting: Copies of notification issued or posted by college or university placement office naming the employer and the date it conducted the interview for employment in the occupation;

Journal advertisement: Copy of the page that the advertisement appeared;

Trade and professional organization: Photocopies of pages of newsletter or trade journals containing the advertisement;

Private employment firms: Copies of contracts between the employer and the private employment firm and copies of advertisements placed by the private employment firm for the occupation;

Employee referral program with incentives: Dated copies of employer notice or memorandum advertising the program specifying the incentive offered;

Campus placement office: Employer's notice of job opportunity provided to the campus placement office (this is for positions that solely require a bachelor's degree);

Local and ethnic newspapers: Copies of page in newspaper that contains employer advertisement; or

Radio and television advertisement: Copy of the employer's text of the employer's advertisement along with a written confirmation from the radio or television station stating when the advertisement was heard.

For college and university teachers there must be a competitive recruitment and selection process. This involves a statement signed by the actual hiring authority outlining the recruitment procedure, the total number of job applicants, the lawful job-related reasons for rejection, a final report of the administrative body making the recommendation or selection of the alien at the completion of the competitive recruitment and a copy of at least one advertisement in a professional journal, as well as evidence of other recruitment sources and a written statement attesting to the degree of the educational or professional qualifications.

For nurses there must be a certificate from CGFNS (Commission of Graduate Foreign Nurses Schools) for a full and unrestricted permanent license to practice in the state of intended employment or passing the NCLEX-RN. For physical therapists there must be a letter or statement signed by the authorized state physical therapy official stating that the alien is qualified to take the state licensing exam.

Nurses and physical therapists are termed as Schedule A occupations. The form and supporting documents must be submitted to the Department of Homeland Security, Citizenship and Immigration Services Office having jurisdiction of the case.

2. Application Process

The electronic filing simplified the labor certification process and also allowed employers and attorneys to check the status of the applications online. When the process was implemented, the Department of Labor (DOL) feared that the online system would raise the chances for fraudulent applications. The PERM process limited the access of attorneys to make changes in the accounts, slowed down the application process. The PERM process was to allow for the certification process to be completed between 45–90 days. The program is severely backed up and some cases are taking up to 8 months to be completed.

Prior to filing the application, the employer must register the company with the permanent online system at http://www.plc.doleta.gov. The following steps must be taken:

Step 1: Initial Registration

In order to register the company, you must go to http://www.plc.doleta.gov and complete the following steps:

1. Click "OK" to the government warning;

2. Click "Register-Become a Registered User for Free";

3. Click "Setup Employer Profile";

4. Click "Accept";

5. Complete the "User Profile" including name, telephone number and e-mail address fields;

6. Create a username which must be 8–15 characters long;

7. Complete the "Employer Business Information" including the EIN, employer name, address and telephone number fields;

8. In the NAICS Code field enter **NAICS NUMBER, NAICS TITLE**

9. Complete the "Employer Contact Information" including name, address, telephone number and e-mail address or check the "Same as Employer Information" box; and

10. Click "Submit."

After this process is complete, you will receive a username and password via e-mail from the U.S. DOL.

Step 2: Change of username and password

Once you receive your username and password, you will be required to change from the one provided to you at the time of registration to a unique username and password of your choice. The new password must also be 8–15 characters long and must contain at least one number and one special character such as @, #, $, %, &, *, etc.

To change the Username and Password, you must once again log onto http://www.plc.doleta.gov and complete the following steps:

1. Login with the username and password provided at the time of registration;

2. Select the "MY PROFILE" tab;

3. Click "LOGIN INFORMATION";

4. In the "Username" field type in a new username of your choice;

5. In the "Password" field type in a new password of your choice and repeat in the "Confirm Password" field; and

6. Click "Save" to save the changes you made.

Be sure to write down the new username and password and keep it in a safe place.

Step 3: Creation of a User Account:

To create a user account you must, once again, log onto http://www.plc.doleta.gov and complete the following steps:

1. Login with your username and password;

2. Select the "USER ACCOUNTS" tab;

3. Click "Activate User Account" (if this is the first time a user account is activated, otherwise skip to step 4);

4. Click "Add New User"; and

5. In the "User Information" section enter the following information:

   • Name of the user

   • Address

   • Telephone number

   • Fax number

   • Sub-account user type: Lawyer/Agent

   • E-mail address

   • In the "Username" field type your username

   • In the "Password" field type your password

   • In the "Security Access" section check "Edit Applications," "Add/Reuse Application" and "Withdraw Applications"

6. Click "Save."

To file the form by mail Employers must file their applications with the National Processing Center with responsibility for the state or territory where the job opportunity is located as shown on the following page:

United States Department of Labor
Employment and Training Administration
Atlanta National Processing Center
Harris Tower
233 Peachtree St., N.E., Suite 410
Atlanta, GA 30303
Telephone: 404-893-0101
Fax: 404-893-4642

Alabama	Connecticut	Delaware	District of Columbia
Florida	Georgia	Kentucky	Maine
Maryland	Massachusetts	Mississippi	New Hampshire
New Jersey	New York	North Carolina	Pennsylvania
Puerto Rico	Rhode Island	South Carolina	Tennessee
Vermont	Virgin Islands	Virginia	West Virginia

United States Department of Labor
Employment and Training Administration
Chicago National Processing Center
Railroad Retirement Board Building
844 N. Rush St.
12th Floor
Chicago, IL 60611
Telephone: 312-886-8000
Fax: 312-886-1688

Alaska	Arizona	Arkansas	California
Colorado	Guam	Hawaii	Idaho
Illinois	Indiana	Iowa	Kansas
Louisiana	Michigan	Minnesota	Missouri
Montana	Nebraska	Nevada	New Mexico
North Dakota	Ohio	Oklahoma	Oregon
South Dakota	Texas	Utah	Washington
Wisconsin	Wyoming		

An application for a Schedule A occupation is filed with the appropriate Department of Homeland Security office and not with a Department of Labor National Processing Center. A prevailing wage determination and an internal posting must be filed with the Form I-140 with USCIS. After the form is filled out and submitted online, it should be printed out and signed by employer and alien.

If the application is rejected, the employer or agent should review the form, try to rectify any deficiencies and resubmit the application to the Department of Labor. If the application is not rejected, the USDOL will send a notice that the case is under final review or pending audit.

It is extremely important that an audit file be created in case the U.S. DOL chooses to conduct an audit. An audit file should include the following:

1. Copy of form ETA 9089;

2. Copy of prevailing wage determination;

3. Employer's business necessity statement and supporting documents; and

4. The following recruitment supporting documents:

   a. Recruitment report;

   b. Notice of job availability;

   c. Advertisements; and

   d. Job order.

Once the Application is certified by USDOL, it may be filed with form I-140 and relevant documents to the petition with USCIS.

B. Schedule A

Schedule A is a list of occupations for which the DOL has determined there are not sufficient U.S. workers who are able, willing, qualified and available. It also establishes that the employment of aliens in these pre-certified occupations will not adversely affect the wages and working conditions for U.S. workers similarly employed 20 C.F.R. §656.10.

The alien may be eligible for one of the following:

- Blanket Schedule A: The DOL has pre-certified certain occupations, because they do not displace U.S. workers (e.g., registered nurses and physical therapists).

- Group I: This group refers to certain medical personnel (i.e. physical therapists that can show qualifications to be state licensed)—20 C.F.R. §656.10, and nurses provided, s/he passed CGFNS or holds a full and unrestricted license to practice—20 C.F.R. §656.22(c)(2).

- Group II: This group refers to persons or exceptional ability (i.e. persons in science or arts, except performing arts, and university teachers; persons who show exceptional ability and international recognition; and persons who have practiced in field for previous year and intends to practice in same field)—20 C.F.R. §§656.10 (b), 656.22(d). (If a performing artist or teacher does not qualify under this category, s/he may possibly apply through regular process.)

1. Forms Required:

The Form I-140 is the application filed with the USCIS Regional Service Center, together with Form G-28. Schedule A requires the approved labor certification. Attached to the application must be the requisite supporting documents. If it is a concurrent filing, the approved Form I-140 or Form I-140 receipt is filed simultaneously with adjustment of status application.

2. Documents Required:

   a. Form I-485, including two recent photographs;
   b. Form G-325A (for applicants 14 and older);
   c. Form ETA 9089;
   d. Form I-693 and supplement (Medical exam);
   e. Form I-765, including two recent photographs;
   f. Notice of Approval and/or USCIS receipt;
   g. Job offer letter or self-petition letter;
   h. Form I-131, including two recent photographs;
   i. Copy of passport and Form I-94;
   j. Evidence of family relationship; and
   k. Required filing fees.

C. Visa Retrogression

Visa retrogression occurs when immigrant visas are not immediately available in certain categories, thus rendering those skilled workers, professionals and other workers ineligible to file for permanent residence at that time. However, those aliens who qualify to file their applications under Schedule A are allowed to do so without delay.

There must be a visa number available to the alien when s/he applies. Whether a visa number is available or not depends on the use of visas in his/her category and country and the rate at which applications are being processed by the government. The alien's place in line is determined by his/her priority date, usually the date their labor certification was filed with the DOL or, for those applications not requiring labor certification, the date a petition was filed with USCIS. When more people apply in a certain category than there are visas available, the

Department of State (DOS) establishes a cut-off date, which is the priority date of the first applicant who could not be issued a visa within the numerical limits. Visa numbers are available only to those applicants with priority dates before the cut-off date.

The date the document is filed establishes the priority date. The priority date is the day the case is put "in line" for permanent residency under the worldwide visa quota system through a relative petition or employment based petition. Priority dates are established as follows:

- EB-1 & EB-2 (Labor Certification waived) — Priority date established when I-140 is filed
- EB-2 (with Labor Certification) & EB-3 — Priority date established when Labor Certification (PERM) is filed with the U.S. DOL or State Agency (Legacy I.N.S.)
- EB-4 — Priority date established when Form I-360 is filed
- EB-5 — Priority date established when Form I-526 is filed

It is important to visit the DOS' visa bulletin at http://travel.state.gov, to see if a visa is currently available. If a visa category is not current ("C"), the visa bulletin will give a cut-off date meaning there is a wait to file permanent residency because the category has retrogressed. "U" or unavailable means there are no more visas available for the month. Under these circumstances, the beneficiary is not eligible to adjust his/her status until a visa number becomes available or the category becomes current.

For example, if you peruse the visa bulletin of October 2006, the First, Second, Fourth and Fifth preferences and Schedule A are categories available under the column for "all chargeability areas except those listed." The Third Preference, which applies to Labor Certification—PERM-Skilled Workers, Professionals and Other Workers has a cut-off date of May 1, 2002, for professional and skilled workers and January 1, 2001, for unskilled workers. This means that for Form I-485 and consular processing applications, the beneficiary must have a priority date up to or prior to said date (e.g., an EB-3 skilled worker must have a priority before May 1, 2002, in order to file for adjustment of status).

(**Note:** Certain categories for beneficiaries from China, India, Mexico and the Philippines are not current as of October 2006.)

Most importantly, retrogression of visas also applies to family based petitions. The visa bulletin should be reviewed when filing a preference relative petition as more fully discussed in Chapter 6.

V. Evidence Required for Categories EB-1, -2 and -3

1. Forms Required:

   The Form I-140 is the application filed with the USCIS Regional Service Center, together with Form G-28. The EB-2 with advanced degrees and EB-3 requires the approved labor certification. Attached to the application must be the requisite supporting documents. If it is a concurrent filing, the approved Form I-140 or Form I-140 receipt is filed simultaneously with adjustment of status application.

2. Documents Required:

   a. Form I-485;

   b. Form G-325A (for applicants 14 and older);

   c. Two recent photographs;

   d. Form I-693 and supplement (Medical exam);

   e. Job offer letter;

   f. Notice of Approval and/or USCIS receipt;

g. Copy of passport and Form I-94;

h. Evidence of family relationship, e.g., marriage and birth certificate(s);

i. Form I-765, including two recent photographs;

j. Form I-131, including two recent photographs; and

k. Required filing fees.

VI. Fourth Preference — Special Immigrants — Religious Worker

To qualify under this category the foreign national must have been member of a religious denomination for at least two years immediately preceding the time of filing of the application. S/he must seek to enter the United States solely for the purpose of carrying on the vocation as a minister of that denomination, to work in a professional capacity or religious vocation or to work in a religious vocation or occupation. The organization must be a bona fide entity which is affiliated with the religious denomination and is exempt from taxation as an organization described by the Internal Revenue Code under section 501(c)(3) of Title 26. INA §101 (a)(27)(C) (ii), 8 U.S.C. §1101 (a)(27)(C)(ii), 8 C.F.R. §204.5 (m); 22 C.F.R. §42.32(d)(1)(ii).

A religious worker includes members of a religious organization such as chorus leaders, religious instructors, cantors, missionaries and religious broadcasters.

Professional ability entails practicing a religious vocation, or holding an occupation which requires a bachelor's degree or foreign equivalent.

Religious vocation means a calling to a traditional religious life, including taking vows (e.g., monks and nuns).

1. Forms Required:

   The Forms I-360 and G-28 are submitted to the USCIS Service Center with transmittal letter and supporting documents. There is no concurrent filing permitted under this category.

2. Documents Required:

   a. Documentation showing that it is a not-for-profit organization exempt from taxation in accordance with section (501)(c)(3) of the Internal Revenue Code;

   b. A letter from an authorized official of the religious organization in the United States which establishes:

      1. That, immediately prior to the filing of the petition, the alien had the required two years of membership in the denomination and the required two years of experience in the religious vocation, professional religious work or other religious work; and

      2. That, if the alien is a minister, s/he has authorization to conduct religious worship and to perform other duties usually performed by authorized members of the clergy, including a detailed description of such authorized duties. In appropriate cases, the certificate of ordination or authorization may be requested; or

      3. That, if the alien is a religious professional, he or she has at least a U.S. baccalaureate or its foreign equivalent required for entry into the religious profession. In all professional cases, an official academic record showing that the alien has the required degree must be submitted; or

      4. That, if the alien is to work in another religious vocation or occupation, he or she is qualified in the religious vocation or occupation. Evidence of such qualifications may include, but need not be limited to, evidence establishing that the alien is a nun, monk, or religious brother, or that the type of work to be done relates to a traditional religious function;

      5. The letter must also describe the job offer. The authorized official of the religious organization in the United States must state how the alien will be solely carrying on the vocation of a minister (including any terms of payment for services or other remuneration) or how the alien will be paid or remunerated if the alien will work in a

professional religious capacity or in other religious work. The documentation should clearly indicate that the alien will not be solely dependent on supplemental employment or solicitation of funds for support.

   c. Current financial statement;

   d. Church membership figures; and

   e. If a professional position, résumé, and copy of degree(s) of worker.

VII. Fifth Preference—EB-5—Investors

A. Employment Creation Visa

This investor visa is one of the employment creation visas. Its purpose is to permit investors to immigrate to the United States to enhance employment opportunities. This category grants conditional residency for two years to individual investors who invest, after November 29, 1990, $1,000,000 or $500,000 in designated rural or high unemployment area with the intention of hiring 10 U.S. workers. Ninety days prior to the expiration of the two year period, the investor must file to remove the condition in order to obtain lawful permanent residency. INA §203(b)(1)(5)(B)(i), 8 U.S.C. §1153(b)(5); 8 C.F.R. §204.6(e).

B. Summary of Statutory Requirements

1. Capital

   a. Investment of $500,000.00 in a rural or high unemployment area and $1,000,000 in all other areas;

   b. Capital includes cash, cash equivalents, debt inventory, equipment or other tangible property; and

   c. Must disclose source of capital, but it need not come from abroad.

2. New Commercial Enterprise

   a. Creation of new original business after November 29, 1990;

   b. Purchase of an existing business with reorganization into a new business; and

   c. Expansion of existing business by creating a 40 percent increase in net worth or a 40 percent increase in number of employees.

3. Creation of 10 Full-Time Positions

   a. Full-time position equals at least 35 hours per week;

   b. Can be in the process of hiring 10 full-time workers or presently employ 10 full-time workers; and

   c. Does not include independent contractors.

4. Troubled Business

Troubled business means a business that has been in existence for at least two years and has incurred a net loss for accounting purposes (determined on the basis of generally accepted accounting principles) during the 12- or 24-month period prior to the filing of the application. The loss for such period is at least equal to forty percent of the troubled business' net worth prior to such loss.

    The Forms I-526 and G-28 are submitted to the USCIS Service Center with transmittal letter and supporting documents. There is no concurrent filing permitted under this category.

C. Regional Centers

USCIS has set up Regional Centers for EB-5 investments. This is a type of geographic franchise for collecting foreign investment and funneling it into job creating businesses. Presently there are more than 15 of these across the United States and more are being added every year. They invest in projects anywhere from a ski resort to state infrastructure. Usually, the center pulls the resources of about 4 investors in order to create an LLC. The immigration attorney should only suggest the center after doing diligence in investigating numbers of cases approved and processing times. It is advisable to suggest 3 after doing the research. The investor will wire the investment amount ($500,000 or $1,000.000) to an escrow account of the investment along with an administrative fee (usually $30,000). The account will be in the name of the investor and the center. The Form I-526 is filed with USCIS requesting conditional residence of two years, along with proof of the investment funds in the account and documentation to show that the funds came from legal sources. Once the I-526 is approved, the center is able to withdraw the funds and invest it in the project. The investor and his family must file to withdraw the condition during the 90day window preceding the two year anniversary of the conditional residence.

D. Documents Required

1. A business plan for the new enterprise;
2. Business license or authorization to transact business in a state or city;
3. For investments in an existing business, proof that the required amount of capital has been transferred to the business and that the investment has increased the number of employees or net worth by 40 percent;
4. Bank statements showing deposits in the U.S. account of the enterprise;
5. Evidence of assets purchased for use in the enterprise;
6. Evidence of property transferred from abroad;
7. Evidence of funds invested in the enterprise in exchange for stock or for stock redeemable at the holder's request;
8. Evidence of debts secured by the investor's assets and for which investor is personally and primarily liable;
9. Copies of the I-9 Forms and tax records or payroll documents;
10. Legal Acquisition of Capital:
    i. Foreign business registration records,
    ii. Business and personal tax returns or other tax returns of any kind anywhere in the world within the previous five years,
    iii. Documents identifying any other source of money;
11. Proof of targeted area (Statistics maintained by each state's unemployment office will provide information on whether the investment has been made or is about to be made in a high unemployment or targeted area).

Appendix

1. Employer/Employee Questionnaire
2. I-140 (EB-1—Intracompany Transferee) Letter
3. Form ETA 9089
4. Results of Recruitment Report
5. Notice of Job Availability

Employer Questionnaire

A. Information Concerning Employer/Petitioner

1. Company name: _____

2. Address: _____

3. Telephone number(s): _____

4. Fax number: _____

5. E-mail address: _____

6. Internet website (www.): _____

7. If employee will work at a different address than above, please state: _____

   _____

8. Date established: _____

9. Employer tax ID #: _____

10. Number of total employees: _____

11. Number of employees on H-1B1 visa: _____

12. Approximate *gross* annual income for current year:

    $ _____

13. Approximate *net* annual income for current year:

    $ _____

14. Please give a detailed description of business:

    _____

    _____

> *Please attach all available information concerning the petitioner (e.g., brochures, advertising material, catalogues, published articles, references, etc).*

Employer Questionnaire

15. Full name of company representative who will sign petitioning documents:

_____

16. Which position does the representative hold with the company (e.g., president, vice president, manager of

    human resources)? _____

_____

17. Name of contact person at petitioning company, if different from above: _____

_____

B. Information Concerning the Position offered

1. Job title: _____

2. Detailed description of duties to be performed:

_____

_____

_____

3. Hours per week: _____

4. Wages per week: _____

5. Would there be additional compensation? If so, please explain: _____

_____

6. If so, what would that compensation be valued at? _____

_____

7. How long do you intend to employ the beneficiary? _____

_____

Employee Questionnaire

1. Full Name: _____

Last   First   Middle

2. Address abroad: _____

_____

_____

3. Place of Birth: _____

City/State/Province   Country

4. Date of birth: _____

Month   Day   Year

5. Country of Citizenship: _____

Profession/Occupation: _____

6. Do you have a university/college degree?   Yes {   }   No {   }

Major/primary field of study: _____

Degree obtained: _____

When and where? _____

7. How many years did you spend at college/university? _____

8. Social Security Number: SSN# _____

9. Alien Registration Number: A# _____

10. Address in the U.S. where you will reside: _____

_____

_____

11. Gender: Male {   }   Female {   }

12. Marital status: Married {   }   Divorced {   }   Single {   }   Widowed {   }

Spouse's Name: _____

Last   First   Middle

Date of birth: _____

Month   Day   Year

Place of Birth: _____

City/State/Province   Country

13. Do you have any children?   Yes {   }   No {   }

Child's Name: _____

Last   First   Middle

Date of Birth: _____

Month   Day   Year

Place of Birth: _____

City/State/Province   Country

Country of Citizenship: _____

I-140 (EB-1—Intracompany Transferee) Letter

John Doe, Inc.
222 S.W. 27 Drive
Weston, Florida 33751
Telephone (305) 332-6673
Fax (305) 223-4229

November 11, 2007

Certified Mail

U.S. Citizenship and Immigration Services
Texas Service Center
P.O. Box 852135
Mesquite, TX 75185-2135

Re: **I-140 Immigrant Visa Petition for Classification as Priority
Worker-Multinational Manager under Section 203(b)(1)(c)
of the Immigration and Nationality Act.**
Petitioner: John Doe, Inc.
Beneficiary: Doe, John

Dear Sir or Madam:

This letter is submitted in support of the I-140 petition of John Doe, Inc., on behalf of Mr. John Doe, a Peruvian national, and President/Chief Financial Officer of our company. We wish to permanently retain Mr. John Doe at our Florida subsidiary.

THE PETITIONER AND CORPORATE RELATIONSHIP

John Doe, Inc., was established and registered on March 13, 2002, in the State of Florida and is involved in the import and export of hardware tools and heavy-equipment machinery. Our company is located at 222 S.W. 27th Drive, Weston, FL 33751.

Currently, the U.S. subsidiary company has a staff of six individuals, and during the year 2002 grossed an income of $24 million.

Our parent company, Chesta & Chesta S.A.C., was incorporated in Lima, Peru, on June 17, 1996. The company is involved in the import, distribution, sales, leasing and operations related to industrial use machinery, equipment and automobiles. Chesta & Chesta S.A.C. is located in the heart of the Peruvian capital, at Avenida Benavides 170, Office 99, Miraflores, Lima 17, Peru. Currently, our company has a staff of 16 employees. The parent company, Chesta & Chesta S.A.C., owns 51 percent of the shares of John Doe, Inc.

TRANSFEREE'S QUALIFICATIONS AND POSITION ABROAD

John Doe was the Manager of our parent company, Chesta & Chesta S.A.C. From 1996–2002. As manager, Mr. John Doe was responsible for conducting general administration affairs of the company including the hiring and firing of staff, acting as liaison and representative of Chesta & Chesta S.A.C. He was responsible for planning, formulating and implementing administrative and operational policies and procedures, managing budget, schedules and contracts.

Since May 2002, Mr. John Doe has held the position of President/Chief Financial Officer of our U.S. subsidiary. In this position he has been responsible for the direction and coordination of activities and operation of the corporation, planning, formulating and implementing administrative and operational policies and procedures. He has been conducting general administrative affairs of the company, acting as a liaison and representative for the subsidiary company in the United States.

In sum, Mr. John Doe has had autonomous control over and exercised wide latitude and discretionary decision-making in establishing the most advantageous courses of action for the successful management and direction of our international development activities. With respect to all matters in his jurisdiction he has exercised broad discretion over day-to-day operations. This has been a senior level position and an essential function at our Miami branch.

THE U.S. POSITION TO BE HELD BY THE TRANSFEREE

We wish to permanently retain Mr. John Doe at our Miami subsidiary in the position of President/Chief Financial Officer. Mr. John Doe will continue to perform the following duties: He will have full responsibility for the direction and coordination of activities and operation of the corporation. He will be responsible for planning, formulating, and implementing administrative and financial policies and procedures. His duties will include conducting general administrative and financial affairs of the company, acting as a liaison and representative for the subsidiary company in the United States, marketing the services of the parent company, engaging in long-range planning and identifying business opportunities in the United States and international markets, directing the business activities and supervising other managers and professionals.

As President/Chief Financial Officer, he will have authority to bind the company in legal contract agreements and will be expected to work autonomously in making key decisions for the company. His duties will include conducting general administration and affairs of the company, analyzing the appropriate market, setting strategic goals for growth, setting sales quotas and managing expenses. Mr. John Doe will supervise the manager, who will be in charge of supervising the staff who will be performing the day-to-day duties and policies that Mr. Doe has implemented.

With respect to all matters in his jurisdiction, he will exercise broad discretion over day-to-day operations. This is a senior level position and an essential function at our Miami branch. Chief Financial Officer is the top position of the branch office. Mr. Doe oversees all financial and accounting functions and formulates and administers the organization's overall financial plans and policies.

Mr. John Doe has complete autonomy and discretion to organize financial goals, objectives, and budgets. He will also review investment of any profits or other monies, supervise cash raising activities and execute all capital raising strategies to support the company's expansion, which means working closely with the accountant and bank officers. Most importantly, he will perform data analysis and use it to offer ideas to the Board of Directors and management personnel on how to maximize profits.

In the time that Mr. John Doe has been in the United States, he has surpassed our expectations concerning our U.S. activities, and his duties are indispensable for the continued success of the business.

In order to prove continuous business activities, we are enclosing among others documents: sale receipts, and purchase receipts. (Please see exhibits)

TERMS OF EMPLOYMENT

We currently intend to continue to employ Mr. John Doe permanently at a salary of $600.00 per week. Mr. Doe will work 40 hours per week with overtime as needed.

We respectfully request that the I-140 petition on behalf of Mr. John Doe be granted.

We would appreciate it if you would give this matter your attention and kind consideration.

Very truly yours,

John Doe, INC.

_____

John Doe
President

Form ETA 9089

OMB Approval: 1205-0451 Expiration Date: 03/31/2008	Application for Permanent Employment Certification ETA Form 9089 **U.S. Department of Labor**

Please read and review the filing instructions before completing this form. A copy of the instructions can be found at 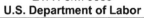 http://workforcesecurity.doleta.gov/foreign/.

Employing or continuing to employ an alien unauthorized to work in the United States is illegal and may subject the employer to criminal prosecution, civil money penalties, or both.

A. Refiling Instructions

1. Are you seeking to utilize the filing date from a previously submitted Application for Alien Employment Certification (ETA 750)?	☐ Yes	☒ No

1-A. If Yes, enter the previous filing date

1-B. Indicate the previous SWA or local office case number OR if not available, specify state where case was originally filed:

B. Schedule A or Sheepherder Information

1. Is this application in support of a Schedule A or Sheepherder Occupation?	☐ Yes	☒ No

If Yes, do NOT send this application to the Department of Labor. All applications in support of Schedule A or Sheepherder Occupations must be sent directly to the appropriate Department of Homeland Security office.

C. Employer Information (Headquarters or Main Office)

1. Employer's name **Doe and Associates**			
2. Address 1 **5525 SW 50 terrace, Suite #250**			
Address 2			
3. City **Miami**	State/Province **FLORIDA**	Country	Postal code **33166**
4. Phone number **305-1234567**		Extension	
5. Number of employees **10**		6. Year commenced business **1998**	
7. FEIN (Federal Employer Identification Number) **123456789**			8. NAICS code **523930**

9. Is the employer a closely held corporation, partnership, or sole proprietorship in which the alien has an ownership interest, or is there a familial relationship between the owners, stockholders, partners, corporate officers, incorporators, and the alien?	☐ Yes	☒ No

D. Employer Contact Information (This section must be filled out. This information must be different from the agent or attorney information listed in Section E).

1. Contact's last name **Richardson**	First name **Kim**	Middle initial
2. Address 1 **5525 SW 50 terrace, Suite #250**		
Address 2		

3. City **Miami**	State/Province **FLORIDA**	Country	Postal code **33166**
4. Phone number		Extension	
5. E-mail address **RK@doeassociates.com**			

Form ETA 9089

OMB Approval: 1205-0451
Expiration Date: 03/31/2008

Application for Permanent Employment Certification
ETA Form 9089
U.S. Department of Labor

E. Agent or Attorney Information (If applicable)

1. Agent or attorney's last name	First name	Middle initial

2. Firm name **Attorney's Firm**		

3. Firm EIN **123456**	4. Phone number **123-456-7890**	Extension

5. Address 1 **265 Le jeune Road, Suite 808**
Address 2

6. City **Miami**	State/Province **FL**	Country **USA**	Postal code **33134**

7. E-mail address **attorney@attorney.com**

F. Prevailing Wage Information (as provided by the State Workforce Agency)

1. Prevailing wage tracking number (if applicable)	2. SOC/O*NET(OES) code **11-2021**

3. Occupation Title **Marketing Manager**	4. Skill Level **1**

5. Prevailing wage   Per: (Choose only one)
$ **29.03**   ☒ Hour   ☐ Week   ☐ Bi-Weekly   ☐ Month   ☐ Year

6. Prevailing wage source (Choose only one)
☒ OES   ☐ CBA   ☐ Employer Conducted Survey   ☐ DBA   ☐ SCA   ☐ Other

6-A. If Other is indicated in question 6, specify: **N/A**

7. Determination date **01/20/2007**	8. Expiration date **06/30/2007**

G. Wage Offer Information

1. Offered wage
From: To: (Optional)   Per: (Choose only one)
$ **29.03** $ ☒ Hour   ☐ Week   ☐ Bi-Weekly   ☐ Month   ☐ Year

H. Job Opportunity Information (Where work will be performed)

1. Primary worksite (where work is to be performed) address 1 **5525 SW 50 terrace, Suite #250**
Address 2

2. City **Miami**	State **FL**	Postal code **33166**

3. Job title **Marketing Manager**

4. Education: minimum level required:

☐ None   ☐ High School   ☐ Associate's   ☒ Bachelor's   ☐ Master's   ☐ Doctorate   ☐ Other

4-A. If Other is indicated in question 4, specify the education required:

4-B. Major field of study
Business Administration

5. Is training required in the job opportunity? ☐ Yes ☒ No	5-A. If Yes, number of months of training required: **N/A**

Form ETA 9089

OMB Approval: 1205-0451
Expiration Date: 03/31/2008

Application for Permanent Employment Certification
ETA Form 9089
U.S. Department of Labor

H. Job Opportunity Information Continued

5-B. Indicate the field of training: **N/A**	

6. Is experience in the job offered required for the job?	6-A. If Yes, number of months experience required:	
☒ Yes ☐ No	**24**	

7. Is there an alternate field of study that is acceptable?	☐ Yes	☒ No

7-A. If Yes, specify the major field of study: **N/A**

8. Is there an alternate combination of education and experience that is acceptable?	☐ Yes	☒ No

8-A. If Yes, specify the alternate level of education required:

☒ None   ☐ High School   ☐ Associate's   ☐ Bachelor's   ☐ Master's   ☐ Doctorate   ☐ Other

8-B. If Other is indicated in question 8-A, indicate the alternate level of education required:

N/A

8-C. If applicable, indicate the number of years experience acceptable in question 8: **N/A**

9. Is a foreign educational equivalent acceptable?	☒ Yes	☐ No

10. Is experience in an alternate occupation acceptable?	10-A. If Yes, number of months experience in alternate occupation required:
☐ Yes ☒ No	

10-B. Identify the job title of the acceptable alternate occupation:

N/A

11. Job duties – If submitting by mail, add attachment if necessary. Job duties description must begin in this space.

Determine the demand of products and services offered by company and its competitors and identify potential customers. Develop pricing strategies with the goal of maximizing company*s profits or share of market while ensuring customer*s satisfaction. Research market conditions in local, regional, or national area to determine potential sales of product or service. Examine and analyze statistical data to forecast future marketing trends. Gather data on competitors and analyze process, sales, and methods of marketing and distribution. Collect data on customer preferences and buying habits. Supervise development of advertising and public relations programs.

12. Are the job opportunity's requirements normal for the occupation? *If the answer to this question is No, the employer must be prepared to provide documentation demonstrating that the job requirements are supported by business necessity.*	☒ Yes	☐ No
13. Is knowledge of a foreign language required to perform the job duties? *If the answer to this question is Yes, the employer must be prepared to provide documentation demonstrating that the language requirements are supported by business necessity.*	☐ Yes	☒ No

14. Specific skills or other requirements – If submitting by mail, add attachment if necessary. Skills description must begin in this space.

Experience in financial services

Verifiable References

Form ETA 9089

OMB Approval: 1205-0451
Expiration Date: 03/31/2008

Application for Permanent Employment Certification

ETA Form 9089

U.S. Department of Labor

H. Job Opportunity Information Continued

15. Does this application involve a job opportunity that includes a combination of occupations?	☐ Yes ☒ No
16. Is the position identified in this application being offered to the alien identified in Section J?	☒ Yes ☐ No
17. Does the job require the alien to live on the employer's premises?	☐ Yes ☒ No
18. Is the application for a live-in household domestic service worker?	☐ Yes ☒ No
18-A. If Yes, have the employer and the alien executed the required employment contract and has the employer provided a copy of the contract to the alien?	☐ Yes ☐ No ☒ NA

I. Recruitment Information

a. Occupation Type – All must complete this section.

1. Is this application for a **professional occupation**, other than a college or university teacher? Professional occupations are those for which a bachelor's degree (or equivalent) is normally required.	☒ Yes ☐ No
2. Is this application for a college or university teacher? **If Yes, complete questions 2-A and 2-B below.**	☐ Yes ☒ No
2-A. Did you select the candidate using a competitive recruitment and selection process?	☐ Yes ☒ No
2-B. Did you use the basic recruitment process for professional occupations?	☐ Yes ☒ No

b. Special Recruitment and Documentation Procedures for College and University Teachers – Complete only if the answer to question I.a.2-A is Yes.

3. Date alien selected: **N/A**
4. Name and date of national professional journal in which advertisement was placed: **N/A**
5. Specify additional recruitment information in this space. Add an attachment if necessary.   **N/A**

c. Professional/Non-Professional Information – Complete this section unless your answer to question B.1 or I.a.2-A is YES.

6. Start date for the SWA job order **02/01/2007**	7. End date for the SWA job order **03/04/2007**
8. Is there a Sunday edition of the newspaper in the area of intended employment?	☒ Yes ☐ No
9. Name of newspaper (of general circulation) in which the first advertisement was placed: **Miami Herald**	
10. Date of first advertisement identified in question 9: **02/04/2007**	
11. Name of newspaper or professional journal (if applicable) in which second advertisement was placed: **Miami Herald**	☒ Newspaper ☐ Journal

Form ETA 9089

OMB Approval: 1205-0451
Expiration Date: 03/31/2008

Application for Permanent Employment Certification
ETA Form 9089
U.S. Department of Labor

I. Recruitment Information Continued

12. Date of second newspaper advertisement or date of publication of journal identified in question 11: **02/11/2007**

d. Professional Recruitment Information – Complete if the answer to question I.a.1 is YES or if the answer to I.a.2-B is YES. Complete at least 3 of the items.

13. Dates advertised at job fair From: To:	14. Dates of on-campus recruiting From: To:
15. Dates posted on employer web site From: To:	16. Dates advertised with trade or professional organization From: To:
17. Dates listed with job search web site From: **02/12/2007** To: **02/28/2007**	18. Dates listed with private employment firm From: To:
19. Dates advertised with employee referral program From: To:	20. Dates advertised with campus placement office From: To:
21. Dates advertised with local or ethnic newspaper From: **02/22/2007** To: **02/22/2007**	22. Dates advertised with radio or TV ads From: **02/28/2007** To: **02/28/2007**

e. General Information – All must complete this section.

23. Has the employer received payment of any kind for the submission of this application?	☐ Yes ☒ No	
23-A. If Yes, describe details of the payment including the amount, date and purpose of the payment :		
24. Has the bargaining representative for workers in the occupation in which the alien will be employed been provided with notice of this filing at least 30 days but not more than 180 days before the date the application is filed?	☐ Yes ☐ No	☒ NA
25. If there is no bargaining representative, has a notice of this filing been posted for 10 business days in a conspicuous location at the place of employment, ending at least 30 days before but not more than 180 days before the date the application is filed?	☒ Yes ☐ No	☐ NA
26. Has the employer had a layoff in the area of intended employment in the occupation involved in this application or in a related occupation within the six months immediately preceding the filing of this application?	☐ Yes ☒ No	
26-A. If Yes, were the laid off U.S. workers notified and considered for the job opportunity for which certification is sought?	☐ Yes ☐ No	☒ NA

J. Alien Information (This section must be filled out. This information must be different from the agent or attorney information listed in Section E).

1. Alien's last name **DOE**	First name **John**	Full middle name

2. Current address 1 **222 S.W. 27th Drive**
Address 2

3. City **Weston**	State/Province **Florida**	Country **USA**	Postal code **33751**

4. Phone number of current residence **(305) 777-4444**	
5. Country of citizenship **England**	6. Country of birth **England**
7. Alien's date of birth **05/20/1986**	8. Class of admission **B2**
9. Alien registration number (A#) **None**	10. Alien admission number (I-94) **123456789 00**

11. Education: highest level achieved relevant to the requested occupation: ☐ None ☐ High School ☐ Associate's ☒ Bachelor's ☐ Master's ☐ Doctorate ☐ Other

Form ETA 9089

OMB Approval: 1205-0451
Expiration Date: 03/31/2008

Application for Permanent Employment Certification
ETA Form 9089
U.S. Department of Labor

J. Alien Information Continued

11-A. If Other indicated in question 11, specify **N/A**	
12. Specify major field(s) of study **Business Administration**	
13. Year relevant education completed **1985**	
14. Institution where relevant education specified in question 11 was received **University of London**	
15. Address 1 of conferring institution **London**	
Address 2	

16. City **London**	State/Province	Country **England**	Postal code

17. Did the alien complete the training required for the requested job opportunity, as indicated in question H.5?	☐ Yes ☐ No ☒ NA
18. Does the alien have the experience as required for the requested job opportunity indicated in question H.6?	☒ Yes ☐ No ☐ NA
19. Does the alien possess the alternate combination of education and experience as indicated in question H.8?	☐ Yes ☐ No ☒ NA
20. Does the alien have the experience in an alternate occupation specified in question H.10?	☐ Yes ☐ No ☒ NA
21. Did the alien gain any of the qualifying experience with the employer in a position substantially comparable to the job opportunity requested?	☐ Yes ☐ No ☒ NA
22. Did the employer pay for any of the alien's education or training necessary to satisfy any of the employer's job requirements for this position?	☐ Yes ☒ No
23. Is the alien currently employed by the petitioning employer?	☐ Yes ☒ No

K. Alien Work Experience

List all jobs the alien has held during the past 3 years. Also list any other experience that qualifies the alien for the job opportunity for which the employer is seeking certification.

a. Job 1

1. Employer name **I & T Financial Advisors, Inc.**	
2. Address 1 **Miami**	
Address 2	

3. City **Miami**	State/Province **Florida**	Country	Postal code **33134**

4. Type of business **Financial services**	5. Job title **Marketing Manager**

6. Start date **12/01/2003**	7. End date **04/01/2007**	8. Number of hours worked per week **40**

Form ETA 9089

OMB Approval: 1205-0451
Expiration Date: 03/31/2008

Application for Permanent Employment Certification
ETA Form 9089
U.S. Department of Labor

K. Alien Work Experience Continued

9. Job details (duties performed, use of tools, machines, equipment, skills, qualifications, certifications, licenses, etc. Include the phone number of the employer and the name of the alien's supervisor.)

Determine the demand of products and services offered by company and its competitors and identify potential customers. Develop pricing strategies with the goal of maximizing company's profits or share of market while ensuring customer's satisfaction. Research market conditions in local, regional, or national area to determine potential sales of product or service. Examine and analyze statistical data to forecast future marketing trends. Gather data on competitors and analyze process, sales, and methods of marketing and distribution. Collect data on customer preferences and buying habits. Supervise development of advertising and public relations programs.

b. Job 2

1. Employer name **Atlantic Financial Corporation**			
2. Address 1 **London**			
Address 2			
3. City **London**	State/Province	Country **England**	Postal code
4. Type of business **Financial Services**		5. Job title **Marketing Manager**	
6. Start date **01/01/1993**	7. End date **08/30/2002**	8. Number of hours worked per week **40**	

9. Job details (duties performed, use of tools, machines, equipment, skills, qualifications, certifications, licenses, etc. Include the phone number of the employer and the name of the alien's supervisor.)

Determined the demand of products and services offered by company and its competitors and identify potential customers. Developed pricing strategies with the goal of maximizing company's profits or share of market while ensuring customer's satisfaction. Researched market conditions in local, regional, or national area to determine potential sales of product or service. Examined and analyzed statistical data to forecast future marketing trends. Gathered data on competitors and analyze process, sales, and methods of marketing and distribution. Collected data on customer preferences and buying habits. Supervised development of advertising and public relations programs.

c. Job 3

1. Employer name **Worldwide Financial bank**			
2. Address 1 **Paris**			
Address 2			
3. City **Paris**	State/Province	Country **France**	Postal code
4. Type of business **Bank**		5. Job title **Marketing Director**	
6. Start date **03/02/1988**	7. End date **12/30/1992**	8. Number of hours worked per week **40**	

Form ETA 9089

K. Alien Work Experience Continued

9. Job details (duties performed, use of tools, machines, equipment, skills, qualifications, certifications, licenses, etc. Include the phone number of the employer and the name of the alien's supervisor.)

Determined the demand of products and services offered by company and its competitors and identify potential customers. Developed pricing strategies with the goal of maximizing company's profits or share of market while ensuring customer's satisfaction. Researched market conditions in local, regional, or national area to determine potential sales of product or service. Examined and analyzed statistical data to forecast future marketing trends. Gathered data on competitors and analyze process, sales, and methods of marketing and distribution. Collected data on customer preferences and buying habits. Supervised development of advertising and public relations programs.

L. Alien Declaration

I declare under penalty of perjury that Sections J and K are true and correct. *I understand that to knowingly furnish false information in the preparation of this form and any supplement thereto or to aid, abet, or counsel another to do so is a federal offense punishable by a fine or imprisonment up to five years or both under 18 U.S.C. §§ 2 and 1001. Other penalties apply as well to fraud or misuse of ETA immigration documents and to perjury with respect to such documents under 18 U.S.C. §§ 1546 and 1621.*

In addition, ***further declare*** *under penalty of perjury that I intend to accept the position offered in Section H of this application if a labor certification is approved and I am granted a visa or an adjustment of status based on this application.*

1. Alien's last name	First name	Full middle name
DOE	**John**	
2. Signature	Date signed	

Note – The signature and date signed do not have to be filled out when electronically submitting to the Department of Labor for processing, but must be complete when submitting by mail. If the application is submitted electronically, any resulting certification MUST be signed *immediately upon receipt* from DOL before it can be submitted to USCIS for final processing.

M. Declaration of Preparer

1. **Was the application completed by the employer?** If No, you must complete this section.	☐ Yes ☒ No

I hereby certify that I have prepared this application at the direct request of the employer listed in Section C and that to the best of my knowledge the information contained herein is true and correct. *I understand that to knowingly furnish false information in the preparation of this form and any supplement thereto or to aid, abet, or counsel another to do so is a federal offense punishable by a fine, imprisonment up to five years or both under 18 U.S.C. §§ 2 and 1001. Other penalties apply as well to fraud or misuse of ETA immigration documents and to perjury with respect to such documents under 18 U.S.C. §§ 1546 and 1621.*

2. Preparer's last name	First name	Middle initial
Attorney's name	**Name**	
3. Title **Attorney**		
4. E-mail address **attorney@attorney.com**		
5. Signature	Date signed	

Note – The signature and date signed do not have to be filled out when electronically submitting to the Department of Labor for processing, but must be complete when submitting by mail. If the application is submitted electronically, any resulting certification MUST be signed *immediately upon receipt* from DOL before it can be submitted to USCIS for final processing.

Form ETA 9089

OMB Approval: 1205-0451
Expiration Date: 03/31/2008

Application for Permanent Employment Certification
ETA Form 9089
U.S. Department of Labor

N. Employer Declaration

*By virtue of my signature below, **I HEREBY CERTIFY** the following conditions of employment:*

1. The offered wage equals or exceeds the prevailing wage and I will pay at least the prevailing wage.
2. The wage is not based on commissions, bonuses or other incentives, unless I guarantees a wage paid on a weekly, bi-weekly, or monthly basis that equals or exceeds the prevailing wage.
3. I have enough funds available to pay the wage or salary offered the alien.
4. I will be able to place the alien on the payroll on or before the date of the alien's proposed entrance into the United States.
5. The job opportunity does not involve unlawful discrimination by race, creed, color, national origin, age, sex, religion, handicap, or citizenship.
6. The job opportunity is not:
    a. Vacant because the former occupant is on strike or is being locked out in the course of a labor dispute involving a work stoppage; or
    b. At issue in a labor dispute involving a work stoppage.
7. The job opportunity's terms, conditions, and occupational environment are not contrary to Federal, state or local law.
8. The job opportunity has been and is clearly open to any U.S. worker.
9. The U.S. workers who applied for the job opportunity were rejected for lawful job-related reasons.
10. The job opportunity is for full-time, permanent employment for an employer other than the alien.

I hereby designate the agent or attorney identified in section E (if any) to represent me for the purpose of labor certification and, by virtue of my signature in Block 3 below, **I take full responsibility** for the accuracy of any representations made by my agent or attorney.

I declare under penalty of perjury that I have read and reviewed this application and that to the best of my knowledge the information contained herein is true and accurate. *I understand that to knowingly furnish false information in the preparation of this form and any supplement thereto or to aid, abet, or counsel another to do so is a federal offense punishable by a fine or imprisonment up to five years or both under 18 U.S.C. §§ 2 and 1001. Other penalties apply as well to fraud or misuse of ETA immigration documents and to perjury with respect to such documents under 18 U.S.C. §§ 1546 and 1621.*

1. Last name **Richardson**	First name **KIM**	Middle initial
2. Title **President**		
3. Signature	Date signed	

Note – The signature and date signed do not have to be filled out when electronically submitting to the Department of Labor for processing, but must be complete when submitting by mail. If the application is submitted electronically, any resulting certification MUST be signed *immediately upon receipt* from DOL before it can be submitted to USCIS for final processing.

O. U.S. Government Agency Use Only

Pursuant to the provisions of Section 212 (a)(5)(A) of the Immigration and Nationality Act, as amended, I hereby certify that there are not sufficient U.S. workers available and the employment of the above will not adversely affect the wages and working conditions of workers in the U.S. similarly employed.

Signature of Certifying Officer	Date Signed
Case Number	Filing Date

Form ETA 9089

OMB Approval: 1205-0451
Expiration Date: 03/31/2008

Application for Permanent Employment Certification
ETA Form 9089
U.S. Department of Labor

P. OMB Information *Paperwork Reduction Act Information Control Number 1205-0451*

Persons are not required to respond to this collection of information unless it displays a currently valid OMB control number.

Respondent's reply to these reporting requirements is required to obtain the benefits of permanent employment certification (Immigration and Nationality Act, Section 212(a)(5)). Public reporting burden for this collection of information is estimated to average 1¼ hours per response, including the time for reviewing instructions, searching existing data sources, gathering and maintaining the data needed, and completing and reviewing the collection of information. Send comments regarding this burden estimate to the Division of Foreign Labor Certification * U.S. Department of Labor * Room C4312 * 200 Constitution Ave., NW * Washington, DC * 20210.
Do NOT send the completed application to this address.

Q. Privacy Statement Information

In accordance with the Privacy Act of 1974, as amended (5 U.S.C. 552a), you are hereby notified that the information provided herein is protected under the Privacy Act. The Department of Labor (Department or DOL) maintains a System of Records titled Employer Application and Attestation File for Permanent and Temporary Alien Workers (DOL/ETA-7) that includes this record.

Under routine uses for this system of records, case files developed in processing labor certification applications, labor condition applications, or labor attestations may be released as follows: in connection with appeals of denials before the DOL Office of Administrative Law Judges and Federal courts, records may be released to the employers that filed such applications, their representatives, to named alien beneficiaries or their representatives, and to the DOL Office of Administrative Law Judges and Federal courts; and in connection with administering and enforcing immigration laws and regulations, records may be released to such agencies as the DOL Office of Inspector General, Employment Standards Administration, the Department of Homeland Security, and the Department of State.

Further relevant disclosures may be made in accordance with the Privacy Act and under the following circumstances: in connection with federal litigation; for law enforcement purposes; to authorized parent locator persons under Pub. L. 93-647; to an information source or public authority in connection with personnel, security clearance, procurement, or benefit-related matters; to a contractor or their employees, grantees or their employees, consultants, or volunteers who have been engaged to assist the agency in the performance of Federal activities; for Federal debt collection purposes; to the Office of Management and Budget in connection with its legislative review, coordination, and clearance activities; to a Member of Congress or their staff in response to an inquiry of the Congressional office made at the written request of the subject of the record; in connection with records management; and to the news media and the public when a matter under investigation becomes public knowledge, the Solicitor of Labor determines the disclosure is necessary to preserve confidence in the integrity of the Department, or the Solicitor of Labor determines that a legitimate public interest exists in the disclosure of information, unless the Solicitor of Labor determines that disclosure would constitute an unwarranted invasion of personal privacy.

Results of Recruitment Report

SAMPLE
(TO BE PRINTED IN COMPANY'S LETTERHEAD)

Date
U.S. Department of Labor
Employment and Training Administration
Harris Tower
233 Peachtree Street, Suite 410Atlanta, Georgia 30303
RE: Application for Alien Employment Certification
       Employer: _____
       Alien: _____

Dear Sir or Madam:

This letter is to report the results of the recruitment efforts developed by our company to hire a U.S. worker for the position of
_____.

We have considered the following U.S. workers for this job opportunity and have not hired them for the stated reasons which we consider to be lawful and job-related reasons:

1. Name: _____
    Address: _____
    _____

	City	State	Zip Code

    Phone: _____
    Reason for not hiring: Applicant does not have the required experience in the job being offered.

2. Name: _____
    Address: _____
    _____

	City	State	Zip Code

    Phone: _____
    Reason for not hiring: Applicant did not accept the position as offered

3. Name: _____
    Address: _____
    _____

	City	State	Zip Code

    Phone: _____
    Reason for not hiring: Applicant does not have the required education in the job being offered.

4. Name: _____
    Address: _____
    _____

	City	State	Zip Code

    Phone: _____
    Reason for not hiring: A letter was mailed to the applicant inviting him to contact our office in order to schedule an appointment for an interview; but s/he did not respond.

All applicants learned of position through _____.
Thank you for your attention to this matter.
Very truly yours,

NAME OF EMPLOYER

_____
                Name of Representative
                        Title

Notice of Job Availability

Title: _____

Duties: _____

Requirements: _____

_____

Salary/Overtime: _____

Hours: _____

Contact: _____

_____

Date Posted: _____

Date Removed: _____

Results: _____

Employer Signature:

_____
Name of Employer's Representative
Title

This notice is posted in connection with the filing of an application for permanent alien labor certification. Any person may provide documentary evidence bearing on the application to the State Workforce Agency and/or the Labor Certification Processing Center at the following address:

U.S. Department of Labor
Employment and Training Administration
Harris Tower
233 Peachtree
Street, Suite 410
Atlanta, Georgia 30303
Phone: (404) 893-0101
Fax: (404) 893-4642

CHAPTER **9**

Claiming Asylum or Protection in the United States

A person physically present or arriving in the United States, who expresses a fear of persecution on account of race, religion, nationality or membership in a particular social group and/or political opinion, is eligible to apply for a discretionary grant of asylum and eventually to adjust his/her status as a lawful permanent resident. Two other forms of relief are available: Withholding of Removal and Relief Under the Convention Against Torture.

I. Legal Standard for Asylum/Refugee Protection

A. International Definition of Refugee

A refugee is any person who is outside their country of nationality or, in such a case, any person having no nationality or being outside any country in which such a person last habitually resided and who is unable or unwilling to return and is unable or unwilling to avail him/herself of the protection of that country because of persecution or a well-founded fear of persecution on account of race, religion, nationality, membership in a particular social group or political opinion. Immigration and Nationality Act, §101(a)(42)(A); 8 USC §1101(a)(42)(a).

B. Definition of Persecution

Persecution is the infliction of suffering or harm in a way that is regarded as offensive physical abuse or threats to life or freedom; the harm experienced cannot be mere harassment. In addition, the cumulative effect of various types of harm can be persecution when added together (e.g., (1) economic disadvantage/inability to procure gainful employment; (2) interference with person's right to privacy; (3) interference with person's right to higher education; (4) being forced to live in substandard housing or conditions; (5) being forced to live ostracized by society or family; (6) being denied a passport; (7) being forced to live under constant surveillance; and (8) being under constant pressure to become an informant).

The persecution must be either by the government or a group that the government cannot control or refuses to control.

C. Well-Founded Fear Test

To establish a "well-founded fear of persecution," an asylum applicant need only show a reasonable expectation that s/he will be persecuted. There is a subjective and objective element. To meet the subjective test, s/he must demonstrate that s/he actually has a fear of returning to their home country. To meet the objective requirement, s/he must demonstrate country conditions through specific and objective evidence or credible testimony.

The regulations at 8 C.F.R. §208.13 (b) sets forth asylum standards:

The applicant may qualify as a refugee either because s/he has suffered past persecution or because s/he has a well-founded fear of future persecution.

If the applicant can provide evidence s/he was persecuted in the past, there is a presumption of future persecution 8 C.F.R. §208.13(b)(1)(i).

The government then has the burden of rebutting the presumption. For example, it can try to establish by a preponderance of the evidence that country conditions have changed and applicant no longer has a well-founded fear.

II. Other Relief

A. Withholding Standard

The Attorney General may not remove a person to a country where his/her life or freedom would be threatened because of the person's race, religion, nationality, membership in a particular social group or political opinion. The applicant for withholding of removal must show a clear probability of persecution or that it is more likely than not that s/he would be persecuted if removed to the home country. Under INA §241(b)(3), 8 U.S.C. §1231(b)(3):

Under withholding, the applicant can remain in the United States, but it is not a grant of lawful permanent residency.

B. Convention against Torture (CAT)

Torture is defined in Article 3 of the United Nations Convention Against Torture and Other Cruel, Inhuman, and Degrading Treatment or Punishment (CAT), as:

"Any act by which severe pain or suffering, whether physical or mental, is intentionally inflicted on a person for such purposes as obtaining from him or a third person information or a confession, punishing him for an act he or a third person has committed or is suspected of having committed, punishing him for an act he or a third person or for any reason based on discrimination of any kind … when such pain or suffering is inflicted by or at the instigation of or with the consent or acquiescence of a public official or other person acting in official capacity …"

CAT is a treaty that prohibits the return of a person to a country where there are substantial grounds for believing that the person would be in danger of being subjected to torture if returned.

There are no bars to eligibility for CAT. The standards for asylum, establishing that his/her fear of torture is on account of race, religion, nationality, political opinion and/or membership in a social group are not required under CAT.

The standard of proof under the CAT is higher than the standard for asylum. The alien must prove that it is "more likely than not" that s/he would be tortured if forced to return. The evidentiary proof for torture is very similar to the proof for asylum or withholding claims.

Like the restriction on withholding, the benefits of CAT are limited. An individual who is successful under a CAT claim cannot be removed from the United States to the country from which s/he fled persecution but can be removed to a third country if one is available. The individual may not adjust his/her status to legal permanent residency, but can obtain work authorization.

C. Bars to Eligibility for Asylum

The Asylum Officer or Immigration Judge will also consider whether any bars apply. The applicant will be barred from being granted asylum under INA § 208(b) (2) if the applicant:

1. Ordered, incited, assisted or otherwise participated in the persecution of any person on account of race, religion, nationality, membership in a particular social group or political opinion;

2. Was convicted of a particularly serious crime (includes aggravated felonies);

3. Committed a serious nonpolitical crime outside the United States;

4. Poses a danger to the security of the United States;

5. Firmly resettled in another country prior to arriving in the United States (see 8 C.F.R. § 208.15 for a definition of "firm resettlement");

6. Has engaged in terrorist activity;

7. Is engaged in or is likely to engage after entry in any terrorist activity (or a consular officer or the Attorney General knows or has reasonable grounds to believe that this is the case.);

8. Has, under any circumstances indicated an intention to cause death or serious bodily harm or incited terrorist activity;

9. Is a representative of (i) a foreign terrorist organization; (ii) is a member of a political, social or other terrorist organization whose public endorsement of acts of terrorist activity undermines United States efforts to reduce or eliminate terrorist activities; and (iii) has used a position of prominence within any country to endorse or espouse terrorist activity or to persuade others to support terrorist activity or a terrorist organization, in a way that undermines United States efforts to reduce or eliminate terrorist activities; or

10. Has previously filed for asylum and was denied.

D. Bar for Failure to File within One Year of Entry

This bar applies if the applicant did not file for asylum within one-year of entry or by April 1, 1997, whichever is later. S/he can show changed circumstances in his or her country or extraordinary circumstances in order not to be barred, as follows:

1. Changed circumstances: 8 C.F.R. § 208.4(a)(4)

    These may include but are not limited to the following:

    a. Changes in condition in the applicant's country of nationality or, if the applicant is stateless, country of last permanent residence;

    b. Changes in the applicant's circumstances that materially affect the applicant's eligibility for asylum, including changes in applicable U.S. law and activities the applicant becomes involved in outside the country of feared persecution that place the applicant at risk; or

    c. In the case of an alien who had previously been included as a dependent in another alien's pending asylum application, the loss of the spousal or parent-child relationship to the principal applicant through marriage, divorce, death or attainment of age 21.

2. Extraordinary Circumstances: 8 C.F.R. § 208.4(a)(5)

    These may include but are not limited to the following:

    a. Serious illness or mental or physical disability, including any effects of persecution or violent harm suffered in the past, during the one-year period after arrival;

    b. Legal disability (e.g., the applicant was an unaccompanied minor or suffered from a mental impairment) during the one-year period after arrival;

c. Ineffective assistance of counsel provided that:

i. The applicant files an affidavit setting forth in detail the agreement with counsel concerning services to be rendered and what counsel failed to do with reference to representation

ii. Proof counsel has been informed of the allegations leveled against him/her and given an opportunity to respond; and

iii. The applicant indicates whether a complaint has been filed with appropriate Bar authorities (indicate why if not);

iv. The applicant maintained temporary protected status, lawful immigrant or nonimmigrant status or was given parole until a reasonable period before the filing of the asylum application;

v. The applicant filed an asylum application prior to the expiration of the one-year deadline, but that application was rejected by the Service as not properly filed, was returned to the applicant for corrections and was re-filed within a reasonable period thereafter; and

vi. The death, serious illness or incapacity of the applicant's legal representative or a member of the applicant's immediate family.

III. Procedure for Filing Asylum Application

There are two methods for filing for asylum, affirmatively:

"Affirmative" Asylum Application Filed with USCIS

In the affirmative asylum, individuals who are physically present in the United States, notwithstanding of how they entered and their current immigration status, may apply for asylum. This should be done within one year of date of entry. An affirmative application (Form I-589) is filed with USCIS. As mentioned, to file after one year, s/he must demonstrate changed circumstances that materially affect his/her eligibility or extraordinary circumstances relating to the delay in filing and that s/he filed within a reasonable amount of time thereafter. The Service Center will forward the application to the USCIS Asylum Office for an asylum interview.

After the interview, the application will be approved for a grant of asylum or referred to the Immigration Court.

If referred to the Immigration Court, the applicant will be placed in removal proceedings by service of a Notice to Appear and other charging documents. Grounds for referring an applicant to the EOIR are found when an alien, who is undocumented or in violation of his/her status when apprehended in the United States, is caught trying to enter the United States without proper documentation (usually at a port of entry) or is found having no credible fear of persecution.

"Defensive" Asylum Process

Before the Immigration Judge (IJ), the applicant, who is named as the respondent, will be allowed to raise his/her asylum claim as a defense against removal. The IJ hears the applicant's claim and also hears any arguments on the validity of the claim raised by the Government, which is represented by a trial attorney. The IJ then makes a determination of eligibility. If the applicant is not found eligible for asylum, the IJ determines whether the applicant is eligible for any other forms of relief from removal such as withholding of removal or relief under CAT and, if not, will order the individual removed from the United States.

IV. Required Documents

A. A complete application, whether for someone in removal proceedings or someone applying affirmatively with the USCIS, includes the following:

1. Request for asylum (Form I-589);

2. Detailed statement from client about his/her asylum claim;

3. USCIS Notice of Appearance (Form G-28);

4. EOIR Notice of Appearance (EOIR-28), only in removal proceedings, unless previously submitted at the Master Calendar hearing. This is not needed for affirmative applications;

5. Certificate of Service upon the USCIS for cases in removal proceedings. This is also recommended, but not required, for affirmative applications;

6. Cover letter from the attorney;

7. Signature of the applicant and anyone, other than an immediate relative, who helped in the preparation of the application under penalty of perjury;

8. Two recent passport photographs of every individual included in the application;

9. Any evidence of claimed relationship for all family members included in the application (e.g., marriage certificate and/or birth certificates);

10. Form I-589 and documentation must be submitted in triplicate (i.e., original plus two copies as well as an additional copy of the applicant's Form I-589 for each dependent included in the application);

11. Properly certified translation in English of any documents in a foreign language;

12. There is no filing fee for the asylum application;

13. Written declaration by the applicant detailing questions contained on the Form I-589;

14. Any materials that help verify the applicant's claim and independent materials such as news articles reports by human rights groups and other proof of cultural, political and social circumstances in applicant's country, region, city or district or any other information on his/her country conditions;

15. Proof of applicant's identity such as passport, identity card or any other form of identification; and

16. Expert testimony or declaration about country conditions and/or medical/psychiatric evaluation, etc.

B. An asylum-seeker may include spouse and unmarried children under 21 who are in the United States in the application. These family members are eligible for derivative asylum status if the principal applicant (the parent or spouse) wins asylum. Children who are married or over 21 must file a separate Form I-589 application.

V. Filing Documents with Government Agencies

If the applicant is currently in proceedings with EOIR, s/he is required to file the application, Form I-589, with the Immigration Court having jurisdiction over the case.

Immigration judges have exclusive jurisdiction over asylum applications filed by an alien who has been served with a Form I-862, Notice to Appear, (formerly known as Order to Show Cause).

If the applicant is not in proceedings in the Immigration Court, s/he should mail the completed Application for Asylum, Form I-589 and any other additional information to the USCIS Service Center as indicated below.

If the applicant lives in Alabama, Arkansas, Colorado, Commonwealth of Puerto Rico, District of Columbia, Florida, Georgia, Louisiana, Maryland, Mississippi, New Mexico, North Carolina, Oklahoma, western Pennsylvania, South Carolina, Tennessee, Texas, United States Virgin Islands, Utah, Virginia, West Virginia or Wyoming, s/he should mail the application to:

Department of Homeland Security
U.S. Citizenship and Immigration Service
Texas Service Center
Attn: Asylum
P.O. Box 851892
Mesquite, TX 75185-1892

If the applicant lives in Alaska, northern California, Hawaii, Idaho, Illinois, Indiana, Iowa, Kansas, Kentucky, Michigan, Minnesota, Missouri, Montana, Nebraska, northern Nevada, North Dakota, Ohio, Oregon, South Dakota, Territory of Guam, Washington or Wisconsin, s/he should mail the application to:

Department of Homeland Security
U.S. Citizenship and Immigration Service
Nebraska Service Center
P.O. Box 87589
Lincoln, NE 68501-7589

If applicant lives in Arizona, southern California or southern Nevada, s/he should mail the application to:

Department of Homeland Security
U.S. Citizenship and Immigration Service
California Service Center
P.O. Box 10589
Laguna Niguel, CA 92607-0589

If applicant lives in Connecticut, Delaware, Maine, Massachusetts, New Hampshire, New Jersey, New York, eastern Pennsylvania, Rhode Island or Vermont, s/he should mail the application to:

Department of Homeland Security
U.S. Citizenship and Immigration Service
Vermont Service Center
75 Lower Welden St.
St Albans, VT 05479-0589

VI. Status of Family Members, Adjustment of Status, Work Authorization and Travel Permit

A. Derivative Status

The applicant must list the spouse and all the children on the Form I-589 regardless of their age, marital status, whether they are in the United States or whether they are included in the application or filing a separate asylum application.

The applicant may ask to have included in the asylum decision the spouse and/or any children who are under the age of 21 and unmarried, if they are in the United States. If s/he is granted asylum, they will also be granted asylum status and will be allowed to remain in the United States. However, if the applicant is referred to the Immigration Court, family members will also be referred to the court for removal proceedings. Marriage certificates and/or birth certificates should be provided to prove family relationships.

Children who are married and/or children who are 21 years of age or older at the time the asylum application is filed must file separately for asylum by submitting their own asylum applications (Form I-589).

Upon the grant of asylum, the applicant may petition to bring the spouse and/or children (unmarried and under the age of 21 as of the date s/he filed the asylum application) to the United States through form I-730.

B. Aged Out or Reaching 21 Years of Age after Filing Application

Under the Child Status Protection (CSPA), the applicant's child will continue to be classified as a child if s/he turned 21 years of age after application was filed but while it was pending. Child must have been unmarried and under 21 years of age on the date Form I-589 was filed. Proof of filing should be kept in the file (e.g., certified mail return receipt or courier service receipt of delivery to USCIS).

There is no requirement that the applicant's child has been included as a dependent on the asylum application at the time of filing, only that the applicant's child be included prior to the decision made on the claim. This means that the applicant may add to the asylum application an unmarried son or daughter who is 21 years of age, but who was 20 at the time of the filing of the asylum application.

C. Obtaining Work Authorization

An asylum applicant does not obtain work authorization upon filing the application. The applicant will be authorized to work in the United States if s/he is granted asylum and as long as s/he remains in asylum status. The applicant is also eligible to apply for employment authorization if s/he is given a recommended approval or conditional grant of asylum. In addition, work authorization will be granted if 150 days have passed since the filing of the application with the Service Center and no decision has been made on the application. The USCIS has 30 days to either grant or deny the request for employment. The application to apply for an Employment Authorization Document (EAD) is the Form I-765.

D. Permission to Travel

If the application for asylum is approved, the applicant may apply for a Refugee Travel Document. This document will allow applicant to travel abroad and return to the United States. However, the attorney should review any "unlawful presence" issues before the departure of the applicant from the U.S.

If the applicant obtains the document and returns to the country of feared persecution, s/he will be presumed to have abandoned his/her asylum request, unless applicant can show compelling reasons for the return.

E. Unlawful Presence

The applicant will not suffer the consequences of unlawful presence mentioned in Chapter 1 while the application is pending because the application tolls the time taken into account in determining the period of "unlawful presence," unless the applicant engages in employment without authorization.

F. Adjustment of Status to Permanent Residency

The applicant may apply for lawful permanent resident status under INA § 209(b) after s/he has been physically present in the United States for a period of one year after the date applicant was granted asylum status. To apply for lawful permanent resident status, the applicant must submit a separate Form I-485, Application to Register Permanent Residence or Adjust Status, for him/herself and each qualifying family member to the USCIS, Nebraska Service Center, P.O. Box 87485, Lincoln, NE 68501-7485.

Appendix

1. Form I-589—Asylum Application
2. Form I-589 Supplement A
3. Form I-589 Supplement B
4. Written Declaration from Client

Form I-589

Department of Homeland Security
U.S. Citizenship and Immigration Services

U.S. Department of Justice
Executive Office for Immigration Review

OMB No. 1615-0067; Expires 03/31/10

I-589, Application for Asylum and for Withholding of Removal

START HERE - Type or print in black ink. See the instructions for information about eligibilty and how to complete and file this application. There is NO filing fee for this application.

NOTE: Check this box if you also want to apply for withholding of removal under the Convention Against Torture. ☐

Part A. I. Information About You

1. Alien Registration Number(s) (A-Number) *(if any)* None	**2.** U.S. Social Security Number *(if any)* None

3. Complete Last Name DOE	**4.** First Name Juan	**5.** Middle Name

6. What other names have you used *(include maiden name and aliases)?*
None

7. Residence in the U.S. *(where you physically reside)*	Telephone Number (305) 777-4444
Street Number and Name 222 SW 27th Drive	Apt. Number

City Weston	State Florida	Zip Code 33751

8. Mailing Address in the U.S. *(if different than the address in No. 7)* In Care Of *(if applicable)*: (Attorney's Name)	Telephone Number ( )
Street Number and Name 222 S.W. 27 Drive	Apt. Number

City Weston	State Florida	Zip Code 33751

9. Gender: ☒ Male ☐ Female   **10.** Marital Status: ☒ Single ☐ Married ☐ Divorced ☐ Widowed

11. Date of Birth *(mm/dd/yyyy)* 05/15/1960	**12.** City and Country of Birth Bogota, Colombia

13. Present Nationality *(Citizenship)* Colombian	**14.** Nationality at Birth Colombian	**15.** Race, Ethnic, or Tribal Group	**16.** Religion Catholic

17. *Check the box, a through c, that applies:* **a.** ☒ I have never been in Immigration Court proceedings.
b. ☐ I am now in Immigration Court proceedings.   **c.** ☐ I am **not** now in Immigration Court proceedings, but I have been in the past.

18. *Complete 18 a through c.*
a. When did you last leave your country? *(mmm/dd/yyyy)*   04/07/2002   **b.** What is your current I-94 Number, if any? *123456789 00*

c. List each entry into the U.S. beginning with your most recent entry.
List date (mm/dd/yyyy), place, and your status for each entry.(Attach additional sheets as needed.)

Date 07/20/2002	Place Miami, FL	Status B2	Date Status Expires: 01/19/2003
Date	Place	Status	
Date	Place	Status	

19. What country issued your last passport or travel document? Colombia	**20.** Passport # 123456789	**21.** Expiration Date *(mm/dd/yyyy)* 10/10/2010
	Travel Document #	

22. What is your native language *(include dialect, if applicable)?* Spanish	**23.** Are you fluent in English? ☐ Yes ☒ No	**24.** What other languages do you speak fluently? None
For EOIR use only.	**Action:** Interview Date: Asylum Officer ID#:	**For USCIS use only. Decision:** Approval Date: Denial Date: Referral Date:

Form I-589 (Rev. 04/07/09) Y

Form I-589

Part A. II. Information About Your Spouse and Children

Your spouse   ☐ I am not married. (Skip to **Your Children** below.)

1. Alien Registration Number (A-Number) *(if any)*	2. Passport/ID Card No. *(if any)*	3. Date of Birth *(mm/dd/yyyy)*	4. U.S. Social Security No. *(if any)*

5. Complete Last Name	6. First Name	7. Middle Name	8. Maiden Name

9. Date of Marriage *(mm/dd/yyyy)*	10. Place of Marriage	11. City and Country of Birth

12. Nationality *(Citizenship)*	13. Race, Ethnic, or Tribal Group	14. Gender ☐ Male ☐ Female

15. Is this person in the U.S.?

☐ Yes *(Complete Blocks 16 to 24.)*   ☐ No *(Specify location):* _____

16. Place of last entry into the U.S.	17. Date of last entry into the U.S. *(mm/dd/yyyy)*	18. I-94 No. *(if any)*	19. Status when last admitted *(Visa type, if any)*

20. What is your spouse's current status?	21. What is the expiration date of his/her authorized stay, if any? *(mm/dd/yyyy)*	22. Is your spouse in Immigration Court proceedings? ☐ Yes ☐ No	23. If previously in the U.S., date of previous arrival *(mm/dd/yyyy)*

24. If in the U.S., is your spouse to be included in this application? *(Check the appropriate box.)*

☐ Yes *(Attach one photograph of your spouse in the upper right corner of Page 9 on the extra copy of the application submitted for this person.)*

☐ No

Your Children. List **all** of your children, regardless of age, location, or marital status.

☐ I do not have any children. *(Skip to Part A. III., **Information about your background.**)*

☐ I have children.   Total number of children: _____ .

(**NOTE:** *Use Form I-589 Supplement A or attach additional sheets of paper and documentation if you have more than four children.*)

1. Alien Registration Number (A-Number) *(if any)*	2. Passport/ID Card No. *(if any)*	3. Marital Status *(Married, Single, Divorced, Widowed)*	4. U.S. Social Security No. *(if any)*

5. Complete Last Name	6. First Name	7. Middle Name	8. Date of Birth *(mm/dd/yyyy)*

9. City and Country of Birth	10. Nationality *(Citizenship)*	11. Race, Ethnic, or Tribal Group	12. Gender ☐ Male ☐ Female

13. Is this child in the U.S. ?

☐ Yes *(Complete Blocks 14 to 21.)*   ☐ No *(Specify location.)* _____

14. Place of last entry in the U.S.	15. Date of last entry in the U.S. *(mm/dd/yyyy)*	16. I-94 No. *(if any)*	17. Status when last admitted *(Visa type, if any)*

18. What is your child's current status?	19. What is the expiration date of his/her authorized stay, if any? *(mm/dd/yyyy)*	20. Is your child in Immigration Court proceedings? ☐ Yes ☐ No

21. If in the U.S., is this child to be included in this application? *(Check the appropriate box.)*

☐ Yes *(Attach one photograph of your child in the upper right corner of Page 9 on the extra copy of the application submitted for this person.)*

☐ No

Form I-589

Part A. II. Information About Your Spouse and Children (Continued)

1. Alien Registration Number (A-Number) *(if any)*	**2.** Passport/ID Card No. *(if any)*	**3.** Marital Status *(Married, Single, Divorced, Widowed)*	**4.** U.S. Social Security No. *(if any)*
5. Complete Last Name	**6.** First Name	**7.** Middle Name	**8.** Date of Birth *(mm/dd/yyyy)*
9. City and Country of Birth	**10.** Nationality *(Citizenship)*	**11.** Race, Ethnic, or Tribal Group	**12.** Gender ☐ Male ☐ Female

13. Is this child in the U.S. ?
☐ Yes *(Complete Blocks 14 to 21.)* ☐ No *(Specify location.)* _____

14. Place of last entry into the U.S.	**15.** Date of last entry into the U.S. *(mm/dd/yyyy)*	**16.** I-94 No. *(If any)*	**17.** Status when last admitted *(Visa type, if any)*

18. What is your child's current status?	**19.** What is the expiration date of his/her authorized stay, if any? *(mm/dd/yyyy)*	**20.** Is your child in Immigration Court proceedings? ☐ Yes ☐ No

21. If in the U.S., is this child to be included in this application? *(Check the appropriate box.)*
☐ Yes *(Attach one photograph of your child in the upper right corner of Page 9 on the extra copy of the application submitted for this person.)*
☐ No

1. Alien Registration Number (A-Number) *(if any)*	**2.** Passport/ID Card No. *(if any)*	**3.** Marital Status *(Married, Single, Divorced, Widowed)*	**4.** U.S. Social Security No. *(if any)*
5. Complete Last Name	**6.** First Name	**7.** Middle Name	**8.** Date of Birth *(mm/dd/yyyy)*
9. City and Country of Birth	**10.** Nationality *(Citizenship)*	**11.** Race, Ethnic, or Tribal Group	**12.** Gender ☐ Male ☐ Female

13. Is this child in the U.S.?
☐ Yes *(Complete Blocks 14 to 21.)* ☐ No *(Specify location.)* _____

14. Place of last entry into the U.S.	**15.** Date of last entry into the U.S. *(mm/dd/yyyy)*	**16.** I-94 No. *(If any)*	**17.** Status when last admitted *(Visa type, if any)*

18. What is your child's current status?	**19.** What is the expiration date of his/her authorized stay, if any? *(mm/dd/yyyy)*	**20.** Is your child in Immigration Court proceedings? ☐ Yes ☐ No

21. If in the U.S., is this child to be included in this application? *(Check the appropriate box.)*
☐ Yes *(Attach one photograph of your child in the upper right corner of Page 9 on the extra copy of the application submitted for this person.)*
☐ No

1. Alien Registration Number (A-Number) *(if any)*	**2.** Passport/ID Card No. *(if any)*	**3.** Marital Status *(Married, Single, Divorced, Widowed)*	**4.** U.S. Social Security No. *(if any)*
5. Complete Last Name	**6.** First Name	**7.** Middle Name	**8.** Date of Birth *(mm/dd/yyyy)*
9. City and Country of Birth	**10.** Nationality *(Citizenship)*	**11.** Race, Ethnic, or Tribal Group	**12.** Gender ☐ Male ☐ Female

13. Is this child in the U.S. ? ☐ Yes *(Complete Blocks 14 to 21.)* ☐ No *(Specify location.)* _____

14. Place of last entry into the U.S.	**15.** Date of last entry into the U.S. *(mm/dd/yyyy)*	**16.** I-94 No. *(if any)*	**17.** Status when last admitted *(Visa type, if any)*

18. What is your child's current status?	**19.** What is the expiration date of his/her authorized stay, if any? *(mm/dd/yyyy)*	**20.** Is your child in Immigration Court proceedings? ☐ Yes ☐ No

21. If in the U.S., is this child to be included in this application? *(Check the appropriate box.)*
☐ Yes *(Attach one photograph of your child in the upper right corner of Page 9 on the extra copy of the application submitted for this person.)*
☐ No

Form I-589

Part A. III. Information About Your Background

1. List your last address where you lived before coming to the United States. If this is not the country where you fear persecution, also list the last address in the country where you fear persecution. *(List Address, City/Town, Department, Province, or State and Country.)*
   *(**NOTE:** Use Form I-589 Supplement B, or additional sheets of paper, if necessary.)*

Number and Street *(Provide if available)*	City/Town	Department, Province, or State	Country	Dates From *(Mo/Yr)*	To *(Mo/Yr)*
Carr. 26 #26-50	Bogota	D.C.	Colombia	05/1960	04/2002

2. Provide the following information about your residences during the past 5 years. List your present address first.
   *(**NOTE:** Use Form I-589 Supplement B, or additional sheets of paper, if necessary.)*

Number and Street	City/Town	Department, Province, or State	Country	Dates From *(Mo/Yr)*	To *(Mo/Yr)*
222 SW 27th Drive	Weston	Florida	USA	7/2002	Present
Carr. 26 #26-50	Bogota	D.C.	Colombia	5/1960	7/2002

3. Provide the following information about your education, beginning with the most recent.
   *(**NOTE:** Use Form I-589 Supplement B, or additional sheets of paper, if necessary.)*

Name of School	Type of School	Location *(Address)*	Attended From *(Mo/Yr)*	To *(Mo/Yr)*
Gran Colombian University	University	Bogota, Colombia	8/1992	6/1997
Escuela de Enfermeria de Colombia	Technical Nurse	Bogota, Colombia	8/1986	6/1988
Gran Colombian High School	High School	Bogota, Colombia	8/1973	6/1978
Gran Colombia School	Elementary School	Bogota, Colombia	8/1967	6/1973

4. Provide the following information about your employment during the past 5 years. List your present employment first.
   *(**NOTE:** Use Form I-589 Supplement B, or additional sheets of paper, if necessary.)*

Name and Address of Employer	Your Occupation	Dates From *(Mo/Yr)*	To *(Mo/Yr)*
ABC Foundation, Bogota, Colombia	Urban Program Advisor	9/2001	3/2002
Colombian University, School of Architecture, Bogota, Colombia	Professor	6/1997	12/1999
Colombian University Hospital, Bogota, Colombia	Nurse	6/1993	8/1996

5. Provide the following information about your parents and siblings (brothers and sisters). Check the box if the person is deceased.
   *(**NOTE:** Use Form I-589 Supplement B, or additional sheets of paper, if necessary.)*

Full Name	City/Town and Country of Birth	Current Location
Mother Maria Restrepo	Bogota, Colombia	☐ Deceased Bogota, Colombia
Father John Doe	Bogota, Colombia	☐ Deceased Bogota, Colombia
Sibling		☐ Deceased
Sibling		☐ Deceased
Sibling		☐ Deceased
Sibling		☐ Deceased

Form I-589

Part B. Information About Your Application

(**NOTE:** *Use Form I-589 Supplement B, or attach additional sheets of paper as needed to complete your responses to the questions contained in Part B.*)

When answering the following questions about your asylum or other protection claim (withholding of removal under 241(b)(3) of the INA or withholding of removal under the Convention Against Torture), you must provide a detailed and specific account of the basis of your claim to asylum or other protection. To the best of your ability, provide specific dates, places, and descriptions about each event or action described. You must attach documents evidencing the general conditions in the country from which you are seeking asylum or other protection and the specific facts on which you are relying to support your claim. If this documentation is unavailable or you are not providing this documentation with your application, explain why in your responses to the following questions.

Refer to Instructions, Part 1: Filing Instructions, Section II, "Basis of Eligibility," Parts A - D, Section V, "Completing the Form," Part B, and Section VII, "Additional Evidence That You Should Submit," for more information on completing this section of the form.

1. Why are you applying for asylum or withholding of removal under section 241(b)(3) of the INA, or for withholding of removal under the Convention Against Torture? Check the appropriate box(es) below and then provide detailed answers to questions A and B below:

I am seeking asylum or withholding of removal based on:

☐ Race

☐ Religion

☐ Nationality

☐ Political opinion

☐ Membership in a particular social group

☐ Torture Convention

A. Have you, your family, or close friends or colleagues ever experienced harm or mistreatment or threats in the past by anyone?

☐ No   ☐ Yes

If "Yes," explain in detail:

1. What happened;
2. When the harm or mistreatment or threats occurred;
3. Who caused the harm or mistreatment or threats; and
4. Why you believe the harm or mistreatment or threats occurred.

(Please see attached statement)

B. Do you fear harm or mistreatment if you return to your home country?

☐ No   ☐ Yes

If "Yes," explain in detail:

1. What harm or mistreatment you fear;
2. Who you believe would harm or mistreat you; and
3. Why you believe you would or could be harmed or mistreated.

(Please see attached statement)

Form I-589

Part B. Information About Your Application (Continued)

2. Have you or your family members ever been accused, charged, arrested, detained, interrogated, convicted and sentenced, or imprisoned in any country other than the United States?

   ☒ No   ☐ Yes

   If "Yes," explain the circumstances and reasons for the action.

   ┌───┐
   │   │
   │   │
   │   │
   │   │
   │   │
   └───┘

3.A. Have you or your family members ever belonged to or been associated with any organizations or groups in your home country, such as, but not limited to, a political party, student group, labor union, religious organization, military or paramilitary group, civil patrol, guerrilla organization, ethnic group, human rights group, or the press or media?

   ☒ No   ☐ Yes

   If "Yes," describe for each person the level of participation, any leadership or other positions held, and the length of time you or your family members were involved in each organization or activity.

   ┌───┐
   │   │
   │   │
   │   │
   │   │
   │   │
   └───┘

B. Do you or your family members continue to participate in any way in these organizations or groups?

   ☒ No   ☐ Yes

   If "Yes," describe for each person your or your family members' current level of participation, any leadership or other positions currently held, and the length of time you or your family members have been involved in each organization or group.

   ┌───┐
   │   │
   │   │
   │   │
   │   │
   │   │
   └───┘

---

4. Are you afraid of being subjected to torture in your home country or any other country to which you may be returned?

   ☐ No   ☒ Yes

   If "Yes," explain why you are afraid and describe the nature of torture you fear, by whom, and why it would be inflicted.

   ┌───┐
   │ (Please see attached statement)   │
   │   │
   │   │
   │   │
   │   │
   └───┘

Employment discrimination against homosexuals is also very common in Colombia, where homosexuals have been stigmatized to work only in beauty salons, and where they are linked to prostitution, considering them immoral people. This interferes with a homosexual working in professional or specialized jobs. Also, being an HIV carrier increases the phobia, rejection and discrimination even more in the work area, since many companies require the employees to take HIV tests in order to start working or keep a job.

In the year 1999, my immediate supervisors made everything they could to get me out of the hospital. They didn't think it was correct for a homosexual nurse to work in the psychiatric unit of the Colombian Hospital in Bogotá, even more because I defended any colleague that was attacked or rejected by other peers or supervisors for having different sexual inclinations or for being an HIV carrier or suffering from AIDS.

Because I helped my colleagues, I began receiving aggressive and abusive phone calls, from 1997 to 1999, at home and also at work, when I was working at the psychiatric unit. These phone calls were made by unknown people, presumably employees of the same hospital where I worked in who said they didn't want fagot nurses, less so if they had AIDS because it was a disparage for the profession and an embarrassment for the other colleagues of the hospital family.

Starting in 1997, I linked myself as an Architect to public institutions in Colombia, During all this time I hid my homosexual inclination, because if I didn't, I would not have been able to be promoted so fast in public administration.

This type of work allowed me to have direct contact with the less fortunate communities, generating in me a sense of community assistance, with democratic and frank rejection against those insurgent groups that force the farming communities to flee to the great cities. This position allowed me to develop programs such as that of urban building recovery, and different investigations that took place for the urban development of the city of Bogotá, providing the urban community better quality of life.

At the same time, I got involved with two universities as professor in the School of Architecture.

During my employment in these universities, I also had to hide my homosexuality, since the dean of the school of architecture of the University was the first to reject any suggestion of the relationship between Architects and Homosexuals, taking on the task to clean up our university, specially his personnel in the school of Architecture, and as soon as the sexuality of any professor was doubted or brought up, his work contract would not be renewed for the next semester, or he would be substituted without explanation.

My work in the university allowed me to create programs where the University and the students could get involved with the communities in order to develop urban development, architectonic (design and construction) projects, technical consulting in urban procedures, making it possible for great projects with high design costs to be developed for those less fortunate communities. We were also able to take to the different neighborhoods, the adequate information regarding urban plans, of which they have a right to receive, but because of lack of information and proper direction they cannot complete.

It was easy for me to execute these projects with the Universities, students and community, since my professional work as an architect in the Institute of Urban Development of the city of Bogotá, allowed me to obtain all the necessary information and facilitate any community urban project.

The position I held within the university also allowed me to express to my students and the community, my democratic ideologies and flat rejection against terrorist groups, such as "FARC" or "Urban Militias", who operate nowadays in the poorest urban areas of Bogotá, and who do not allow the development of projects, such as the ones we developed with the University, and even less the diffusion of any ideas that go against their own terrorist objectives. Young people feel they have no other alternative but to link themselves to these groups, such as the "Urban Militias", who operate in the most depressive areas of Ciudad Bolivar in Bogotá.

These projects provided a better quality of life, since informational seminars were given about urban projects, informing the population about the ways they could finish their projects, allowing them to design community centers, police stations, fire stations, schools, arenas, in this way generating in these towns a series of activities where they participated with the University. This created in the students a great attitude for community care, and at the same time they were able to design and give consultations about real projects.

All these activities I was involved in, gave me a sense of leadership, creating discomfort on the part of the Urban Militias, composed of insurgents located in the areas where I was developing my community activities, and this was enough for them to threaten me in different occasions.

The threats were made by people from the community who would come up to me and tell me that there were some individuals in the area who were against the development of programs of the government, and that the best thing would be for us to take our projects somewhere else, because it would be very dangerous for us to continue with these urban programs, knowing that the "Urban Militias" operated in this area and they were the ones who made decisions for anything that affected this community, and for this reason it would be better if we didn't insist, since our lives could be in danger. I never paid attention to these threats, since I believed the project I was developing was very important to my people and my ideals were always clear.

In addition to this, I couldn't make my homosexuality public. If I did, I would not be able to continue my promotion within the public administration area, which in fact happened at the end of the second semester of 1999, when my homosexuality was made public, generating a series of discriminations and persecution by the dean of the school of Architecture, as a result, terminating my employment contract with the university, receiving, at the same time, threatening pamphlets in my classes where it was stated that they didn't want gay professors at Colombian University. Moreover, in my employment with the government as professional specialized in projects and programs created by me, with the pretext that I wasn't discreet to declare my rejection against FARC (Urban Militias) and with the comments of my sexual inclination, which was not convenient for the institution I was working for, I was fired without justification in February 2001.

This made me realize that life in my country had no meaning and anyone who declares their ideals publicly, anyone having the means to make our people realize the importance of conserving our democracy, runs a great risk because you never know if the person next to you supports those illegal groups or homophobic groups, who greatly discriminate and persecute homosexuals in our institutions and our entire country.

On September 1, 2001, almost a year unemployed, I had the chance to start working with XXXXXXX (XXXXXXX Foundation), giving professional and technical advice to different urban programs and residential improvement in dejected areas of the city of Bogota, participating in the self-sufficient development project of urban progress in those areas of the city. Taking advantage of my previous employment experience, I began designing projects to be presented to the mayor, together with the community action councils, in order to improve the residential living in these areas. Once again I got in touch with the communities, where years earlier I was already known for my programs with the University.

This type of work was always developed with meetings where the inhabitants of the area participated, and there was always fear that any community project had to be approved by certain individuals that were never present but who administered from the shadows, making decisions for the community, by means of fear instilled by firearms, for their own benefit and interests, and what they wanted was a person, like me, to lead this type of project, because I always emphasized that it was important to improve the life of our youth with projects that would favor democracy and not let the terrorist groups intimidate us. All the terrorists want is to immerse them in under developing conditions and fear, through ignorance, facilitating their terrorist activities and in this way, giving easy access to the youth and force them to enlist and continue their terrorist ideologists.

From that moment on, I was warned that I shouldn't mention to the community my ideas against these marginal groups, because it would be dangerous for me. But I didn't pay attention and continued with my work for two reasons: 1 — I was convinced that by means of urban development of these areas, these people would have a better quality of life, minimizing fear. 2 — I was always clear of my political ideals in favor of democracy and I felt it was better to continue doing my job.

The threats of the guerrilla groups was made more concrete on March 16, 2002, at about four a.m., in the community hall of Bogota, when two unknown men, with hostile appearance, after a community meeting, came up to me and forced me to leave the hall with a pistol pointed at me under their ponchos. They took me two blocks away, where I was threatened with pistols pointed at my head, and later throwing me on the floor, they put their rubber boots on my face, beginning to attack me verbally with insults, clearly and emphatically saying that they didn't want me working in any kind of project for the communities and that I should never return or they would give me a lesson I would never forget. They kicked me and shot my legs, telling me that for being a fagot I didn't need my male sexual organs, and that next time they wouldn't shoot at my legs but straight at my testicles. After beating me up, they put me face down and with the gun on my head they warned me that they didn't want fagots like me living in the country, since there were SOBs like me who poisoned the minds of the people with capitalist ideas, specially people who publicly declared to be against the revolutionary groups that favored the interests of the people, such as FARC or the Urban Militias, and because of this I had signed my death sentence, and if I wanted to meet the same fate as other fagots who had appeared dead, without motives or explanations, I should abandon the country in one month, and if I didn't, not only would I die but also my family.

These people also warned me that if I filed a report with the authorities I would not have die immediately, and that most of the police stations had informants that would let them know if I filed a report.

Still with their boots on my head and with the gun pointed at me, they told me to remain face down for a while, if not they would shoot. So I waited several minutes and finally I slowly turned my head and realized nobody was there anymore. With much effort I went home, took a shower, and went to bed after calling my friends and asking for their help since I was hurt, especially in my stomach, gluteus, and legs.

Even with their warning, I filed a report against them two days later, without many details since I was still afraid.

After filing a report on March 18, 2002, they began calling my apartment and my mother's house the following week, announcing that I had two days left to live, since I had signed my own death sentence. From that day on, fear and terror empowered me, and when I saw on television and the newspapers, that these individuals kill so many innocent people for less important reasons, I could not go out on the streets feeling safe anymore, and everyone that came near me I thought wanted to kill me.

In my state of panic, because of everything that had happened to me and the threats and persecution that these people from FARC had subjected me to, as well as the homophobic groups, threats against my life, as well as the lack of protection from the security organizations of the State, I realized that my only way out was to escape from my country in order to protect my life and that of my family, and with great pain and the greatest frustration of my life, I decided to abandon Colombia on April 7, 2002.

I had to flee Colombia and will not be able to return since my life is in danger ever since I publicly rejected all the activities of the guerrilla, specially those insurgent groups located in the urban perimeter of Bogotá, with the name of "Urban Militias", who are in charge of eliminating and shutting up anyone who expresses against their objectives. To this, I have to add that I have been a declared Homosexual, worsening my situation, since this has generated more threats and persecution against my life.

In the month of March 2003, while in the United States, I found out I was an HIV carrier, and my life suddenly changed. Once again I was fearful and afraid to return to my country. Not only would I be persecuted because of my political position against FARC and for being a homosexual, but now also for carrying the HIV virus, and with my knowledge of the lack of medicine, mistreatment, phobia and discrimination against patients infected with HIV by the society in general, as well as the indifference of the government and the authorities in my country, Colombia, my return would be a serious death sentence, a sure death.

Because of all the experiences I lived, my own and that of others, related to my homosexual condition, carrier of HIV, and the political persecution I was submitted to by the "Urban Militias" of Bogotá, I am afraid to return to my country. If I am returned to Colombia, I would be discriminated not only socially, but politically as well as by my family, and financially; persecuted and mistreated because of my sexuality and my condition of HIV positive, since this disease is considered a Divine punishment imposed on homosexuals. Also, my life would be in constant danger due to the lack of adequate treatment for my disease, the lack of financial resources generated by the lack of employment, the economic crisis lived in the country, the deficiency of the Colombian social security system to attend to these cases in particular, the lack of medicine and their high cost make me lose hope of ever receiving the proper medical treatment, which would condemn me to a sure death, aggravated by the psychological and even physical torture originated by the social environment and the eminent danger I would run, as well as my family, if I return, because of the FARC (Urban Militias), since my profession as Architect is specialized in Urbanism, making me deal directly with the community, and the threats are clearly against me on the part of FARC. Therefore, my only hope to live a safe and dignified life would be in this country, which offers me the necessary conditions to continue living; and I am sure that I have the human and professional skills to contribute to this country. I have clearly understood here that life has an incalculable value; that safety is the axle of all of society and that here, those patients with HIV do not die because of lack of medical care and medicines. All of this generates in me a great sense of tranquility and allows me to contribute to this country all my knowledge and desire to serve the society.

Because of these reasons, I respectfully petition for political asylum in the United States.

_____

Juan Doe

CHAPTER 10

Seeking Relief before the Courts (IJ, BIA and Federal Courts)

I. Introduction

When an application or petition is denied by USCIS or USCIS fails to act, there are several venues to seek relief before the courts. Depending on the type of application submitted the case may be appealed or transferred to another forum. The denial may either be appealed to the Administrative Appeals Office (AAO) (formerly the Administrative Appeal Unit) or the USCIS may refer it to an immigration judge.

A case denied by the IJ may be appealed to the Board of Immigration Appeals (BIA). If the BIA affirms the decision of the immigration judge and denies the appeal, a petition for review may be filed with the U.S. Court of Appeals. The U.S. Court of Appeals falls under the jurisdiction of the Federal Courts.

When a DHS agency fails to act or has acted outside of its legal scope, you may bring action before a federal court in the form of a writ of mandamus or habeas corpus.

II. The Immigration Court

The Office of the Immigration Judge falls under the EOIR. If, for example, an asylum application is not approved by the officer who interviews the applicant, the case may be referred to an IJ. 8 C.F.R. § 1003.10.

There are other ways in which an individual may be placed in proceedings before an IJ. If an individual is caught violating a visa (e.g., working illegally, found with fraudulent documents or is simply illegal), the individual will be scheduled for a hearing before an IJ.

A. The Charging Document

The charging document starts the procedure before an IJ. The charging document is titled Notice to Appear (NTA). The NTA will set out facts such as the allegations against the alien and a section with charges.

The NTA is usually given directly to the applicant or sent via mail. If the individual receives it personally or it is mailed to the individual's last known address, the NTA has been officially served and proceedings may begin.

B. Master Calendar

The first hearing before an IJ is the Master Calendar Hearing, where the individual admits or denies the allegations in the NTA and requests relief. There are several forms of relief available before an IJ. We will only discuss the ones that require an application and evidence. A formal request for asylum may be a form of relief. The procedures for going forward on that relief are discussed in Chapter 8.

An individual who has been present in the United States for 10 years or more before the date on the NTA and has a qualifying relationship may request cancellation of removal. An individual who has an approved relative petition or immigrant worker petition with a current priority date may request adjustment of status before the IJ.

(For relief of adjustment of status based on a petition and re-adjudication of a petition, as well as for the evidence needed and the forms to present to the IJ, refer to the previous chapters on the topic of residence.)

C. Individual Hearing

The IJ will schedule a date to present testimony similar to a trial. That hearing is called Individual Hearing. At the hearing, the IJ will review the evidence before him, the attorney for the respondent will call witnesses and the government attorney will cross-examine the witnesses and present evidence. At the conclusion of the hearing, the IJ will make a decision to grant or deny the relief being sought.

III. The Board of Immigration Appeals

The Board of Immigration Appeals is part of the EOIR, which, in turn, is part of the Department of Justice. The decisions of immigration judges are appealed to the BIA within 30 days of the decision. Relative petitions that have been denied by USCIS are appealed to the BIA. Traditionally, three board member panels had decided the appeals. The BIA has been reduced to 11 members. Decisions by the BIA may be summary decisions by one board member. A three-board-member review panel shall remain for complex cases, for cases requiring interpretations of law and for corrections of clear errors of fact.

1. Forms Required:

   The Forms EOIR-26, Notice of Appeal and EOIR-27 must be submitted to the Board of Immigration Appeals. A photocopy of the evidence submitted to the BIA must be submitted to the government attorneys.

2. Documents Required:

   a. Decision of the district director;

   b. Legal brief; and

   c. Documents to support the facts of the Brief.

IV. Federal Court Relief

A. Writ of Mandamus

A Writ of Mandamus is a civil lawsuit brought against the government and filed with the Federal District Court to compel a government agency to perform a duty owed to a plaintiff. This action may be used to force USCIS to perform its duty in adjudicating a petition or application that has been pending for a long time. It is most commonly used in adjudication delays for naturalization.

B. Writ of Habeas Corpus

A Writ of Habeas Corpus is a legal procedure filed with the Federal District Court to object and review the lawfulness of an individual's detention or imprisonment. If granted, the Court will order the prison official to release the individual. It is most commonly used when the government is holding someone without filing the charging document with immigration court.

C. Petition for Certiorari

A Petition for Certiorari may be filed with the U.S. Supreme Court in instances where there is conflicting precedent on the same issue in different Circuits.

Appendix

1. Form I-290B
2. Form EOIR-26
3. Form EOIR-27
4. Form EOIR-28
5. Brief to AAO
6. Brief to BIA

Form I-290B

OMB No. 1615-0095; Expires 02/28/10

Department of Homeland Security
U.S. Citizenship and Immigration Services

**Form I-290B, Notice
of Appeal or Motion**

In the Matter of:	File Number: A -

START HERE - Please Type or Print (Use black ink)

For USCIS Use Only

Part 1. Information About You *(Individual/Business/Organization filing appeal or motion)*

Family Name	Given Name	Middle Name

Name of Business/Organization *(if applicable)*

Mailing Address - Street Number and Name   Apt. #

C/O (*in care of*):

City	State or Province	Zip/Postal Code

Country	Daytime Phone # *(Area/Country Code)*
	( )

Fax # *(Area/Country Code)*	E-Mail Address *(if any)*
( )	

☐ I am an attorney or representative. If you check this box, you must provide the following information about the person or organization for whom you are appearing. (**NOTE:** You must attach a Form G-28, Notice of Entry of Appearance as Attorney or Representative.)

Family Name	Given Name	Middle Name

Complete Name of Business/Organization/School *(if applicable)*

A # *(if any)*	Daytime Phone # *(Area/Country Code)*
	( )

Fax # *(Area/Country Code)*	E-mail Address *(if any)*
( )	

For USCIS Use Only

Returned	Receipt
Date	
Date	
Resubmitted	
Date	
Date	
Reloc Sent	
Date	
Date	
Reloc Rec'd	
Date	
Date	
Remarks	

Part 2. Information About the Appeal or Motion

Check the box below that best describes your request. *(Check one box.)*

A. ☐ I am filing an appeal. My brief and/or additional evidence is attached.

B. ☐ I am filing an appeal. My brief and/or additional evidence will be submitted to the AAO within 30 days.

C. ☐ I am filing an appeal. No supplemental brief and/or additional evidence will be submitted.

D. ☐ I am filing a motion to reopen a decision. My brief and/or additional evidence is attached.

E. ☐ I am filing a motion to reconsider a decision. My brief is attached.

F. ☐ I am filing a motion to reopen and a motion to reconsider a decision. My brief and/or additional evidence is attached.

Form I-290B (Rev. 02/10/09) Y

United States Department of Justice
Texas Service Center
P.O. Box 279030
Mesquite, TX 75227-0930

Petitioner: A to Z Construction & Management, Inc.
Beneficiary: Melinda Doe
File: SRC-00-205-52373

Brief of Appeal for Administrative Appeals Office

FACTS

The petitioner is a construction company located in South Florida. It filed a petition for an H-1B for a Contract Specialist on July 22, 2004. In support of the petition for a specialty occupation, the petitioner submitted evidence of industry standards such as advertisements from monster.com which demonstrated that construction companies require at least a bachelor's degree for entry into this position.

The case was denied without requesting additional evidence. The District Director finding the petitioner had failed to establish the position met the requirements of Title 8, Code of Federal Regulations, Part 214.2(h)(4)(ii) which defines "specialty occupation."

The service stated the following:

• You have not submitted documentary evidence to support that it is the industry standard among similar organizations to hire an individual with a bachelor's degree or an equivalent for this position."

• The beneficiary has not established that a bachelor degree is common to the industry in parallel positions among similar organizations or, in the alternative, that the employer showed that this particular position is so complex or unique that it can only be performed by an individual with a degree."

• The critical element is not the title of the position or an employer's self-imposed standard, but whether the position actually requires theoretical and practical application of a body of highly specialized knowledge, and the attainment of a bachelor's degree in the specific specialty as minimum for entry into the occupation as required by the Act."

• The service recognizes that certain Contract Specialist positions are a specialty occupation, however, given how the Contract Specialist position will be utilized within your organization, the position does not qualify as a specialty occupation."

ARGUMENT

The regulations at 8 C. F. R. 214.2(h)(4)(iii)(A) states that to qualify as a specialty occupation, the position must meet **one** of four criteria. One of those criteria is 8 C.F.R. 214.2(h)(4)(iii)(A)(2) which states:

The degree requirement is common to the industry in parallel positions, or the particular position is so complex or unique that it can be performed only by an individual with a degree.

One of the ways to meet the standards of the industry is to show evidence of entry requirements for the position with the same type of companies, in this case construction companies. The advertisements from monster.com were advertisements of those same types of companies seeking individuals for an entry level position as a Contract Specialist. All those companies require at least a bachelor's degree as a minimum for entry into the position, as evidenced in their advertisements. An alternative method to meet the industry standard requirements is to have other companies of similar size provide evidence of the industry standard. This can be done in the form of a letter from such companies.

The service has based its decision on the fact that the advertisements supplied as evidence of industry standards named large companies and therefore cannot be compared to the petitioner's company. The Service did not allow the petitioner to respond with evidence that a bachelor's degree is required for smaller companies as well. The Service is not only discriminating against small companies by assuming that they should not be entitled to the same type of employees with full credentials such as with large companies it is also not allowing a small company to respond to this assumption.

The Yates memo, dated May 4, 2004, states that "an REF is not required for every case prior to adjudication and clarifies when an adjudicator may deny an application or petition without issuing an RFE," was written as a policy directive to streamline the process of petitions and applications. Mr. Bill Yates has stated personally that it was not intended to be used by the Service for denials every single time that evidence is not sufficient. It was only to be used in instances where there is evidence of clear ineligibility.

In the instant case, the Service states that it recognizes that certain Contract Specialist positions are a specialty occupation. Therefore, this denial contravenes policies and the intentions of the Service because it denies, without a Request for Evidence, a case that is approvable in some instances. We are enclosing industry letters from small construction companies showing that the requirement for a bachelor's degree is common to the industry in parallel positions among similar organizations.

CONCLUSION

The Service's decision that the beneficiary has not established that a bachelor degree is common to the industry in parallel positions among similar organizations or, in the alternative, that the employer showed that its particular position is so complex or unique that it can only be performed by an individual with a degree is an incorrect assumption. The beneficiary was not allowed to present additional evidence that would have clearly indicated that he was eligible for the relief sought.

Therefore, the petitioner requests that this case be approved on its merits.

Respectfully submitted,

Maria Doe
Smith & Doe, P.A.
444 Main St.
Miami, FL 3311
305-555-5555

U.S. Department of Justice
Executive Office for Immigration Review
Board of Immigration Appeals
5201 Leesburg Pike, Suite 1300
Falls Church, VA 22041

In the Matter of   File No.
Doe, Jane   A 55 555 555

Brief in Support of Appeal

FACTS

Respondent is a 46-year-old native and citizen of Colombia who entered the United States on February 9, 1986.

The respondent, her son, mother and other siblings entered the United States after having received special visas from the U.S. Embassy in Colombia. The visas were a result of the co-operation of Tony Doe, respondent's brother, with the U.S. government. Respondent's brother was a diplomat and willingly cooperated with the U.S. government. Due to this co-operation, the respondent, her legal permanent resident mother, son and siblings were threatened. After the kidnapping of Tony Doe in Colombia, the family believed the death threats and the threats of kidnapping were likely. Respondent's brother Tony Doe was granted asylum by the Honorable Judge Jones, in Miami, Fla., on September 8, 1998. At-tached is an affidavit from Tony Doe.

Respondent informed her attorney of the specific problems they as a family had endured in Colombia. She requested that the attorney file asylum applications on behalf of herself and her son. Respondent was told that asylums are not granted to Colombian nationals and re-fused to file the application.

Respondent's attorney filed applications for cancellation of removal based on respondent's ten year presence in the country. Respondent's attorney also filed a cancellation of removal application on behalf of respondent's twelve-year-old son, who did not have a qualifying rel-ative for the application and was therefore ineligible.

At the hearing, the respondent and her mother testified as to the statutory requisites for cancellation of removal. The Immigration Judge found all statutory requisites were met for relief with the exception of whether the removal would result in exceptional and extremely unusual hardship to the applicant's spouse, parent, or child who is a United States citizen or lawful permanent resident, in this case, the respondent's permanent resident mother.

The IJ held that though there would be hardship to the permanent resident relative, it does not rise to the level of exceptional and extremely unusual hardship necessary to a grant of cancellation of removal. The main reason for this holding is that there was an inevitable severance of the family unit, the twelve-year-old son would have to leave the United States because he was not eligible for cancellation of removal and had not applied for any other relief.

The IJ also stated that the legal permanent resident mother would be able to reside with her other daughter and two sons. The court also stated that the return of the lead respondent to Colombia and the economic detriment to the permanent resident mother was not sufficiently demonstrated to the extent of being exceptional and extremely unusual hardship.

In addition, the IJ noted that the permanent resident mother has traveled to Colombia three times since she came to the United States. However the testimony is clear in that it was for specific reasons.

ARGUMENT

WHETHER RESPONDENT WAS PREJUDICED BY COUNSEL

Previous counsel's actions clearly prejudiced respondent. The Immigration Judge held that respondent's qualifying relatives, her legal permanent resident mother; hardship did not rise to the level of exceptional and extremely unusual hardship necessary to a grant of cancellation of removal. The transcript is showered with the immigration judge's comment that evidence was not developed to substantiate the claim. One of the main reasons for this determination was that upon the child being granted voluntary departure, the family unit was already severed. This is a result of counsel filing for relief that the child was clearly not eligible for and not filing for asylum relief as the respondent had requested for her and her son.

The court incorrectly stated that the mother could reside with another daughter who has a husband and children, despite the fact that both the respondent and mother stated she would not be able to reside with the other daughter. The court's conclusion is not based on any evidence such as the capacity of the home to allow for another adult, the ability of the husband of the daughter to accept his mother in law to be permanently residing with them or the capacity of the married daughter to provide for her aging mother in the future (i.e., home and personal care, etc.). This is important in light of the fact that the mother is seventy five years old. None of this information or evidence was presented. And additionally, this testimony was never developed. The IJ determined the case only involved economic detriment to the legal permanent resident mother. The IJ states the Board's position on the factor of economic detriment in a suspension context, in that economic detriment absent other hardships is not extreme hardship. Matter of Ige, 20 I&N Dec. 880 (BIA 1994); Matter of Sangster, 11 I&N Dec. 309 (BIA 1965). The additional information provided were the country reports of not only the economic hardship in Colombia but the danger to individuals in Colombia, evidence of the fact that special visas had to be arranged for them to leave Colombia, and evidence that the permanent resident mother is 75 years old, and though may appear to be "youthful" to the IJ, the factor of her age should be seriously considered in determining who will car for her. Should we permit the daughter who has lived with her all her life or our tax dollars to care for her? The IJ states that the lead respondent did not offer any testimony that she would not be able to acquire similar employment upon her return to Colombia. He ignored the fact of the circumstances of how they had left Colombia and that the country conditions have not only changed but are actually worse. The IJ stated that there was no testimony regarding the inability to sell the property in Colombia or that it would not generate sufficient income. However, the transcript clearly reflects the mother's testimony wherein she states that she would not be able to sell the property now (page 62). Additionally she testified that the property had not generated any income for two years and in fact she had to pay expenses or lose the property. The IJ considered only the reduction in the standard of living for Graciella Doe, the permanent resident mother. However, this case encompasses more than that.

The IJ also stated that the legal permanent resident mother visited Colombia three times while she has resided in the United States. The IJ knew that the mother had actually lived in the United States for 13 years. Clearly, three visits in 13 years are insignificant. Additionally the testimony presented made it clear that the visits were for specific reasons. The last trip was after she had not received income for two years from her property and was about to lose the property. She testified that she stayed at a pervious domestic employee's house in Colombia and was constantly guarded by the husband of that employee. It should be noted that Ms. Doe did not stay with her daughter in Colombia but chose to stay at the house of domestic employee. This fact was not developed.

The IJ erred in not finding exceptional and extremely unusual hardship to the applicant's permanent resident mother. And part if not all of the error was contributed by previous counsel.

WHETHER RESPONDENT DESERVES A MOTION TO REMAND BASED ON
INEFFECTIVE ASSISTANCE OF COUNSEL

A motion to reopen based on alleged ineffective representation must be supported by a specific showing of the alleged inadequacy and of prejudice to the client, show that prior counsel was informed of charged inadequacy, give an opportunity to respond and indicate whether a complaint against former counsel was made to appropriate disciplinary authorities. Matter of Lozada, 19 I & N Dec. 637, 6 Immig. Rptr. B1-31 (BIA 1988). The requisite should be similar in a remand context.

The attorney respondent hired to represent her failed to meet with respondent before the hearing and prepare evidence both testimonial and documentary for hearing. She did not prepare an asylum application on behalf of respondent, despite the fact that it was an available relief and that it was the only relief available to her son and this inaction caused irreparable harm to her case.

The attorney told the respondent that asylum is never granted to Colombian nationals. She did not review the information of respondent. Additionally, respondent's and respondent's witness' testimony was never developed.

Respondent is providing photocopies of cancelled receipts of fees paid to the firm of the attorney.

Respondent has notified the attorney of the charged inadequacy by providing her with this Appeal Brief and Motion to Remand. Further, attached is a Certificate of Service evidencing this matter, giving her the opportunity to respond.

Respondent is providing an affidavit stating that she has contacted the Florida Bar to file a grievance against the attorney for their ineffective assistance as counsel.

All the requisites to establish a case for a motion on ineffective assistance of counsel in accordance with Matter of Lozada, supra, have been met. These actions constitute the ineffective assistance of counsel and respondent deserves a favorable decision on the motion.

WHETHER RESPONDENT HAS ESTABLISHED A PRIMA FACIE CASE OF ASYLUM

A movant must establish a prima facie case for the underlying substantive relief sought <u>Ogbemudia v. INS</u> 988 F.2d 595,600 (5th Cir. 1993).

Respondent is attaching an asylum application explaining the threats and persecution she and her family suffered in Colombia, which consist of bomb and death threats.

In order to establish eligibility for a grant of asylum, an alien must demonstrate that he is unwilling or unable to return to his country because of persecution or a "well-founded fear" of persecution on account of race, religion, nationality, membership in a particular social group or political opinion.

According to the Status of Refugees in International Law 217 (1966) G. Goodwin-Gill, the Refugee in International law 30 (1983), "social group" persecution must be based on a "characteristic is either beyond the power of an individual to change or is so fundamental to individual identity or conscience that it ought not to be required to be changed." Inarguably, Ms. Doe being singled out because of her support for Mr. Doe in the determination to aid in the conviction and arrests of narcotraffickers and her position as a family member of a high ranking government official, are fundamental traits to her identity and conscience and ought not to be required to be changed.

In <u>Matter of Fuentes,</u> 19 I&N Dec. 658 (BIA 1988), the BIA held that status as a former policeman is an immutable characteristic and mistreatment occurring because of such status in appropriate circumstances could be found to be persecution on account of political opinion or membership in a particular social group. However, the BIA did not grant asylum, due to the fact that the police and guerrillas were considered to be victims of persecution based solely on attacks by one against the other. This is different form Ms. Doe's case because she belonged to the family of high ranking official who was a member of a particular social status as a diplomat and who worked with the DEA. These are not people who are simply performing a service which entails defending people against guerrillas such as simple police duties. These actions are at a higher aggressive level acting in an active and voluntary capacity as a member of a U.S. agency which investigates and pursues the conviction of international criminals. This is different from the policeman in Fuentes which was considered by the BIA to be part of a group of victims of "attacks on each other." Additionally, the Doe family was not doing this because of a "job," but because they believed in a cause.

In <u>Ananeh Firempong v. INS</u>, 766. F.2d 621 (1977), the court held that social class together with other facts placed the applicant in the enumerated ground of "membership in a social group" as required by the statute. The status of Ms. Doe's social class combined with the facts of the country conditions and the actions to support the U.S. Government make her clearly a member of a social group in accordance with case law.

It is important to note that Ms. Doe belonged to a particular social group that is persecuted by a group the government cannot control and that while there is a serious conflict in Colombia, it is not an "embattling nation."

In conclusion, respondent belongs to one of the enumerated groups which make her eligible for asylum in the United States. She is a member of a social group. She belongs to a family of high ranking government officials who have cooperated with the U.S. Government and the Colombian government to prosecute and bring to justice Cartel members, narcotraffickers and members of guerrilla forces. Respondent's brother was granted asylum by the Honorable Judge in Miami, Fla. The asylum grant was based on his being a member of a social group for the exact same activities as previously mentioned.

Presently, the situation in Colombia has gotten worse. Attached are numerous clippings of the threats and consequences suffered by individuals similarly situated as the respondent.

Respondent is filing her asylum application after the one year date of entry which is not allowed but for a few exceptions (8 C.F.R. 208.4). An exception to filing within the one year is for ineffective assistance of counsel (8 C.F.R. 208.4(5)(iii).

Therefore, respondent is prima facie eligible for asylum.

CONCLUSION

The Respondent has been a victim of ineffective assistance of counsel. Due to the attorney's actions, the Immigration Court erred in its finding because the evidence was not developed sufficiently nor was it presented adequately. Furthermore, previous counsel failed to present an asylum application on behalf of respondent and her son, causing both cases to be severed. Respondent was and is prima facie eligible for asylum, the relief sought. Previous counsel has been notified of their inadequacies, and the respondent has been extremely prejudiced by the attorney's actions.

Wherefore, respondent respectfully requests that the appeal be sustained and the case remanded to the IJ in order for her to pursue her case as an asylum applicant.

This 9th day of August, 2004.

Respectfully submitted,

Maria Doe
Attorney for Respondent
Smith and Doe, P.A.
555 Main St.
Miami, FL 33131

CERTIFICATE OF SERVICE

Matter of: Doe, Jane

File No.: A55 555 555

I, Maria Doe, certify that on this date I have served via first-class mail, a copy of the attached brief to the Office of the Chief Counsel at 333 S. Miami Ave., 2nd Floor, Miami, FL 33131.

Date: _____

Signature: _____

CHAPTER **11**

Citizenship in the United States

I. Introduction

U.S. citizenship can be acquired either by operation of law (e.g., birth in the United States or birth abroad to U.S. citizens or nationals) or by naturalization, which requires an affirmative application. There is also derivative citizenship to certain children whose parent or parents naturalize for whom citizenship is automatically granted as a matter of law. INA § 316, 8 USC § 1427, 8 C.F.R. § 316.

A. Statutory Requirements

No person shall be naturalized unless s/he either:
- is a lawful permanent resident for at least five years prior to filing;
- is a lawful permanent resident for at least three years and has been married to and living with the same U.S. citizen for the last three years, and said spouse has been a U.S. citizen for the last three years;
- is a person who has served in the U.S. Armed Forces and is a lawful permanent resident with at least three years of U.S. Armed Forces service being on active duty or filing within six months of honorable discharge;
- has served during a period of recognized hostilities and enlisted or re-enlisted. (**Note:** Applicant does not have to be a lawful permanent resident).

Other basic requirements for naturalization in the United States are:
1. Physical presence in the United States for at least half the time of permanent residency;
2. Good moral character;
3. Basic knowledge of U.S. government and history as determined by passing civics test;
4. Ability to read, write and speak simple English;
5. Attainment of at least 18 years of age;
6. As a minor, being in the custody of at least one parent who becomes a citizen, which often confers automatic citizenship;
7. Legal competence to take the citizenship oath; and
8. Expressed allegiance to the U.S. government

B. Bars to Naturalization

An applicant is not a person of good moral character if during the last five years s/he:
- has committed and been convicted of one or more crimes involving moral turpitude;

- has committed and been convicted of two or more offenses for which the total sentence imposed was five years or more;
- has committed and been convicted of any controlled substance, except for a single offense of simple possession of 30 grams or less of marijuana;
- has been confined to a penal institution during the statutory period as a result of a conviction for an aggregate period of 180 days or more;
- has committed and been convicted of two or more gambling offenses;
- is or has earned his/her principal income from illegal gambling;
- is or has been involved in prostitution or commercialized vice;
- is or has been involved in smuggling illegal aliens into the United States;
- is or has been a habitual drunkard;
- is practicing or has practiced polygamy;
- has willfully failed or refused to support dependents;
- has given false testimony, under oath, in order to receive a benefit under the Immigration and Nationality Act;
- is of has been involved in subversive activities;
- is or has been a member of the Communist Party;
- is or has been a deserter during war time, unless s/he had received a pardon or general amnesty;
- is or has been an alien who has removal proceedings pending, outstanding and/or a final order of deportation, unless eligible for citizenship due to military service;
- has failed to register with the selective service; or
- has any other criminal history.

It is very important to note that filing a naturalization application may lead to the applicent being placed in removal proceedings if the crime is deemed serious enough for the permanent residence to be revoked.

C. Exemptions to English or Government and History Requirement

An individual who has been a legal permanent resident of the United States for twenty years and is 55 years old or a legal permanent for fifteen years and at least 60 years old may take the government and history requirement in his/her native language.

An individual may also request a medical waiver to waive the English or government and history requirement in cases where the applicant has a mental impairment not withstanding their age or period of legal permanent residence. The Form N-648 is proposed and submitted with the N-400 application.

D. Filing for Naturalization

1. Forms Required:
   a. USCIS Form N-400 and filing fees;
   b. Form G-28;
   c. Form N-648, if requesting a medical waiver.
2. Documents Required:
   a. Copy of Alien Registration Card—Form I-551;
   b. Copy of any criminal record including indictment, disposition and arrest report;

c. Certified copy of divorce decree or marriage if claiming citizenship as married to a U.S. citizen; and

d. Two recent passport photographs (taken within the last 30 days prior to filing the application).

Appendix

1. Form N-400
2. Form G-28

Form N-400

OMB No. 1615-0052; Expires 12/31/09

Department of Homeland Security
U.S Citizenship and Immigration Services

N-400 Application
for Naturalization

Print clearly or type your answers using CAPITAL letters. Failure to print clearly may delay your application. Use black ink.

Part 1. Your Name *(Person applying for naturalization)*	Write your USCIS A-Number here: A

A. Your current legal name.

Family Name *(Last Name)*

> DOE

Given Name *(First Name)*

> John

Full Middle Name *(If applicable)*

For USCIS Use Only

Bar Code	Date Stamp
	Remarks
	Action Block

B. Your name **exactly** as it appears on your Permanent Resident Card.

Family Name *(Last Name)*

> DOE

Given Name *(First Name)*

> John

Full Middle Name *(If applicable)*

C. If you have ever used other names, provide them below.

Family Name *(Last Name)*	Given Name *(First Name)*	Middle Name

D. Name change *(optional)*

Read the Instructions before you decide whether to change your name.

1. Would you like to legally change your name?   ☐ Yes   ☐ No

2. If "Yes," print the new name you would like to use. Do not use initials or abbreviations when writing your new name.

Family Name *(Last Name)*

Given Name *(First Name)*   Full Middle Name

Part 2. Information About Your Eligibility *(Check only one)*

I am at least 18 years old **AND**

A. ☒ I have been a lawful permanent resident of the United States for at least five years.

B. ☐ I have been a lawful permanent resident of the United States for at least three years, **and** I have been married to and living with the same U.S. citizen for the last three years, **and** my spouse has been a U.S. citizen for the last three years.

C. ☐ I am applying on the basis of qualifying military service.

D. ☐ Other *(Explain)* _____

Form N-400 (Rev. 01/22/09) Y

Form N-400

Part 3. Information About You	Write your USCIS A-Number here: A

A. U.S. Social Security Number

`123-45-1234`

B. Date of Birth *(mm/dd/yyyy)*

`05/20/1986`

C. Date You Became a Permanent Resident *(mm/dd/yyyy)*

D. Country of Birth

`United Kingdom`

E. Country of Nationality

`United Kingdom`

F. Are either of your parents U.S. citizens? *(If yes, see instructions)* ☒ Yes ☐ No

G. What is your current marital status? ☒ Single, Never Married ☐ Married ☐ Divorced ☐ Widowed

☐ Marriage Annulled or Other *(Explain)* _____

H. Are you requesting a waiver of the English and/or U.S. History and Government requirements based on a disability or impairment and attaching Form N-648 with your application? ☐ Yes ☒ No

I. Are you requesting an accommodation to the naturalization process because of a disability or impairment? *(See instructions for some examples of accommodations.)* ☐ Yes ☒ No

If you answered "Yes," check the box below that applies:

☐ I am deaf or hearing impaired and need a sign language interpreter who uses the following language: _____

☐ I use a wheelchair.

☐ I am blind or sight impaired.

☐ I will need another type of accommodation. Explain: _____

_____

Part 4. Addresses and Telephone Numbers

A. Home Address - Street Number and Name *(Do **not** write a P.O. Box in this space.)*   Apartment Number

`222 SW 27th Drive`

City	County	State	ZIP Code	Country
Weston		FL	33751	USA

B. Care of

`Blank Attorney, P.A.`

Mailing Address - Street Number and Name *(If different from home address)*   Apartment Number

`2655 S Le Jeune Road  1001`

City	State	ZIP Code	Country
Coral Gables	FL	33134	USA

C. Daytime Phone Number *(If any)*

(954) 777-8855

Evening Phone Number *(If any)*

(305) 777-4444

E-Mail Address *(If any)*

Form N-400

Part 5. Information for Criminal Records Search	Write your USCIS A-Number here: A

NOTE: The categories below are those required by the FBI. See instructions for more information.

A. Gender

☒ Male ☐ Female

B. Height

Feet	Inches

C. Weight

Pounds

D. Are you Hispanic or Latino? ☐ Yes ☐ No

E. Race *(Select one or more)*

☐ White ☐ Asian ☐ Black or African American ☐ American Indian or Alaskan Native ☐ Native Hawaiian or Other Pacific Islander

F. Hair color

☐ Black ☐ Brown ☐ Blonde ☐ Gray ☐ White ☐ Red ☐ Sandy ☐ Bald (No Hair)

G. Eye color

☐ Brown ☐ Blue ☐ Green ☐ Hazel ☐ Gray ☐ Black ☐ Pink ☐ Maroon ☐ Other

Part 6. Information About Your Residence and Employment

A. Where have you lived during the last five years? Begin with where you live now and then list every place you lived for the last five years. If you need more space, use a separate sheet of paper.

Street Number and Name, Apartment Number, City, State, Zip Code, and Country	Dates *(mm/dd/yyyy)*	
	From	To
Current Home Address - Same as Part 4.A	7/2002	Present
56 Mainstream Drive Apt 25, London England	05/1986	07/2002

B. Where have you worked (or, if you were a student, what schools did you attend) during the last five years? Include military service. Begin with your current or latest employer and then list every place you have worked or studied for the last five years. If you need more space, use a separate sheet of paper.

Employer or School Name	Employer or School Address *(Street, City, and State)*	Dates *(mm/dd/yyyy)*		Your Occupation
		From	To	
None		8/1991	Present	Student

Form N-400

Part 7. Time Outside the United States *(Including Trips to Canada, Mexico and the Caribbean Islands)*	Write your USCIS A-Number here: A

A. How many total days did you spend outside of the United States during the past five years? ☐ days

B. How many trips of 24 hours or more have you taken outside of the United States during the past five years? ☐ trips

C. List below all the trips of 24 hours or more that you have taken outside of the United States since becoming a lawful permanent resident. Begin with your most recent trip. If you need more space, use a separate sheet of paper.

Date You Left the United States *(mm/dd/yyyy)*	Date You Returned to the United States *(mm/dd/yyyy)*	Did Trip Last Six Months or More?	Countries to Which You Traveled	Total Days Out of the United States
		☐ Yes ☐ No		
		☐ Yes ☐ No		
		☐ Yes ☐ No		
		☐ Yes ☐ No		
		☐ Yes ☐ No		
		☐ Yes ☐ No		
		☐ Yes ☐ No		
		☐ Yes ☐ No		
		☐ Yes ☐ No		
		☐ Yes ☐ No		

Part 8. Information About Your Marital History

A. How many times have you been married (including annulled marriages)? ☐ If you have **never** been married, go to Part 9.

B. If you are now married, give the following information about your spouse:

1. Spouse's Family Name *(Last Name)*   Given Name *(First Name)*   Full Middle Name *(If applicable)*

2. Date of Birth *(mm/dd/yyyy)*   **3.** Date of Marriage *(mm/dd/yyyy)*   **4.** Spouse's U.S. Social Security #

5. Home Address - Street Number and Name   Apartment Number

City   State   Zip Code

Form N-400

Part 8. Information About Your Marital History *(Continued)*	Write your USCIS A-Number here: A

C. Is your spouse a U.S. citizen?   ☐ Yes   ☐ No

D. If your spouse is a U.S. citizen, give the following information:

    1. When did your spouse become a U.S. citizen?   ☐ At Birth   ☐ Other

    If "Other," give the following information:

    2. Date your spouse became a U.S. citizen

    3. Place your spouse became a U.S. citizen (*See instructions*)

                                               City and State

E. If your spouse is **not** a U.S. citizen, give the following information :

    1. Spouse's Country of Citizenship

    2. Spouse's USCIS A- Number (*If applicable*)   A

    3. Spouse's Immigration Status

    ☐ Lawful Permanent Resident   ☐ Other

F. If you were married before, provide the following information about your prior spouse. If you have more than one previous marriage, use a separate sheet of paper to provide the information requested in Questions 1-5 below.

    1. Prior Spouse's Family Name (*Last Name*)   Given Name (*First Name*)   Full Middle Name (*If applicable*)

    2. Prior Spouse's Immigration Status

    ☐ U.S. Citizen

    ☐ Lawful Permanent Resident

    ☐ Other

    3. Date of Marriage (*mm/dd/yyyy*)

    4. Date Marriage Ended (*mm/dd/yyyy*)

    5. How Marriage Ended

    ☐ Divorce   ☐ Spouse Died   ☐ Other

G. How many times has your current spouse been married (including annulled marriages)?   ☐

If your spouse has **ever** been married before, give the following information about **your spouse's** prior marriage.
If your spouse has more than one previous marriage, use a separate sheet(s) of paper to provide the information requested in Questions 1 - 5 below.

    1. Prior Spouse's Family Name (*Last Name*)   Given Name (*First Name*)   Full Middle Name (*If applicable*)

    2. Prior Spouse's Immigration Status

    ☐ U.S. Citizen

    ☐ Lawful Permanent Resident

    ☐ Other

    3. Date of Marriage (*mm/dd/yyyy*)

    4. Date Marriage Ended (*mm/dd/yyyy*)

    5. How Marriage Ended

    ☐ Divorce   ☐ Spouse Died   ☐ Other

Form N-400

Part 9. Information About Your Children	Write your USCIS A-Number here: A

A. How many sons and daughters have you had? For more information on which sons and daughters you should include and how to complete this section, see the Instructions.

B. Provide the following information about all of your sons and daughters. If you need more space, use a separate sheet of paper.

Full Name of Son or Daughter	Date of Birth *(mm/dd/yyyy)*	USCIS A- number *(if child has one)*	Country of Birth	Current Address *(Street, City, State and Country)*
		A		
		A		
		A		
		A		
		A		
		A		
		A		
		A		

Add Children		Go to continuation page

Part 10. Additional Questions

Answer Questions 1 through 14. If you answer "Yes" to any of these questions, include a written explanation with this form. Your written explanation should (1) explain why your answer was "Yes" and (2) provide any additional information that helps to explain your answer.

A. General Questions.

1. Have you **ever** claimed to be a U.S. citizen *(in writing or any other way)*? ☐ Yes ☒ No

2. Have you **ever** registered to vote in any Federal, State, or local election in the United States? ☐ Yes ☒ No

3. Have you **ever** voted in any Federal, State, or local election in the United States? ☐ Yes ☒ No

4. Since becoming a lawful permanent resident, have you **ever** failed to file a required Federal, State, or local tax return? ☐ Yes ☒ No

5. Do you owe any Federal, State, or local taxes that are overdue? ☐ Yes ☒ No

6. Do you have any title of nobility in any foreign country? ☐ Yes ☒ No

7. Have you ever been declared legally incompetent or been confined to a mental institution within the last five years? ☐ Yes ☒ No

Form N-400

Part 10. Additional Questions *(Continued)*	Write your USCIS A-Number here: A

B. Affiliations.

8. a Have you **ever** been a member of or associated with any organization, association, fund foundation, party, club, society, or similar group in the United States or in any other place? ☐ Yes ☐ No

   b. If you answered "Yes," list the name of each group below. If you need more space, attach the names of the other group(s) on a separate sheet of paper.

Name of Group	Name of Group
1.	6.
2.	7.
3.	8.
4.	9.
5.	10.

9. Have you **ever** been a member of or in any way associated *(either directly or indirectly)* with:

   a. The Communist Party? ☐ Yes ☒ No

   b. Any other totalitarian party? ☐ Yes ☒ No

   c. A terrorist organization? ☐ Yes ☒ No

10. Have you **ever** advocated *(either directly or indirectly)* the overthrow of any government by force or violence? ☐ Yes ☒ No

11. Have you **ever** persecuted *(either directly or indirectly)* any person because of race, religion, national origin, membership in a particular social group, or political opinion? ☐ Yes ☒ No

12. Between March 23, 1933, and May 8, 1945, did you work for or associate in any way *(either directly or indirectly)* with:

   a. The Nazi government of Germany? ☐ Yes ☒ No

   b. Any government in any area (1) occupied by, (2) allied with, or (3) established with the help of the Nazi government of Germany? ☐ Yes ☒ No

   c. Any German, Nazi, or S.S. military unit, paramilitary unit, self-defense unit, vigilante unit, citizen unit, police unit, government agency or office, extermination camp, concentration camp, prisoner of war camp, prison, labor camp, or transit camp? ☐ Yes ☒ No

C. Continuous Residence.

Since becoming a lawful permanent resident of the United States:

13. Have you **ever** called yourself a "nonresident" on a Federal, State, or local tax return? ☐ Yes ☒ No

14. Have you **ever** failed to file a Federal, State, or local tax return because you considered yourself to be a "nonresident"? ☐ Yes ☒ No

Form N-400

Part 10. Additional Questions *(continued)*	Write your USCIS A-Number here: A

D. Good Moral Character.

For the purposes of this application, you must answer "Yes" to the following questions, if applicable, even if your records were sealed or otherwise cleared or if anyone, including a judge, law enforcement officer, or attorney, told you that you no longer have a record.

15. Have you **ever** committed a crime or offense for which you were **not** arrested? ☐ Yes ☒ No

16. Have you **ever** been arrested, cited, or detained by any law enforcement officer (including USCIS or former INS and military officers) for any reason? ☐ Yes ☒ No

17. Have you **ever** been charged with committing any crime or offense? ☐ Yes ☒ No

18. Have you **ever** been convicted of a crime or offense? ☐ Yes ☒ No

19. Have you **ever** been placed in an alternative sentencing or a rehabilitative program (for example: diversion, deferred prosecution, withheld adjudication, deferred adjudication)? ☐ Yes ☒ No

20. Have you **ever** received a suspended sentence, been placed on probation, or been paroled? ☐ Yes ☒ No

21. Have you **ever** been in jail or prison? ☐ Yes ☒ No

If you answered "Yes" to any of Questions 15 through 21, complete the following table. If you need more space, use a separate sheet of paper to give the same information.

Why were you arrested, cited, detained, or charged?	Date arrested, cited, detained, or charged? *(mm/dd/yyyy)*	Where were you arrested, cited, detained, or charged? *(City, State, Country)*	Outcome or disposition of the arrest, citation, detention, or charge *(No charges filed, charges dismissed, jail, probation, etc.)*

Answer Questions 22 through 33. If you answer "Yes" to any of these questions, attach (1) your written explanation why your answer was "Yes" and (2) any additional information or documentation that helps explain your answer.

22. Have you **ever**:

    a. Been a habitual drunkard? ☐ Yes ☒ No

    b. Been a prostitute, or procured anyone for prostitution? ☐ Yes ☒ No

    c. Sold or smuggled controlled substances, illegal drugs, or narcotics? ☐ Yes ☒ No

    d. Been married to more than one person at the same time? ☐ Yes ☒ No

    e. Helped anyone enter or try to enter the United States illegally? ☐ Yes ☒ No

    f. Gambled illegally or received income from illegal gambling? ☐ Yes ☒ No

    g. Failed to support your dependents or to pay alimony? ☐ Yes ☒ No

23. Have you **ever** given false or misleading information to any U.S. Government official while applying for any immigration benefit or to prevent deportation, exclusion, or removal? ☐ Yes ☒ No

24. Have you **ever** lied to any U.S. Government official to gain entry or admission into the United States? ☐ Yes ☒ No

Form N-400

Part 10. Additional Questions *(Continued)*	Write your USCIS A-Number here: A

E.   Removal, Exclusion, and Deportation Proceedings.

25. Are removal, exclusion, rescission, or deportation proceedings pending against you?   ☐ Yes ☒ No

26. Have you **ever** been removed, excluded, or deported from the United States?   ☐ Yes ☒ No

27. Have you **ever** been ordered to be removed, excluded, or deported from the United States?   ☐ Yes ☒ No

28. Have you **ever** applied for any kind of relief from removal, exclusion, or deportation?   ☐ Yes ☒ No

F. Military Service.

29. Have you **ever** served in the U.S. Armed Forces?   ☐ Yes ☒ No

30. Have you **ever** left the United States to avoid being drafted into the U.S. Armed Forces?   ☐ Yes ☒ No

31. Have you **ever** applied for any kind of exemption from military service in the U.S. Armed Forces?   ☐ Yes ☒ No

32. Have you **ever** deserted from the U.S. Armed Forces?   ☐ Yes ☒ No

G. Selective Service Registration.

33. Are you a male who lived in the United States at any time between your 18th and 26th birthdays   ☐ Yes ☒ No
in any status except as a lawful nonimmigrant?

If you answered "NO," go on to question 34.

If you answered "YES," provide the information below.

If you answered "YES," but you did not register with the Selective Service System and are still under 26 years of age, you must register before you apply for naturalization, so that you can complete the information below:

Date Registered (mm/dd/yyyy) [   ]   Selective Service Number [   ]

If you answered "YES," but you did not register with the Selective Service and you are now 26 years old or older, attach a statement explaining why you did not register.

H. Oath Requirements. *(See Part 14 for the text of the oath)*

Answer Questions 34 through 39. If you answer "No" to any of these questions, attach (1) your written explanation why the answer was "No" and (2) any additional information or documentation that helps to explain your answer.

34. Do you support the Constitution and form of government of the United States?   ☒ Yes ☐ No

35. Do you understand the full Oath of Allegiance to the United States?   ☒ Yes ☐ No

36. Are you willing to take the full Oath of Allegiance to the United States?   ☒ Yes ☐ No

37. If the law requires it, are you willing to bear arms on behalf of the United States?   ☒ Yes ☐ No

38. If the law requires it, are you willing to perform noncombatant services in the U.S. Armed Forces?   ☒ Yes ☐ No

39. If the law requires it, are you willing to perform work of national importance under civilian direction?   ☒ Yes ☐ No

Form N-400

Part 11. Your Signature	Write your USCIS A-Number here: A

I certify, under penalty of perjury under the laws of the United States of America, that this application, and the evidence submitted with it, are all true and correct. I authorize the release of any information that the USCIS needs to determine my eligibility for naturalization.

Your Signature

Date *(mm/dd/yyyy)*

Part 12. Signature of Person Who Prepared This Application for You *(If applicable)*

I declare under penalty of perjury that I prepared this application at the request of the above person. The answers provided are based on information of which I have personal knowledge and/or were provided to me by the above named person in response to the *exact questions* contained on this form.

Preparer's Printed Name

Ryan Attorney, Esq.

Preparer's Signature

Date *(mm/dd/yyyy)*

Preparer's Firm or Organization Name *(If applicable)*

Blank Attorney, PA

Preparer's Daytime Phone Number

(123)987-6543

Preparer's Address - Street Number and Name

2655 Le Jeune Road Suite 1001

City

Coral Gables

State

FL

Zip Code

33751

NOTE: Do not complete Parts 13 and 14 until a USCIS Officer instructs you to do so.

Part 13. Signature at Interview

I swear (affirm) and certify under penalty of perjury under the laws of the United States of America that I know that the contents of this application for naturalization subscribed by me, including corrections numbered 1 through _____ and the evidence submitted by me numbered pages 1 through _____ , are true and correct to the best of my knowledge and belief.

Subscribed to and sworn to (affirmed) before me

Officer's Printed Name or Stamp

Date *(mm/dd/yyyy)*

Complete Signature of Applicant

Officer's Signature

Part 14. Oath of Allegiance

If your application is approved, you will be scheduled for a public oath ceremony at which time you will be required to take the following Oath of Allegiance immediately prior to becoming a naturalized citizen. By signing, you acknowledge your willingness and ability to take this oath:

I hereby declare, on oath, that I absolutely and entirely renounce and abjure all allegiance and fidelity to any foreign prince, potentate, state, or sovereignty, of whom or which I have heretofore been a subject or citizen;

that I will support and defend the Constitution and laws of the United States of America against all enemies, foreign and domestic;

that I will bear true faith and allegiance to the same;

that I will bear arms on behalf of the United States when required by the law;

that I will perform noncombatant service in the Armed Forces of the United States when required by the law;

that I will perform work of national importance under civilian direction when required by the law; and

that I take this obligation freely, without any mental reservation or purpose of evasion, so help me God.

Printed Name of Applicant

Complete Signature of Applicant

Form G-28

OMB No. 1615-0105; Expires 04/30/2012

G-28, Notice of Entry of Appearance as Attorney or Accredited Representative

Department of Homeland Security

Part 1. Notice of Appearance as Attorney or Accredited Representative

A. This appearance is in regard to immigration matters before:

[x] USCIS - List the form number(s): N-400   ☐ CBP - List the specific matter in which appearance is entered:

☐ ICE - List the specific matter in which appearance is entered:

B. I hereby enter my appearance as attorney or accredited representative at the request of:

List Petitioner, Applicant, or Respondent. **NOTE:** Provide the mailing address of Petitioner, Applicant, or Respondent being represented, and **not** the address of the attorney or accredited representative, except when filed under VAWA.

Principal Petitioner, Applicant, or Respondent			A Number or Receipt Number, if any	
Name: Last	First	Middle		☐ Petitioner
DOE	John		None	[x] Applicant
				☐ Respondent

Address: Street Number and Street Name	Apt. No.	City	State	Zip Code
Applicant's Address				

Pursuant to the Privacy Act of 1974 and DHS policy, I hereby consent to the disclosure to the named Attorney or Accredited Representative of any record pertaining to me that appears in any system of records of USCIS, USCBP, or USICE.

Signature of Petitioner, Applicant, or Respondent	**Date**
	11/08/2009

Part 2. Information about Attorney or Accredited Representative *(Check applicable items(s) below)*

A. [x] I am an attorney and a member in good standing of the bar of the highest court(s) of the following State(s), possession(s), territory(ies), commonwealth(s), or the District of Columbia: State of _____   Supreme Court

I am not [x] or ☐ **am subject to any order of any court or administrative agency disbarring, suspending, enjoining, restraining, or otherwise restricting me in the practice of law (If you are subject to any order(s), explain fully on reverse side).**

B. ☐ I am an accredited representative of the following qualified non-profit religious, charitable, social service, or similar organization established in the United States, so recognized by the Department of Justice, Board of Immigration Appeals pursuant to 8 CFR 1292.2. Provide name of organization and expiration date of accreditation:

C. ☐ I am associated with _____ .

The attorney or accredited representative of record previously filed Form G-28 in this case, and my appearance as an attorney or accredited representative is at his or her request *(If you check this item, also complete item A or B above in **Part 2**, whichever is appropriate).*

Part 3. Name and Signature of Attorney or Accredited Representative

I have read and understand the regulations and conditions contained in 8 CFR 103.2 and 292 governing appearances and representation before the Department of Homeland Security. I declare under penalty of perjury under the laws of the United States that the information I have provided on this form is true and correct.

Name of Attorney or Accredited Representative	Attorney Bar Number(s), if any
Attorney or Accredited Representative's Name	
Signature of Attorney or Accredited Representative	Date 11/08/2009

Complete Address of Attorney or Organization of Accredited Representative (Street Number and Street Name, Suite No., City, State, Zip Code)
Attorney or Accredited Representative's Address

Phone Number *(Include area code)*	Fax Number, if any *(Include area code)*	E-Mail Address, if any
(305) 442-1322	(305) 444-7578	Valid E-mail Address

Form G-28 (Rev. 04/22/09)N

CHAPTER 12

Representation before Department of Homeland Security Agencies

I. Introduction

As mentioned earlier in this book, the Department of Homeland Security has several agencies. The client may need representation before some of them while seeking an immigration benefit. This chapter will cover in more detail representation/relief before USCIS, AAO, CBP and ICE. It seems that lately cases have become more complicated and require specialized attention to issues that did not use to arise previously.

II. USCIS

A. Requests for Evidence

When an application is filed with USCIS, USCIS may send a request for evidence (RFE) depending on the type of cases. It is advisable to address the issues that may generate an RFE in the original submission. Even a typographical mistake can cause an RFE and will request not only the correction but will delve into other issues.

If you are filing an H1B case and the beneficiary does not have a formal degree, but is qualifying due to an evaluation on experience and some education, you should submit an advisory opinion. An advisory opinion is a type of evaluation given by the educational evaluation company which is usually prepared by a professor who has knowledge of the courses necessary to complete the bachelor's degree in the United States. He evaluates the experience of the beneficiary and equates it to the courses for the attainment of the degree. It is also advisable to send an "industry standard" letter. This is a letter from another company similarly situated with the petitioner which states that it is common in the industry to require at minimum a bachelor's degree for an entry level position in their company.

If you are filing an H3, be prepared for an RFE that requests how the petitioner will benefit in the United States when the employee returns abroad. It is advisable that the petitioner have a company abroad where the beneficiary will return upon completion of the training. This shows that the U.S. petitioner will benefit by training the employee in the U. S. and placing him abroad.

If you are filing an L1A extension and the employment based category EB1 for multi national executive or managers, you will most likely receive an RFE to prove that the position of the beneficiary is that of a manager or executive. USCIS usually looks at the subordinates of the beneficiary. If you can show that the subordinates are professionals you are in good shape. Try to include the degrees and resumes of those subordinates to show that they are professionals. For employment based residence, the most common RFE is for "ability to pay". If the beneficiary is not working for the petitioner at the proffered salary indicated on the PERM, you should do your research of secondary evidence and provide it. If the beneficiary is working for less, you can include the W2s of the beneficiary along with the tax returns to demonstrate that what is lacking on the W2 can be made up by the net income/assets on the tax returns.

B. Motions to Reopen

In the event that USCIS denies a case, the beneficiary or petitioner may file a motion to reopen and or reconsider and an appeal.

Motions to Reopen request the government to reopen a case when there are new facts or evidence that was not available previously. For example if a case is denied by USCIS for failure to be present at a interview, but there is evidence that the applicant or petitioner were in the hospital or involved in an accident you could request the Service to reopen your case along with evidence of either hospital admission information or traffic/accident report. Motions to reopen can also be filed in cases where there was service error. Evidence of the error would have to be submitted with the motion and in some instances USCIS may waive the filing fee for the waiver. The filing fee for a motion is presently $585.00.

C. Motions to Reconsider

In some cases USCIS may deny the case based on an error of law. If USCIS denies the case using a wrong standard such as a heightened standard or using incorrect case law, a motion to reconsider should be filed in order for USCIS to reopen the case.

D. H1B and L1A Audits

When an H1B petition or L1A petition is filed, an anti-fraud fee is included. This fee is for the investigation of vulnerabilities in the H1B and L1A process that may lead to fraud. This is different from an audit for compliance with the LCA performed by DOL. DOL is looking for labor law violations. USCIS is looking for H1B or L1A vulnerabilities. Some violations may be technical but other violations may be egregious. USCIS contracts private investigators who will carry a business card identifying themselves as an employee of USCIS. They are supposed to go to the work location and obtain information on the beneficiary. The information is the rate of pay, the date of hire and the duties of the position. You should inform the petitioner of these visas that they may be visited. They are entitled to have their attorney present during this interview. If someone in the business is approached, they should ask the investigator to contact the attorney. If the person contacted does not have the information because this information is usually kept with the human resources department, they should make it very clear that they are not authorized to have that information and that they may also contact the human resources department or the person who is in possession of that information. Once a petition is approved, you should send a letter to the petitioner explaining this and clearly delineating the duties, salary and date of hire.

III. Appeals before the Administrative Appeals Office (AAO)

The AAO has jurisdiction on any decision under the immigration laws in any type of proceedings over which the Board of Immigration Appeals (BIA) does not have appellate jurisdiction. 8 C.F.R. § 103.3 and § 103.5. For example, if an Immigrant Petition for an Alien Worker, Form I-140, is filed with USCIS and is denied, an appeal to the AAO is the next step, unless a motion to reopen or reconsider is filed.

For an appeal or motion to reopen or reconsider the Form I 290B is used. The Form I-290B must be filed with the Service Center that denied the matter within 30 calendar days after service of the decision. If the decision is mailed, the form must be filed within 33 days. There are certain instances where the appeal must be filed earlier, such as in the event of a revocation. You must always research the time allotted to file the appeal as it may change.

Appeals

1. Brief

Filing a brief is not mandatory. If you wish to file a brief you may submit the brief with any pertinent evidence within 30 days of the dated you signed the Form I-290B. You must submit the brief and any supporting documentation to:

> USCIS Administrative Appeals Office
> U.S. Citizenship and Immigration Services
> 20 Massachusetts Avenue, N.W., Room 3000
> Washington, D.C. 20529

2. Oral Argument

Appellant may request oral argument before the AAO in Washington, D.C. in a letter attached to the form explaining why oral argument is necessary.

IV. Customs and Border Protection (CBP)

It is common knowledge that individuals do not have constitutional rights if they are outside our borders. The U. S. government has taken the position that if an individual is at a port of entry, they have not "entered" and are therefore not accorded any constitutional protections, such as the right to an attorney. In some instances, you may call the port and speak to a duty CBP inspector or supervisor and make the case for your client, such as being able to fax relevant information that is being questioned at entry. However, in most cases, the individual is sent back to their country or they are allowed to enter the United States and given a date to present themselves at "deferred inspection". Deferred inspection is a process where the individual presents himself to a CBP office off site the airport at a later date to have inadmissibility issues reviewed. If upon further inspection, CBP finds that the individual is admissible, he is issued a Notice to Appear and may either be released or arrested and detained. It is very important that complete and thorough research be conducted of the legal issues involved and that a memorandum be prepared along with documentation to be presented to the interviewing inspector.

If the individual has been returned to their country, you should ask him what was the reason for his being returned and research the issue. If he was returned for having overstayed his visa, he needs to request a new visa before he returns to the United States. However, it is very likely that he will be issued a visa such as a tourist or student visa.

V. Immigration and Customs Enforcement (ICE)

A. Enforcement and Removal Operations (ERO)

If an individual has overstayed their voluntary departure or they have overstayed their visa waiver program 90 day stay or have a removal order that has been issued, ERO will either send them a "bag and baggage" letter or will go to their home in the early hours of the morning to arrest them and detain them in order to remove them from the United States. A "bag and baggage" letter is a letter that is sent to the individual for him to present himself voluntarily at a ERO office and bring an airline ticket to be processed for removal.

B. Homeland Security Investigations

Investigations is another unit of ICE. It is charged with investigating benefits fraud and employer violations. Raids and arrests that gain media attention are usually performed by this department.

1. Employer Compliance

Compliance with I-9 and the hiring of those not authorized to work have caused civil fines and sometimes criminal penalties for employers. The Social Security Administration attempted to update their records with no match letters. And most recently the once experimental and voluntary "E-Verify" program has become mandatory for employers of certain states and federal contractors.

Part of employer compliance is "worksite enforcement". The basic goal of worksite enforcement is to remove incentives to enter illegally by cracking down on employers who hire undocumented immigrants. Immigration and Customs Enforcement (ICE) is the agency charged with regulatory enforcement of Form I-9 employment eligibility verification and worksite inspections. This began in 1986 with the Immigration Reform and Control Act of 1986 (IRCA) when employers were required to verify the identity and employment eligibility of all persons hired for employment after November 6, 1986. The law imposed administrative sanctions for Form I-9 hiring and verification violations and made it unlawful to knowingly hire or continue to employ unauthorized aliens. The new I-9 form became effective on April 3, 2009. Changes to the form are an additional attestation box in Section 1, the requirement of unexpired documents, the updating of the list of acceptable documents, and the clarification of rules on technical changes to the language. The employer must be careful not to over request documents. In other words if the employee submits a document from list A, a passport or passport card, permanent resident card or alien registration receipt card (Form I-551), a foreign passport that contains an I-551 stamp or temporary I-551 printed notation on a machine readable immigrant visa, an Employment Authorization document that contains a photograph, a foreign passport with form I-94 bearing the name on the passport and containing an endorsement of the alien's nonimmigrant status or passport from the Federated States of Micronesia (FSM) or Republic of the Marshall Islands (RMI) with Form I-94 or Form I-94A indicating nonimmigrant admission under the Compact of Free Association Between the United States and the FSM or RMI, the employer is not allowed to ask for more documents. If the employee is not able to produce a document from list A, then and only then can the employer request one document from list B (to establish identity) and one document on list C (to establish employment authorization). ICE may audit the files of the employer and initiate this by sending a Notice of Inspection (Appendix 5). Upon examination of the I-9 and documents and investigation of the status of the employees, ICE may give a variety of notices such as a Notice of Suspect Documents, a Notice of Unauthorized Aliens, a Notice of Technical or Procedural Failures, a Warning Notice and or a Final Order to Cease Violations and Pay Fine. As mentioned earlier, the penalties imposed may be a civil fine or criminal misdemeanor or felony charges.

2. E-Verify Program

E-Verify is an online system used to verify employment eligibility of new hires and is to be used regardless of national origin or citizenship status after the employee has completed the I-9 form. Any type of profiling or discrimination may expose the employer to labor discrimination complaints. The Employer must provide any referral notice from the SSA or DHS to the employee to contest any non confirmation. The Employee should be allowed to continue working during the period of re confirmation. The employer can check E-Verify daily for updates and should contact E-Verify if they believe the final non confirmation is in error. The Employer is required to post notices of employer's participation in E-Verify along with the anti discrimination notice issued by the Office of Special Counsel for Immigration-Related Unfair Employment Practices (OSC). The employer should accept any Form I-9 List B document with a photo from the employee who chooses to provide list B documents. He should also secure the privacy of the employees' personal information. The employer should delay running the E-Verify query for an employee who has not yet been issued a Social Security number until the Social Security number is issued and allow the employee to work through the period of waiting for the social security number. The employer should not use the program to verify current employees, or selectively based on a 'suspicion" due to national origin or that they believe may not be eligible to work. The employer should not use the program to pre-screen employment or influence or coerce an employee's decision whether to contest a tentative non confirmation or terminate or take adverse action against an employee such as unacceptable conditions who is contesting a tentative non confirmation. The employer should not request additional documents or request specific documents in order to activate the E-Verify photo tool feature or run the program for any employee who is waiting for their Social Security number.

3. No Match Letters

In 1993, the Social Security Administration (SSA) started sending no match letters to employers referencing employees whose names did not match their social security number. This was generated when the employer would report the income of the employee to IRS on a W2. The purpose of these letters was to ensure that wages are correctly reported and credited towards an employee's SSA benefits, etc. The employer was not required to respond to the SSA letters. The SSA stopped the program due to the voluminous letters that were going out and the lack of resources. Moreover, an injunction was issued barring the SSA from continuing to issue the letters. Though, IRS regulations allow for a fine to be imposed on an employer who files a document with an incorrect Tax Identification Number or Social Security Number, this penalty may be waived if the employer has a Form W4 with the number that he is reporting and signed by the employee even if the number is incorrect.

Appendix

1. Request for Evidence
2. Sample Motion to Reopen and Reconsider
3. Motion to Reconsider and.or Reopen Template
4. Form I-9
5. Notice of Inspection
6. Notice of Suspect Documents
7. Notice of Unauthorized Aliens
8. Notice of Technical or Procedural Failures
9. Warning Notice
10. Final Order to Cease Violations and Pay Fine

Request for Evidence

U.S Department of Homeland Security	Notice of Action
U. S. Citizenship and Immigration Services	Page 1 of 3

Applicant/Petitioner A #	Application/Petition
	PETITION FOR A NONIMMIGRANT WORKER (Form I129)
Notice Date	**Response due by**
September 11, 2009	October 26, 2009

444 BRICKELL AVE 416
MIAMI FL 33131

EAC0921651371

Applicant/Petitioner
Beneficiary
Receipt Number

IMPORTANT: THIS NOTICE CONTAINS YOUR UNIQUE NUMBER AND MUST BE SUBMITTED IN THE ORIGINAL WITH THE REQUESTED EVIDENCE.

1. The evidence submitted with your form is insufficient. U. S. Citizenship and Immigration Services (USCIS) requires certain additional evidence to process your form. Please respond with the evidence listed on the attached page(s).

2. Your response must be received in this office on or before **October 26, 2009**.

3. All requested evidence should be submitted at the same time. Incomplete submission of the requested evidence will be considered a request for a decision on the record [8 CFR 103.2(b)(11)].

4. An extension of time will not be granted for you to submit the requested evidence.

5. You will be notified separately about any other applications or petitions you have filed.

6. You should save a copy of this notice for your records.

7. From the date this office receives your submission, it will take a minimum of 14 days to process your form. If you have not heard from USCIS within **60 days**, you may contact the USCIS National Customer Service Center (NCSC) at **1-800-375-5283**. If you are hearing impaired, please call the NCSC TDD at **1-800-767-1833**.

8. Responses, inquiries or correspondence must include this notice and be mailed to:

> U. S. CITIZENSHIP AND IMMIGRATION SERVICES
> VERMONT SERVICE CENTER
> 75 LOWER WELDEN STREET
> ST. ALBANS, VT 05479-0001

FOR OFFICE USE ONLY
S

Form I-797 (8/03/90) Y

Request for Evidence

U.S Department of Homeland Security **U. S. Citizenship and Immigration Services**	Notice of Action Page 2 of 3

━━━━━━━━━━━

It is not presently evident that an employer-employee relationship exists between the petitioner and the beneficiary because it appears the beneficiary may be an owner/partner of the petitioning company.

To establish that an employer-employee relationship exists between the petitioner and the beneficiary, submit evidence which clearly establishes who supervises and assigns work to the beneficiary, who has the authority to hire, fire, pay, and change the beneficiary's job duties, or otherwise control his or her work. Such documentation may include, but is not limited to, an organizational chart, employment contract, or any other document describing the beneficiary's claimed employment relationship with the petitioner. Include a statement concerning:

- the beneficiary's influence on the petitioning business if he or she reports to a higher authority,
- whether it is intended that the beneficiary be an employee, and
- whether the beneficiary shares in profits, losses, and liabilities of the business.

In addition, submit evidence which will establish the ownership and control of the petitioning company. The evidence to submit may include, but is not limited to, copies of stock ledgers, stock certificates, articles of incorporation, joint-venture agreements, etc., which delineate the ownership and control of the U.S. petitioner.

How many other individuals do you employ in similar positions? Of these, how many hold at least a baccalaureate degree? In what field of study?

Please submit evidence showing that you hire individuals with a baccalaureate degree in a specific field of study as a standard minimum requirement for the job offered.

Submit a list of individuals that you currently employ in this position and the degree and field of study held by the employees listed may satisfy this requirement.

In your explanation of your company you state that ▆▆▆▆▆▆▆▆▆ is an agent of ▆▆▆▆▆▆▆▆▆. Please submit an explanation of the company description as "agent". As an "agent" of the ▆▆▆▆▆▆▆▆▆, please submit a organizational chart from ▆▆▆▆▆▆▆▆▆ indicating how many other "agent" businesses they have under their business umbrella.

You also state that your company offers financial services, including various options such as stocks, bonds, mutual funds, along with trading and investment services. Please explain to whom you are offering this information and advice.

You also state that your company requires employees with advanced knowledge of economics and business who will maintain and render professional and reliable financial services. Please explain how the beneficiary will accomplish this task working on a part-time basis. Also explain how you can expect this business acumen from employees when according to the petition that was filed, there is only one employee.

It is not clear that the beneficiary is coming to the United States to perform services in a "specialty occupation." The proffered position does not appear to involve such specialization or complexity as to require the knowledge associated with the attainment of a baccalaureate degree or is commensurate with the nature, scope, and/or size of the employer's business enterprise. It is also not clear how the beneficiary will be relieved from performing non-qualifying functions. Therefore, evidence is required to establish that the petitioner can sustain an employee performing duties at the level required for consideration as a "specialty occupation" per 8 CFR 214.2(h)(4)(ii).

Submit documentation highlighting the nature, scope, and activity of the petitioner's business enterprise(s) in order to

FOR OFFICE USE ONLY
S ▆▆▆▆

Form I-797 (8/03/90) Y

Request for Evidence

establish the beneficiary will be employed with the duties you have set forth. Such evidence may include, but is not limited to:

- A detailed description of the proffered position, to include approximate percentages of time for each duty the beneficiary will perform;
- Copies of any written contracts (or work orders) between the petitioner and the beneficiary or, if there is no written contract, a summary of the terms of the oral agreement under which the beneficiary will be employed that indicates the services being provided by your company and/or the beneficiary;
- Documentation of how many other individuals in your establishment are currently, or were, employed in this position or similar positions (document with copies of the former employees' degrees and evidence of employment such as pay stubs or Form W-2s or W-3s); and/or
- Brief job descriptions for the majority of positions within the petitioner's employ and approximately how many individuals occupy such positions (to include job titles, duties and education requirements).

Form I-797 (8/03/90) Y

FOR OFFICE USE ONLY
S

Sample Motion to Reopen and Reconsider

United States Citizenship and Immigration Service
California Service Center

Applicant: ▇▇▇▇▇▇▇▇▇▇▇▇▇▇▇▇▇▇
FILE: ▇▇▇▇▇▇▇▇▇▇

Motion to Reopen and Reconsider and
Appeal Brief
Facts

This brief is being filed as a motion to reopen based on new material evidence and a motion to reconsider based on the erroneous interpretation of law and guidance in not issuing an RFE for missing evidence.

The applicant filed an application for change of status from E-2 to B-1 (visitor for business). The petition was filed on ▇▇▇▇▇▇▇ under section 101(a) (15) (B) of the Act. The applicant included her spouse on the application; they wished to stay in the US for 3 more months to evaluate some business opportunities. The applicant presented a reason letter stating their reasons, attached a bank statement reflecting substantial funds sufficient for a short business stay and attached airline tickets as proof of their intentions to return to France, their home country. The case was filed with the Vermont Service Center then transferred to the California Service Center

The Service determined "*Although the applicant submitted a reason for the extension of stay, the reason appears to be very a general statement, not a detailed explanation as required by regulation*" and "*the applicant has provided no documentation showing definitive arrangements to depart the United States have been secured*". "*Because the applicant failed to file the I-539 application with <u>all</u> initial evidence required by regulation or by the instructions on the form, the applicant failed to establish the required burden of proof for the requested benefit…. As such, the Application to Extend/Change Nonimmigrant Status must be, and is hereby denied*"..

Sample Motion to Reopen and Reconsider

Argument

The decision was based on an erroneous determination of policy. The standard for adjudication of an application or petition is "preponderance of the evidence" "which means that the matter asserted is more likely than not to be true. Filings are not required to demonstrate eligibility beyond a reasonable doubt" [1] The regulations state that deference should be given to the form instructions. The form states that the individual must submit a written statement explaining in detail the reason for the request, why the stay would be temporary, including arrangements to depart and any effect the extended stay may have on the employment or foreign residency.

The Service admits in the denial notice that the application was NOT submitted with incomplete evidence. The Service states that the applicant submitted a reason letter, but the Service find the letter not detailed enough for CIS to be able to determine if the proposed activity is qualifying and consistent with the visitor for business classification. The statement explained that they had scheduled business meetings with potential suppliers, they stated that they only needed 3 months to conduct this business (clearly a statement that this is temporary), the arrangements to depart were submitted in the form of airline tickets (which had to be cancelled ultimately because of the extensive delays of USCIS), since there was no effect on their residence or employment abroad this is a non-issue. The instructions and regulations are not giving exact terms of how detailed the explanations should be. In our case, the applicants are requesting to change the status for a business related classification (E-2) to the B-1 visitor for business. It is very likely that having directed and developed an investment opportunity in the U. S. that the applicants would want to exploit those contacts before they return to ███████ Also, the applicants are attaching a bank statement reflecting substantial funds in the amount of $███████ In order to determine the preponderance evidence the adjudicator should look at the totality of the circumstances.

---

1. Memorandum by William R. Yates, *Request for Evidence(RFE) and Notices for Intent to Deny (NOID)*, HQOPRD(February 16, 2005)

Sample Motion to Reopen and Reconsider

Moreover, the applicants included in their application package their airline tickets for the return to France. The tickets were secured, then since the application was pending and the requested time passed, the applicants canceled the tickets to avoid loosing the funds intending to acquire the new tickets as soon as their application will be approved and the applicants would be able to know a more specific date. The Service is wrong stating that the applicants have provided no documentation showing definitive arrangements to depart the US.

The Neufeld RFE Memorandum[2], dated June 01, 2007 gives guidance in the issue of the RFEs. *"USCIS will have the option to deny incomplete applications, though it will exercise this option judiciously".* *" If an application or petition lacks required initial evidence, USCIS may deny the incomplete application or petition, though adjudicators are urged to exercise this option judiciously, or issue a request for additional evidence (RFE).*

The Service ignores the guidance offered by its Acting Associate Director in the June 01, 2007 Memo. The Service denied the application without issuing an RFE. A judicious decision should be characterized by wisdom, marked by deep understanding. The decision maker is aware of or informed about a particular matter. The Webster dictionary defines judicious as defined above.

In our case, the Service states *"Generic statements such as business meetings encompass a wide range of activities, which may or may not be qualifying"* and admits that a deep understanding can not be made and the Services feels that details are missing to determine with certainty if the stated reasons are or not qualifying. The RFE Memo in this situation urges the USCIS to issue an RFE to clarify its doubts. The Service ignores the Memo and denies the application without the RFE. The RFE would have given the opportunity to the applicants to explain in more detail their intentions, the applications should have been approved and the applicant would have been spared of the uncomfortable situation of being out of legal status and paying for a motion out of pocket.

2.Donald Neufeld, June 01, 2007 *Removal of Standardized Request for Evidence Processing Timeframe* (Neufeld RFE Memorandum)

Sample Motion to Reopen and Reconsider

The Yates RFE Memo provides guidance to adjudicators on whether to issue an RFE or NOID under current regulations of 8 C.F.R. 103.2(b)(8). The memo instructs the adjudicators to deny " *if there is clear evidence of ineligibility"*.

Clear ineligibility exist when the adjudicator can be sure that the applicant or petitioner cannot meet statutory or regulatory requirement, even if the filer were to be given the opportunity to present additional information"

In our case, the adjudicator in the denial letter states that he has doubts whether the stated reason may or may not be qualifying the applicants for the visitor for business category. The adjudicator is not sure about the reasons because of the lack of detail not because of the lack of reasons. The adjudicator can not be sure that the applicants can not give these details if they were given the opportunity to present additional information. The Memo instructs the adjudicators that *"The standard to be met by the applicant or petitioner is "preponderance of the evidence" which means that the matter asserted is more likely than not to be true. Filings are not required to demonstrate eligibility beyond a reasonable doubt"* .

The applicants at the time of filing, are in the US under E-2 status, always followed the US immigration laws. It is not beyond the reasonable doubt that after a period of time doing business in the US to need three more months to explore some business opportunities, having $▓▓▓▓▓▓ in their bank account.

There is new material evidence to support the motion to reopen. Attached is a detailed letter from the applicant which sets out the three requirements according to the regulations and instructions to the form. Attached is an itinerary of the business meetings, copy of airline tickets, original I-94 Forms and statement reflecting that there is no effect on the residency and employment abroad. The itinerary of the business meetings can attest of the numerous meetings attended by the applicants.

Sample Motion to Reopen and Reconsider

The denial notice was received by mail; the present Motion to Reopen and Reconsider is being timely filed via overnight services inside the allowed 33 days from the date of the denial.

Respectfully submitted on this ██ᵗʰ day of ████████ 200█

Motion to Reconsider and/or Reopen Template

UNITED STATES DEPARTMENT OF HOMELAND SECURITY
CITIZENSHIP AND IMMIGRATION SERVICES
MIAMI DISTRICT OFFICE
7880 Biscayne Boulevard, Miami, Florida 33138
Attention: Officer

IN THE MATTER OF:

ALIEN

A#
Type of Process:
_____   *

MOTION TO RECONSIDER AND/OR REOPEN
DENIAL OF AN APLICATION FOR ADJUSTMENT OF STATUS

Alien hereby and through undersigned counsel request per 8 C.F.R. § 103.5 that his application

for marriage based adjustment be reconsidered or reopened. for the reasons set forth herein:

1.   [State the facts of the case and reason for denial] Alien is a native and citizen of

Rumania who applied for adjustment of status based on an I-130 filed on his behalf by his

American Citizen wife, Alien's Wife. He also filed concurrently an I-485. His

application was denied on May 5, 2007 for failure to provide evidence that had been

requested.

2.   [Cite the applicable rule whether you are requesting Reopening or Reconsideration: "A

motion to reopen must state the new facts to be provided in the reopened proceeding and

be supported by affidavits or other documentary evidence.// A motion to reconsider must

state the reasons for reconsideration and be supported by any pertinent precedent

decisions to establish that the decision was based on an incorrect application of law or

Service policy." Read 8 CFR 103.5]

Motion to Reconsider and/or Reopen Template

3.   The Response to the Request for Evidence was mailed on time to USCIS on October 1, 2007. See copy of certified mail attached and copy of the response submitted. As such, USCIS erred in finding that the applicant had failed to respond to the request for evidence and therefore had abandoned his application.

4.   Both petitioner and beneficiary/applicant would like to request that their cases be reopened so that an interview can take place to adjudicate his application for permanent residence.

WHEREAS, all premises considered, we request that this case be reconsidered or reopened so that applicant's application for residence be adjudicated.

Dated: <u>December 25, 2007</u>

Respectfully submitted.

_____

Attorney for Alien

Form I-9

OMB No. 1615-0047; Expires 08/31/12

**Form I-9, Employment
Eligibility Verification**

Department of Homeland Security
U.S. Citizenship and Immigration Services

Read instructions carefully before completing this form. The instructions must be available during completion of this form.

ANTI-DISCRIMINATION NOTICE: It is illegal to discriminate against work-authorized individuals. Employers CANNOT specify which document(s) they will accept from an employee. The refusal to hire an individual because the documents have a future expiration date may also constitute illegal discrimination.

Section 1. Employee Information and Verification *(To be completed and signed by employee at the time employment begins.)*

Print Name: Last	First	Middle Initial	Maiden Name

Address *(Street Name and Number)*	Apt. #	Date of Birth *(month/day/year)*

City	State	Zip Code	Social Security #

I am aware that federal law provides for imprisonment and/or fines for false statements or use of false documents in connection with the completion of this form.

I attest, under penalty of perjury, that I am (check one of the following):

☐ A citizen of the United States

☐ A noncitizen national of the United States (see instructions)

☐ A lawful permanent resident (Alien #) _____

☐ An alien authorized to work (Alien # or Admission #) _____
until (expiration date, if applicable - *month/day/year*) _____

Employee's Signature	Date *(month/day/year)*

Preparer and/or Translator Certification *(To be completed and signed if Section 1 is prepared by a person other than the employee.) I attest, under penalty of perjury, that I have assisted in the completion of this form and that to the best of my knowledge the information is true and correct.*

Preparer's/Translator's Signature	Print Name

Address *(Street Name and Number, City, State, Zip Code)*	Date *(month/day/year)*

Section 2. Employer Review and Verification *(To be completed and signed by employer. Examine one document from List A OR examine one document from List B and one from List C, as listed on the reverse of this form, and record the title, number, and expiration date, if any, of the document(s).)*

	List A	OR	List B	AND	List C
Document title:					
Issuing authority:					
Document #:					
Expiration Date *(if any)*:					
Document #:					
Expiration Date *(if any)*:					

CERTIFICATION: I attest, under penalty of perjury, that I have examined the document(s) presented by the above-named employee, that the above-listed document(s) appear to be genuine and to relate to the employee named, that the employee began employment on *(month/day/year)* _____ and that to the best of my knowledge the employee is authorized to work in the United States. (State employment agencies may omit the date the employee began employment.)

Signature of Employer or Authorized Representative	Print Name	Title

Business or Organization Name and Address *(Street Name and Number, City, State, Zip Code)*	Date *(month/day/year)*

Section 3. Updating and Reverification *(To be completed and signed by employer.)*

A. New Name *(if applicable)*	B. Date of Rehire *(month/day/year)* *(if applicable)*

C. If employee's previous grant of work authorization has expired, provide the information below for the document that establishes current employment authorization.

Document Title:	Document #:	Expiration Date *(if any)*:

I attest, under penalty of perjury, that to the best of my knowledge, this employee is authorized to work in the United States, and if the employee presented document(s), the document(s) I have examined appear to be genuine and to relate to the individual.

Signature of Employer or Authorized Representative	Date *(month/day/year)*

Form I-9

LISTS OF ACCEPTABLE DOCUMENTS
All documents must be unexpired

LIST A	LIST B	LIST C
Documents that Establish Both Identity and Employment Authorization OR	**Documents that Establish Identity** AND	**Documents that Establish Employment Authorization**
1. U.S. Passport or U.S. Passport Card	1. Driver's license or ID card issued by a State or outlying possession of the United States provided it contains a photograph or information such as name, date of birth, gender, height, eye color, and address	1. Social Security Account Number card other than one that specifies on the face that the issuance of the card does not authorize employment in the United States
2. Permanent Resident Card or Alien Registration Receipt Card (Form I-551)		2. Certification of Birth Abroad issued by the Department of State (Form FS-545)
3. Foreign passport that contains a temporary I-551 stamp or temporary I-551 printed notation on a machine-readable immigrant visa	2. ID card issued by federal, state or local government agencies or entities, provided it contains a photograph or information such as name, date of birth, gender, height, eye color, and address	3. Certification of Report of Birth issued by the Department of State (Form DS-1350)
4. Employment Authorization Document that contains a photograph (Form I-766)	3. School ID card with a photograph	
	4. Voter's registration card	4. Original or certified copy of birth certificate issued by a State, county, municipal authority, or territory of the United States bearing an official seal
5. In the case of a nonimmigrant alien authorized to work for a specific employer incident to status, a foreign passport with Form I-94 or Form I-94A bearing the same name as the passport and containing an endorsement of the alien's nonimmigrant status, as long as the period of endorsement has not yet expired and the proposed employment is not in conflict with any restrictions or limitations identified on the form	5. U.S. Military card or draft record	
	6. Military dependent's ID card	
	7. U.S. Coast Guard Merchant Mariner Card	5. Native American tribal document
	8. Native American tribal document	6. U.S. Citizen ID Card (Form I-197)
	9. Driver's license issued by a Canadian government authority	
	For persons under age 18 who are unable to present a document listed above:	7. Identification Card for Use of Resident Citizen in the United States (Form I-179)
6. Passport from the Federated States of Micronesia (FSM) or the Republic of the Marshall Islands (RMI) with Form I-94 or Form I-94A indicating nonimmigrant admission under the Compact of Free Association Between the United States and the FSM or RMI	10. School record or report card	8. Employment authorization document issued by the Department of Homeland Security
	11. Clinic, doctor, or hospital record	
	12. Day-care or nursery school record	

Illustrations of many of these documents appear in Part 8 of the Handbook for Employers (M-274)

Notice of Inspection

Office of Investigations

U.S. Department of Homeland Security
[Address]
[Address]

 U.S. Immigration
and Customs
Enforcement

NOTICE OF INSPECTION

[Date]

[Name of Company Official]
[Company Name]
[Company Address]

Dear Sir/Madam:

Section 274A of the Immigration and Nationality Act, as amended by the Immigration Reform and Control Act of 1986, requires employers to hire only United States citizens and aliens who are authorized to work in the United States. Employers must verify employment eligibility of persons hired after November 6, 1986 using the Employment Eligibility Verification Form I-9.

U.S. Immigration and Customs Enforcement (ICE) regulations require the provision of three days notice prior to conducting a review of an employer's Forms I-9. This letter serves as advance notice that ICE has scheduled a review of your forms for *Insert date and time*. You may, however, waive the three-day period, should you wish to do so, by annotating and signing the bottom of this letter and advising this office of your decision.

During the review, *Insert name and title of ICE point of contact* will discuss the requirements of the law with you and inspect your Forms I-9. The purpose of this review is to assess your compliance with the provisions of the law. ICE will make every effort to conduct the review of records in a timely manner so as not to impede your normal business routine.

Sincerely,

Insert name
Insert title (GS or above)

I wish to waive the three day notice to which I am entitled by regulation.

_____   _____   _____
(Printed Name)   (Signature)   (Date)

Notice of Suspect Documents

Office of Investigations

U.S. Department of Homeland Security
[Address]
[Address]

U.S. Immigration and Customs Enforcement

NOTICE OF SUSPECT DOCUMENTS

[Date]

File Number

Name of Company Official
Company Name
Company Address

Dear Sir/Madam:

On *Insert date of inspection* agents from U.S. Immigration and Customs Enforcement (ICE) conducted an inspection of *Insert name of employer* to determine compliance with Section 274A of the Immigration and Nationality Act. During that inspection, the requirements of the law were discussed and I-9 Forms were inspected.

This letter is to inform you that, according to the records checked by the ICE, the following individuals appear, at the present time, not to be authorized to work in the United States. The documents submitted to you were found to pertain to other individuals, or there was no record of the alien registration numbers being issued, or the documents pertain to the individuals but the individuals are not employment authorized or their employment authorization has expired. Accordingly, the documentation previously provided to you for these employees does not satisfy the I-9 Form employment eligibility verification requirements of the Immigration and Nationality Act.

Attach a list if more appropriate

Unless the above employees present valid identification and employment eligibility documentation acceptable for completing the I-9 Form, other than the documentation noted above, they are considered by the ICE to be unauthorized to work in the United States. If you continue to employ these individuals without valid documentation, you may be subject to a civil money penalty ranging from $275 to $2,200 per unauthorized alien for a first violation. Higher penalties can be imposed for a second or subsequent violation. Further, criminal charges may be brought against any person or entity which engages in a pattern or practice of knowingly hiring or continuing to employ unauthorized aliens. This is a very serious matter that requires your immediate attention.

Notice of Suspect Documents

SUBJECT: Notice of Suspect Documents
Page 2

If you or the employees feel that this determination is in error and the employees are authorized to work, immediately call *Insert name and title of ICE point of contact* at *Insert phone number*. The ICE agent will re-verify the information provided about the employees, including any new information provided by you or the employees. You will then be notified of the employees' status in writing. In these instances, do not terminate the employees whose status is in question until you receive written notification from ICE. If you or the employees have any other questions, please call the ICE contact noted above.

Sincerely,

Insert name
Assistant Special Agent in Charge

Notice of Unauthorized Aliens

Office of Investigations

U.S. Department of Homeland Security
[Address]
[Address]

U.S. Immigration
and Customs
Enforcement

NOTICE OF UNAUTHORIZED ALIENS

[Date]

[Case Number]

[Name of Company Official]
[Company Name]
[Company Address]

Dear Sir/Madam:

On *Insert date of apprehension,* U.S. Immigration and Customs Enforcement (ICE)
apprehended the following individual(s):

Insert name(s) or attach list

You employed the individuals at your place of business, *Insert name of employer.* The
individuals have been deemed by ICE to be unauthorized to work in the United States.

Unless they present valid identification and employment eligibility documentation acceptable
for completing the Form I-9, other than the documents previously presented, they are
unauthorized to work in the United States.

Any continued employment of the individuals without satisfying the employment eligibility
verification requirements may subject you to civil penalties for knowingly continuing to
employ unauthorized aliens in violation of Section 274A(a)(2) of the Immigration and
Nationality Act. A civil money penalty ranging from $375 to $3,200 per unauthorized alien
may be imposed for a first violation of knowingly hiring or continuing to employ an
unauthorized alien. Higher monetary penalties can be imposed for a second or subsequent
violation. Further, criminal charges may be brought against any person or entity which
engages in a pattern or practice of knowingly hiring or continuing to employ unauthorized
aliens. This is a very serious matter that requires your immediate attention.

Notice of Unauthorized Aliens

SUBJECT: Notice of Unauthorized Aliens
Page 2

If you or the employees feel that this determination is in error and the employees are authorized to work, or if you or the employees have any other questions, you or the employees may call *Insert name and title of ICE point of contact* at *Insert telephone number*.

Sincerely,

Insert name
Insert title (GS or above)

Notice of Technical or Procedural Failures

Office of Investigations

U.S. Department of Homeland Security
[Address]
[Address]

 U.S. Immigration
and Customs
Enforcement

NOTICE OF TECHNICAL OR PROCEDURAL FAILURES

[Date]

[Case Number]

[Name of Company Official]
[Company Name]
[Company Address]

Dear Sir/Madam:

On *Insert date of inspection,* Special Agents of U.S. Immigration and Customs Enforcement conducted an inspection of *Insert name of employer* to determine compliance with Section 274A of the Immigration and Nationality Act (INA). At that time, *Insert number of Forms I-9* Employment Eligibility Verification Forms (Forms I-9) were presented for inspection. During the inspection of the Forms I-9 presented, technical or procedural failures to meet the employment verification requirements of Section 274A(b) of the INA were discovered. Pursuant to Section 274A(b)(6) of the INA, these technical or procedural failures are considered violations of Section 274A(b) of the INA if they remain uncorrected.

Note: Additional failures to meet the employment verification requirements of Section 274A(b) of the INA may have been discovered. These failures are not included in this notification and may result in the issuance of a Notice of Intent to Fine. If a Notice of Intent to Fine is issued, it will be served separately from this notification.

This letter and accompanying documents are to notify *Insert name of employer* of the technical or procedural failures encountered and to provide *Insert name of employer* a period of not less than ten business days within which to correct these failures. Accompanying this letter are copies of *Insert number of Forms I-9 being returned* Forms I-9 that contain technical or procedural failures. The technical or procedural failures found on each Form I-9 have been highlighted or circled in ink. They include one or more of the following technical or procedural failures:

☐ Employee's maiden name, address or birth date missing in Section 1
☐ No alien registration number next to the phrase in Section 1, "A Lawful Permanent Resident" where the number is in Sections 2 or 3 of the I-9 (or on a document retained with the Form I-9 and presented at the I-9 inspection)

Notice of Technical or Procedural Failures

SUBJECT: Notice of Technical or Procedural Failures
Page 2

☐ No alien registration number or admission number next to the phrase in Section 1, "An alien authorized to work until" where the number is in Sections 2 or 3 of the I-9 (or on a document retained with the Form I-9 and presented at the I-9 inspection)

☐ Employee attestation date missing in Section 1

☐ Employee attestation not completed at the time of hire in Section 1

☐ Name, address or signature of the preparer and/or translator missing in Section 1

☐ No date in the preparer and/or translator certification box in Section 1

☐ No document identification number of a List A, B or C document in Section 2 where a copy of document(s) is retained with the Form I-9 and presented at the I-9 inspection

☐ No document expiration date of a List A, B or C document in Section 2 where a copy of document(s) is retained with the Form I-9 and presented at the I-9 inspection

☐ Business title, name or address missing in Section 2

☐ Date of hire missing in Section 2

☐ No employer attestation date in Section 2

☐ Employer attestation in Section 2 not completed within 3 business days of the hire or, if the employee is hired for 3 business days or less, at the time of hire

☐ No document identification number of a List A, B or C document in Section 3 where a copy of document(s) is retained with the Form I-9 and presented at the I-9 inspection

☐ No document expiration date of a List A, B or C document in Section 3 where a copy of document(s) is retained with the Form I-9 and presented at the I-9 inspection

☐ Date of rehire missing in Section 3

You must correct the noted failures directly on the Form I-9. Initial and date the corrections made. A written explanation must be provided for corrections that cannot reasonably be made (e.g., information unavailable, individual's employment terminated). Verification failures that are not technical or procedural have not been highlighted or circled on the Forms I-9 accompanying this letter.

Insert name of employer is being provided until *Insert date by which Forms I-9 must be corrected* to correct the highlighted or circled failures on the accompanying Forms I-9. Within one week of this date, ICE will make arrangements to review these forms to ensure that the noted failures have been corrected. Be aware that any uncorrected technical or procedural failures may result in the issuance of a Notice of Intent to Fine.

If you have any questions regarding this notification or your requirements under the law, you may call *Insert name and title of ICE point of contact* at *Insert telephone number*.

Sincerely,

Insert name
Insert title (GS or above)

Enclosures   AILA InfoNet Doc. No. 09031660. (Posted 03/16/09)

Notice of Technical or Procedural Failures

SUBJECT: Notice of Technical or Procedural Failures
Page 3

AILA InfoNet Doc. No. 09031660. (Posted 03/16/09)

Warning Notice

DEPARTMENT OF HOMELAND SECURITY
U.S. Immigration and Customs Enforcement

WARNING NOTICE

Name: _____   Date: _____

Address: _____   File Number: _____

_____

On _____, officers of U.S. Immigration and Customs Enforcement conducted an inspection of Forms I-9 and related employment records for:

_____

_____

_____

(Business Name and Address)

The following deficiencies were identified:

SEE ATTACHMENT

The U.S. Government encourages voluntary compliance with the law. As a matter of discretion, we have chosen to issue only this WARNING NOTICE in lieu of imposing any sanctions at this time. However, we anticipate your full cooperation in correcting the violation or violations which resulted in the issuance of this WARNING NOTICE and any other violations which may exist in your Forms I-9. If it is determined that the listed violations are not immediately corrected or other violations are detected, civil or criminal proceedings may be instituted against you.

A follow-up inspection of Forms I-9 and related employment records is scheduled for _____.

Should you have any questions, you may contact this office at _____.

(Telephone Number)

Sincerely,

_____   _____

(Signature)

_____   _____

(Title)   (Address)

SERVICE OF WARNING NOTICE

I hereby certify that, on _____, I served the above Warning Notice and The Handbook for Employers

(Month/Day/Year)

to _____

(Name and Title)

of _____

(Name of Entity)

by _____

(Personal Service or Certified Mail)

at _____

(Street Address)

_____   _____

(Name & Signature)   (Title)

Warning Notice

PURPOSE OF THIS WARNING NOTICE

This WARNING NOTICE is issued to bring to your attention your responsibilities under the Immigration and Nationality Act (Act), as amended. Representatives of U.S. Immigration and Customs Enforcement (ICE) are available to discuss these responsibilities with you. The Handbook for Employers (M-274) provided to you with this WARNING NOTICE discusses the requirements of the law. Should you have any questions, you may contact the office noted in the front of the WARNING NOTICE.

PROHIBITED PRACTICES

Section 274A of the Act renders it unlawful for a person or entity, after November 6, 1986, to hire, or to recruit or refer for a fee for employment, an individual, knowing that he or she is not authorized by law to work in the United States. The Act prohibits a person or entity from continuing to employ an individual hired after November 6, 1986, knowing that he or she is or has become unauthorized to work in the United States. The Act also prohibits a person or entity from requiring a person to post bond or security, to pay or agree to pay an amount, or otherwise to provide a financial guarantee or indemnity, against any potential liability for employer sanctions violations.

In addition, under this law you may not discriminate against any individual (other than an unauthorized alien) in hiring, discharging, or recruiting or referring for a fee because of that individual's national origin or, in the case of a citizen or protected individual, because of his or her citizenship status. The Office of Special Counsel for Immigration-Related Unfair Employment Practices, U.S. Department of Justice, enforces the anti-discrimination provisions of the Act.

VERIFICATION REQUIREMENTS

The law requires employers and those recruiters or referrers for a fee who are agricultural associations, agricultural employers, or farm labor contractors to verify on the "Employment Eligibility Form," Form I-9, the identity and employment eligibility of all individuals hired, or recruited, or referred for a fee for employment in the United States after November 6, 1986. However, a Form I-9 need not be completed for individuals who were hired after November 6, 1986, but who quit or were terminated prior to June 1, 1987.

Employers and recruiters or referrers for a fee must produce Forms I-9 for inspection upon request of officers of ICE, the Employment Standards Administration, or the Office of Special Counsel.

ADDITIONAL INFORMATION

The law imposes civil penalties consisting of fines up to $10,000 per unauthorized alien for violations of the provision pertaining to the hiring, recruiting, or referring for a fee, or continued employment of an individual hired after November 6, 1986, knowing that he or she has become unauthorized to work in the United States, fines up to $11,000 per violation occurring on or after September 29, 1999, and fines up to $16,000 per violation occurring on or after March 27, 2008. For those who engage in a pattern or practice of violations of these provisions, the law imposes criminal penalties consisting of a fine of up to $3,000 for each unauthorized alien, imprisonment for up to 6 months for the entire pattern or practice, or both. Failure to adhere to the verification requirements of the law will result in civil penalties consisting of a fine ranging from $100 to $1,000 per violation for each individual with respect to whom such a violation occurred before September 29, 1999 and not less than $110 and not more than $1,100 per violation occurring on or after September 29, 1999.

Warning Notice

- NOTICE -

Failure to comply with this final order may result in ICE filing suit in the appropriate district court to seek compliance with this order.

In the Matter of (Respondent):

Certificate of Service

Served by (print name) _____

Date served _____

Method of service _____

Person or entity served _____

Title of person served _____

Place of service _____

Signature of employee or officer _____

Name and title of employee or officer _____

Final Order to Cease Violations and Pay Fine

DEPARTMENT OF HOMELAND SECURITY
U.S. Immigration and Customs Enforcement

FINAL ORDER TO CEASE VIOLATIONS AND PAY FINE

Pursuant to:

Section 274A of the Immigration and Nationality Act and Part 274a, Title 8, Code of Federal Regulations

or

Section 274C of the Immigration and Nationality Act and Part 270, Title 8, Code of Federal Regulations

United States of America	Office Address
A-File Number	Fines Case Number
In the Matter of (Respondent):	
Address (Street Number and Name)	
City, State, and ZIP Code	

On _____ , a Notice of Intent to Fine (copy attached) was served upon you stating the allegation(s) and charge(s), and the penalty to be assessed against you.

The **Notice of Intent to Fine** advised you of your right to contest the fine by requesting a hearing before an administrative law judge within 30 days of the service of the Notice. The Notice also advised you that failure to request a hearing on a timely basis would result in the issuance of a final and unappealable order by U.S. Immigration and Customs Enforcement (ICE).

☐ ICE has not received on a timely basis a written request for a hearing before an administrative law judge.

☐ Your request for a hearing before an administrative law judge was withdrawn in writing pursuant to an agreement between the parties.

☐ The parties have agreed to settle this matter without an administrative hearing.

Therefore, it is ordered that you: Pay a fine in the amount of $_____
and cease and desist from such violations (with the exception of Section 274A(a)(1)(b) violation(s)).

Payment must be in the form of a cashier's check, money order, or bank check made payable to "U.S. Immigration and Customs Enforcement." Payment must be submitted within 30 days of the receipt of this order to the following address:

Signature of Issuing Officer
Name of Issuing Officer
Title of Issuing Officer
Date

Glossary and Acronyms

Adjustment to Immigrant Status: Procedure allowing certain aliens already in the United States to apply for immigrant status. Aliens admitted to the United States in a nonimmigrant, refugee or parolee category may have their status changed to that of lawful permanent resident if they are eligible to receive an immigrant visa and one is immediately available. In such cases the alien is counted as an immigrant as of the date of adjustment, even though the alien may have been in the United States for an extended period of time.

Beginning in October 1994, section 245(i) of the Immigration and Nationality Act allowed illegal residents who were eligible for immigrant status to remain in the United States and adjust to permanent resident status by applying at an Immigration and Naturalization Service office and paying an additional penalty fee. Section 245(i) is no longer available unless the alien is the beneficiary of a petition under section 204 of the Act or of an application for a labor certification under section 212(a)(5)(A), filed before Jan. 15, 1998 and May 1, 2001. Prior to October 1994, most illegal residents were required to leave the United States and acquire a visa abroad from the Department of State.

Alien: Any person not a citizen or national of the United States.

Beneficiary: Alien on whose behalf a U.S. citizen, legal permanent resident or employer has filed a petition to receive immigration benefits from USCIS. The beneficiary generally receives lawful status as a result of his/her relationship to an U.S. citizen, lawful permanent resident or U.S. employer.

Border Crosser: An alien resident of the United States re-entering the country after an absence of less than six months in Canada or Mexico, or a non-resident alien entering the United States across the Canadian border for stays of no more than six months or across the Mexican border for stays of no more than 72 hours.

Business Nonimmigrant: An alien coming temporarily to the United States to engage in commercial transactions which do not involve gainful employment in the United States (i.e., engage in international commerce on behalf of a foreign firm, not be employed in the U.S. labor market and receive no salary from U.S. sources).

Cancellation of Removal: A discretionary benefit adjusting an alien's status from that of removable alien to one lawfully admitted for permanent residence. Application for cancellation of removal is made during the course of a hearing before an immigration judge.

Certificate of Citizenship: Identity document proving U.S. citizenship. Certificates of citizenship are issued to derivative citizens and to persons who are naturalized (see Derivative Citizenship).

Child: Generally, an unmarried person under 21 years of age, who is: a child born in wedlock; a stepchild, provided that the child was under eighteen 18 years of age at the time that the marriage creating the stepchild relationship occurred; a legitimated child, provided that the child was legitimated while in the legal custody of the legitimating parent; a child born out of wedlock, when a benefit is sought on the basis of its relationship with its mother or to its father, if the father had or has a bona fide relationship with the child; a child adopted while under 16 years of age who has resided since adoption in the legal custody of the adopting parents for at least 2 years; or an orphan under 16 years of age who has been adopted abroad by a U.S. citizen or has an immediate relative visa petition submitted on his/her behalf and is coming to the United States for adoption by a U.S. citizen.

Country of Birth: The country in which a person is born.

Country of Chargeability: The independent country to which an immigrant entering under the preference system is accredited for purposes of numerical limitations.

Country of Citizenship: The country in which a person is born (and has not renounced or lost citizenship) or naturalized and/or to which that person owes allegiance and by which s/he is entitled to be protected.

Country of (Last) Residence: The country in which an alien habitually resided prior to entering the United States.

Crewman: A foreign national serving in a capacity required for normal operations and service on board a vessel or aircraft. Crewmen are admitted for 29 days, with no extensions. Two categories of crewmen are defined in the Immigration and Nationality Act: D-1, departing from the United States with the vessel or aircraft on which s/he arrived or some other vessel or aircraft; and D-2, departing from Guam with the vessel on which s/he arrived.

Customs and Border Protection (CBP): Besides the former INS Inspections and Border Patrol, this bureau includes agricultural quarantine inspections and the Customs Service. CBP focuses on movement of people and goods across borders and ports of entry; the interior enforcement is delegated to Immigration and Customs Enforcement.

Deferred Inspection: Usually occurs when it is not clear to the examining officer whether the alien is eligible to be admitted or refused entry; may be conferred when the alien appears at a port of entry with documentation and when some questions remain about their admissibility that may be best answered at their point of destination.

Department of Homeland Security (DHS): The new agency into which INS was folded effective March 1, 2003. The benefits functions of the former INS transferred to USCIS, while the enforcement functions transferred to Customs and Border Protection and Immigration and Customs Enforcement.

Deportable Alien: An alien in and admitted to the United States subject to any grounds of removal specified in the Immigration and Nationality Act. This includes any alien illegally in the United States, regardless of whether the alien entered the country by fraud or misrepresentation or entered legally but subsequently violated the terms of his/her Non Immigrant classification or status.

Deportation: The formal removal of an alien from the United States when the alien has been found removable for violating immigration law. Deportation is ordered by an immigration judge without any punishment being imposed or contemplated. Prior to April 1997, deportation and exclusion were separate removal procedures. The Illegal Immigration Reform and Immigrant Responsibility Act of 1996 consolidated these procedures. After April 1, 1997, aliens in and admitted to the United States may be subject to removal instead of deportation.

Derivative Citizenship: Citizenship conveyed to children through the naturalization of parents or, under certain circumstances, to foreign-born children adopted by U.S. citizen parents, provided certain conditions are met.

Exchange Visitor: An alien coming temporarily to the United States as a participant in a program approved by the Secretary of State for the purpose of teaching, instructing or lecturing, studying, observing, conducting research, consulting, demonstrating special skills or receiving training.

Exclusion: Prior to the Illegal Immigration Reform and Immigrant Responsibility Act of 1996, exclusion was the formal term for denial of an alien's entry into the United States. The decision to exclude an alien was made by an immigration judge after an exclusion hearing.

Since April 1, 1997, the process of adjudicating inadmissibility may take place in either an expedited removal process or in removal proceedings before an immigration judge.

Fiancé(e) of U.S. Citizen: A nonimmigrant alien coming to the United States to conclude a valid marriage with a U.S. citizen within 90 days after entry.

Immediate Relatives: Certain immigrants who, because of their close relationship to U.S. citizens, are exempt from the numerical limitations imposed on immigration to the United States. Immediate relatives are: spouses of citizens; children (under 21 years of age and unmarried) of citizens; and parents of citizens 21 years of age or older.

Immigrant: See Permanent Resident Alien.

Immigration and Customs Enforcement (ICE): It is responsible for enforcement within the interior of the nation, and includes functions of the Customs Service, Federal Protection Service and the investigative and enforcement functions of the former INS (other than those border functions assumed by CBP).

Immigration and Nationality Act (INA): The Act, which along with other immigration laws, treaties and conventions of the United States, relates to the immigration, temporary admission, naturalization and removal of aliens.

Immigration Marriage Fraud Amendments of 1986: Public Law 99-639 (Act of Nov. 10, 1986), which was passed in order to deter immigration-related marriage fraud. Its major provision stipulates that aliens deriving their immigrant status based on a marriage of less than two years are granted conditional immigrant status. To remove their conditional status the immigrants must apply at an Immigration Service office during the 90-day period before their second-year anniversary of receiving conditional status. If the aliens cannot show that the marriage through which the status was obtained was and/or is a valid one, their conditional immigrant status may be terminated and they may become removable.

Inadmissible: An alien seeking admission at a port of entry who does not meet the criteria in the Immigration and Nationality Act for admission. The alien may be placed in removal proceedings or, under certain circumstances, allowed to withdraw his or her application for admission.

Intracompany Transferee: An alien employed for at least one continuous year out of the last three by an international firm or corporation, who seeks to enter the United States temporarily in order to continue to work for the same employer or a subsidiary or affiliate, in a capacity that is primarily managerial, executive or involves specialized knowledge, as well as the alien's spouse and minor unmarried children.

Labor Certification: Requirement for U.S. employers seeking to employ certain persons whose immigration to the United States is based on job skills or nonimmigrant temporary workers coming to perform services for which qualified authorized workers are unavailable in the United States. Labor certification is issued by the Secretary of Labor and contains attestations by U.S. employers as to the numbers of U.S. workers available to undertake the employment sought by an applicant, and the effect of the alien's employment on the wages and working conditions of U.S. workers similarly employed. Determination of labor availability in the United States is made at the time of a visa application and at the location where the applicant wishes to work. As of March 2005, there is a new procedure for the electronic filing of Labor Certification titled Program Electronic Review Management (PERM).

Lawful Permanent Resident (LPR): An alien who has the right to live permanently in the U.S. "Green Card" holders are LPRs. LPRs are also called permanent residents or resident aliens.

Master's Degree: Academic degree usually awarded for completion of a graduate or postgraduate course of one to three years in duration.

National: This means almost the same thing as citizen. It only applies to persons from America Samoa or the Swain Islands.

Naturalization: The conferring, by any means, of citizenship upon a person after birth.

Nonimmigrant: An alien who seeks temporary entry to the United States for a specific purpose. The alien must have a permanent residence abroad (for most classes of admission) and qualify for the nonimmigrant classification sought. The nonimmigrant classifications include: foreign government officials; visitors for business and for pleasure; aliens in transit through the United States; treaty traders and investors; students; international representatives of foreign information media; exchange visitors;, fiancé(e)s of U.S. citizens; intracompany transferees; NATO officials; religious workers; and some others. Most nonimmigrants can be accompanied or joined by spouses and unmarried minor (or dependent) children.

North American Free Trade Agreement (NAFTA): Public Law 103-182 (Act of Dec. 8, 1993), which superseded the United States-Canada Free Trade Agreement as of Jan. 1, 1994. It continues the special, reciprocal trading relationship between the United States and Canada (see United States-Canada Free Trade Agreement) and establishes a similar relationship with Mexico.

Not-for-Profit: An organization whose primary objective is to support some issue or matter of private interest or public concern for non-commercial purposes.

Order to Show Cause (OSC): This was the charging document issued by INS under the pre-Illegal Immigration Reform and Immigrant Responsibility Act law, which asked alien to show why INS should not deport him/her from the United States. (Now called Notice to Appear.)

Out of Wedlock (Born Out of Wedlock): A child born of parents who were not legally married to each other at that time.

Advance Parole: Authorized by the United States Citizenship and Immigration Services in advance of alien's arrival; may be issued to aliens residing in the United States in status other than lawful permanent resident status who have an unexpected need to travel and return and whose conditions of stay do not otherwise allow for readmission to the United States if they depart.

Port-of-Entry Parole: Authorized at the port upon alien's arrival; applies to a wide variety of situations and is used at the discretion of the supervisory immigration inspector, usually to allow short periods of entry. Examples include allowing aliens who could not be issued the necessary documentation within the required time period, or who were otherwise inadmissible, to attend a funeral and permitting the entry of emergency workers, such as fire fighters, to assist with an emergency.

Humanitarian Parole: Authorized at Immigration Service headquarters or overseas District Offices for "urgent humanitarian reasons" specified in the law. It is used in cases of medical emergency and comparable situations.

Overseas Parole: Authorized at an USCIS District or sub-office while the alien is still overseas; designed to constitute long term admission to the United States. In recent years, most of the aliens the Immigration Service has processed through overseas parole have arrived under special legislation or international migration agreements.

Significant Public Benefit Parole: Authorized at USCIS headquarters for "significant public benefit" specified in the law. It is generally used for aliens who enter to take part in legal proceedings.

Program Electronic Review Management (PERM): The Department of Labor's most recent program for permanent labor certification processing.

Permanent Resident Alien: An alien admitted to the United States as a lawful permanent resident. Permanent residents are also commonly referred to as immigrants. Lawful permanent residents are legally accorded the privilege of residing permanently in the United States. They may be issued immigrant visas by the Department of State overseas or adjusted to permanent resident status by the USCIS in the United States.

Petition: An immigration form asking for a certain benefit (e.g., Form I-130).

Petitioner: Person, corporation (or company) or organization requesting that a relative/employee be permitted to immigrate to the United States.

Public charge: Individuals who are likely to become public charges are inadmissible. The 1996 Act changed the beneficiary's income requirement. The beneficiary is required to show that the sponsor on an affidavit of support (or other person) has income or resources that are at least 125 percent of the Federal Poverty Guidelines.

Refugee: Any person who is outside his/her country of nationality who is unable or unwilling to return to that country because of persecution or a well-founded fear of persecution. Persecution or the fear thereof must be based on the alien's race, religion, nationality, membership in a particular social group or political opinion. People with no nationality must generally be outside their country of last habitual residence to qualify as a refugee. Refugees are subject to ceilings by geographic area set annually by the President of the United States in consultation with Congress and are eligible to adjust to lawful permanent resident status after one year of continuous presence in the United States.

Respondent: Under the Executive Office for Immigration Review (EOIR) system, the excludable, inadmissible deportable or removable aliens are called respondents because they have to respond to the EOIR Notice to Appear (formerly Order to Show Cause).

Schedule A: List of occupations for which the Department of Labor has determined there are not sufficient U.S. workers who are able, willing, qualified and available and establishes that the employment of aliens in these pre-certified occupations will not adversely affect the wages and working conditions for U.S. workers similarly employed.

Student: As a nonimmigrant class of admission, an alien coming temporarily to the United States to pursue a full course of study in an approved program in either an academic (college, university, seminary, conservatory, academic high school, elementary school, other institution or language training program) or vocational or other recognized non-academic institution.

Temporary Worker: An alien coming to the United States to work for a temporary period of time. The Immigration Reform and Control Act of 1986 and the Immigration Act of 1990, as well as other legislation, revised existing classes and created new classes of nonimmigrant admission. The nonimmigrant temporary worker classes of admission are as follows:

> **H-1B:** Workers with "specialty occupations" admitted on the basis of professional education, skills and/or equivalent experience.

> **H-2A:** Temporary agricultural workers coming to the United States to perform agricultural services or labor of a temporary or seasonal nature when authorized workers are unavailable in the United States.

> **H-2B:** Temporary non-agricultural workers coming to the United States to perform temporary services or labor if unemployed persons capable of performing the service or labor cannot be found in the United States.

> **H-3:** Aliens coming temporarily to the United States as trainees, other than to receive graduate medical education or training.

> **H-4:** Spouse and children of H visa recipients.

> **O-1, O-2, O-3:** Temporary workers with extraordinary ability or achievement in the sciences, arts, education, business or athletics; those entering solely for the purpose of accompanying and assisting such workers; and their spouses and children.

> **P-1, P-2, P-3, P-4:** Athletes and entertainers at an internationally recognized level of performance; artists and entertainers under a program that is "culturally unique"; and their spouses and children.

Q-1, Q-2, Q-3: Participants in international cultural exchange programs; participants in the Irish Peace Process Cultural and Training Program; and spouses and children of Irish Peace Process participants.

R-1, R-2: Temporary workers to perform work in religious occupations and their spouses and children.

Transit without Visa (TWOV): A transit alien traveling without a nonimmigrant visa under section 233 of the Immigration and Nationality Act. This visa was recently eliminated.

United States-Canada Free Trade Agreement: Public Law 100-449 (Act of Sept. 28, 1988) established a special reciprocal trading relationship between the United States and Canada. It provided two new classes of nonimmigrant admission for temporary visitors to the United States, Canadian citizen business persons and their spouses and unmarried minor children. Entry is facilitated for visitors seeking classification as visitors for business, treaty traders or investors, intracompany transferees or other business people engaging in activities at a professional level. Such visitors are not required to obtain nonimmigrant visas, prior petitions, labor certifications or prior approval, but must satisfy the inspecting officer they are so qualified. The United States-Canada Free Trade Agreement was superseded by the North American Free Trade Agreement as of Jan. 1, 1994.

United States Citizenship and Immigration Services (USCIS): The division of the Department of Homeland Security responsible for the "benefits" side of the former INS.

Visa Waiver Program (VWP): Allows citizens of certain selected countries, traveling temporarily to the United States under the nonimmigrant admission classes of visitors for pleasure and visitors for business, to enter the United States without obtaining nonimmigrant visas. Admission is for no more than 90 days.

Voluntary Departure: The departure of an alien from the United States without an order of removal. The departure may or may not have been preceded by a hearing before an immigration judge.

Keywords

– A –

AAO, Administrative Appeals Office, 277, 316
Ability, 221–250
    exceptional, 221, 223–224, 229, 293–295
    extraordinary, 14–15, 51, 91, 93, 101–102,
    104–105, 112, 221–222, 253–254, 349
Adjustment of status, 18, 20, 123, 190–191, 194–195,
    199, 229–230, 256–258, 278
Administrative Appeals Office (AAO) authority and
    procedures, 67–68, 315–317
Advance degrees, professionals, 223–224, 277,
    292–299
Affidavit of support, 21, 80–81, 191–192, 349
Appeals, 277–278, 289–292, 316, 317
Asylum, 13, 251–258, 276
    affirmative/defensive, 254
Agricultural worker, 32
Athletes, 20, 91–93, 349
Audits, 316

– B –

B Visas, 21, 36, 39, 81, 93, 190–191, 194
Bar to asylum-Filing within one year, 253
Board of Immigration Appeals (BIA), 278, 316
Business, extraordinary, 14, 91, 93, 221, 349

– C –

CBP, 317
Child defined, 345–346
Child Status Protection Act (CSPA), 257
Citizenship, 15, 34–35, 43, 66, 76, 89, 112, 191–194,
    199, 226, 236–237, 256, 301–303, 317–318
Consular processing, 36, 192, 230
Civics requirements, 301
Conditional permanent residence, 193
Convention Against Torture, (CAT), 252
Crimes/bars to asylum, 253
Crimes/bars to citizenship, 237–238

– D –

Deportation, 12–13, 302

– E –

E Visas, 35, 93
Educators/extraordinary, 91, 159
Employer/Employee Questionnaire, 41–43, 98–100,
    234–236

Employment-based immigration, 221–233
    First preference, 93, 189–190, 221
Extraordinary ability (EB-), 91, 221
    Fifth preference-Investor, 232
    Fourth preference-Special immigrant/religion, 231
    International executives & managers, 222
    Outstanding professors & researchers, 221–222
    PERM, (see PERM entry)
    Schedule A, 221, 224, 226, 228–230, 278, 349
    Second preference-Exceptional ability, 223–224
    Third preference-Labor certification, 224–228
Entry without Inspection, 3
E-Verify program, 318, 319
Executive Office for Immigration Review (EOIR), 4,
    254–255, 278, 282–288

– F –

F Visas, 93, 189–190
Family-sponsored immigration, 182, 219
Fear of persecution, well-founded, 251–252, 297, 349
Fiancés and fiancées, 189,193–194
First Preference, 221–223
    Employment-based preferences, 221–233
    Family-based preferences, 189–195
    Fourth Employment-based Preferences, 231–232

– G –

Good moral character-citizenship, 301

– H –

H Visas, 31

– I –

ICE, 315, 317–318
Illegal Entry (EWI), 3
Issues, 1, 3, 4, 12, 79, 257, 315, 317
Immigrants, 189–195, 221–233
    Employment based, 221–233
    Family sponsored, 189–195
Immigration Court, 254–256, 277–278, 299
Individual Hearing, 277–278
Ineligible for citizenship, 301–302
International
    Cultural exchange aliens-Q-1, 95
Interview techniques, 3
Intracompany transferees, 348, 350
Investor, immigrant, 221–233

– J –

J-1- Exchange Visitor, 80–81

– K –

K-1 Visa, 193
K-3 Visa, 194

– L –

L Visas, 37
Labor Certification, 3, 12, 15, 31–32, 221–230, 250
    Second employment-based preference, 223–224
    Third employment-based preference, 224–230
L1-A Visa, 38
L1-B Visa, 39

– M –

M Visa, 81, 193
Managers, international, 222, 238
Master Calendar, 255, 277–278
Motions, 296–299, 316, 323–329
    Reopen, 296–299, 316, 323–329
    Reconsider, 316, 319, 323–329

– N –

Naturalization, 278, 301–302
No Match Letters, 318–319
Non-Immigrant Categories, 14, 19–124, 193–194
    B-visitors, 19–21
    E-treaty trader and investors, 35–37
    F-academic students, 79
    H1-B-specialty occupation, 31
    H2-A-temporary agricultural workers, 32
    H2-B-temporary non-agricultural workers, 32
    H-3-trainees, 33
    J-exchange visitors, 80
    K-fiancés and fiancées, 125–126
    L-intracompany transferees, 37–39
    M-vocational students, 81
    O-extraordinary ability, entertainers, 91–93
    P-entertainers and athletes, 93–95
    Q-international cultural exchange aliens, 95
    R-ministers and religious workers, 96
    T-Victims of Trafficking, 121–122
    U–Victims of Criminal activity, 122–124
Notice of Entry, Forms
    EOIR, 280–288
    G-28, 30, 53, 69, 78,88–89, 111, 120, 198, 203, 208, 210, 314
Notice to Appear (NTA), 277

– O –

O-1 Visa, employment based, 91–92
O-2 Visa, 92
Outstanding professors and researchers, 221–222
Opening a file, 4

– P –

P Visa, 93–94
Parent-child relationship, 35, 253
Performing artist with exceptional ability, 91, 221–222
PERM, 221, 223–230, 315

Persecution, definition, 251
Petition letter, 40, 50–52, 66–68, 76–77, 93, 97, 101–105, 112–114, 195, 198, 237–238
Petition process, 190–191
Political opinion (Persecution on account of), 297
Preferences, 189, 221–233, 271
Presence, physical citizenship, 301
Professionals (with advanced degrees) 221–223, 230

– Q –

Q Visa, 94, 96
Quota System, 189, 230

– R –

R Visa, 96
Refugees, 251–276, 297
Religion, religious workers, 96, 231–232
Requests for Evidence, 315–316
Retainer agreement, 3–5, 15

– S –

Schedule A precertification, 229
Science, extraordinary ability in, 91,93, 221–222, 224, 229
Second employment-based preference, 223–224
Second family-based preference, 189
Skilled workers, 221, 224, 229–230
Special immigrants, 221, 231

– T –

T Visas, 121–124
Travel permit, 256
Third employment-based preference, 224–229
Third family based preference, 190
TN-North America Free Trade Agreement (Canada/Mexico), 34–35
Trainees, 31–34
Treaty trader and investors (E-1, E-2), 35–37
Tickler system, 4–5

– U –

U Visas, 122–124
Undergraduate degrees, alien professionals, 31
University teachers, 226, 229
Unlawful presence, 3–4, 257
Unskilled workers, 230

– V –

V Visa, 194–195, 317
Victims, 121–187
    Criminal activity, 121–123, 145–153
    Trafficking, 121–123, 272
Visa Waiver Program (VWP), 3, 19,–21, 317
Visitors, 19–21, 348, 350
Vocational students, 80–81

– W –

Well-founded fear of persecution, 251–252, 297
Withholding standard, 252
Writ of Habeas Corpus, 278
Writ of Mandamus, 277